Value Stream Management

In an increasingly competitive world, it is quality of thinking that gives an edge. An idea that opens new doors, a technique that solves a problem, or an insight that simply helps make sense of it all.

We work with leading authors in the fields of management and finance to bring cutting-edge thinking and best learning practice to a global market.

Under a range of leading imprints, including *Financial Times Prentice Hall*, we create world-class print publications and electronic products giving readers knowledge and understanding which can then be applied, whether studying or at work.

To find out more about our business and professional products, you can visit us at
www.business-minds.com

For other Pearson Education publications, visit
www.pearsoned-ema.com

Value Stream Management

Strategy and Excellence in the Supply Chain

Peter Hines, Richard Lamming, Daniel Jones, Paul Cousins, Nick Rich

FINANCIAL TIMES

Prentice Hall

An imprint of Pearson Education

Harlow, England • Reading, Massachusetts • Menlo Park, California
New York • Don Mills, Ontario • Amsterdam • Bonn • Sydney • Singapore
Tokyo • Madrid • San Juan • Milan • Mexico City • Seoul • Taipei

PEARSON EDUCATION LIMITED

Head Office:
Edinburgh Gate
Harlow CM20 2JE
Tel: +44 (0)1279 623623
Fax: +44 (0)1279 431059

London Office:
128 Long Acre
London WC2E 9AN
Tel: +44 (0)207 447 2000
Fax: +44 (0)207 240 5771

First published in Great Britain in 2000

© Peter Hines, Richard Lamming, Daniel Jones, Paul Cousins, Nick Rich 2000

The rights of Peter Hines, Richard Lamming, Daniel Jones, Paul Cousins and Nick Rich to
be identified as authors of this work have been asserted by them in accordance with the
Copyright, Designs, and Patents Act 1988.

ISBN 0 273 64202 2

British Library Cataloguing in Publication Data
A CIP catalogue record for this book can be obtained from the British Library.

10 9 8 7 6 5 4 3

Typeset by Northern Phototypesetting Co. Ltd, Bolton.
Printed and bound in Great Britain by Biddles Ltd, Guildford & King's Lynn.

The Publishers' policy is to use paper manufactured from sustainable forests.

Contents

PART THREE

Thinking Strategically About Supply   187

PART FOUR

Making the Change in Supply Management   271

PART FIVE

Making the Change in Other Linked Processes 383

About the Authors

Professor Peter Hines

Professor Peter Hines, is Professor of Supply Chain Management and Co-Director of the Lean Enterprise Research Centre at Cardiff Business School. He holds a BA (MA) in geography from Cambridge University and an MBA and PhD from the University of Cardiff. Peter followed a successful career in distribution and manufacturing industry before joining Cardiff Business School in 1992. Since that time he initially led the Materials Management Unit and now leads the 20 strong Lean Enterprise Research Centre together with Professor Dan Jones.

He has undertaken extensive research into the Supply Chain in both the automotive and other industries and has pioneered a number of key concepts, methods and applications in the UK, including: Supplier Associations (now involving over 500 UK firms), Value Stream Mapping, Network Sourcing, the Three Tier System of Management and the Value Stream Analysis Tool. He has written several books including *Creating World Class Suppliers* published by Pitman in 1994 and *The Lean Enterprise* (with Dan Dimancescu and Nick Rich) published by Amacom in 1997. He is editor-in-chief of the *International Journal of Logistics: Research & Applications* and the present chairman of the Logistics Research Network.

Professor Richard Lamming BSc DPhil CEng MIEE FRSA FCIPS

Professor Richard Lamming holds the CIPS Chair of Purchasing and Supply Management at the School of Management, University of Bath, in the UK, where he is Director of the Centre for Research in Strategic Purchasing and Supply (CRiSPS), and Director of Corporate Development for the School itself.

He began his career in the automotive industry, holding several posts, including five years as a management consultant. His academic career began in 1982. From 1986–90 he was a senior member of the International Motor Vehicle Programme, based at Massachusetts Institute of Technology (USA) and Brighton Business School (UK). He was subsequently part of a small team which contributed to the best-selling book, *The Machine That Changed the World* (1990). It was this book that launched the concept of lean production.

In addition to his roles at Bath, he now carries out research, teaching, consultancy and presentation work, on an international basis, specialising in the conceptual and practical development of lean supply in several industrial and commercial sectors. He is a member of the steering group of Partnership Sourcing Ltd and an adviser to the UK Department of Trade and Industry.

Professor Daniel T Jones

Professor Jones's career has been devoted to understanding the causes of differing industrial performance and to the concept of lean thinking or lean production.

He co-directed two major international studies of the automobile industry with Dr James P Womach of MIT and co-authored the resulting books *The Future of the Automobile* (1984) and *The Machine that Changed the World* (1990). In 1996 they published the best-selling *Lean Thinking*.

In 1989 he was appointed Professor of Management and in 1993 he founded the Lean Enterprise Research Centre at Cardiff Business School, Cardiff University. He is now a co-director of the centre with Professor Peter Hines.

He lectures extensively around the world and is a consultant to several companies trying innovative approaches in making the transition to Lean Management.

Dr Paul D Cousins BA (Hons) MBA PhD MCIPS

Paul began his working life with Westland Helicopters Limited, based in Yeovil, Somerset, where he worked as an expeditor, chief expeditor, buyer and finally chief buyer. His academic career started with a degree in Informatics at Sheffield University. He continued, at the University of Bath, to study for an MBA degree and Doctorate.

In 1993, Dr Cousins and Professor Lamming began work on the RAP project, a study that developed methodologies for assessing and developing supplier/buyer relationships. The current project is ESSCMo – Environmentally Sound Supply Chain Management.

Dr Cousins has also worked as a senior consultant with A.T.Kearney. He now balances both academia and industry with posts at the University of Bath, A.T.Kearney and a range of other major blue chip firms.

Finally, Paul has authored a wide range of academic papers, as well as two books which are due to be published in 1999/2000.

Nick Rich, BSc (Cardiff), MBA (Cardiff)

Nick is a Senior Research Associate. After a number of years' international industrial management and consultancy experience, he returned to join the university at Cardiff. He was one of the original members of the Lean Enterprise Research Centre and has conducted many of the 'world famous' research programmes of the centre. These programmes have included the Andersen Consulting Lean Enterprise Benchmarking studies, the Supply Chain Development Programme and the Lean Processing Programme (LEAP). Nick has published many papers and books including *Creating The Lean Enterprise* (1997) with Professor Peter Hines. He received the International Benchmarking Award in 1998. He has also spent extensive periods of study in Japan studying supply chain management practices. His research interests are policy deployment, lean production, quality management and total productive maintenance.

Foreword

The Supply Chain Development Programme was a unique experiment from the start. Here were a group of academics with a novel set of ideas, drawn in the main from studying Toyota and the Japanese motor industry, looking for a group of interested firms to join them to explore whether they had relevance to other sectors. Indeed they were asking not just for financial support and interest but for us to act as guinea-pigs in carrying out live proof of concept experiments. I think most of the industrial sponsors were intrigued by ideas and by the willingness of the academics to get their hands dirty – but were equally sceptical about the outcome!

When the programme started lean, production ideas had only really been applied within a factory environment. This was the first time they were being tried across whole supply chains outside the auto industry. As we began to explore these lean ideas, it became clear they opened up new possibilities for improving supply chain performance and were as relevant to grocery distribution and retailing as in the auto industry. Indeed some of the work carried out within SCDP has had a significant impact within Tesco and its supply chain, which we are continuing to this day.

For me that lasting image from this research was that it opened my eyes to waste – or *Muda* as Toyota calls it. This was brought home to me walking with several senior managers through all the stages of a complete supply chain in a day with the team's value stream mapping results in our hands. We all suddenly saw waste everywhere – it really opened our eyes! Shortly afterwards teams from both companies reviewed the process to address these wastes, with good results. This began to give real direction and focus to our efforts to improve our supply chain performance.

SCDP raised as many questions as it answered and there is a long way to go from the successful pilot projects reported in this book to implementation across whole supply chains. Lean thinking is not easy to implement and quickly runs up against many obstacles. However, I am convinced that these ideas represent some of the essential building blocks of supply chain management in the next century.

Graham Booth
Supply Chain Development & Planning Director
Tesco Stores Ltd,
Cheshunt.
25 August 1999.

CHAPTER 1

Introduction[1]

The need for rapid and sustainable development within supply chains is one of the key imperatives of today's business environment. Indeed it is undoubtedly a key source of competitive advantage as the locus of competition moves increasingly from the company to the supply chain.

However, the central questions with this are: how the enlightened manager should begin to understand their business environment; how they should start thinking strategically about change; or indeed how they should undertake the implementation of an improved supply chain. These were the types of question posed by a group of innovative companies in mid-1993 at the start of a four-year, £1million research programme. This research programme was named the 'Supply Chain Development Programme' (or SCDP) and involved a group of nearly twenty leading UK-based manufacturing, retail and service companies[2] all with a common desire to develop supply chain excellence and thereby to create a sustainable source of advantage to themselves and the other firms in their customer and supplier chains.

The need for rapid and sustainable development within supply chains is one of the key imperatives of today's business environment.

The firms involved will become known to the reader through the pages of this text as they became implementers of change. At the conception of SCDP firms were drawn from three leading industries: automotive,

---

[1] This chapter was prepared by Peter Hines, Daniel Jones, Richard Lamming, Paul Cousins and Nick Rich.

[2] The firms involved in the Supply Chain Development Programme during some or all of its duration were: Bass Brewers, Birds Eye Walls, Britvic Soft Drinks, Calsonic Llanelli Radiators, Clarks Shoes, Dalgety Food Ingredients, ICI Chemicals, IBM UK, Kuwait Petroleum, Lever Brothers, London Underground, Northern Telecom, Pedigree Petfoods, RS Compo-

electronics and fast-moving consumer goods (FMCG). The reason for this choice was that at the start of 1993 these sectors were felt to be the most innovative in the UK. During the following fifteen months the group increased in size to include firms from both service and process manu-facturing industries.

The research itself was carried out by staff at the Lean Enterprise Research Centre (LERC) at Cardiff Business School and the Centre for Research in Strategic Purchasing and Supply (CRiSPS) at Bath Univer-sity's School of Management. The programme in overview entailed input from almost twenty members of the research and administration team at these two leading centres.[3]

In many ways the rather large grouping of managers and researchers was unusual, since it involved a wide range of industries as well as a dis-parate group of functional specialisms. Indeed, taking the knowledge of the core managers and university staff into account, expertise was drawn from the fields of purchasing, logistics, manufacturing, information tech-nology and marketing, thus allowing for a good coverage of both the inter-nal and external elements of supply chain management.

The Supply Chain Development Programme

The Supply Chain Development Programme was designed to offer spon-soring companies some of the answers to the important strategic and operational questions and issues that they will be faced with into the next century. The research work has accordingly been designed to stand out-side the traditional academic 'ivory towers' and to focus on the partici-pating companies together with other exemplar companies from around the world. The focus has been as much on providing practical implemen-tation routes as on understanding and extrapolating best practice.

The research work consisted of *four* concurrent stages as shown in Figure 1.1 and described below:

Stage 1: Requirement Definition

This first stage was designed to arrive at an understanding of the key issues and areas where companies could be assisted, particularly over the medium- to long-term timeframe. Discussion of the particular benefits to an individual organization were set up. These discussions provided the research team with a clear focus for the programme, based on the needs

---

[3] The complete research and administration team involved in the Supply Chain Develop-ment Programme was: Debbie Bolton, Sara Bragg, Dr Paul Cousins, Ann Esain, Mark Fran-cis, Robin Frewer, Jon Hampson, Professor Peter Hines, Richard James, Professor David Jessop, Professor Daniel Jones, Owen Jones, Professor Richard Lamming, Bob Lowson, Donna Marshall, David Nicol, Nick Rich, Donna Samuel and David Simons.

FIGURE 1.1   Supply Chain Development Programme: research
methodology

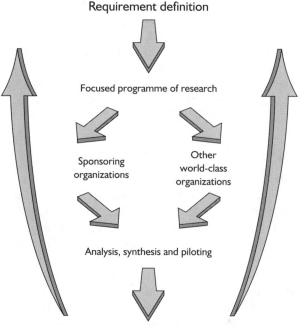

Requirement definition

Focused programme of research

Sponsoring
organizations

Other
world-class
organizations

Analysis, synthesis and piloting

Dissemination and implementation

and requirements of the world-class organizations of the future. These
requirements were combined with the views of the research team to provide an agenda for research. This process was initially undertaken in the
autumn of 1993.

Stage 2: Focused Programme of Research

The requirement definition stage highlighted the general areas in which
sponsors felt research would be required. The initial focusing event at
which all the sponsors came together identified five such areas. As a result
specific research projects were developed which it was felt, would help fill
the gaps identified by the sponsors. Each project was designed to run for
between six months and two years depending on their individual complexity and whether the work was carried forward into an implementation
stage. Because of the close synergy between the needs and requirements
of the sponsors a correspondingly close agreement has been reached
about which projects should run at any one time.

Stage 3: Analysis, Synthesis and Piloting

Once the primary research work had been undertaken with the sponsoring companies and, in some cases other world-class organizations, the resulting data was analyzed and synthesized into working methods that could be employed by each participant in their particular journey to excellence. In some cases, in order to provide a clear implementation route plan it was felt to be useful to undertake piloting work with one or more of the sponsors. This allowed these firms to gain priority access to the resulting models, but also provided the other participants with an opportunity to learn from a practical implementation programme. This subsequently allowed all the firms to gain useful insights that could substantially reduce their learning curves when they came to implement such strategies and tools for themselves.

Stage 4: Dissemination and Implementation

The fourth stage that ran concurrently with the first three was a series of regular workshops involving the sponsoring companies and the combined research team. These meetings allowed for the active dissemination and implementation to companies of a range of strategies, tools and techniques. This information was then subsequently diffused to a wider audience within these firms. The workshops were used to report on the latest research and pilot implementation programmes, as well as other research carried out by the universities and significant advances made by other academics or companies outside the group. In addition, the events provided an important networking opportunity between leading practitioners and academics for discussion, debate and exchange of information for the benefit of everyone. One of the advantages of this networking was that even though they worked in completely different industrial sectors, many of the companies found that they had issues, problems and opportunities in common. This networking allowed a sense of common purpose, vision and language to develop.

Underlying Lean Philosophy

One of the reasons why it was possible for such a wide-ranging group of companies and researchers to come together and work so closely was an underlying belief by the research team in the development of a 'lean philosophy' within each and every research programme. This common lean philosophy runs through the past research work at both Cardiff and Bath and is illustrated in the bibliography of the team.[4]

Although the reader should study these texts in order to understand the lean philosophy in detail, it will perhaps be useful to summarize some

---

[4] Past books written by the research team include:
Andrew Cox and Peter Hines, *Advanced Supply Management: The Best Practice Debate*, Earlsgate Press, Boston, Lincs., 1997

of the key underlying points of this philosophy. Ten central elements of this thinking are shown in Table 1.1.

The starting point in the lean approach is that value needs to be created in the eyes of the final consumer, who is, after all, paying for the product or service they consume. This focus on value is therefore translated across functional and company boundaries in both the design and delivery of the appropriate product–service bundle. In order to do this, the lean message suggests that the focus of attention should not be on the company or functional department but instead on the complete value stream. The value stream is those set of tasks and activities required to design and make a family of products or services that are undertaken with a group of linked functions or companies from the point of customer specification right back to the raw material source. Any company may focus its attention on a variety of value streams depending on which market segments or categories they are seeking to work within.

> *The starting point in the lean approach is that value needs to be created in the eyes of the final consumer.*

In order to maximize the value of products and services as they are delivered throughout the value stream it is necessary to concentrate attention on a rapid and uninterrupted flow that is 'pulled' by the final demand profile. This allows for a minimum of wasteful activities, such as storage, waiting, excess transportation and quality failures. However, in order to ensure that this flow avoids waste, it is imperative to create a dynamic transparency between companies both upstream and downstream. This transparency ensures that strategies, costs and information are appropriately shared between value stream members.

In order to ensure that all the relevant functions and companies are involved in this sharing process and that maximum competitive advantage is obtained, attention needs to be directed to the complete network of organizations involved. Value stream thinking goes beyond simplistic academic models of single buyer/single supplier relationships or even supply chains involving one customer, a focal firm and its single supplier. Instead, a more realistic approach is adopted involving a complete network of companies arrayed in each tier of supply. In addition, the lean approach seeks

Dan Dimancescu, Peter Hines and Nick Rich, *The Lean Enterprise: Designing and Managing Strategic Processes for Customer-Winning Performance*, AMACOM, New York, 1997

Peter Hines, *Creating World Class Suppliers: Unlocking Mutual Competitive Advantage*, Pitman Publishing, London, 1994

Richard Lamming, *Beyond Partnership: Strategies for Innovation and Lean Supply*, Prentice Hall, Hemel Hempstead, 1993

James Womack and Daniel Jones, *Lean Thinking: Banish Waste and Create Wealth in Your Corporation*, Simon and Schuster, New York, 1996

James Womack, Daniel Jones and Daniel Roos, *The Machine that Changed the World*, Rawson Associates, New York, 1990.

TABLE 1.1 The Ten Key Elements of the Lean Value Stream

1. Specify what does and does not create *value* from the customer's perspective rather than from the perspective of individual firms, functions and departments

2. Identify all the steps necessary to design, order and produce across the whole *value stream* to highlight non-value-adding waste

3. Make those actions that create value *flow* without interruption, detours, backflows, waiting or scrap

4. Only make what is *pulled* by the customer just-in-time

5. Create a dynamic *transparency* of strategies, costs and information in the value stream

6. Address competitive advantage at the value stream *network* level, moving past simple buyer/supplier partnership rhetoric

7. Use a new toolkit called *value stream mapping* for analysis, diagnosis and implementation of change

8. Focus on key *processes*, not just separate business departments

9. Address *whole industries* over the long term rather than on short-term improvement of individual firms

10. Strive for *perfection* by continually removing successive layers of waste as they are uncovered

---

to go beyond partnership rhetoric and seeks solutions at the value stream level that will benefit all the organizations involved.

In order to understand what to do and where to prioritize attention within the value stream, a new diagnostic method is called for – one that draws upon tools, and methods from a variety of functional backgrounds. Such a toolkit, called 'Value Stream Mapping', has been developed during the Supply Chain Development Programme. In brief, however, the method seeks to identify areas of waste in terms of excess time (lead time or inventory), excess cost and poor quality or product or service supplied. The approach will be illustrated in detail later in the text.

To gain maximum effect from this type of mapping, attention needs to be directed at key processes in the value stream. The decision on which are the key processes is best made in a contingent way, value stream by value stream. However, in many cases key processes may include order fulfilment, supplier integration, promotions management as well as new product design and introduction. Each of these processes will be described and discussed within this text.

For achieving a true lean approach it is also necessary to develop the habit of thinking about complete industries and the importance of improvement initiatives. An example of this is the massive attention that has been directed to just-in-time delivery in the automotive components sector upstream of the car assemblers. Here success is measured in reducing inventory or lead time by a further few minutes or hours. However, a more holistic vision of the industry would show that in many cases there are weeks or even months of finished product upstream of the car assemblers. Hence, attention needs to be at a complete industry level to focus attention on to where the largest gains are to be made.

The final lean message is that, whenever a programme of waste elimination has been undertaken, it is necessary to set up a process of maintenance to ensure gains are not immediately lost. A period of maintenance will allow successful change to bed in before starting another round of improvement, perhaps in the same area, in order to move ever closer to the ultimate goal of perfection.

The Research Programme

For the purpose of constructing an appropriate research programme as discussed above a review was undertaken of the needs and requirements of the companies. Although this was initially undertaken in 1993, it was constantly updated as new developments and needs were identified. As a result a highly industry-focused programme was developed. In all, 19 research projects have been carried out either by the Cardiff or Bath teams or in several cases jointly. These are illustrated in Figure 1.2. Each of these projects was undertaken separately, but with a view to fitting within the holistic lean value stream agenda discussed above.

In order for the findings of this work to be discussed in a logical flow, this text will seek to provide a flow of incremental ideas rather than simply report the results of the research project by project. However, for the interested reader a listing of research papers produced directly as a result of the Supply Chain Development Programme is given at the conclusion of this book.

This text is divided into five parts. Part One provides a more detailed background to the programme by developing an understanding of the value stream. This covers four chapters. Chapter 2 provides an introduction to the value stream, what wastes there may be to remove as well as an outline of the Value Stream Mapping method. Chapters 3 and 4 illustrate how this general approach may be applied within a physical product and information flow environment respectively. Chapter 5 demonstrates the use of the Value Stream Analysis Tool (or VALSAT). This method is applied within value streams to help focus improvements by ensuring a focus on customer requirement. Taken altogether Part One provides the reader with an analysis and diagnostic toolkit to help decide what strategic and operational tasks need to be undertaken within their value stream.

Part Two entitled 'Thinking Strategically about Change' follows the general diagnostic methods described before by providing an outline of how the company (and value stream) can start to develop and deploy strategies and policies effectively. Chapter 6 provides an overview model for this activity with Chapter 7 demonstrating how this approach may be applied to different key processes within the value stream such as order fulfilment and supplier integration. Chapter 8 shows how over time high performing systems can be standardized into holistic operating systems whether this be on the shop floor, the warehouse or the office environment. Part Two attempts to provide the reader with a strategic management approach for applying improvements to the value stream.

Part Three takes this lean change philosophy into the supply area of the value stream. In Chapter 9 a case is developed for a move from the traditional purchasing function to a new strategic supply process. Chapter 10 applies this type of thinking to a larger company environment where the supplier integration process has been complicated by purchasing being undertaken in a number of different locations. It returns the reader to the old chestnut debate of centralization vs. de-centralization, but in this case within a lean thinking environment. Chapter 11 focuses on the strategic performance measurement system required to support the strategic supply area. Part Three thus provides the reader with a framework for applying value stream thinking into a traditional purchasing environment.

Part Four called 'Making the Change in Supply Management' pulls together many of the theoretical or strategic ideas from the preceding parts to focus on what you actually do. Central to this task is the creation of a dynamic transparency in the value stream. Chapter 12 illustrates how this can be achieved for cost and other more general information. This is followed by Chapters 13 and 14 on supplier development and the control of inventory. To complete this section Chapter 15 deals with environmental thinking and how to ensure that a lean value stream does not occur at the expense of a polluted or socially unsound value stream. Part Four thus provides the reader with guidance on how the new value stream thinking can actually be applied in practice.

Throughout this text to this point the emphasis has been on the flow of materials and information within the value stream. However, increasingly during the Supply Chain Development Programme it became obvious that focusing just on these processes, important though they are, would not provide any value stream with a complete answer to their problems and issues. As a result Part Five reviews how the lean approach can be applied to other key processes within the value stream.

Three other such processes are discussed here, namely, the management of promotions, new product introduction/development and distribution. The reason why three chapters have been dedicated to these other supply chain processes is that for the more advanced value stream, once considerable advantage has been gained within more traditional supply chain areas, further advantage is more readily available by

FIGURE 1.2 The Supply Chain Development Programme Project Chart

Date columns: 9/93, 11/93, 1/94, 3/94, 5/94, 7/94, 9/94, 11/94, 1/95, 3/95, 5/95, 7/95, 9/95, 11/95, 1/96, 3/96, 5/96, 7/96, 9/96, 11/96, 1/97, 3/97, 5/97, 7/97, 9/97, 11/97, 1/98

Activities:
- Supplier Development
- Supply Chain Responsiveness
- Communicating between Organizations
- Quality Function Deployment
- Environmental Supply Chain Management
- Demand Amplification
- Promotions Management
- Cost Transparency
- Effective Supplier Response
- Purchasing Performance
- Warehouse Operations
- Policy Deployment
- Value Stream Mapping
- Multi Site Purchasing
- Vendor Managed Inventory
- Information Mapping
- Strategic Purchasing
- New Product Introduction
- New Product Development

addressing other key processes and, in particular, how these integrate with processes such as order fulfilment and supplier integration. This part will provide the reader with a far wider viewpoint for their application of lean value stream management and how they need to integrate with a wider range of personnel than just their traditional purchasing and logistics colleagues.

Chapter 19 concludes the book and provides the reader with a new agenda for thinking strategically and acting operationally to create competitive advantage for themselves and their value stream colleagues as we move further into the era of competing value streams.

Understanding
the Value Stream

CHAPTER 2

Understanding Improvement Areas in the Value Stream

The starting point for the development of a lean approach to the supply chain is an understanding of value and waste within this environment. Part One of this text demonstrates an approach developed within the Supply Chain Development Programme to do this by clearly differentiating between waste and value. The generic method described here is called 'Value Stream Mapping'. The approach will be discussed from a theoretical viewpoint within this chapter, and from a more practical one using various case material in the subsequent chapters.

The starting point for the development of a lean approach to the supply chain is an understanding of value and waste within this environment.

This chapter[1] explores a theoretical approach to the question of how companies can identify where to focus improvement and how to identify appropriate methods to make radical or incremental change. Work over the course of the Supply Chain Development Programme has shown that, in order fully to understand the different value streams (Womack and Jones, 1994) within which the sponsors operate, it is necessary to map these inter- and intra-company value-adding processes. These value-adding processes make the final product or service more valuable to the end consumer than it would have been otherwise. The difference between the traditional supply or value chain and the value stream is that the former includes the complete activities of all the companies involved, whereas the latter refers only to the specific parts of the firms that actually add value to the product or service under consideration. The value

[1] This chapter first appeared as: Peter Hines and Nick Rich, 'The Seven Value Stream Mapping Tools', *International Journal of Operations & Production Management*, Volume 17, Number 1, pp. 46–64. The authors would like to thank the editors and publishers of IJOPM for agreeing to its reproduction here in a slightly revised form.

stream is, therefore, a far more focused and contingent view of the value-adding process.

Unfortunately, there is at present only an ill-defined and ill-categorized toolkit to understand the value stream, although several workers have developed individual tools (for instance: New, 1993; Forza *et al.*, 1993; Beesley, 1994 and Jessop and Jones, 1995). However, in general, these authors have viewed their creations as *the* answer, rather than a part of the jigsaw. In addition, these tools derive from functional ghettos and, on their own, do not fit well with the more cross-functional toolbox required by today's best companies. It is the purpose of this paper to construct a typology or total jigsaw to allow for an effective application of sub-sets of the complete suite of tools. The tools themselves can then be effectively applied, singularly or in combination, to match the requirements of the individual value stream.

Waste Removal Inside Companies

The underlying logic for the collection and use of this suite of tools is to help researchers or practitioners to identify waste within individual value streams and then to find an appropriate route to remove or at least to reduce this waste. The use of such waste removal to drive competitive advantage inside organizations was pioneered by Toyota's chief engineer Taiichi Ohno and *sensei* Shigeo Shingo (JPA, 1985; Shingo, 1989) and is fundamentally productivity-oriented, rather than quality-oriented. The reason for this is that improved productivity leads to leaner operations which in turn help to expose further waste and quality problems within the system. Thus the systematic attack on wastes is also a systematic assault on the underlying causes of poor quality and fundamental management problems (Bicheno, 1994).

In an internal manufacturing context, there are three types of operations that are undertaken, according to Yasuhiro Monden (Monden, 1993). These can be categorized into: Non-Value-Adding (NVA), Necessary but Non-Value-Adding (NNVA) and Value-Adding (VA). The first of these is pure waste and involves unnecessary actions which should be eliminated completely. Examples would include: waiting time; stacking intermediate products; and double handling.

Necessary but Non-Value-Adding operations are wasteful, but may be necessary under the current operating procedures. Examples would include: walking long distances to pick up parts; unpacking deliveries; and transferring a tool from one hand to another. In order to eliminate these types of operation, it would be necessary to make major changes to the operating system, such as creating a new layout or arranging for suppliers to deliver unpacked goods. This type of change may not be possible immediately.

Value-Adding operations involve the conversion or processing of raw materials or semi-finished products through the use of manual labour. This would involve activities such as: sub-assembly of parts; forging raw materials; and painting body work. Value-Adding operations may also include partially 'manned' or 'unmanned' machining operations.

The Seven Wastes

There are seven commonly accepted wastes within the Toyota Production System (TPS):

1. Overproduction.
2. Waiting.
3. Transportation.
4. Inappropriate Processing.
5. Unnecessary Inventory.
6. Unnecessary Motion.
7. Defects.

Overproduction is regarded as the most serious waste as it discourages a smooth flow of goods or services and is likely to inhibit quality and productivity. Such overproduction also tends to lead to excessive lead- and storage-times. As a result, defects may not be detected early, products may deteriorate and artificial pressures on work rate may be generated. In addition, overproduction leads to excessive work-in-progress stocks resulting in the physical dislocation of operations and poorer communications. This state of affairs is often exacerbated by bonus systems that encourage the push of unwanted goods. The pull or *kanban* system was employed by Toyota as a way of overcoming this problem.

When time is being used ineffectively, the waste of *waiting* occurs. In a factory setting, this waste occurs whenever goods are not moving or being worked upon. This waste affects goods and workers, both of whom spend a part of their time waiting. The ideal state should be no waiting time with a consequent faster flow of goods. Waiting time for workers may be used for training, maintenance or *kaizen* activities and should not result in overproduction.

The third waste, that of *transportation*, involves goods being moved about. Taken to its extreme, any movement in the factory could be viewed as waste, and so transportation minimization rather than total removal is usually sought. In addition, double handling and excessive movements are likely to cause damage and deterioration with the distance of communication between processes proportional to the time it takes to feed back reports of poor quality and so take corrective action.

Inappropriate processing happens where overly complex solutions are found to simple procedures, such as a large inflexible machine instead of several small flexible ones. The over-complexity generally discourages ownership and encourages the employees to overproduce to recover the large investment in the complex machines. Such an approach encourages poor layout, leading to excessive transport and poor communication. The ideal, therefore, is to have the smallest possible machine, capable of producing the required quality, located next to preceding and subsequent operations. Inappropriate processing also occurs when machines are used without sufficient safeguards, such as poke yoke or *jidoka* devices, so that poor quality goods result.

Unnecessary inventory tends to increase lead time, prevents the rapid identification of problems and increases space, thereby discouraging communications. Thus, problems are hidden by inventory. To correct these problems, they first have to be found. This can only be achieved by reducing inventory. In addition, unnecessary inventories cause significant storage costs and hence lower the competitiveness of the organization or value stream within which they exist.

Unnecessary motion involves the ergonomics of production where operators have to stretch, bend and pick up when this could be avoided. Such waste is tiring for the employees and is likely to lead to poor productivity and often to quality problems.

The bottom line waste is that of *defects*, as these cost money directly. The Toyota philosophy is that defects should be regarded as opportunities to improve, rather than something to be traded off against what is ultimately poor management. Thus defects are seized upon for immediate *kaizen* activity.

In systems such as the Toyota Production System, it is the continuous and iterative analysis of system improvements using the seven wastes, that results in a *kaizen*-style improvement system. The majority of such improvements are on a small but incremental basis as opposed to a radical or breakthrough one.

Waste Removal Inside Value Streams

As the focus of the value stream includes the complete value-adding (and non-value-adding) process from conception of requirement back through to raw material source and back again to the consumer's receipt of product, there is a clear need to extend this internal waste removal to the complete supply chain. However, there are a number of difficulties involved. These include a lack of visibility along the value stream and of the appropriate tools to create this visibility. This paper is designed to help researchers and practitioners to remedy this. In addition, the waste terminology described above has been drawn from a manufacturing environment, and the automotive industry specifically, and what is more, from a Japanese perspective. As a result, some translation of the general terminology will be required to fit a particular part of the value stream and particular industries in a non-Japanese setting. To do this, some use of a contingency approach is required.

Such an approach has been the subject of considerable work at the Lean Enterprise Research Centre. It would include the application of the *kyoryoku kai* (Supplier Association) into a range of UK-based industry sectors by Hines (Hines, 1994) and the translation of the Toyota Production System philosophy into a warehouse environment by Jones (Jones, 1995). In the latter case, Jones showed that the seven wastes needed to be reworded to fit an after-market distribution setting. He therefore retitled the seven wastes as:

- faster than necessary pace;
- waiting;
- conveyance;
- processing;
- excess stock;
- unnecessary motion;
- correction of mistakes.

The Seven Value Stream Mapping Tools

The typology of the seven new tools will be the same as the seven wastes that have already been described. In addition the delineating of the overall combined value stream structure will be useful and will also be combined in the way shown in the left-hand column in Figure 2.1. Thus, in

FIGURE 2.1 The Seven Value Stream Mapping Tools

Mapping Tool Wastes/ Structure	1. Process Activity Mapping	2. Supply Chain Response Matrix	3. Production Variety Funnel	4. Quality Filter Mapping	5. Demand Amplification Mapping	6. Decision Point Analysis	7. Physical Structure a) Volume b) Value
1. Overproduction	L	M		L	M	M	
2. Waiting	H	H	L		M	M	
3. Transportation	H						L
4. Inappropriate Processing	H		M	L		L	
5. Unnecessary Inventory	M	H	M		H	M	L
6. Unnecessary Motion	H	L					
7. Defects	L			H			

H   High Correlation and Usefulness
M   Medium Correlation and Usefulness
L   Low Correlation and Usefulness

order to make improvements in the supply chain, it is suggested here that at least an outline understanding of the particular wastes to be reduced must be gained before any mapping activity takes place.

At this point it should be stressed that many of the seven mapping tools were already well known before the writing of this paper. However, at least two can be regarded as new, and most will be unfamiliar to a wide range of researchers and practitioners. However, until now, there has been no decision-support mechanism to help chose the most appropriate tool or tools to use.

The tools themselves are drawn from a wide range of sources as show in Table 2.1. These sources include engineering (tools 1 & 5), action research/logistics (tools 2 & 6) operations management (tool 3) and two that are new (tools 4 & 7). As may be seen, they are generally from specific functional ghettos and the full range will not be familiar to many researchers, although a small number may be well known to individual readers. Each of these will be reviewed in turn before we discuss how they can be selected for use.

TABLE 2.1 Origins of the Seven Value Stream Mapping Tools

Mapping Tool	Origin of Mapping Tool
1. Process Activity Mapping	Industrial Engineering
2. Supply Chain Response Matrix	Time Compression/Logistics
3. Production Variety Funnel	Operations Management
4. Quality Filter Mapping	New Tool
5. Demand Amplification Mapping	Systems Dynamics
6. Decision Point Analysis	Efficient Consumer Response/Logistics
7. Physical Structure Mapping	New Tool

The Tools Themselves

1. Process Activity Mapping

As noted above, Process Activity Mapping has its origins in industrial engineering. Industrial engineering is a group of techniques that can be used to eliminate waste, inconsistencies, and irrationalities from the workplace and provide high quality goods and services easily, quickly and inexpensively (Ishiwata, 1991). The technique is known by a number of names in this context, although Process Analysis is the most common (PMRG, 1993). There are five stages to this general approach:

1. The study of the flow of processes.
2. The identification of waste.
3. A consideration of whether the process can be rearranged into a more efficient sequence.

> *Process Activity Mapping has its origins in industrial engineering.*

4. A consideration of a better flow pattern involving different flow layout or transportation routing.
5. A consideration of whether everything that is being done at each process is really necessary and what would happen if superfluous tasks were removed.

In order to do this, several simple stages are to be followed. First, a preliminary analysis of the process should be undertaken, followed by the detailed recording of all the required items in each process. The result of this will be a map of the process under consideration (Figure 2.2). As can be seen from this process industry example, each step has been categorized from 1 to 23 within a variety of types of activity (operation, transport, inspection and storage). The machine or area used for each of these activities is recorded, together with the distance moved, time taken and number of people involved. A simple flow chart of the types of activity being undertaken at any one time can then be made. This is depicted by the dark shaded boxes in Figure 2.2.

After this, the total distance moved, time taken and people involved can be calculated. This calculation is then recorded. The final diagram (Figure 2.2) can then be used as the basis for further analysis and subsequent improvement. This is often achieved through the use of techniques such as 5W1H (Why does an activity occur? Who does it? On What machine? Where, When and How?). The basis of this approach is to try to eliminate activities that are unnecessary, simplify or combine others and seek sequence changes that will reduce waste. Various contingent improvement approaches can be similarly mapped before the best approach is selected for implementation.

2. Supply Chain Response Matrix

The origin of the second tool lies in the Time Compression and Logistics movement and goes under a variety of names. It was used by New (New, 1993) and Forza et al. (Forza et al., 1993) within a textile supply chain setting. In a more wide-ranging work, Beesley applied what he termed 'Time-Based Process Mapping' to a range of industrial sectors including automotive, aerospace and construction (Beesley, 1994). A similar, if slightly refined, approach was adopted by Jessop and Jones in the electronics, food, clothing and automotive industries (Jessop and Jones, 1995).

The fundamentals of this mapping approach, as shown in Figure 2.3, are that the approach seeks to portray in a simple diagram the critical lead

FIGURE 2.2 Process Activity Map

#	Step	Flow	Area	Dist (m)	Time (min)	People	Operation	Transport	Inspect	Store	Delay	Comments
1	Driver takes paperwork to office	T	Outside/office	50	0.5		O	T	–	S	D	
2	Check booked in/issue ticket	I	Office	10	1	1(+1)	O	T	■	S	D	(Driver)
3	Driver to vehicle	T	Office/outside	50	0.5		O	T	–	S	D	
4	Open back of truck	O	Outside				O	T	–	S	D	
5	Back on to bay	D	Outside/bay	30	15		O	T	–	S	D	
6	Wait for pump truck	D	Bay				O	T	–	S	D	
7	Unload lorry	O	Splitting	25	20	1(+1)	O	T	–	S	D	10 pallets
8	Wait for total unloading	D	Splitting		10	2(+1)	O	T	–	S	D	Driver (total 30)
9	Wait for paperwork	D	Splitting		0.5	(1)	O	T	–	S	D	
10	Driver to office for paperwork	T	Outside/office	20		1(+1)	O	T	■	S	D	
11	Get paperwork	I	Office		3		O	T	–	S	D	
12	Delay to start splitting	D	Splitting		120		O	T	–	S	D	
13	Splitting	O	Splitting	20	50	2	O	T	–	S	D	
14	Move pallet to quantification	T	Quantification				O	T	–	S	D	Pump truck
15	Delay to quantify	D	Quantification		240		O	T	–	S	D	
16	Quantify	O	Quantification		10		O	T	■	S	D	
17	Move to lift and load	T	Inspection/lift	3	2		O	T	–	S	D	
18	Move to WIP	T	Lift to WIP	5	0.3		O	T	–	S	D	
19	Delay	D	Lift top		5		O	T	–	S	D	
20	Remove from lift	T	Lift top	2	2		O	T	–	S	D	
21	Place in storage area	T	Floor	10	2		O	T	–	S	D	
22	Storage	D	Floor		2880		O	T	–	S	D	
23	Collect production order	T	To office	25	15		O	T	–	S	D	
24	Pull stock to production area	T	To packing	10	2		O	T	–	S	D	Hand pump
25	Delay	D	Packing		15		O	T	–	S	D	Setup
26	Load machine and cycle	O	Packing	2	0.1	1	O	T	–	S	D	
27	Place in tote	T	Packing	0.5	0.1	(1)	O	T	–	S	D	
28	Wait for batch	D	Packing		30		O	T	–	S	D	
29	Load conveyor	T	Packing to conveyor	12	0.5	1	O	T	–	S	D	
30	Travel to crane	T	To crane	150	5		O	T	–	S	D	
31	Wait for crane	D	Crane		5		O	T	–	S	D	
32	Put into main store	T	Crane/store	75	1	1	O	T	–	S	D	
33	Store	D	Store		155.4 33.6		O	T	–	S	D	

| | Total | | | 489.5 | 158.8
84.1
51.1
322 mpm | 29 | | | | | | |

Operations — 4

Percentage operations — 13.8%

FIGURE 2.3   Supply Chain Response Matrix

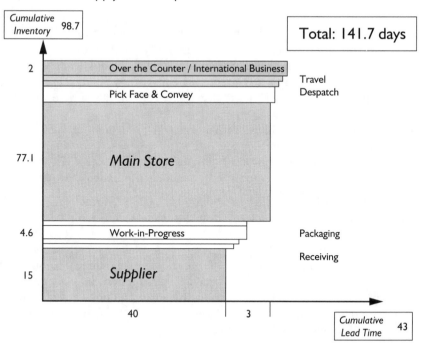

time constraints for a particular process. In this case it is the cumulative lead time within a distribution company, its suppliers and its downstream retailer. In Figure 2.3 the horizontal measurements shows the lead time for the product both internally and externally. The vertical plot shows the average amount of standing inventory (in days) at specific points in the supply chain.

In this example the horizontal axis shows the cumulative lead time as 43 working days. In addition the vertical axis shows that another near 99 working days of material is held within the system. Thus a total response time of just over 141 working days can be seen to be typical in this system. Once this is understood, each of the individual lead times and inventory amounts can be targeted for improvement activity as was shown with the Process Activity Mapping approach.

3. Production Variety Funnel

The Production Variety Funnel is shown in Figure 2.4. This approach originates in the operations management area (New, 1974) and has been applied by New in the textile industry (New, 1993). A similar method is IVAT analysis which views internal operations in companies as consisting of activities that conform to an I, V, A or T shape (Macbeth and Ferguson, 1994).

- 'I' plants consist of unidirectional, unvarying production of multiple identical items such as a chemical plant.
- 'V' plants consist of a limited number of raw materials processed into a wide variety of finished products in a generally diverging pattern. 'V' plants are typical in textile and metal fabrication industries.
- 'A' plants, in contrast, have many raw materials and a limited range of finished products with different streams of raw materials using different facilities. Such plants are typical in the aerospace or other major assembly industries.
- 'T' plants have a wide combination of products from a restricted number of components made into semi-processed parts held ready for a wide range of customer-demanded final versions. This type of site is typical in electronics and household appliance industries.

Such a delineation using the Production Variety Funnel (Figure 2.4) allows the mapper to understand how the firm or the supply chain operates and the accompanying complexity that has to be managed. In addition, such a mapping process helps potential research clients to understand the similarities and differences of their industry to one that may have been more widely researched. The approach can be very useful in helping to decide where to target inventory reduction and making changes to the processing of products. It is also useful in gaining an overview of the company or supply chain being studied.

FIGURE 2.4   Production Variety Funnel: a Brewing Industry Case

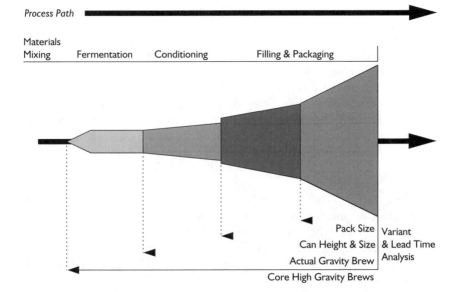

4. Quality Filter Mapping

The Quality Filter Mapping Approach is a new tool that is designed to identify where quality problems exist in the supply chain. The resulting map itself shows where three different types of quality defects occur in the supply chain (Figure 2.5). The first of these is *product* defects. Products defects are defined here as defects in goods produced that are not caught by in-line or end-of-line inspection and are therefore passed on to customers.

The second type of quality defect is what may be termed *service* defects. Service defects are problems given to a customer that are not directly related to the goods themselves, but relate to the accompanying level of service. The most important of these service defects is inappropriate delivery (late or early), together with incorrect paperwork or documentation. In other words such defects include any problems caused to customers that are not concerned with a faulty product.

The third type of defect is *internal scrap*. Internal scrap refers to defects made within a company that have been caught by in-line or end-of-line inspection. The in-line inspection methods will vary and may con-

FIGURE 2.5   The Quality Filter Mapping Approach: an Automotive Example

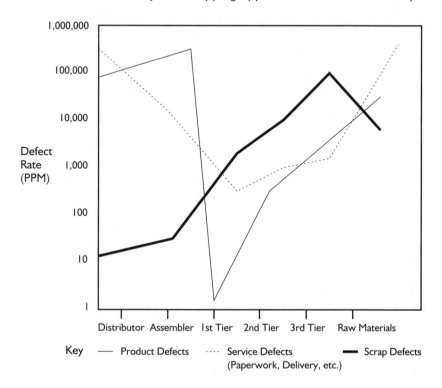

sist of traditional product inspection, statistical process control or through poke yoke devices.

Each of these three types of defect are then mapped latitudinally along the supply chain. In the automotive example given (Figure 2.5), this supply chain is seen to consist of distributor, assembler, first tier supplier, second tier supplier, third tier supplier and raw material source. This approach has clear advantages in identifying where defects are occurring and hence in identifying problems, inefficiencies and wasted effort. This information can then be used for subsequent improvement activity.

5. Demand Amplification Mapping

Demand Amplification Mapping has its roots in the systems dynamics work of Jay Forrester and John Burbidge (Forrester, 1958; Burbidge, 1984). What has now become known as the 'Forrester Effect' was first described in a *Harvard Business Review* article in 1958 by Jay Forrester. This effect is primarily linked to delays and poor decision-making concerning information and material flow. The Burbidge effect is linked to the Law of Industrial Dynamics which states 'if demand is transmitted along a series of inventories using stock control ordering, then the amplification of demand variation will increase with each transfer' (Burbidge, 1984). Thus, in unmodified supply chains excess inventory, production, labour and capacity are generally found as a result. It is therefore quite likely that on many day-to-day occasions manufacturers will be unable to satisfy retail demand, even though they are on average able to produce more goods than those being sold. Within a supply chain setting, manufacturers have consequently sought to hold, in some cases sizeable, stocks to avoid such problems. Forrester likens this to driving an automobile blindfolded with instructions being given by a passenger.

In unmodified supply chains excess inventory, production, labour and capacity are generally found as a result.

The use of various mapping techniques loosely based on Forrester's and Burbidge's pioneering work is now quite common (e.g. Wikner *et al.*, 1991), and in at least one case the basic concept has even been developed into a game called the 'Beer Game', which looks at the systems dynamics within a retail-brewing situation (Senge, 1990). The basis of the mapping tool in the supply chain setting is given in Figure 2.6. In this instance an FMCG food product is being mapped along its distribution through a leading UK supermarket retailer. In this simple example two curves are plotted. The first, in lighter shading, represents the actual consumer sales as recorded by EPOS (Electronic Point Of Sale) data. The second, darker, curve represents the orders placed to the supplier to fulfil this demand. As can be seen, the variability of consumer sales is far lower than for supplier orders. It is also possible subsequently to map this product further upstream. An example may be the manufacturing plant of the cleaning

FIGURE 2.6 FMCG Demand Amplification Mapping: an FMCG Food Product Example

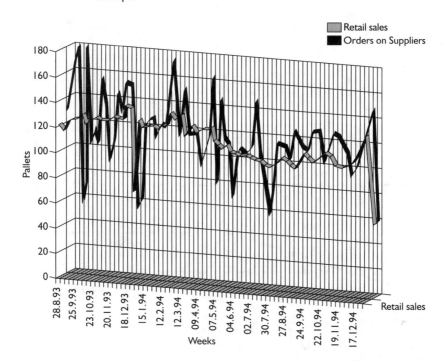

products company or even the demand they place on their raw material suppliers.

This simple analysis tool can then be used to show how demand changes along the supply chain within varying time buckets, and this information will form the basis for decision-making and further analysis to try to redesign the value stream configuration, manage or reduce the fluctuation or set up dual mode solutions where regular demand can be managed in one way and exceptional or promotions demand in a separate way (James, 1995).

6. Decision Point Analysis

Decision Point Analysis is of particular use for 'T' plants or supply chains that exhibit similar features, although it may be used in other types of industries. The Decision Point is the point in the supply chain where actual demand pull gives way to forecast driven push. In other words, it is the point at which products stop being made in accordance with actual demand and start to be made against forecasts alone (Hoekstra and Romme, 1992). Thus with reference to Figure 2.7, an example from the FMCG industry, the decision point can be at any point from Regional Distribution Centres to National Distribution Centres through to any point

FIGURE 2.7 Decision Point Analysis

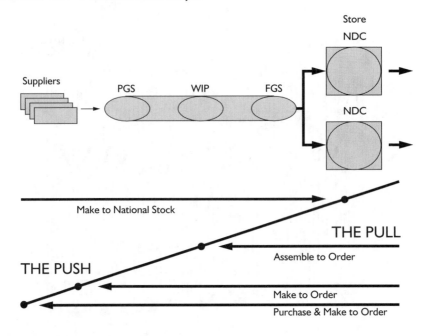

inside the manufacturer or indeed at any tier within the supply chain (Rich, 1995).

Gaining a basic understanding of where this point lies is useful for two reasons. First, at the immediate level, with this knowledge it is possible to assess the processes that operate both downstream and upstream from this point. The purpose of this is to ensure that they are aligned with the relevant pull or push philosophy. Second, at a more fundamental and longer-term level, it is possible to design various 'what if' scenarios to view the operation of the value stream if the decision point is moved. This may allow for a better design of the value stream.

7. Physical Structure

Physical structure mapping is a new tool that has been found to be useful in understanding what a particular supply chain looks like at an overview or industry level. This knowledge is helpful in understanding what the industry looks like, how it operates and in particular in directing attention to areas that may not be receiving sufficient developmental attention.

The tool is illustrated in Figure 2.8 and can be seen to be split into two parts: volume structure and cost structure. The first diagram (Figure 2.8A) shows the structure of the industry according to the various tiers that exist in both the supplier area and the distribution area, with the assembler located at the middle point. In this simple example there are three supplier tiers mirrored by three distribution tiers. In addition, the supplier area is seen to include raw material sources and other support suppliers (such as tooling, capital equipment and consumable goods firms). These two sets of firms are not given a tier level as they can be seen to interact with the assembler as well as the other supplier tiers.

The distribution area of Figure 2.8 includes three tiers as well as a section representing the after-market (in this case for spare parts) as well as various other support organizations providing consumables and service items. This complete industry map therefore captures all the firms involved with the area of each part of the diagram proportional to the number of firms in each set.

The second diagram maps the industry in a similar way with the same

FIGURE 2.8   Physical Structure Mapping: an Automotive Industry Example

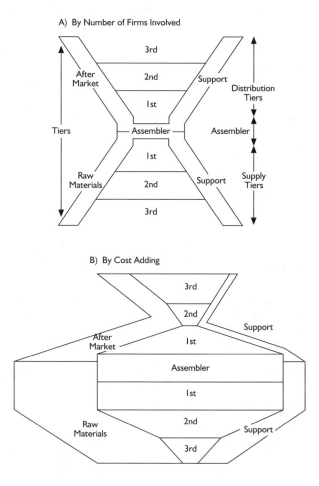

sets of organizations. However, instead of linking the area of the figure of the diagram to the number of firms involved, it is directly linked to the value-adding process (or, strictly speaking, to the cost-adding process). As can be noted in this automotive case, the major cost-adding occurs within the raw material firms, the first tier suppliers and the assembler themselves. The distribution area is not seen to be a major cost-adding area.

However, the basis of use of this second figure is that it is then possible to analyze the value adding that is required in the final product as it is sold to the consumer. Thus Value Analysis or Function Analysis tools employed by industrial engineers can be focused at the complete industry or supply chain structure (Miles, 1961; Akiyama, 1989). Such an approach may result in a redesign of the way in which the industry itself functions. Thus, in a similar way to the discussion of the Process Activity Mapping tool above, attempts can be made to eliminate activities that are unnecessary, simplify others, combine others and seek sequence changes that will reduce waste.

Using the Toolkit

The use of this toolkit should not at this stage be confined to any particular theoretical approach to ultimate implementation. Thus the options can be left open at this stage whether to adopt a *kaizen* or Business Process Re-engineering approach once the tools have been used (Imai, 1986; Hammer, 1990). It is the author's belief that this framework does not constrain this choice process.

Value Stream Mapping Tools

The specific focusing of which tools to use in which circumstances is done using a simplified version of the Value Stream Analysis Tool (VALSAT) (Hines *et al.*, 1998) also described in more detail in a later chapter. The first part of this process is to identify the specific value stream to be reviewed; the second, through a series of preliminary interviews with managers in the value stream, is to identify the various wastes that exist in the value stream that the managers believe can and should be removed (reference should be made to the earlier discussion of the seven wastes). In addition, it is important to gain the views of these managers on the importance of understanding the complete industry structure, irrespective of which wastes are to be removed.

To identify the various wastes that exist in the value stream that the managers believe can and should be removed.

This focusing is achieved by giving the interviewees a written overview of each of the wastes as well as what is meant by the industry structure. At this stage, if necessary, the seven wastes can be reworded into a more sympathetic form for the industry under consideration. For instance, in the healthcare industry the concept of overproduction may not have great value. However, a rewording to call this potential waste 'doing things too early' may be more useful so that the interviewees can relate the concept to their own situations.

Once this has been done, the reworded seven wastes and overall structure are recorded as eight rows in the VALSAT diagram, or as eight rows in area A of Figure 2.9. Comparison of Figure 2.1 and Figure 2.9 will show that the former is a simplification of the latter but with sections A, B and C already completed. Thus, using this VALSAT method, the different approaches to identifying how these eight variables can be mapped has already been completed by the addition of the seven value stream mapping tools (B). In addition, area C of Figure 2.9 has already been completed, as the correlation between tools and wastes was carried out within the main body of Figure 2.1.

At this point it is useful to ask the firm or firms involved who they would regard as the benchmark company within their sector for each of the eight wastes/structure (D). In other words, by opening these discussions at this stage it forces the firm/firms to think about which of their competitors is best at reducing particular wastes and managing their com-

FIGURE 2.9   Using the VALSAT Approach to Select Effective Value Stream Mapping Tools

		TOOLS	
WASTES/ STRUCTURE	WEIGHT	[B]	COMPETITOR ANALYSIS
[A]	[E]	[C]	[D]
	TOTAL WEIGHT	[F]	

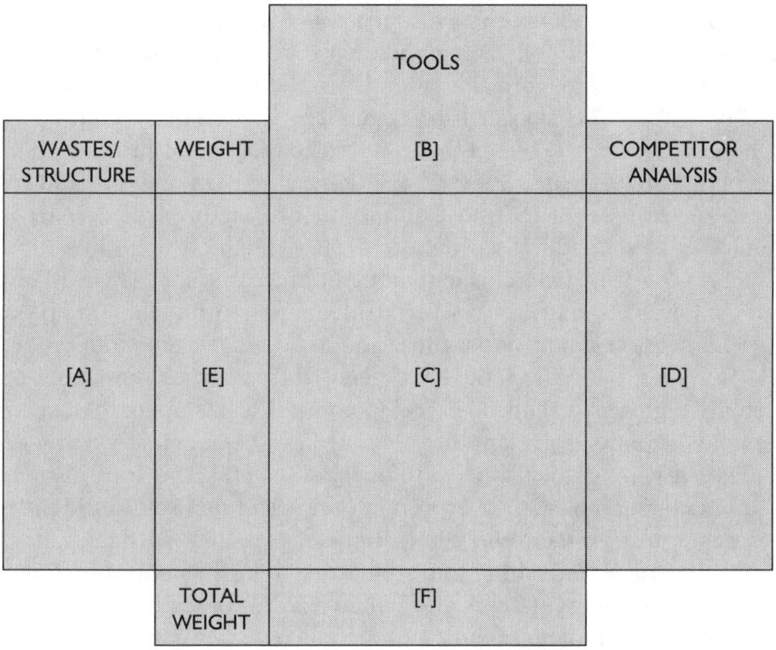

plete supply/distribution chain. This knowledge may then lead on to more formal benchmarking with these companies if this is felt appropriate or at least may form a good focus for subsequent mapping activities.

The next stage (E) is to ascertain the individual importance weighting of the seven wastes and the overall industry structure. This is best achieved by allocating a total of 40 points for the eight factors and asking the interviewee to apportion these on an importance rating basis between the factors, with the proviso that no one factor can attract more than 10 points. If there is more than one interviewee, the different scores can be aggregated and rebased to total 40 points.

The last arithmetical stage of this approach is to create total weights for each tool. In effect, what is being done here is to give a rating to each tool according to how useful it is in identifying the various wastes that are regarded by the organization or organizations as the most important. This is achieved by awarding each of the different correlations given in Figure 2.1 a score. High correlations are equivalent to 9 points, medium 3 points and low 1 point. Then for each correlation a total importance score is calculated. This is achieved by multiplying the weighting of each of the waste/structure by the correlations. Thus, referring to the correlations in Figure 2.1, if the weighting for overproduction is 6 points, the usefulness of the tools in addressing this will be 6 for Process Activity Mapping (6x1), 18 for Supply Chain Response Matrix (6x3), 0 for Production Variety Funnel (6x0), 6 for Quality Filter Mapping (6x1), 18 for Demand Amplification Mapping (6x3), 18 for Decision Point Analysis (6x3) and 0 for Physical Structure Mapping (6x0).

This type of calculation is next applied to each other row so that scores are recorded for each individual correlation. Once this is complete, the total scores for each column are then summed and recorded in the Total Weight section or F in Figure 2.9. The columns that have the highest scores are the ones that contain the most appropriate tools. As a rule of thumb it is usually useful to choose more than one tool. Indeed, as a final check each of the most important two or three wastes/structure should have been addressed by a tool with a high correlation with it or, failing this, at least two tools with a medium correlation. This will ensure that each waste/structure is covered adequately in the mapping process.

This section should assist the reader to identify which tool or tools to use. However, once the tools have been run it may be that some unexpectedly high wastes have become apparent. For instance, the use of the Demand Amplification Mapping tool may have been employed to identify unnecessary inventory and waiting. However, as the tool also has a medium correlation with overproduction, it will be useful in identifying this waste, if it exists, although at first not recognized by the managers involved. This backflushing may therefore identify some unanticipated potential improvement areas and hence lead to some breakthroughs.

After this complete mapping process is complete the researcher will be able to use each individual tool with its associated benefits to undertake more detailed analysis of the value stream with a view to improvement. As stated above it is not the purpose of this paper to constrain other researchers into adopting a *kaizen* or Business Process Re-engineering approach in this subsequent work. However, the various mapping tools described will help with whichever approach is chosen for adoption. In general the removal of Non-Value-Adding waste is best done using a *kaizen* approach, whereas the removal of Necessary but Non-Value-Adding waste requires a more revolutionary approach where the application of Business Process Re-engineering may be more appropriate.

Conclusion

This paper has outlined a new typology and decision-making process for the mapping of the value stream or supply chain. This general approach is grounded in a contingency approach as it allows the researcher to choose the most appropriate methods for the particular industry, people and type of problems that exist. The typology is based around a choice of which particular wastes the researcher/company/value stream members wish to reduce or eliminate. As such it allows for an extension of the effective internal waste reduction philosophy pioneered by leading companies such as Toyota. However, in this case such an approach can be widened and so extended to a value stream setting. This extension process lies at the heart of creating Lean Enterprises with each of the value stream members actively reducing wasteful activity both inside and between their organizations.

CHAPTER 3

Mapping Physical Flows[1]

Introduction

The management of change within a supply chain is perhaps the key role of the enlightened logistics, purchasing and supply manager. However, the task is not easy when the manager is faced with a plethora of fads and 'cure-all' solutions such as TQM, BPR and Lean Thinking (Cox, 1995). The problem here is that 'these fads can, if not properly understood and rigorously analysed, be implemented incorrectly or out of context and can do far more harm than good ... the major reason why fads fail is that those who rush to implement new concepts and ideas often fail to understand that the relationships which work successfully in one business environment may not be as successful when transplanted elsewhere' (Cox, 1995, pp. 72–3). Cox goes on to challenge the academic community to '(develop) a coherent body of empirically verified knowledge concerning which types of sourcing and supply relationships might best be used under what circumstances, and with what costs and benefits to business profitability' (Cox, 1995, p. 73).

Whatever purchasing or supply chain solution is already in place or further development attempted, the costs and benefits should be fully understood.

Inherent in this challenge is that, whatever purchasing or supply chain solution is already in place or further development attempted, the costs and benefits should be fully understood. However, when such costs are based on traditional cost accounting methods, this assumption may be unrealistic because of the weaknesses of these approaches. What is really needed is a more dynamic approach, one linked to the key wastes and

---

[1] This chapter was prepared by Peter Hines and Nick Rich.

value-adding areas of the business. The Value Stream Mapping approach as demonstrated in Chapter 2 provides just such a method and is not only able to capture the existing costs but can also help pinpoint where the opportunities are for future development.

This chapter[2] charts the early trial period of Value Stream Mapping as it was first piloted within both a distribution and manufacturing environment with SCDP sponsor organizations, RS Components and Q8 Lubricants respectively, in late 1995. At this point in time the main activities that were mapped tended to be the physical activity although, as the reader will observe, there was also some attention to information flows. However, this second area was further developed within later research described in the next chapter.

Physical Mapping Within a Distribution Industry Environment

The term 'lean' was popularized by Womack *et al.* (1990) as embodying a system that uses fewer of all inputs to create outputs similar to the mass production system, but offers an increased choice to the end customer. The logic behind lean thinking is that companies jointly identify the value stream for each product from concept to consumption and optimize this value stream regardless of traditional functional or corporate boundaries. This is done by teams organized between functions and between companies, supported by the relevant functional specialists.

In order to facilitate this change process it is necessary to define corporate strategy and to identify key customer-facing processes such as order fulfilment and new product development together with key non-customer-facing processes such as supplier integration or environmental control. Once this is complete, roles and responsibilities can be defined and appropriate structures for improvement put in place (Dimancescu *et al.*, 1997).

The choice for first empirical testing was the UK division of RS Components, a leading distributor of electronic, electrical and mechanical components and instruments. The firm has a UK range of over 80,000 products, which it sells from its two main warehouses based in central England as well as from a network of regional 'over-the-counter' operations. It dispatches more than 15,000 orders per day and employs more than 3,000 people in its UK operations.

---

[2] The first case study discussed here first appeared as: Peter Hines, Nick Rich and Ann Esain, 'Creating a Lean Supplier Network: A Distribution Industry Case', *European Journal of Purchasing and Supply Management* (1998). The authors would like to thank the editor and publishers of EJPSM for agreeing to its reproduction here in a modified form.

The Mapping Programme

At the outset of the change process it was decided by the research team and company alike that a Lean Enterprise perspective would be adopted in the work. It was not, however, determined where in the company or extended enterprise the work would take place. This was to be decided on the basis of need. In order to identify where this need existed, considerable time was spent with the company, involving a range of senior staff. This group represented a spread of different functions in the business. The focus here was on unstructured or semi-structured interviews with representatives from purchasing, inventory control, goods inwards, warehousing operations, marketing, quality and finance. As a result of these discussions it was possible to identify the strategy being enacted by RS Components in terms of market definition, expansion path, warehousing location and growth path, service requirements of customer base and their internationalization programme.

This information was vital in understanding not only what the company was wishing to do, but also what their key customer-facing and non-customer-facing processes were. It was possible to identify the following *four* key processes within the business:

1. *Order Fulfilment*, covering all the activities required from the receipt of an actual order from a customer to its ultimate delivery the next morning to the customer.
2. *New Product Introduction*, covering all the activities required to bring a new product to market. New products were generally offered to RS Components by a manufacturer or distributor who already supplied them with other products.
3. *Sales Acquisition*, involving all activities required to market the existing product range and actually obtain the order from the customer.
4. *Supplier Integration*, involving all activities required to coordinate the various suppliers' activities with RS Components including the reduction of inter-company and intra-company waste (Hines, 1994a).

A review of these key processes showed that the company was exceptional good at the first and third with the New Product Introduction being highly effective. New Product Introduction was not as rapid as RS Components would like and the company had already identified this opportunity and set up an improvement programme.

The present case study therefore focuses on the Supplier Integration process, which was identified as the key process that was at the time underdeveloped and had the potential to yield significant benefits if addressed.

Mapping the Value Stream

Scope

In order to identify the opportunities for improvement of the Supplier Integration process it was decided by the authors and the RS Components management team to map the activities between the buyer and suppliers. In doing so it was necessary to decide where the handover lay between the Supplier Integration process and the customer Order Fulfilment process. A decision was taken to divide the processes at the pick face where goods were available for despatch to RS Components customers. In choosing which products to map it was decided to concentrate on one product category but to look at products with different demand and revenue profiles. The company already defined all of its products according to a Pareto split (A, B, C for both volume of sales and a separate A, B, C for value of sales). As a result there were nine category areas ranging from AA (high volume, high total value) to CC (low volume, low total value).

Organization

In order to simplify data capture, one product was chosen from each of the Pareto categories from one product range area. This was particularly effective as the company had already organized its Order Fulfilment process along value stream lines, that is, with mixed teams of buyers, inventory controllers and marketers co-located and controlling all activities for one of the 17 product areas. These cross-functional teams were supported by a number of small competency centres focusing on purchasing, inventory control and marketing, who provided training and access to knowledge and new developments that could be used by team members. The product range chosen was lighting products, as the earlier discussions with the senior managers had identified this as a 'difficult' range due to its seasonal variability and fragility.

Approach

The Value Stream Mapping approach was adopted. This method involves the identification of value-adding and wasteful activities based around Ohno's seven wastes as shown in Table 3.1 (Monden, 1993). This was achieved through structured interviews with the senior management team described above, representing a wide spectrum of functional responsibilities. This broad range of views allowed for necessary cross-checking, triangulation and outlier identification. Each participant was given a description of the seven wastes (based on Bicheno, 1994) and was asked to apportion 35 points to the wastes according to how important they felt that they were to RS Components.

TABLE 3.1   The Seven Wastes

1.	Overproduction
2.	Waiting
3.	Transportation
4.	Inappropriate Processing
5.	Unnecessary Inventory
6.	Unnecessary Motions
7.	Defects

Within this exercise participants were asked to give between 0 and 10 points to each waste with a total of 35 points. The result of this exercise proved that unnecessary inventory was by far the largest perceived waste. Indeed the company was achieving stock turns of only around three per year at the start of the work in late 1995. In addition, due to the rapid increase in sales such a situation would lead to the requirement for a new warehouse in the UK every five years.

Applying a weighted average of the wastes it was possible to identify which of the available mapping tools would be most appropriate, using the waste/tool correlation chart (Figure 3.1). Five tools were selected and the results of their application are illustrated in Figures 3.2–3.6 with only one product displayed for simplicity in Figures 3.2–3.4 and an average or overview in Figures 3.5–3.6. Some key learning points from the mapping exercise will be briefly summarized below. It should be noted that only

FIGURE 3.1   The Seven Value Stream Mapping Tools

Mapping Tool — Wastes/ Structure	1. Process Activity Mapping	2. Supply Chain Response Matrix	3. Production Variety Funnel	4. Quality Filter Mapping	5. Demand Amplification Mapping	6. Decision Point Analysis	7. Physical Structure a) Volume b) Value
1. Overproduction	L	M		L	M	M	
2. Waiting	H	H	L		M	M	
3. Transportation	H						L
4. Inappropriate Processing	H		M	L		L	
5. Unnecessary Inventory	M	H	M		H	M	L
6. Unnecessary Motion	H	L					
7. Defects	L			H			

H   High Correlation and Usefulness
M   Medium Correlation and Usefulness
L   Low Correlation and Usefulness

FIGURE 3.2 Process Activity Map

#	Step	FLOW	Area	Dist (m)	Time (min)	People	Operation	Transport	Inspect	Store	Delay	Comments
1	Driver takes paperwork to office	T	Outside/office	50	0.5	–	O	T		S	D	
2	Check booked in/issue ticket	I	Office	10	1	1(+1)	O		▬	S	D	(Driver)
3	Driver to vehicle	T	Office/outside	50	0.5	–	O	T		S	D	
4	Open back of truck	O	Outside		–	–	●	T		S	D	
5	Back on to bay	T	Outside/bay	30	–	–	O	T		S	D	
6	Wait for pump truck	D	Bay		15	–	O	T		S	D	
7	Unload lorry	D	Splitting	25	20	1(+1)	O	T		S	D	10 pallets
8	Wait for total unloading	D	Splitting		10	2(+1)	O	T		S	D	Driver (total 30)
9	Wait for paperwork	D	Splitting		0.5	(1)	O	T		S	D	
10	Driver to office for paperwork	T	Outside/office	20	3	1(+1)	O	T		S	D	
11	Get paperwork	D	Office		120		O			S	D	
12	Delay to start splitting	D	Splitting		50		O	T		S	D	
13	Splitting	O	Splitting	20	–	2	●	T	▬	S	D	Pump truck
14	Move pallet to quantification	T	Quantification		240	1	O	T		S	D	
15	Delay to quantify	D	Quantification		10		O	T		S	D	
16	Quantify	I	Quantification		2	–	O	T	▬	S	D	
17	Move to lift and load	T	Inspection/lift	3	0.3	–	O	T		S	D	
18	Move to WIP	T	Lift to WIP	5	5		O	T		S	D	
19	Delay	D	Lift top		2	–	O	T		S	D	
20	Remove from lift	T	Lift top	2	2	–	O	T		S	D	
21	Place in storage area	T	Floor	10			O	T		S	D	
22	Storage	D	Floor		2880		O	T		S	D	
23	Collect production order	T	To office	25	15	–	O	T		S	D	
24	Pull stock to production area	T	To packing	10	2		O	T		S	D	
25	Delay	D	Packing		15		O	T		S	D	
26	Load machine and cycle	O	Packing	2	0.1	1	●	T		S	D	Hand pump
27	Place in tote	T	Packing	0.5	0.1	(1)	O	T		S	D	Setup
28	Wait for batch	D	Packing		30		O			S	D	
29	Load conveyor	T	Packing to conveyor	12	0.5	1	O	T		S	D	
30	Travel to crane	T	To crane	150	5		O	T		S	D	
31	Wait for crane	D	Crane		5		O			S	D	
32	Put into main store	T	Crane/store	75	1	1	O	T		S	D	
33	Store	D	Store		155.4		O			S	D	
					33.6							
Total				489.5	158.8	29						
					84.1							
					51.1							
					322 mpm							
Operations						4						
Percentage operations						13.8%						

about 50 per cent of the learning points are drawn directly from the maps, with the others based on the researchers' observations made during and after the mapping project.

The Process Activity Map (Figure 3.2) showed that for most of the time that products are within the defined supply chain no value is being added and, indeed, a new term 'Minutes Per Million (MPM)' was used to describe the ratio of operating time to total time because of the extremely low ratio found. In addition, many delay points were identified in goods inwards but a very low product failure rate was identified at the incoming quality check. It was also noted that the inherent high urgency of products inside RS Components was rarely found in the external supply chain.

The Supply Chain Response Matrix (Figure 3.3) identified that the supplier lead times were on average very long, with other internal lead times considerably shorter. It also showed that there was a very high level of available stock in the main storage area with other stock holdings relatively low. There also appeared to be no direct pull of goods from market needs; instead, an inventory-based push system was in place. This issue was further exacerbated by the less even demand profile of product shipped to the 'over-the-counter' operations.

The Demand Amplification Map (Figure 3.4) showed that the company was good at forecasting the demand of products with the forecast and actual demand curves in close parallel. However, there was a fundamental

FIGURE 3.3 Supply Chain Response Matrix

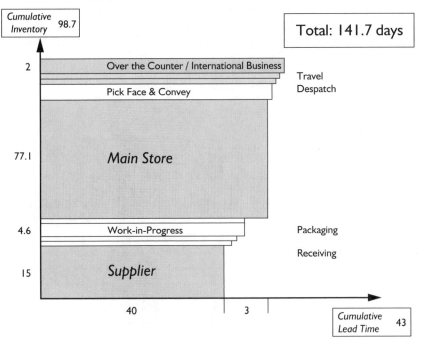

FIGURE 3.4 Demand Amplification Map

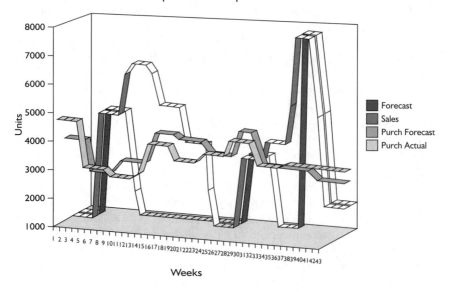

dislocation between actual demand and actual purchases required. In addition the on-time delivery performance of suppliers was poor, with often lengthy delays occurring.

The Quality Filter Map illustrated (Figure 3.5) was based on an average of the products surveyed. As can be clearly seen the quality of incoming products, especially allowing for the very fragile nature of the lighting products measured, is very high and there is relatively little internal

FIGURE 3.5 Quality Filter Map

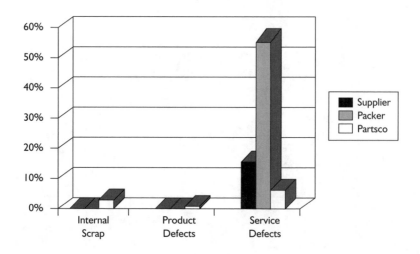

damage. However, the service defects are very considerable, mostly as a result of late delivery. Some of this is a result of the product suppliers' performance, but more was attributable to problems caused by the third-party packer being used.

The Decision Point Analysis map (Figure 3.6) was used to identify where customer product pull reached in the total supply chain. The dislocation point where customer pull met supply chain push was found to be at the pick face, the point indeed which the researchers had earlier defined as being the cut-off point between the Supplier Integration and Order Fulfilment processes. This decision-point definition was used to challenge the storage culture that was prevalent in RS Components and the industry in general. The question 'What do you call a distributor with no stock' was asked with most answers being something like 'in trouble', rather than perhaps a lean thinking response of 'slick'.

These maps, together with a much more detailed analysis of the existing situation, were fed back to the senior management team at RS Components. Following this feedback a discussion was facilitated about how the company and its Supplier Integration process could move forward. In order to aid the discussion, a 'chocolate box' of possible options correlated with the seven wastes was used (Figure 3.7). The result of this discussion was that it was decided by the management team to test the use of a Supplier Association as a structural mechanism to facilitate a Supplier Integration Process and to make radical improvements in RS Components'

FIGURE 3.6   Decision Point Analysis

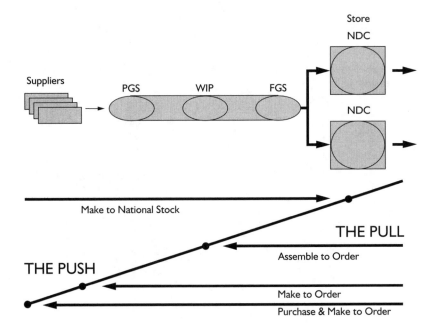

FIGURE 3.7 The Partsco Chocolate Box

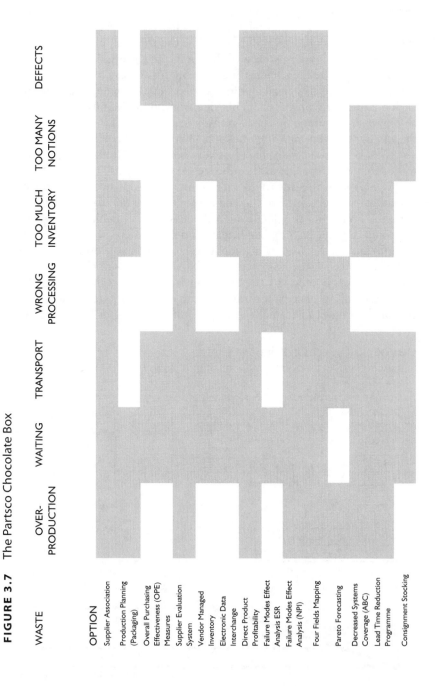

supply chain. Exactly how this was undertaken and the results of this work will be reviewed later in this text.

The Value Stream Mapping provided RS Components not only with a detailed analysis of where waste and opportunity lay but also with a framework for decision-making as to how to make rapid developments in their Supplier Integration process. The work has been described by one senior RS Components executive as 'not rocket science but very effective ... and who wants rocket science anyway'.

Physical Mapping Within a Manufacturing Environment

The ability to portray graphically the complex arrangements of flows of information and material throughout the supply chain to a focal organization is one dimension of the Value Stream Mapping suite of techniques. The second dimension contributing to the effectiveness of these techniques is the ability to conduct several cross-sectional analyses of the internal value chain or that element which the management of the company can control directly. The ability to assess periodically the performance of the business is important in assessing the rate of internal improvement in factory performance as well as providing the ability to re-focus the deployment of internal resources on the weakest elements of the customer service equation.

The ability to assess periodically the performance of the business is important in assessing the rate of internal improvement in factory performance.

Identifying The Key Processes Of Customer Service

For any manufacturing or service operation, there are three key processes that create a return on investment for the company and also serve as the basis on which the company is measured by its customers. These three processes are 'Quality', 'Delivery' and 'Cost', and these elements of the customer service equation span the business in an end-to-end flow of activities that is conducted by many business departments and whose combined effort determines the output for the entire business. The objective of any manufacturing business is therefore to optimize the flow of materials through the factory by constantly improving the quality of the conversion process and its inputs; next, to ensure that the materials are provided in a timely fashion; and finally to streamline the administrative activities and other costs associated with the management of this process. These primary measures of business efficiency can be supplemented with additional processes that concern the development of key competences and capabilities on which the future success of the organization will depend. In contemporary times, these capabilities include the ability to offer a short lead time within the design or 'time to market' cycle, the protection of the environment and customer and supplier partnerships. The latter activities represent investments made by the management of the business today, to protect the competitive position of the organization of tomorrow.

The objective of any manufacturing business is to optimize the flow of materials through the factory by constantly improving the quality of the conversion process and its inputs.

This case study is drawn from work conducted with Q8 Lubricants in Leeds, UK. The site operates two distinct value streams, the first producing neat oils and the second, soluble oils. Both value streams share a similar process path in that the lubricants are blended, quality assured and then packaged into a variety of container types.

Mapping the Internal Value Stream

The scope of the mapping exercise, determined by the management of the factory, covered a mix of high-volume products (termed 'runners'), medium-volume products (termed 'repeaters') and a selection of low-volume and special products (termed 'strangers'). These products were representative of the cross-section of products that were processed by both the soluble and neat internal value chains.

The Organization of the Mapping Activity

The mapping exercise was conducted following the 'seven wastes' ranking exercise by the senior management team, the middle managers and the factory team leaders. The ranking exercise was not 'limited' as in the case of the RS Components exercise where only 35 points were available to be distributed across the seven wastes. Instead, the ranking exercise was 'open' and each individual waste was ranked on a scale of 1 to 10. A score of 10 represented a major form of waste, while a score of 1 represented an insignificant level of waste as perceived by the factory team. The key wastes identified by the team included overproduction, delay, transportation and defects (seen in terms of the level of inspection operated by the factory and not the actual production of defective products). From this point onwards a 'bore down' approach was used to understand the nature of the business. In this process, the decision-point analysis, the supply-chain responsiveness matrix and the demand-amplification chart were used to assess the organization in its wider supply chain, and the quality filter and process activity maps were used to understand the control of the internal value stream.

The maps selected for the Value Stream Mapping included the following :

1. The Decision Point Analysis.
2. The Supply Chain Responsiveness Matrix.
3. The Demand Amplification Chart.
4. The Quality Filter Map.
5. The Production Variety Funnel.
6. The Process Activity Map.

The Results of the Maps

The 'power' of the Value Stream Mapping exercise does not lie with any single map. Each has its own merits and demerits, the real advantage to the application of this 'toolbox' being in the generation of multiple 'cuts' of the same or similar information. It is these dissections that provide the most fruitful avenues for investigation. The next section will address the findings of each chart independently before collating the mapping information and describing the way forward taken by the company.

The Decision Point Analysis demonstrated that the business could be divided into a number of generic elements which included:

1. Material supplies from the refinery operations (a member of the same company but located in the Netherlands). The materials used by the factory were stored in bulk tank farms and also in specialist drums.
2. Primary blending operations where base oils and additive oils were blended using large tanks that were agitated for a time.
3. The next stage represented the conditioning of the lubricant.
4. Following the period of conditioning, the lubricant could be transferred to the automated and manual packaging lines where they were packed and palletized.
5. The products were then sent to the local third party warehouse to await shipment to the European customer base serviced by the company.

The decision point analysis demonstrated that the company had traditionally 'pushed' the production of the site to the stage of the warehouse where the product could be 'pulled' by the customer. This system, using finished goods stocks as the primary buffer to meet customer service, provided high levels of customer service but effectively competed on distribution efficiency. The map provided certain alternatives for the company, namely the use of the finishing operations to begin a programme of 'package to order' or to go further upstream in the value stream to engage in a production system of 'one tank flow'. In the 'package to order' situation, the company could postpone the manufacturing of products until such time as an actual order was received from customers to trigger the finishing of products and the timely movement of finished products through the warehouse (as a consolidation and staging point only, rather than as a stocking point) and into the hands of the customer. For the 'one tank flow' system, the levels of finished goods would be monitored so that reaching predetermined levels of inventory would trigger the replenishment of a single tank (or less) of lubricants. However, these systems would be contingent on the capacity of the packaging lines and the 'level' nature of customer demand being placed on the factory.

The second chart employed, of a high-level, macro view of the factory, was the supply-chain responsiveness matrix. This mapping technique plots the cumulative inventory holding of the company against the cumulative lead time involved in the planning and movement of the materials throughout the system. This map revealed a relatively even spread of inventory between the 'supplier' and 'finished goods' buffers with a small (finite) amount of work-in-progress held in the conditioning vessels and tanks. The lead times affecting the factory were comparatively high for 'additive' oils from the refinery, yet all other processes in the factory and the distribution chain were highly responsive and accounted for negligible amounts of lead time. The map suggested that the process efficiency of the factory was very high, and that the 'natural' break in the process path (the conditioning vessels) could be used as a buffer to protect the packaging lines as well as to allow the development of a 'pack to order' style of production system.

The third chart to be used in the Value Stream Mapping exercise was the demand amplification chart. The chart was constructed using an analysis of individual customer accounts for 'repeating' and 'stranger' categories of products and for a portfolio of the key accounts for the 'runner' category. For the most part, the regular products offered by the company experienced seasonality but no true traumatic 'feasts' and 'famines' through the trading cycle. When this analysis was decomposed to the 'monthly bucket' level, certain order patterns emerged that reflected a 'peak' in orders received at the end of the month. The major sources of demand amplification came from the medium-volume repeaters and the low-volume strangers as customers engaged in periodic reviews of inventory which triggered orders. A second element of the demand amplification, affecting the soluble oils (used as equipment and cutting tool coolants and lubricants) were the processing volumes of the customer. As volume rose in the customer organizations, but the monthly review of stocks held at the customer remained the same, amplification was created. In turn, the blending operations started to produce a batch of products to replenish the finished goods at the factory and, after a small amount of time, the highly responsive packaging lines became energized and sent through the batch of packed product (creating two slightly offset peaks in the amplification chart). The demand amplification, produced as a result of the consumption of materials by the blending plant, had no effect on the base oil cycle of level orders placed on the supplier, but the specialist additives (on a long lead time) exaggerated the sudden short-term uplift in packaging requirements.

The Quality Filter Map was used to trace the 'losses' in the supply, production, and distribution elements of the supply chain. In this case, the level of physical defects was low and the level of service defects was equally low at the point of receiving oils from the supply base. Internally, the paperwork and scrap figures did not record any incident and only a minor level of product re-work was found. In the distribution chain, the service and defect figures were also insignificant with only a small amount of paperwork losses discovered. The map clearly demonstrated that the physical production process was well managed and in control with only minor levels of paper-related and procedural issues to draw the attention of the continuous improvement teams.

The Production Variety Funnel was constructed for the factory by identifying several key additive oils (the base oils used by the factory are integral elements of all products packaged by the site). These additives, starting from a single additive grade, then expanded as the additive was introduced to different oil formulations in the tanks at the factory and 'blossomed' as the blend (containing the additive) was packaged into a wide variety of different packaging media. The amount of variety at the latter end of the internal value chain is common to most FMCG and process industries and results from the offering of the same product in a multitude of different container sizes. In this case, this included such packaging as small pack (500ML plastic bottles), 1L plastic bottles, 2L plastic bottles, and steel cans, as well as a variety of labels for each type of package that depended on the market being serviced or on the branding of the customer. The implication of the variety analysis was that the best and most flexible location of products in the value stream was in a 'pre-packaged' state (or the products should be held in the conditioning tanks). The great 'tail' of packaging specifications meant that to produce and package lubricants and place them in the warehouse against a forecast of sales consumed production capacity and held many commercial risks. The variety funnel therefore suggests that the lubricants should be 'packaged to order' to avoid these risks and to make the most use of the flexibility of the factory and its personnel.

The final mapping technique employed was the process activity map. These maps, conducted for the three categories of products using the two different process paths, demonstrated that the process route through the factory was not simple but included a period of time in storage, a fixed amount of time as the lubricants were blended and conditioned, a period of storage or delay before the blend was 'pulled' into the filling heads at the packaging line and then an insignificant amount of time as the bottles were filled. From this point, the packaged products would wait until the haulier arrived at the site and then the products could be taken to the warehouse for storage. The maps demonstrated that there was a long travel distance involved in the production process and that the value added could be improved in the factory by revising procedures, controlling the amount of time in the production process and relocating processes.

Value Stream Mapping : The Synthesis

The result of the many different individual maps was a series of questions raised by one map, confirmed by a second, and solved by a third. In this respect, the decision-point analysis raised questions about the most advantageous point at which to allow the 'pull' of customer orders to trigger production, the identification of holding pre-packaged stocks was confirmed by the production variety funnel and the demand amplification chart demonstrated that this form of manufacturing to order was possible as a means of levelling the workload of the blending operations. In parallel, the other charts demonstrated areas of 'quick win' that could be achieved through the focusing of improvement projects by the team leaders.

The feedback presentation was attended by the entire management team involved in the 'waste ranking' exercise, and the formal presentation of all the maps as a suite provided a powerful insight into the key variables that served to destabilize the current production system, as well as acting as a forum for individuals to explain, in greater detail, the problems faced as part of their role in the organization and their ability to contribute to the quality, cost and delivery of products. The latter part of the day was spent engaged in a brainstorming exercise to identify the 'quick hit' immediate solutions to the issues identified and also to scope a longer term series of improvement projects. These projects included customer-facing programmes, operational and planning improvement activities as well as a supplier-development initiative. The core underlying objectives for each of the programmes were derived from the VALSAT approach and each project was focused on the improvement of one or a combination of the key 'customer service generating' business processes (quality, cost, delivery, design and external partnerships).

The core underlying objectives for each of the programmes were derived from the VALSAT approach.

As the programme of events was introduced and individuals began to adopt positions of 'empowerment' for the processes under their control, the factory began to change physically and visually. The shopfloor teams excelled under the new regime and began to introduce increasingly tighter specifications to the conversion process (the development of a standardized production system), employees began to transfer to the third party warehouse to undertake improvement activities there, and the entire factory began to 'up skill' through the use of local training courses and study for national qualifications (Dimancescu *et al.*, 1997).

The management-led revitalization of the factory also created a 'tidal wave' of reform including the relocation of assets, the revisiting of existing procedures in the factory, and the determination of 'value' and 'waste' in the production process. Some of the key activities undertaken by the teams included:

1. The complete re-layout of the factory focusing on the elimination of non-value-added time and distance.

2. The relocation of secondary materials stores (such as labels and packaging) to the point at which the materials were consumed.

3. The development of a regular 'shuttle' between the factory and the warehouse.

4. A series of visits to the suppliers to understand their processes and exchange tactical and strategic information relating to the Leeds site.

5. A series of visits to key customers to understand their processes and to evaluate the effectiveness of their ordering activities as well as the future requirements of the customer.

6. The streamlining and removal of unnecessary administrative procedures for the movement of materials through the factory.

7. Colour-coding to differentiate assets, dedicated components for specific assets, and to assist in the appraisal of the technology when it was in process.

8. The housekeeping of the factory site and the development of audit procedures to maintain the highest level of discipline in the factory.

9. The development of technological improvement projects to support the 'ease of use' and 'ease of changeover' in the factory.

10. The introduction of a new product and packaging line without incident or disturbance to the existing production lines.

However, of all the major improvements and the amount of effort expended by the business, the greatest single achievement was derived from the people in the factory. The mapping exercise provided a common frame of reference for all the different administrative and operational departments in the factory, but without an 'enlightened' management approach to the employees the rate of change in the factory could not have been created or sustained. The mapping exercise was, therefore, only a catalyst that allowed all employees to determine 'value' and 'waste' in their own operations and in the activities of their internal customers and suppliers. This activity forges a link between the external dimension of customer service and the internal development of the concept, and as a consequence, the greater number of employees in the factory began to question, rather than accept, customary practice and to develop their own team territories. These invisible territories marked areas of control that were owned by the team and for which standards of discipline were maintained by the team. In this sense, the mapping exercise became 'personalized' and served as a means of tracking the rate of improvement and performance of the team as much as it generated new ideas and questions concerning future improvements.

Value Stream Mapping : A Manufacturing Perspective

In conclusion, the application of the mapping techniques provided a basis for understanding the factory and its supply chain in simple terms that were based on observing the operations rather than discussing the many anecdotal pieces of evidence that tend to be forwarded by employees who are close to the production process and naturally seek to explain 'why' the system could not be applied to 100 percent of products. Instead, the mapping techniques show and provide facts that allow the improvement of the customer service levels achieved by the regular 'runners' and 'repeaters' that account for the bulk of the annual volumes processed by the factory. The 'strangers' (or the 'trivial many' in volume terms) provided the exceptions and generated the need to introduce policies to manage such products.

The real 'upshot' for the use of the Value Stream Mapping methodology developed is derived from the cost-benefit analysis, which is to say that the use of all the techniques takes very little time and effort but the ability of the diagnosis to offer new opportunities, confirm the opinions of employees or run completely counter to the perceptions of individuals is invaluable to the management of the internal and external value streams. The mapping exercise therefore serves to evaluate the many different 'like to do' or 'hobby horse' projects of each manager and employee by taking an holistic view of the organization and its role in generating 'customer service', rather than in implementing 'solutions' based on opinion or current management fashion. The tools also concentrate on the key products through which a small percentage saving has a 'multiplier' effect created through the annual volume of the product, rather than attempting to find isolated products where large savings could be made but with no multiplier. The mapping toolbox is therefore a powerful means of systematically analyzing the 'health' or 'leanness' of a business over time rather than a unique or 'one off' event which provokes debate but no action.

The mapping toolbox is a powerful means of systematically analyzing the 'health' or 'leanness' of a business over time.

The future development of the mapping techniques, based on the pioneering efforts of the SCDP sponsor organizations is likely to take three key routes:

1. The continuous improvement of the current techniques through an iterative process of revisiting the lessons learned through the appli-

cation of the techniques across the many different implementation programmes.

2. The development of a more specialized approach to key business processes (such as the mapping of the 'environmental' citizenship of the organization, etc.).

3. The development of a suite of mapping techniques for the 'jobbing shop' manufacturing sector. This sector of industry operates with low-down to nil levels of repetitive products, has very low levels of formal management controls and often lacks a sufficiently detailed amount of 'process' information.

The authors would like to express their gratitude to the many SCDP sponsor companies who took part in the Value Stream Mapping programme and assisted in the development, and the future refinements, of this research.

CHAPTER 4

Mapping Information Flows

Introduction

This chapter[1] summarizes the findings of the author's research into the role of information as a determinant of Supply Chain effectiveness. In doing so it extends the earlier work carried out within SCDP (demonstrated in the last two chapters) that focused primarily on physical flows within the internal or external supply chain.

The current Lean paradigm (Womack and Jones, 1996) is rooted in the physical dimension. The origins of Lean Thinking can be traced to the Toyota Production System (Monden, 1983) and the automotive shop floor. Here the key driver of business success is perceived to be the effective management of material through the supply chain, encompassing inventory management, production processes, materials management and supplier development. In general the term 'world class', when given to a supply chain setting, is defined in terms of physical and financial performance metrics (Andersen Consulting, 1992 and 1994).

Widespread dissemination of Toyota-related techniques have resulted in a highly evolved body of knowledge regarding this physical dimension. This is witnessed by the number of books and journal articles discussing aspects of the Toyota Production System (Ohno, 1988; Shingo, 1989; Monden 1983 and 1993) and Lean Production (Womack *et al.*, 1990).

The information dimension encompasses the communication and

---

[1] This chapter is based on Mark Francis, 'Lean Information and Supply Chain Effectiveness', *International Journal of Logistics: Research and Applications*, Volume 1, Number 1, 1998. I would like to thank the editors and publishers of this journal for giving permission for the article to be reproduced here in a slightly modified form.

> *The information dimension encompasses the communication and decision-making infrastructure which overlays and is interwoven with the physical dimension.*

decision-making infrastructure which overlays and is interwoven with the physical dimension. With few exceptions (Jones, 1997), the literature regarding the specific role of information within the Lean paradigm is severely lacking. However the pivotal role of information was identified during numerous SCDP research projects (James *et al.*, 1996). The symptoms detailed in Table 4.1 were repeatedly conveyed to researchers via observation, semi-structured interview and anecdotal evidence.

The *Lean Information Project* was founded to redress these deficiencies. Specific project aims were to research the role of information as a deter-

TABLE 4.1 Some Symptoms of Information Waste

1. Long, unpredictable processing lead times
2. Presence of bottleneck departments
3. Lack of consensus regarding priority (especially within bottleneck departments)
4. Proliferation of error and query routes
5. Multiple iterations (of unpredictable duration) for problem resolution
6. Proliferation of validation checks, and validation of the validation checks!
7. Simultaneous multiple error resolution with multiple external entity staff
8. Inability to recall an occurrence of a key document which was completely 'right first time' from an external supplier
9. Lack of standard work practice and disparate routing
10. Absence of auditability and accurate retrospective root cause analysis
11. Multiple, uncontrolled document copies in simultaneous circulation
12. Presence of unofficial and/or uncontrolled expedite path (fast-track)
13. Batching of documents
14. Ineffective (or non-existent) workload scheduling
15. Personal filing systems with incomplete, inconsistent and erroneous file sets (official and unofficial)
16. Expediting and inter-departmental recrimination
17. Multiple, departmental computer applications for project tracking
18. High levels of data entry errors and re-keying
19. Production of reports which nobody uses
20. Computer applications which automate existing manual tasks

minant of Supply Chain effectiveness and to synthesize new concepts, tools and techniques to facilitate effective change in this dimension. Its objectives are listed in Table 4.2.

It was decided to adopt a case study approach. Multiple SCDP sponsor involvement was sought in each of the following key value streams (Hines *et al.*, 1997):

1. *New Product Development (NPD)*: All activity involved in the design and development of a new product.

2. *New Product Introduction (NPI)*: All activity required to bring a new product to market, up to the point where stock is allocated to the Distribution Centre or point of sale.

3. *Promotion*: All activity involved in creating and servicing a programme of product promotion, from inception to delivery of the product to its point of sale.

4. *Order Acquisition*: All activity required to market the existing product range, obtain an order from a customer and enter it into the order entry system.

5. *Order Fulfilment*: All activity required to ensure the timely delivery of the customer's order, from order receipt to physical delivery.

This paper summarizes the key findings of the following cases:

1. *New Product Introduction (NPI)*: UK Retailer.
   2. *Pricing (Order Acquisition and Price Entry)*: Lubricant Manufacturer.

3. *Promotions*: Brewing industry.

4. *Software Application Development*: Automotive sector.

Information is a holistic topic related to cost and quality. In order to confine the cases within manageable proportions, guidance criteria were established with participants. All cases were to be problem-driven. As indicated in Figure 4.1 the scope of the project was to encompass Information Systems (IS) and not to be limited to Information Technology (IT),

TABLE 4.2 The Objectives of the Lean Information Project

1. Produce an expanded body of knowledge.

2. Test the applicability of the *Five Lean Principles* in the information domain (Womack and Jones, 1996).

3. Generate a codification of 'Information Waste'.

4. Produce a profile of Value-Added/Non-Value-Added and Necessary but Non-Value-Added for information driven domains.

FIGURE 4.1   Information Systems (IS) and Information Technology (IT)

Information Systems (IS)	Ascertaining demand for applications
Information Technology (IT)	Satisfying demand for applications

Adapted from Edwards *et al.* (1995).

thus differentiating between information demand (IS) and supply (IT). The initial focus was to be on the information drivers of physical material through the internal supply chain.

Methodology

A case-driven, applied, problem-solving approach was adopted, congruent with previous research carried out at the Lean Enterprise Research Centre at Cardiff Business School. The methodology was a derivative of the Value Stream Mapping framework proposed by Hines and Rich (1997) and modified by the author for the information domain. Semi-structured interviews and participant observation were conducted within this framework. Triangulation was achieved by analyzing multiple map perspectives and also by correlating this quantitative output with the qualitative information derived by interview and observation. Interview participants and senior management were given copies of the resultant report and asked to challenge the content to achieve validation.

Multiple maps were constructed, the focal map being a Two-Phase Process Activity Map (PAM). The Phase-1 PAM was a standard map of the type employed in industrial engineering (Figure 4.2). This involved documenting the distance, duration and number of people involved in each activity step comprising a sub-process (logical part of the process with a defined entry and exit point). Each such step was classified as either an *Operation, Transportation, Inspection* or *Storage* activity ('OTIS').

The characteristics of the information domain necessitated a wider interpretation of these activity types. *Decision-making* (thinking time) was consequently incorporated within the *Operation* classification on the basis that a decision can add value. *Delay* was incorporated within the *Storage* classification.

During Phase 2 an additional codification was superimposed onto each activity step. This involved translating each of the above activities

TABLE 4.3   Phase 1 Process Activity Map

EG/10: Receive Specification and Produce Legal Copy

	Description Product Code: ABC1	Dist (Yds)	Time (Mins)	Staff	○	➡	◻	▲
1	Delay until receive spec. is picked up by Secretary	0	30	0				x
2	Carry it from mail area to Secretary's desk	5	1	1		x		
3	Wait until convenient to 'process' it	0	60	0				x
4	Log receipt onto Project Tracking system and create file	0	1	1	x			
5	Store file in Out-Tray	0	15	0				x
6	Move file to Legal expert's In-Tray	5	1	1		x		
7	Await Legal expert's attention (busy)	0	1440	0				x
8	Legal expert processes copy	0	20	1	x			
9	Store processed copy in Out-tray	0	2880	0				x
10	Move copy to Secretary's desk when convenient	5	1	1		x		
11	Delay until Secretary logs completion on Project Tracking	0	180	0				x
12	Take copy file to photocopier	10	2	1		x		
13	Photocopy x 3	0	2	1	x			
14	Return with copies to desk	10	2	1		x		
15	Collate, staple and 'stuff' internal mail envelopes (immed.)	0	15	1	x			
16	Take 3 x envelopes to departmental Out-Tray	5	1	1		x		
17								
18								
19								
20								
21								
22								
23								
24								
	TOTALS	**40**	**4651**	**10**	**38** **x4**	**8** **x6**	**0** **x0**	**4605** **x6**

KEY: ○ Operation   ➡ Transport   ◻ Inspection   ▲ Storage

TABLE 4.4 Phase 2 Process Activity Map

EG/10: Receive Specification and Produce Legal Copy

	Description / Product Code: ABC1	Dist (Yds)	Time (Mins)	Staff	○	➡	☐	▲
1	Delay until receive spec. is picked up by Secretary	0	30	0				–
2	Carry it from mail area to Secretary's desk	5	1	1		–		
3	Wait until convenient to 'process' it	0	60	0				–
4	Log receipt onto Project Tracking system and create file	0	1	1	+			
5	Store file in Out-Tray	0	15	0				–
6	Move file to Legal expert's In-Tray	5	1	1		0		
7	Await Legal expert's attention (busy)	0	1440	0				0
8	Legal expert processes copy	0	20	1	+			
9	Store processed copy in Out-tray	0	2880	0				–
10	Move copy to Secretary's desk when convenient	5	1	1		0		
11	Delay until Secretary logs completion on Project Tracking	0	180	0				–
12	Take copy file to photocopier	10	2	1		–		
13	Photocopy x 3	0	2	1	–			
14	Return with copies to desk	10	2	1		–		
15	Collate, staple and 'stuff' internal mail envelopes (immed.)	0	15	1	+			
16	Take 3 x envelopes to departmental Out-Tray	5	1	1		0		
17								
18								
19								
20								
21								
	TOTALS	40	4651	10	36	8	0	4605
	VA (34 mins)				34			
	NVA (3172 mins)				2	5		3165
	NNVA (1443 mins)					3		1440

KEY: + VA   – NVA   0 NNAVA

TABLE 4.5 The 'Rules' of Phase 2 Translation

1. Only an *Operation* can be Value-Adding (VA).

2. Not all *Operations* will be Value-Adding (VA).

3. *Transportation, Inspection* and *Storage* activities can be either Non-Value-Adding (NVA) or Necessary but Non-Value-Adding (NNVA); Classification is subjective based upon the time scale, resource and future state model envisaged by the classifier.

Value-Adding (VA), *Non-Value-Adding* (NVA) and *Necessary but Non-Value-Adding* (NNVA) – the three generic activities suggested by Yasuhiro Monden (1993). The latter two categories encompass all the waste in the system.

Table 4.4 illustrates the Phase 2 map for the *'Receive Specification and Produce Legal Copy'* sub-process. The translation criteria are outlined in Table 4.5.

Monden's generic activities were originally developed for the manufacturing shop floor. These definitions have limited applicability within the administrative environment. The following interpretation was applied for the case.

Value Adding (VA)

Originally defined as 'a conversion process on the (shop floor)', this type of activity results directly in the accrual of 'value' in the eyes of the end customer. VA activity is that activity considered essential for the perceived quality of final offering and regulatory compliance. It is that activity which it is unthinkable *not* to conduct in any future state model or scenario. For example, accurate entry of pricing information into the computer (Pricing case) or the first-occasion scrutiny of labelling information by a legal expert to ensure statutory compliance (New Product Introduction case).

Non-Value-Adding (NVA)

Any activity which clearly creates no value (and adds cost), which can be removed immediately (short run) with minimum or no capital investment and with no detrimental impact on end value, NVA is also characterized as possessing minimum knock-on effect if removed. This is classified as 'Type Two Muda' by Womack and Jones (1996:p. 20). It is pure waste and should be targeted for immediate elimination. For example, documents sitting in a departmental in-tray awaiting attention.

Necessary but Non-Value-Adding (NNVA)

Any activity which again creates no value but is unavoidable, given the current operating constraints of technology, production assets and operating procedures of the system under examination. This is 'Type One Muda' (Womack and Jones, 1996:p. 20) and includes the physical movement of documents between departments. This activity will ideally be eliminated in the long run, but it is envisaged that this will require capital investment and/or re-engineering activity.

Findings

The methodology derived both quantitative and qualitative findings. The following represents the quantitative element of one of the cases. Tables 4.6 and 4.7 are incorporated to indicate proportionate activity levels rather than magnitudes. Table 4.6 displays the 'OTIS' summary for the Phase 1 Process Activity Map. As indicated in the previous section the *Operation* category incorporates *Decisions* and the *Storage* category incorporates *Delay*. Key observations are summarized in Table 4.6.

Table 4.8 provides insight into the equivalent Value Adding profile (Phase 2). Key observations are summarized in Table 4.7.

The generic root causes of information domain waste are summarized in Table 4.8. These were drawn from the cases listed in the introductory section and help explain the magnitude of waste witnessed in Tables 4.3 and 4.4.

TABLE 4.6   Phase 1 Process Activity Map – OTIS Summary

1. *Total activity* represents only that associated directly with servicing the critical path. The total absolute workload necessary to support and service the above will be many times greater.

2. *Operational activity* represents less than 1% of total *critical path* activity. This component contains the *raison d'être* for the existence of the sub-process.

3. *Inspection* is very low. Whilst the *raison d'être* for many of the sub-processes is inspection activity, the actual inspection task itself is very brief.

4. The whole *Transportation* element involves physical transportation of batches of documents from one functional department to another. This is 'hand-off' activity.

5. *Storage* (and delay) represents a massive proportion of the time. This data is for *internal* (commercial) processes only. This is controllable.

TABLE 4.7   Phase 2 Process Activity Map – Value-Adding Profile

1. VA activity is less than 1%.

2. There is a small difference between VA (0.86%) and *Operation* activity (0.88%). Therefore not all Operations are value adding.

3. The VA-NVA-NNVA metrics differ markedly from the generic physical benchmark equivalents:[1]

Commercial (Information)			*World Class Physical Supply Chain*		
VA	=	1%	VA	=	5%
NVA	=	49%	NVA	=	60%
NNVA	=	50%	NNVA	=	35%

[1] Womack and Jones, 1996. Derivatives of this benchmark are widely quoted, commonly agreed but of no fixed origin. For example, the *5-Percent Rule* (Levit, 1994); Inger, R. (1997).

A major contributor to waste was *dependent decision cycles* – the inability of key decisions or operations to start prior to the receipt of one or more key dataflows from another part of the process. Findings indicated that over 90 per cent of internal critical path activities were dependant on external stimulus. In the NPI case, 100 per cent of internal critical path activity was dependent on external suppliers. *Push-pull conflicts* were another major cause of delay, resulting in the 'hand-off' issue noted by Hammer and Champy (1995). These are incongruent dataflow triggers between two or more sequential parts of the process. An example would be a document pushed by the originating department into the in-tray of the recipient department without a signal to the recipient decision-maker

TABLE 4.8   The Generic Root Causes of Information Domain 'Waste'

1. *Dependent decision cycles.*

2. *Push–pull conflicts.*

3. *Complex interface* with external entities and suppliers.

4. *Bottleneck* functions and inappropriate capacity planning.

5. Lack of *standard work practice* and *document control.*

6. Existence of *fast-track*/expedite path for strategically important products. This is often unofficial and uncontrolled.

7. *Myopic corporate prioritization* procedure.

8. *Functional Siloism.*

9. Existing computer applications are *'stovepipes'.*

10. *Fragmented* file stores.

11. Extensive utilization of *'Batch and Queue'.*

that it was available. The greater the disparity and span of conflict, the greater the push–pull delay wastage. Conflicts can span one or more of the *three* following levels:

1. Inter-organizational.
2. Inter-departmental.
3. Intra-departmental.

Unlike the (physical) replenishment process where the organization typically interacts on a one-to-one basis with a supplier, the information domain often exhibits a *complex interface* with its suppliers. For example, the NPI case involved the choreography of four primary suppliers. These included a manufacturer of an own-brand product, a design agency, a reprographic agency and a printer/supplier of carton packaging. The complexity was exacerbated by a mutual dependency between the suppliers. This situation was replicated in the Promotions case.

Such relationships more closely approximate the 'network' model discussed by Hines (1994) than the more traditional 'chain'. They compound push–pull conflicts due to dataflow triggers residing in separate external entities where they are subject to a lower level of direct control.

When viewed as a production system, an administrative process is composed of a series of work centres with differing capacities. One or more of these work centres (departments/functions) will form a *bottleneck*. These bottlenecks are often neither identified nor managed effectively. For example, if a validation check exists (a *Necessary but Non-Value-Adding* activity) it is common to see it placed after the bottleneck rather than before it. This leads to the potential utilization of scarce bottleneck resource to process a defective dataflow. As argued by Goldratt and Cox (1993) 'A minute (wasted) at a bottleneck is a minute (wasted) by the whole system'.

> **When viewed as a production system, an administrative process is composed of a series of work centres with differing capacities.**

Application of *standard work practice* and *document version control* varied widely in the cases. Both of these mechanisms introduced conformance and discipline. Their main benefits were to minimize the cost of controlling the system and to facilitate audit. Even in organizations where standard work practice did exist, it was not uncommon to find unofficial 'work arounds' for expediency. Such mechanisms introduce 'noise', generate waste and recess system control.

The most obvious manifestation of work around was the expedite path or *fast-track*. This was an express route involving an expedited version of existing process activity steps. It was usually reserved for products deemed 'strategically important'. The fast-track was typically unofficial and had no formal entry criteria. It was uncontrolled. The reason for its existence was a dissatisfaction with the performance of the normal process. This included responsiveness, lead time and predictability. The net effect of the fast-track was to introduce further noise into the uncontrolled system as existing projects were put on hold to process priority projects. This sub-optimized the process as a whole, further generating the very characteristics which led to the fast-track utilization in the first place.

A further tranche of waste occurred when the corporate prioritization procedure was myopic and based upon decentralized function and/or departmental priorities rather than a higher-level, corporate mechanism. This was true in the NPI case. Here, individual trading teams were allocated clear portfolio development priorities. However, the bottleneck department was a centralized corporate resource. This department acted as a passive service and was not party to the prioritization criteria used by the trading teams, which resulted in the subjective interpretation of 'real' priority by the bottleneck decision-maker. Decisions were based on little or no objective criteria. They often revolved around 'who shouted the loudest?' This inevitably resulted in waste. This is especially apparent when two or more fast-tracks simultaneously competed for the bottleneck.

Many of these previous problems were symptomatic of the deeper rooted problem of *functional siloism* (Hammer and Champy, 1995). Each functional component of the organizations were configured locally to optimize the process, looking inward and upward instead of outward toward the customer. Vertical information flows were facilitated within the confines of the function, whilst horizontal flows were constrained by departmental barriers (Dimancescu, 1992:91). This sub-optimized the wider process and encouraged 'process fragmentation', resulting in an increased number of 'hand-offs' (Hammer and Champy, 1995:28).

Information constraint was exacerbated by the presence in each case of *stovepipe applications* (Martin, 1995:126). These are computer software applications that are designed to satisfy the demands of the hierarchical, functional organization structure. They often reside on stand-alone computers and/or exist as bespoke software packages (creating computer connectivity constraints). Their effect is to institutionalize the existing functional structure, propagating siloism. Stovepipes also produce direct waste in the form of computer batch updates, data re-keying, push–pull conflicts and the development of duplicate manual backup systems to overcome the stovepipe deficiencies.

File stores were often found to be fragmented. In some cases each department, and even each individual had a personal filing area (physical *and* electronic). The lack of centralized control contributed to a situation where individual files were incomplete, inconsistent and contained errors. Stovepipe applications contributed to the fragmentation of electronic file-stores. In one case three separate stand-alone computer-based Project Tracking systems were used. Lack of document version control and standard work practice were other major contributory factors to frag-mentation.

Finally, the cases displayed a uniform proliferation of 'batch & queue' activity, that had a number of sources. Historical system design was founded on functional siloism, resulting in the geographical dispersion of departments. Batching was conducted on the basis either of efficiency or as a matter of convenience – for example, batching documents so as to require a single journey to transfer them to the next department instead of many journeys. As in the physical world this had negative time and quality implications. The net result was again to suboptimize the process.

TABLE 4.9   Specific Recommendations – a Short-run Action Plan

- Introduce document control. Incorporate version number, date, circulation list and routing on every document.
- Attempt to instigate only a single copy of each key dataflow document.
- DO NOT *Batch and Queue*.
- DO NOT *fast-track* / Expedite.
    - Improve the 'normal' process so that total lead time and confidence are adequate to obviate the need for expediting.
    - Prioritize strategically important products, but introduce them to the process singly, not in batches.
- Identify *push–pull triggers*. Instigate continuity. Ideally these should all be in the *same direction* – and that direction should be *pull*.
- Educate staff on how to identify and process VA activities. Also instruct on waste identification.
- Instigate a *corporate-wide* project planning and prioritization procedure.
- Implement a process-wide workflow system to replace the disparate and ineffectual systems currently in place. Ensure all team members have access and training.
- Multi-skill staff to provide operational flexibility.
- Perform only a single validation check.
- Position the validation check immediately before entry into the bottleneck department.
- Do not allow amendments to documents that have been processed by the bottleneck.
- Push validation of dataflows as close to the originator as possible. Attempt to *prevent* errors from entering the system.
- Ensure a single coordination person is allocated at the supplier. Reciprocate. All liaison and queries should be routed through these people.

Interestingly, fast-tracks were also often batched, producing a 'double whammy' wastage effect.

The identification of the causal factors for the waste outlined in the previous section provides valuable insight for any waste elimination exercise in the information domain. Table 4.9 provides a short-run action plan to increase the value-added profile of any supply chain organization. This action will make a significant contribution to the bottom line.

Conclusions

Issues such as the dysfunction of 'batch and queue' in the case environments confirmed the applicability of the 'Five Lean Principles' in the information domain (Table 4.10). The concepts of *value* and the *value stream* are at the heart of the Lean paradigm.

> *The concepts of* value *and the* value stream *are at the heart of the Lean paradigm.*

Womack and Jones (1996:p. 19) argue that the identification of the entire value stream for each product or product family is an essential step towards Lean thinking. They define a value stream as:

> ...the set of all the specific actions required to bring a specific product (whether a good, a service, or, increasingly, a combination of the two) through the three critical management tasks of any business: the *problem-solving task* running from concept through detailed design and engineering to product launch, the *information management task* running from order-taking through detailed scheduling to delivery, and the *physical transformation task* proceeding from raw materials to finished product in the hands of the customer.

Hines *et al.* (1997) have elaborated upon this concept. Both sets of authors place the product at the centre of the value stream concept. The Lean Information Project has built upon this foundation to derive the generic value streams illustrated in Figure 4.2. Value streams are illustrated in relation to the familiar Product Life Cycle (PLC) model.

From this perspective, the only value stream for which the manage-

TABLE 4.10 The Five Lean Principles

1. Specify *Value* by Product.
2. Identify the *Value Stream*.
3. Make the Product *Flow*.
4. At the *Pull* of the Customer.
5. In Pursuit of *Perfection*.

Adapted from Womack and Jones, 1996.

FIGURE 4.2 The Generic Value Streams – Lean Information Project

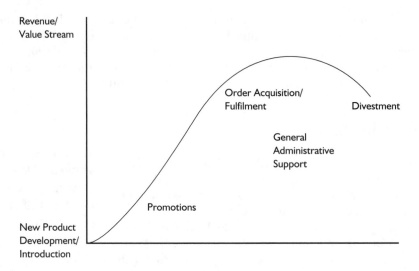

SOURCE: Mark Francis, SCDP.

ment of physical assets is the key driver of business effectiveness is *Order Fulfilment*, and only for an organization with a 'physical' operating core (Mintzberg, 1979). Information management in this environment makes an efficiency contribution. For all other value streams the relationship is inverted and the key driver of effectiveness is the choreography of key dataflow transactions, decision-making, communication and dependent events. These information-driven value streams are typically conducted within the office environment. This subset represents the administrative environment.

It is rare to find an individual through which only a single value stream flows. At any point in time individuals may be observed conducting one of the three types of activity groupings indicated in Figure 4.3:

1. *Value Stream Activity*: Adds value directly.
2. *Direct Support Activity*: Directly supports one or more of the value streams which run 'through' the individual. For example expediting (fast-track), query and problem resolution or processing value stream mail.
3. *Displacement Activity*: Not related to any of the value streams. For example processing general mail, reading the paper, checking e-mail or chatting.

Value stream identification, along with recognition and prioritization of the above activity groupings, should be the first step in any improvement

FIGURE 4.3   Three Workplace Activity Groupings

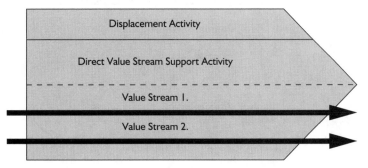

SOURCE: Mark Francis, SCDP.

programme. Significant benefit will accrue to any organization making this tentative step.

An indication of a supply chain's current information domain capability can be gauged by its ability to overcome the *dependent decision cycle* issue. In both the Promotion and NPI cases delay impacted stock availability at the point of sale. It was concluded that an organization's physical and information capabilities are symbiotic. Improvement in either dimension will therefore ultimately be constrained by underdevelopment in the other (Figure 4.4). The effective flow of material through the supply chain will therefore be contingent upon that supply chain's ability to manage its information effectively.

Value stream indentification should be the first step in any improvement programme.

A more tangible metric of capability is the supply chain's value-added contribution. The findings suggest a VA–NVA–NNVA profile of 1–49–50 per cent in the information dimension. This differs markedly from the 5–60–35 percent profile established for world-class (physical) supply chains. Value-added contribution of (up to) 1 per cent can currently be expected as the norm in the information-driven domain.

Such a metric has major implications for investment decisions. Based on the argument that physical and information capabilities are mutually dependent and that physical capabilities are more developed than their information counterparts, an organization is likely to obtain a better return on investment (ROI) for a targeted waste elimination programme in the information domain because there is wider scope for improvement. This logic is more compelling when the organization is world class as, by definition, the gulf will be wider.

The goal of many progressive supply chain organizations is clear: becoming a *Lean Enterprise* (Womack and Jones, 1994). The Lean Information Project has enriched this vision, demonstrating the potential for

FIGURE 4.4 Symbiotic Physical and Information Capabilities

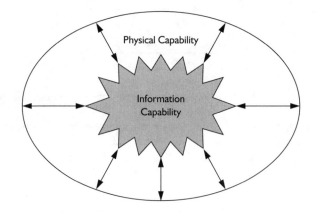

application of Lean techniques in the administrative environment. This is *Lean Administration*.

Whilst the goal is clear, the process of change is fraught with risk and waste. It is the author's belief that the mismatch between capabilities in the physical and information dimensions is reflected in the level of waste witnessed in the resulting systems and in the 'growing pains' associated with Lean change programmes. The challenge is therefore to enrich the Lean paradigm whilst simultaneously developing techniques for achieving this goal with the minimum possible waste.

Future Directions For Research

The Lean Information Project case studies have found existing tools and techniques lacking in the information domain. These need to be improved systematically. For example, the Process Activity Map suffered from inappropriate activity labels and was based upon a linear, sequential world viewpoint. It was unable to capture the subtleties of constraint, multiple paths, dependency, iteration, feedback and recursion which are typical of the information domain.

Additionally work is required on the foundation concepts in this domain. This will include *value, value stream identification* and *core activity*, as well as the codification of sector and value-stream-specific *information waste* in line with the deliverables of the Lean Information Project. Taken in conjunction, these will facilitate a review of the VA–NVA–NNVA concept as prerequisite to the development of a *Lean Change* methodology.

CHAPTER 5

Understanding Improvement Programmes in the Value Stream[1]

This chapter[2] describes the use of the Value Stream Analysis Tool (VALSAT) as a rigorous analysis and decision-making tool in the supply chain or value stream context. The tool can employ both tacit and explicit knowledge to the advantage of the supply chain in which it is used. Although the approach owes its origins to new product development in the Japanese shipbuilding industry, it can provide many advantages over traditional analysis approaches in a value stream setting.

The Value Stream Analysis Tool is demonstrated from both a theoretical and practical viewpoint, the latter involving cases from SCDP companies. As will be demonstrated, the qualities of the tool lie in focusing knowledge so as to aid decision-making where there is a complex web of supply chain interrelationships and especially where data are a mix of subjective and objective assessments. Additionally it creates the right environment for increased intra- and inter-company coordination, allowing for improvement implementation programmes.

Introduction

In order to achieve the delivery of excellent products and services to end consumers it is necessary to harness the expertise, enthusiasm and

[1] This chapter was prepared by Nick Rich and Peter Hines.

[2] The theoretical discussion in this chapter is drawn primarily from Peter Hines, Nick Rich and Malaika Hittmeyer, 'Competing Against Ignorance: Advantage Through Knowledge', *International Journal of Physical Distribution and Logistics Management*, Volume 28, Number 1, 1998. The authors would like to thank the editors and publishers of *IJPDLM* for agreeing to its reproduction here in a modified form.

dynamism of all the firms that contribute to the final consumable. To do this, it is essential to view each of the value-adding processes in each of the companies responsible as a part of a value stream dedicated to the final consumer's requirements. In so doing a truly Lean Enterprise can be created (Womack and Jones, 1994).

In order to achieve the delivery of excellent products and services to end consumers it is necessary to harness the expertise, enthusiasm and dynamism of all the firms that contribute to the final consumable.

However, such a utopian goal is not without its difficulties. The first of these is that there is at present an overemphasis on time and a consequent underplaying of other factors in transforming enterprises. This is not to say that time is not important, but that it is only one of many factors involved. In addition, and partly as a result of the former, there is a dearth of tools and techniques that academics or practitioners can use to create world-class value streams. Third, where there is some evidence of the development of such excellence, it is usually in a component-based industry, such as automotive or electronics and usually in a Japanese-based, or -owned, organization.

The purpose of this chapter is to try to redress the balance. This will be achieved, after a brief literature review, by trying to understand the supply chain development needs of a group of 14 SCDP member companies. This micro perspective will then be placed in a broader context of the importance of understanding and using knowledge within a more macro environment. After this, a new dynamic methodology for helping to create effective value streams will be introduced called the Value Stream Analysis Tool (VALSAT). This will subsequently be demonstrated by its application within a number of SCDP companies.

Past Research

During the first half of the 1990s considerable attention has been paid by both academics and practitioners to 'competing against time'. This has resulted from the seminal work of Stalk and Hout (Stalk, 1988; Stalk and Hout, 1990) as well as a wider discussion of the Japanese experience (Harrison, 1992; Suzaki, 1987). Although these works are not specifically in a supply chain setting, other academics have followed their path to apply these approaches within such a setting (New, 1993; Forza *et al.*, 1993). In more wide-ranging work, Beesley applied what he termed 'Time-Based Process Mapping' to a range of industrial sectors including automotive, aerospace and construction (Beesley, 1994). A similar, if slightly more refined, approach was adopted by Jessop and Jones in the electronics, food, clothing and automotive industries (Jessop and Jones, 1995).

This approach to 'competing against time' is mirrored in the considerable attention paid at practitioner level. The Just-In-Time (JIT) approach has long been important, at least at the level of rhetoric, in the component-based industries such as automotive and electronics. In addition, Quick Response (QR) and Efficient Consumer Response (ECR) now command considerable interest in the textile and grocery industries respectively. However, a key point is that their usage is often confined to the conference circuit or, at best, to an assault on time, rather than a more fundamental approach to the company-wide improvement envisioned by the practitioner forefathers (Ohno, 1988; Monden, 1983).

One of the major impediments to significant improvements at practitioner level has been the lack of a suitable toolkit which could be used to achieve the change towards effective value streams. The most important gap would appear to be a simple but rigorous analytical tool that could be used at a variety of locations in the supply chain to help us to understand the exact situation, quantify the need for change and provide a framework for scenario planning to help ascertain and prioritize the best cause of action. The use of Quality Function Deployment (QFD) within this setting has been suggested (Hines, 1994 and Rich, 1995a). QFD is a well-established, if rarely well-applied, tool from new product development (Mizuno and Akao, 1994; Clausing, 1994) and would appear to offer certain possibilities when deployed in the supply chain context.

Improvements Companies Want to Make

In order to understand more thoroughly the types of improvement that companies want to make in their supply chains and in particular where the academic world can help, a focusing exercise was undertaken with 14 SCDP sponsoring companies. These companies were from a range of industries including grocery, automotive, textile, electronics, petro-chemical, transportation and services, and were drawn from the public and private sectors in the areas of manufacturing, distribution and retailing.

Each of the organizations was given a series of ten propositions concerning improvements in the supply chains they operate within (Table 5.1). They were then asked to allocate an importance rating between 0 and 10 for each factor, with the caveat that their total importance rating for the ten factors was to be 50 points. Thus a mean of 5 could be expected. The same 50-total-point exercise was undertake for the ten factors on the basis of their difficulty. Thus a factor with a score of 0 would be immediately possible and one with a score of 10 impossible. Again a mean of 5 could be expected. The scores for the 14 companies were then averaged. In order to aid their visual representation, the difficulty scores were rebased to run as ease scores from 0 to 10 where higher numbers correspond to 'very easy'.

The resulting 14 company averages are given in Figure 5.1 which, due to the averaging process, hides the more extreme scores of the organiza-

TABLE 5.1 Propositions for Effective Supply Chain Improvement

1. Stocks should be at least halved.

2. Benefits of improvement should be shared between buyer and supplier.

3. Stocks in one company can and perhaps should be managed by another company.

4. The time it takes to get products through the supply chain and to end customers should be reduced by half.

5. Late delivery performance of final products to the end consumer should be reduced by at least half.

6. Improvements in one company in a supply chain should often be made by another company in the same supply chain.

7. In order to make improvements it is essential for customers and suppliers to make suggestions to each other on how this may be done.

8. In order to make improvements in the supply chain a clear sense of openness, honesty and interdependence must exist between the different company members.

9. In order to make improvements in the supply chain it is essential to empower internal cross-functional teams in each company.

10. In order to make improvements in supplier response a crisis must exist or be created in at least one of the member organizations.

tions for some of the factors. This said, it can be seen that time compression (factor 4) could be viewed as a breakthrough for the average company. Likewise, the development of a supply chain with a clear sense of openness, honesty and interdependence would fall into the same category. In addition, in their respective improvement programmes the firms should additionally 'probably consider' at least 5 other aspects, 'possibly consider' a further 2 and reap an early harvest by creating a system of inter-company suggestion exchange (factor 7).

This brief exercise can of course be used for further project focusing either by academics or practitioners. The important point in the context of the present chapter is the obvious importance of the various non-time factors. It may be that a complex interrelationship of a large number of 'wants' may be more appropriate than the selection of one attribute, such as time. In addition, the emphasis on time is by no means felt to be healthy by companies across a wider range of industry sectors not traditionally researched by academics. It should also be stated that the demands of companies will inevitably change over time with perhaps 'time-based competition' being just a phase in their development.

FIGURE 5.1   Supply Chain Improvements Required

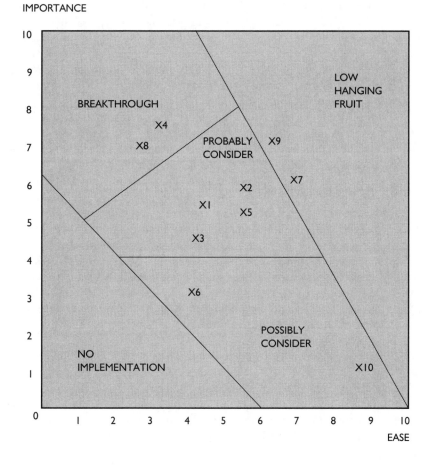

IMPORTANCE

Analyzing the Value Stream

This suggests the need for a dynamic analysis, prioritization and focusing tool, which if possible should be capable of using tacit or subjective, as well as explicit or quantifiable, information. As such, it may be possible to say that the use of such an approach may help researchers and organizations to go beyond a narrow focus to an approach to managing their value streams based on knowledge. This knowledge-based approach to managing the value stream is the logical extension of the work of a small but recently growing group of writers who believe companies should become knowledge-creating organizations (Toffler, 1990; Reich, 1991; Quinn, 1992; Drucker, 1993; Nonaka and Takeuchi, 1995; Rich, 1995a and 1995b) or manage by fact (Kobata, 1995).

In this context, Toffler argues that knowledge is the source of the highest quality power and the key to the *powershift* that lies ahead

(Toffler, 1990). Reich contends that the only true competitive advantage will reside among those he calls 'symbolic analysts' who are equipped with the knowledge to identify, solve and broker new problems (Reich, 1991). In addition Quinn, giving a marketing perspective, points out that the value of most products and services depends primarily on how 'knowledge-based intangibles', like technological know-how, product design, marketing presentation, understanding of the customer, personal creativity, and innovation, can be developed (Quinn, 1992).

Drucker argues that in the new society, knowledge is not just a factor of production like land, labour or capital, but is *the* only meaningful resource today (Drucker, 1992). He goes on to add that in this new society based on knowledge the 'knowledge worker' is the single greatest asset. Included in the list of knowledge workers is the 'knowledge executive' who knows how to allocate knowledge to productive use, just as the capitalist knows how to allocate capital to productive use. Nonaka and Takeuchi take this argument a stage further and note that, 'The realisation that knowledge is the new competitive resource has hit the West like lightning ... despite all the attention by leading observers of business and society, none of them has really examined the mechanisms and processes by which knowledge is created' (Nonaka and Takeuchi, 1995, p. 7). It is the authors' belief that the approach adopted here is not only able to do this within a single company environment but, critically, in a value stream or supply chain setting.

The tool developed for this purpose has been called the 'Value Stream Analysis Tool' (VALSAT) and is to a large extent a refinement and re-application of the Quality Function Deployment (QFD) method employed for new product development by many companies, particularly in the automotive industry and/or with Japanese origins. The use of the term 'Quality Function Deployment' will be avoided as it is a rather unfortunate translation of the Japanese *kanji* characters and does not adequately describe the method in general, let alone when it is used in a supply chain setting.

As mentioned above, there is a limited and growing literature on the use of this type of approach in the new product development arena (Mizuno and Akao, 1994; Clausing, 1994) following its origins in the Kobe shipyards of Japan. However, the potential for use in the supply chain remains considerable in spite of its origins within another function, industry and culture.

Within any supply chain setting any one company or group of companies has to make certain improvements. However, it is often difficult to decide upon an action plan because many of the individual requirements for improvement have not been defined or are difficult to articulate or to score objectively. As a result, subjective factors are often ignored. The VALSAT approach, however, enables both subjective and objective measures to be taken into account. The outline of the method is given in Figures 5.2 and 5.3. The following section will describe the method from a theoretical viewpoint before using a case example to show how it may be used in practice.

The Value Stream Analysis Tool: Theoretical Perspective

Once the appropriate part of the supply chain has been selected for analysis, the first part of the process (A) is to understand the types of improvement that customers require – where customers are defined as the downstream supply chain members (see Figures 5.2 and 5.3). These downstream customers may be internal, external, or both. Indeed, at this stage the VALSAT process forces the researcher or practitioner to define exactly who the different customers are before their requirements can be understood. Taking a food manufacturing plant as an example, the customers can be defined to include potentially: the distribution part of the company; the sales and marketing part of the company; the retail store;

FIGURE 5.2   The Value Stream Analysis Tool (VALSAT) Matrix

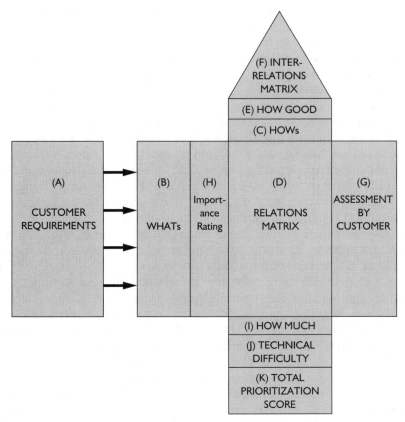

and the ultimate product consumer. Indeed, further customer segmentation may be possible or desirable (Kotler, 1988). However, the important point is that this debate is brought out into the open so that the various customers' requirements can be taken into account.

The most important information will be that obtained by understanding the customer's words, deeds or actions.

The collection of the data can be done in a variety of ways. It can be achieved through participant observation/contextual inquiry (Delbridge and Kirkpatrick, 1994; Parikh, 1992), a grounded theory approach (Glaser and Strauss, 1967), or through semi-structured or structured interviews. The purpose is to obtain information driven by the different stakeholders' requirements. The most important information will be that obtained by understanding the customer's words, deeds or actions. However, the needs of the other stakeholders such as the different corporate functions, shareholders, suppliers and even government can be taken into consideration.

These customer requirements can then be turned into their specific needs, or in the VALSAT terminology the WHATs (or what they want). It may appear that this second stage (B) is very little different from simply recording the stated customer requirements. However, this is often not the case as it is usually necessary to translate the customer's words into a more usable form. A simple example will show why this is necessary. A customer has suggested to the manufacturing company discussed above that they require 48 hours of safety stocks of finished goods to be retained by the manufacturer. The reason given for this is to avoid retail stockouts, so, if the specified customer requirements were used in their existing form, the design of the distribution process would involve a minimum of 48 hours of finished goods at the food processor. Whereas, in reality, the reason for holding this stock is to provide a rapid response to exceptional demand or to cover for certain difficult supply chain contingencies.

The customer's original demand can thus be re-worded or translated into a more specific need, in this case 'the avoidance or stockout' and perhaps 'rapid response to emergency situations'. This rewording process allows the researcher to avoid being artificially constrained in the system's redesign. However, care must be taken to explain the eventual solution to the customer in such a way as to convince them that it will satisfy their needs more fully than the original, and constraining, customer requirement.

The collection of customer needs can be presented either as a simple list of perhaps 15 factors, or, if the number of factors is greater, within a Systemic/Tree Diagram or Analytic Hierarchy Approach (Ozeki and Asaka, 1990; Saaty, 1980). In this way a small number of major customer needs can be split down into subsets. As an example, a need for 'quicker response' may be split into 'quicker response to new business enquiries', 'quicker new product development' and 'short lead times'. Indeed, these

FIGURE 5.3   Steps in the Value Stream Analysis Tool (VALSAT)

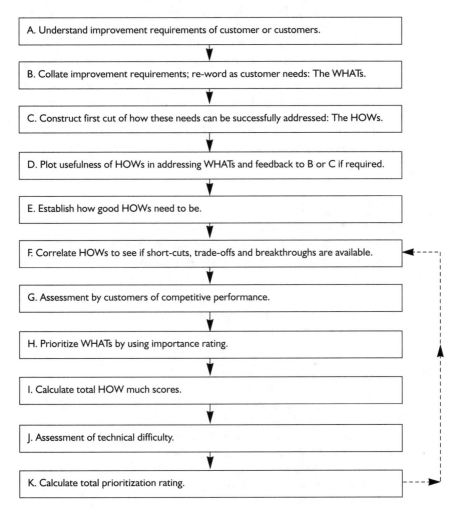

three sub-needs may be split further if the approaches to satisfying these needs are likely to be different.

The third stage (C) is to construct a first cut of how these re-worded customer needs (or WHATs) may be addressed. This stage involves the development of a list of appropriate approaches, or HOWs. Thus for any one need there will be one or more possible ways of achieving it. Continuing with the above example, in order to achieve 'the avoidance of stock-outs' the manufacturer may wish to do a number of things. These may involve holding 48 hours' safety stock as suggested by the retailer or a number of other approaches such as:

- making every product more regularly;
- producing goods in line with customer's actual sales through the accessing and use of EPOS (Electronic Point Of Sale) data;
- controlling the stocks in their customer's premises by the application of VMI (Vendor Managed Inventory).

At this stage a number of competing or complementary approaches can be included in the control matrix (Figure 5.2). In addition, brainstorming of potential solutions could be productive as it might provide the opportunity for breakthrough ideas based on lateral thinking. These ideas may come from the researchers or from the researched.

HOWs

It is useful to check the system in terms of the general effectiveness of the defined HOWs. Thus for each HOW a decision is made as to whether such an approach will go any way towards addressing the needs of the customer as shown in Figure 5.4A. There are *four* grades of relationship that may be apparent:

- A strong relationship shown by a circle in a circle.
- A medium relationship shown by a circle.
- A weak relationship shown by a triangle.
- No relationship where the square would be left blank.

The purpose of this checking exercise is twofold, as suggested in Figure 5.4B. First, there may be HOWs not specifically addressing WHATs. If this were not caught at this stage, a company could spend a great deal of time and effort designing systems that did not actually specifically address customers' needs. If this is the case then these HOWs can be removed from the matrix and from future consideration.

Second, it may be that the articulation of HOWs has not been sufficiently precise to allow for some of the WHATs to be addressed at all. There may therefore be unanswered WHATs. The solution to this is to rerun stages B, C and D with a further quantity of HOWs deemed appropriate to correct the problem and to continue to do so until a satisfactory result is achieved (as illustrated in the feedback loop in Figure 5.3).

After the HOWs suitable for further consideration have been identified, it is then necessary to establish how good the organization has to be in addressing these HOWs (stage E). Thus, continuing the above example, if the HOW is 'making every product more regularly' it is necessary to decide how regularly this should be done. The answer to this could be, for instance, once a day for all products, or a more time-segmented approach involving A-class products being made once a day, B-class twice a week and C-class once a week. The VALSAT approach does not suggest the answer, but triggers the debate within a rigorous framework to ensure the right discussions take place *before* action is undertaken.

FIGURE 5.4   Find Relationships in the Value Stream Analysis Tool
A) Plot Relationship of WHAT to HOWs

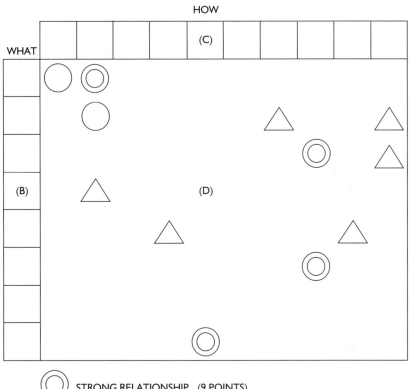

The next stage of the process (F) is to correlate the HOWs in order to see if there are short-cuts, trade-offs or breakthroughs available between the different improvement approaches under consideration as illustrated in Figure 5.5. There may be *five* types of relationship between the different HOWs:

- A strong positive relationship shown by a circle in a circle.
- A positive relationship shown by a circle.
- No relationship shown by a blank square.
- A negative relationship shown by a cross.
- A strong negative relationship shown by a double cross.

The particular character is drawn in the intersection of the diagonal

FIGURE 5.4 continued

B) Check Relationships

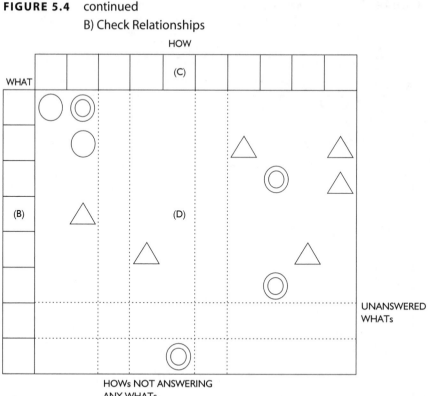

extensions of the HOW columns. In Figure 5.5 there is a negative relationship between the first two HOWs and a strong positive relationship between the first and the last factors.

This analysis is particularly important when it reveals strong negatives and strong positives. A strong negative relationship would suggest that by doing one thing it is almost impossible to do something else. An example of this might be where two HOWs are 'controlling the stocks in their customer's premises by the application of VMI (Vendor Managed Inventory: where stock is managed at customer's premises either physically and/or remotely by suppliers in line with their customer's requirements)' and 'allow customer greater flexibility in stocking'. These two approaches would appear at first sight to be negatively correlated. However, if both of these approaches are later proved to be highly desirable, then finding a way to combine them may provide a very useful competitive advantage that may be very hard for competitors to copy. This could therefore suggest areas in which breakthroughs could occur if sufficient resources were invested in them.

The second result that is particularly useful is that of a strong positive correlation such as that perhaps between 'controlling the stocks in

FIGURE 5.5   Creating the Interrelationship Matrix

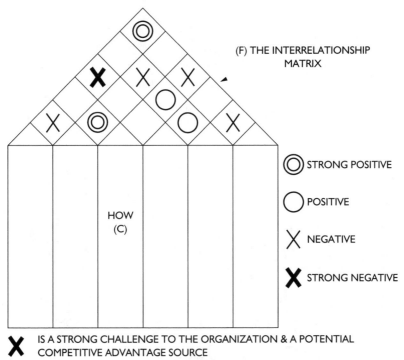

their customer's premises by the application of VMI (Vendor Managed Inventory)' and 'reducing on-site finished goods stocks'. Such a finding might suggest that when one of these is done, the other would automatically follow. Thus, controlling customer's stocks is quite likely to mean that on-site finished stock levels can be reduced. So taking one action may automatically achieve another with its accompanying list of need satisfaction, thus reducing wasteful duplication of actions. It is of course important to bear in mind that many of these relationships may be uni-directional. Reducing on-site finished stocks is most unlikely to result in Vendor Managed Inventory. However, understanding the appropriate relationship and causality flows between HOWs may help increase the effectiveness of any supply chain improvement programme.

Customer Assessment

After this stage it may be useful to go back to the (various types of) customers and ascertain the performance of the organization against its competitors in achieving the specified customer needs or WHATs (stage G).

FIGURE 5.6 Conduct Competitive Assessment

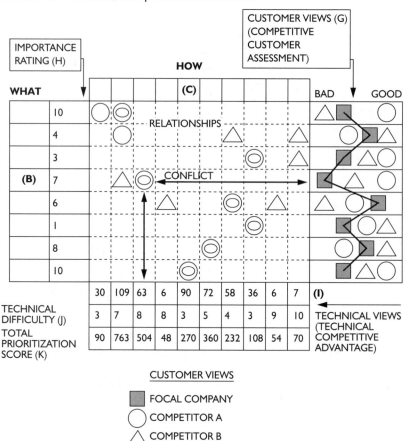

Although this can be done quite objectively with scientifically calculated scores, this is usually not the most appropriate approach. The reason for this is the customer's perception. Indeed, in this exercise (stage G) it may be as important to measure the customer's perceptions as the actual reality, and merely employing a subjective assessment of the organization's performance against the customer's needs is usually satisfactory.

In Figure 5.6 this is shown on a simple 'Good to Bad' scale with the focal company being recorded with a rectangle and two competitors designated by a circle and a triangle respectively. This benchmarking helps the organization concerned to understand where its core competences lie and where improvements are required.

If there are a number of different customers, a series of scores can be collected, which can either be aggregated or weighted and averaged depending on the importance of the different customers to the organization under consideration.

The next stage of the process (stage H) is usually achieved through the same structured interview as stage G. During this discussion it is necessary to gauge the strength of customers' feelings regarding their different needs to allow for needs prioritization. This can be achieved in a number of ways. If there is only one customer, they may be asked to score the importance of each need on a 1 to 10 scale or simply to rank the factors in order of importance with the most important given the highest ranking. If there is more than one customer, a similar aggregation process should be employed as in stage G.

Stage I involves calculating the total usefulness of the delineated HOWs. This is done by multiplying the importance rating against each correlation in the relations matrix (D) and then summing by column. When this multiplication is undertaken a double circle scores nine points, a circle three and a triangle one. To illustrate, for the first column in Figure 5.6:

$$\text{total column score} = 10 \ (\text{importance rating for row 1}) \times 3 \text{ points}$$
$$(\text{medium correlation})$$

$$= (10 \times 3) + (7 \times 1) = 37 \text{ points}$$

This procedure is then repeated for each column.

Technical Difficulty

The next stage (J) is to judge the relative difficulty of the different tasks or HOWs under consideration. This can be done either on a 1 to 10 scale (where 1 is impossible and 10 is very easy) or on a ranking basis with the easiest HOW given the highest ranking. In Figure 5.6 a simple 1 to 10 grading has been given. Such scores should be based on the experience and knowledge of the researcher and the researched. After this is achieved it is a simple job to calculate the total prioritization score (K). This is done by multiplying the HOW much score (I) by the technical difficulty score (J). In Figure 5.6 the resulting scores range from 763 to 48 where higher numbers suggest that implementation is advisable.

As discussed above, in stage F various opportunities may present themselves for trading off two or more positively related factors. As mentioned, in some cases these may be linked only in one causal direction, whereas in other cases they can be bi-directional. These apparent trade-offs can prove useful in re-interpreting the first run of the data and perhaps allowing for an even better prioritization (this feedback mechanism is shown between Stage K and Stage F in Figure 5.3).

This is best illustrated by a simple example. If the organization under consideration could only implement one improvement programme at any one time it would be likely to select the one yielding 763 points. If it were found that the programmes yielding 763 and 504 points were highly positively correlated, then, by doing one, the benefits of the other might be gained. If the two programmes showed bi-directional causality, then the firm could either do the 763 project or the 504 project. The decision on which to do can be made on the basis of the technical difficulty. In this case, the 504 programme would be chosen as it is very easy (scoring 8 for technical difficulty). This approach would yield more benefit than the 763 project and additionally would be far easier to achieve.

The second decision that may be worthy of consideration at this point is whether any of the projects have a negative influence on each other. Thus, if for instance two projects have been selected that would take an organization in opposing directions, some type of reassessment is necessary. This could involve either abandoning one of the projects or trying to overcome the inherent conflict between the approaches. The second of these, although certainly more difficult, may be considerably more rewarding, as such a focus might provide the possibility of developing breakthroughs that are difficult for competitors to imitate and yield sustainable competitive advantage.

The Value Stream Analysis Tool: Practical Perspective

Although the VALSAT approach is, after a little experience, relatively easy to use, it is not easy to grasp at first glance. This observation is the result of working with the tool with a number of value streams in several industrial sectors. It should help, therefore, to briefly illustrate the tool in the context of actual SCDP improvement programmes.

In the case of the assembler of electronic telephonic products, Nortel, the VALSAT technique was used to evaluate the performance of alternative suppliers by product groupings. The objective of the exercise was to create a supplier evaluation system which reflected the need for continuous improvement to the levels of customer service provided to Nortel. Once the evaluation system had been constructed, the high-performing suppliers in each category could be assessed in terms of their ability to forge 'partnership' relationships with Nortel and be integrated into the strategic direction of the purchasing company. The VALSAT technique was implemented using a team comprising the 'lead buyer' for the category and specialist support provided by the supplier's quality assurance department.

To commence the process, the team engaged in a brainstorming exercise to assess the impact of the future strategies and vision of the organization regarding the role and performance required from supplier companies. This exercise created a generic list of corporate-level 'wants' from suppliers over the medium term. It was repeated with the lead buyer and their staff for each category of purchases to assess the operational and 'short-to-medium' term definition of customer service. The combination of the two analyses permitted a good insight into the transactional and operational performance levels required to support the manufacturing site, as well as the key capabilities (and standards) required to expand volumes with the company.

The category teams then listed all the corporate 'wants' and operational 'wants' to form the rows of the matrix and the suppliers (by the site of the company rather than by the company group) in order to assess the performance of each supplier in 'meeting' or 'exceeding' the time-phased expectations of the customer. As each category of suppliers was completed, the comparatively higher scoring supplier companies became targets for development and the deployment of the limited amount of purchasing department resource. In parallel, the 'WANTs' of the matrix were used as the general supplier evaluation system to focus the efforts of all suppliers on the key performance measures (the operational definition of customer service) and the average score of all the suppliers in the purchase category was used as the target performance level for the 'acceptable' standard of customer service in the coming year. Also, the ability to deconstruct the matrix allowed each supplier to see their individual rating against the performance evaluation matrix so that the suppliers could target areas of performance for which improvements would bring quick advances in their supplier ratings.

The combination of the two analyses permitted a good insight into the transactional and operational performance levels required to support the manufacturing site.

Q8 Lubricants (Leeds) is a manufacturing facility which converts base refined oils into soluble (industrial) and neat (engine-related) lubricants. The process involves both blending and packaging processes for a wide range of prestigious customers and the Q8 brand itself. The company holds many accreditations and is ranked as one of the leading European lubricant sites by the P.I.M.S. annual survey. The company employed the VALSAT approach to assist in the development of the Q8 Production System and to focus on the development of key manufacturing capabilities to service a growing range of customers and accreditation systems. During the first stage of the programme, the VALSAT technique was used to evaluate the market environment and market segments for products in terms of the 'order qualification' and 'order winning' criteria of customers in the segments (Hill, 1985). Initially, the VALSAT matrix was constructed using the 'HOWs' to represent the market segments for products with the 'WANTs' being drawn from sales meetings, customer contact and also from the objectives deployed from the Head Office operations. The outcome of the matrix was a visual representation of the 'voice of the customer' and the ability to plot the performance of the site against its competitors, in each segment, by assessing whether the company was better, average or worse than the key players in that segment.

Once the assessment of the current and potential 'customer' clusters had been determined and evaluated by the management team, a second iteration of the matrix was conducted by maintaining the same 'WANTs' but this time using a process of internal departmental brainstorming to assess the key projects which could be undertaken to achieve the goals of the business. This resulted in a wide range of potential departmental projects and programmes which could be launched by the company. However, with finite human and financial resources, the company had to identify the difficulty of undertaking each project, the cost and contribution of the project, and the impact of undertaking the project on the ability of the other projects to realize their proposed contributions. In terms of the latter, the 'roof' of the matrix was used to assess the relationship between one project 'how' and all others.

From this point, the management team selected projects that were fundamental or created a 'platform' on which all projects could be founded (as well as the introduction of projects which were not selected in the time period but were worthy of investment during future rounds of budgeting). Having selected the key themes and programmes, the internal departmental representatives were formed into cross-functional teams to determine the actual implementation projects. These projects were then proposed to the management team, the resources required were allocated to the improvement efforts and the project performance-monitoring and review committees were established. At the close of the project, the matrix could be updated and the customer service improvement by the team could be displayed visually (together with the current standard of performance achieved and the competitive assessment of the company against other manufacturers in the market segment).

For London Underground Limited, the VALSAT technique was employed to reduce the complexity of a capital expenditure project involving many different internal customers and a vast range of vendor selection criteria. The long 'pay back' associated with such a purchase, combined with the public sector procurement regulations that affect the company, the VALSAT tool was a means of providing a logical and equitable means of evaluating different products offered by potential vendors, of integrating many different customer needs, and also of providing a full audit trail to support any procurement decision taken by the company. This process involved the formation of a cross-functional management team, drawn from the many 'customer' directorates engaged in the programme, to create the 'voice of the customer' by determining the 'tree diagram' of 'WANTs' and performance specifications attached to each want.

The customer 'WANTs' were then weighted by the cross-functional team (out of an importance rating of 1 to 10, with 10 being fundamental for all departments and 1 representing a 'nice to have' addition) and the vendors solutions were then listed as the 'HOWs'. After the completion of the evaluation matrix for each vendor, the subsections representing a portfolio of generic purchasing requirements (i.e. ease of use, speed, etc.)

and the functional portfolio (i.e. the actual 'WANTs' assessed on a depart-ment-by-department basis), the overall matrix was scored. Following this process, each vendor was informed of their weaknesses, particularly areas where fundamental 'WANTS' were not satisfied, and requested to re-tender. The second phase of the evaluation process represented a re-evaluation of the original matrix and a final assessment of the 'worthiness' and 'value for money' of each proposal. In this particular case example, the purchasing team within the cross-functional group maintained an holistic and objective view of the purchasing decision despite the complex nature of such a deci-sion.

The purchasing team within the cross-functional group maintained an holistic and objective view of the purchasing decision despite the complex nature of such a decision.

Discussion

The foregoing sections have demonstrated the use of the VALSAT approach from a theoretical and practical point of view. In this section we shall discuss the method in terms of its strengths and weaknesses. How-ever, before doing this the wider implication of such an approach will be made.

The approach may be extended further to 'fine tune' the implementa-tion of a number of potential solutions. This may be done by recategoriz-ing the HOWs from the first matrix and re-configuring these as WANTs to facilitate a more detailed implementation approach. Drawing from an automotive example to illustrate this process, the primary selected 'HOW', from the first matrix that forms the 'WANT' for the second level of analysis may have been the need 'to make products more regularly'. With this as the objective function for the analysis, the team must decide how this can be achieved by conducting a second series of brainstorming exer-cises (aimed at identifying the key causes to provide the effect). The result of these brainstorming activities is a list of potential and viable alternative courses of action. However, the finite level of resources available to con-duct all these different alternatives will mean that only the 'vital few' ini-tiatives can be undertaken in any one time period and the 'many' must be de-listed as they represent less beneficial allocations of business resource.

To identify the projects that represent 'value for money' to the busi-ness, a second matrix is constructed, but this time the selected 'HOWs' from the first level of analysis are transformed into the 'WANTs' for the second level of detailed analysis. In this respect, the objective 'to produce products more regularly', previously a 'HOW', now becomes the objective target for the development of the new 'HOW' practices to achieve. Two of the possible alternatives offered by the members of the case study included a reduction in the size of batches and another alternative

FIGURE 5.7 Second Generation Matrix Analysis

	HOW 1	HOW 2	
WANTS	Reduce Batch Size	Improve Set Up Times	Performance Standards Required
Produce Products More Regularly (How from 1st Matrix)	⊚	⊚	Reduce WIP by 25% & Finished Goods by 10%
Reduce Quality Defects (How from 1st Matrix)	⊚	⊚	
SCORE	18	18	
DIFFICULTY			
Die Cast	MEDIUM	EASY	
Current : Target	200 : 100 pcs	60 : 30 mins	30 mins by 4/1997
Drill	EASY	EASY	
Current : Target	200 : 50 pcs	15 : 5 mins	5 mins by 4/1997
COSTS			
Die Cast	£5 Per 250 castings	£25,000 Tooling	Reduce Finished Goods by £128,000 & WIP by £45,000
Drill	NIL	£1,200 Jigs	
AGREED TIMING			
Die Cast	150 pcs (8/1996) 100 pcs (4/1997)	40 mins (2/1996) 30 mins (1/1997)	
Drill	150 pcs (8/1996) 100 pcs (4/1997)	10 mins (2/1996) 5 mins (6/1996)	

included a reduction in the time needed to change dies from one product to another (set up time). In this level of analysis, the vital few 'HOWs' of the first level analysis create vital few 'WANTs' from the second level of analysis – a similar process to the use of 'Pareto analysis'.

In the development of this matrix, there is little need to score and rank the current 'WANTs' unless the matrix is large. In the same process as before, the relationship matrix is plotted using the appropriate symbols and the team must ensure that there are no blank columns (potential implementation projects with no bearing on the key 'WANTs') and that there are no blank rows (the inability of the team to determine any form of potential solution implementation). The illustration shows only 2 'HOWs' related to 2 'WANTs', but in reality there are likely to be between 6 to 10 'WANTs' and up to 30 'HOWs'. The relationship matrix is scored in the same manner as before, but this time in the absence of the 'multiplier' effect (by summing the columns). Finally, the 'HOWs' are triangulated using the 'roof' of the matrix. This roof is used to relate each second generation 'HOW' to all other 'HOWs'. In this manner, any conflicts will become evident so that the implementation of a specific 'HOW' will diminish the return and contribution or another. At this stage, the team must decide which is the more important route to pursue and therefore de-list the 'HOW' that causes the reduction of improvement.

Once the second generation 'HOWs' have been constructed as a portfolio of 'worthy' projects in which to invest financial and human resources, the team must identify the precedence of the implementation programme. In the illustrative figure, this would involve the promotion of set-up time reduction as a precursor to the ability to reduce batch sizes in the factory. For this the team can develop a critical path (and associated timings) for the implementation of projects as a suite of ongoing initiatives that are mutually reinforcing. This approach allows the many different activities that form a suite of improvement efforts in an area of the factory or workplace to be related to a theme of overall improvement with concrete and goals. The continuous improvement activities are related to the goals of the business and are measured in a mutually reinforcing series of performance evaluators. In this respect, each iteration of the analytical matrices represents a continuously refined approach to the 'HOWs' of project management and the actual practices that will be introduced to each area of the factory. The approach therefore is 'upwardly compatible' and each iteration supports the achievement of the superordinate goals, including the concurrent management of improvement activities, on a company-wide scale, as well as deploying factory effort in a logical and structured manner.

A second point worthy of discussion is the use of this tool by the authors in a number of other areas showing its range of versatility in addressing different problems and opportunities at various points in the value stream. During the lifetime of SCDP, including the above examples, *six* different individual projects have employed the VALSAT method. These include working with:

- an automotive component supplier to assist in the focusing of competitive strategy;
- a food manufacturing company to analyze how improvements can be made in manufacturing and logistics performance;
- a transport provider to assist in their decision-making process for IT purchases (Bouverie-Brine and Rich 1997);

- a lubricant company to help develop their strategic agenda;
- an automotive component manufacturer to focus and drive their supplier development activity (Rich, 1995b);
- a regional development agency to assist their role in attracting inward investors into the region (Rich, 1995a).

As can be seen from this wide variety of applications, this tool is designed to act at a far more fundamental level than simply addressing single issues such as time in the supply chain. This is not to say that the latter is unimportant, but it should be regarded as only one factor in the menu of customer requirements.

Advantage of the VALSAT Approach

There are clearly a number of distinct advantages or strengths in applying the VALSAT approach into the value stream as suggested in Table 5.2. These benefits are considerable compared with traditional analysis approaches that far too often revolve around the implementation of the latest buzz word without really understanding if these are the most appropriate approaches. The technique itself tends to force both cross-functional and cross-organizational working. Another critical area is that it tends to help to de-select 'hobby horse' projects that minority interests in an organization want to pursue, if such projects are inappropriate. This means that greater consensus can be gained and the company can obtain greater focus and cohesion by concentrating on a limited number of critical programmes in its value stream allowing for faster project implementation.

The approach also highlights where potential breakthroughs may occur and gives an indication of whether these, perhaps longer-term, projects are worth developing. As such, VALSAT can be used across a range of time horizons. In addition, the tool can be used at a variety of positions in the value stream but, critically, all are focused on customer requirements, so that the tool will appeal to those from a marketing or quality assurance background.

It should be noted that the approach has a few weaknesses which are summarized in Table 5.3. The first of these is that it appears at first sight

VALSAT can be used across a range of time horizons.

rather complex. However, once a researcher or practitioner has worked through the process it becomes a very manageable approach, one which, however, does not allow for major external or environmental changes between iterations. If it is to be used in a rapidly changing environment, it requires frequent reiteration. The last apparent drawback is that VALSAT forces organizations to spend considerable time in the analysis and planning stage and this can delay

TABLE 5.2   Strengths of the Value Stream Analysis Tool (VALSAT)

1. Involvement of at least two level of the value stream in the analysis process.
2. A rigorous approach that allows subjective and objective measures to be combined.
3. Allows for effective de-selection of 'hobby-horses'.
4. Facilitates consensus within cross-functional management environment.
5. Allows opportunity to analyze how major breakthroughs could be achieved that would be hard for competitors to copy.
6. Is a useful framework to force hidden issues and problems out into the open so they can be addressed early on.
7. A good method of saving time in implementation as clear implementation approaches can be identified particularly if second-stage matrix is constructed.
8. Can be applied at any position in the value stream.
9. Can be simplified with a number of the stages left out if circumstances warrant this.
10. Useful as a scenario planning tool especially where complex web of value stream relationships exist that are difficult to separate.
11. Reality-based approach that can be used within most wider research methodologies.
12. Capable of coping with many requirements not just one, such as time.
13. A quality tool that is based on changing the value stream along lines defined by customers function(s) or organization(s).
14. A dynamic tool that allows for continual reassessment and refocusing of value stream improvements.
15. A tool that can cope with variable horizons from immediate to very long-term horizons.

implementation. However, in every case in which the authors have used it, this lost time is more than made up by a more straightforward implementation programme than might otherwise have been possible.

TABLE 5.3   Weaknesses of the Value Stream Analysis Tool (VALSAT)

1. Initial appears complex and difficult to understand.
2. Has to assume a relatively stable environment between iterations.
3. Increases time spent on analysis stage of projects.

Conclusion

This chapter has attempted to demonstrate the use of a dynamic methodology for creating value stream effectiveness called the Value Stream Analysis Tool or VALSAT. The origins of this approach lie in the Quality Function Deployment approach used in the Japanese shipyards for new product development purposes.

The tool has been demonstrated here both from a theoretical and practical viewpoint. It is contended that the VALSAT approach is a methodology that has significant advantages over traditional methods of analysis of improvement approaches in the value stream arena. Early implementation work with this method has shown a wide variety of potential uses, all to date proving successful. The authors believe that the use of this approach will help those interested in the various value stream or logistics processes to develop approaches that go far beyond the latest 'hobby horses', buzz words or rhetoric to the attainment of true world-class performance.

PART TWO

Thinking Strategically About Change

The 1990s are often characterized as an environment of frequent, unpredictable and accelerating levels of 'change'.[1] The continuous flux of changing requirements has increased the level of competition between companies who share the same market for the goods and services they provide; it has also transcended the 'private' and 'public' sectors and has left virtually no company unaffected by some degree of turbulence in the planning and management of operations. The sources of these rapid changes in the operating environment of the company can be traced to a number of origins that include: increased levels of competition; deregulation of markets; more sophisticated customers; and pressures to re-organize the resources within the organization itself. The pressure to change working structures, working relationships and to develop a strategic response to an uncertain market environment is not a new phenomena and has always been an element of strategic planning and environmental scanning activities. However in recent times the frequency and severity of change has created a renewed interest in the strategy and structure debate, including the externalization of business strategy to the structure of the supply chain itself. The latter analysis and reformations that have sought to rationalize the numbers of suppliers have also created a three-dimensional puzzle of change management. As a result, the management of change has an internal and an external dimension which require orchestration in order to yield beneficial results for the entire supply chain.

A common denominator that unites the many different management authors in this vital field of academic research is the notion that companies who fail to understand the market or supply chain in which they operate and/or fail to develop strategies and structures to accommodate or

[1] Prepared by Nick Rich and Peter Hines.

exploit the competitive opportunities that such change brings, will cease to exist (Kanter, 1989). The dramatic levels of change associated with modern marketplaces has stimulated the development of many different models of management in the 1990s, including the promotion of new management concepts, strategies, processes and practices with which to rejuvenate the organization or equip it with the necessary mechanisms better to 'cope' with the uncertainty of changes in its trading position. Some of these concepts have included introspective changes to the way in which the organization is structured (including concepts such as 'downsizing', 'de-layering', 'right sizing' and Business Process Re-engineering (BPR)), whilst others have focused on the management of the external resources to the business (supplier partnerships, trust, supply-base rationalization and supplier evaluation systems). However, few of these models have taken a holistic view of the organization in its context or a long-term perspective towards the evolution of business structures to meet the needs of future consumers, but instead have tended towards the short-term and reactive solution of problems which may have sources that are much deeper than the models acknowledge. There is also an element of 'fad' and 'blind emulation' of organizations that currently hold titles such as 'exemplar' (Cox, 1995). These strategies do not measure up to the unique contingencies that face each individual company and therefore their implementation is often associated with failure or the inability to restructure the invisible administrative routines that are needed to support such new changes in the operating procedures of the organization, which causes confusion and resistance within the organization itself.

Few of these models have taken a holistic view of the organization in its context.

Part Two of this textbook draws from international applied research, conducted as part of the Supply Chain Development Programme (SCDP), into the strategy and structure of 'lean' organizations. This research has culminated in the development of the four-pillar model which is examined in Chapter 6. This paper highlights the policies, practices and methods adopted by such companies in order to gain a 'fit' within the internal organization of the company and also how the relationships with the supply market and customer market are integrated to form a 'value chain' that is responsive to, and accommodates change in, the supply chain. This chapter should equip the reader with an insight into the strategy and structure of such organizations and provides a model which the reader can use to interpret the changes within their own unique business and environmental constraints.

Chapter 7 deals with the strategic management of the internal 'value-adding process' (those operations that are conducted by the organization itself) and the 'extended value stream (the flow of value and materials throughout the network of suppliers to the consumer). Chapter 7 identifies the common denominator of 'customer service' and how the 'voice of the customer' can be localized within the management and day-to-day improvement efforts in the factory or service centre. It argues for the reinforcement of the traditional Western organizational structures of departmental specialization, through the use of 'lateral' or cross-functional key process management as a means of developing and sustaining the level of 'value' established by the organization.

Chapter 8 extends the top-down and bottom-up restructuring of the organization and its planning systems by providing the reader with an appreciation of standard operating systems. Chapter 8 has two parts: the first concentrates on the development of a standard 'lean' manufacturing system as typified by Toyota Motor Corporation; and the second extends this 'lean thinking' into a non-production setting – the warehouse environment has been chosen to illustrate this 'transference'. The key argument contained in this chapter is that the strategic planning and change management systems adopted by an organization will be severely blunted if the day-to-day operations of the factory or warehouse are not standardized and do not form a base on which 'change management' or improvement decisions can be taken with certainty of success. In this respect, the efforts of the middle managers in the factory (highlighted Chapter 7) and the business strategists (discussed in Chapter 6) cannot be optimized or realize significant business benefits unless the planning cycle is reinforced with a parallel effort to standardize the approach and procedures within the business at the point of 'value adding' or 'waste elimination'.

Deploying Strategic Management in the Value Stream[1]

Introduction

The current global business environment is characterized by frequent and often unpredictable change created through the combination of many interrelated forces. These include more enlightened and demanding customers, technological innovation and growing competition from rival organizations on an international scale (Achrol, 1991; Porter, 1980; Kanter, 1989). Indeed, few, if any, industries have escaped some aspect of this macro change process to remain in an industry that is still stable. The increase in the environmental uncertainty that lies beyond the control and influence of the organization has major implications for the manner in which business strategy is synthesized with the internal operating structure of the company and the way its external relations are conducted. This chapter draws from the research which has been undertaken during the Supply Chain Development Programme and provides a model of how 'world class' companies accommodate change and use the supply chain to create competitive advantage.

Modern Responses to Turbulent Environments

During the 1990s there has been a plethora of new organizational models and new working practices proposed by both academic and practitioner

---

[1] This paper is based on Nick Rich and Peter Hines 'Purchasing Structures, Roles, Processes and Strategies: Is It A Case Of The Tail Wagging The Dog', *European Journal of Purchasing and Supply Management*, Vol. 4, 1, pp. 51–63, March 1998.

communities. For many of these models, the academic community has lagged behind developments in organizations and the academic contribution has tended towards the prescriptive development of 'all-encompassing' models and descriptive account of change management cases. Cox (1995) contends that these models have tended to be adopted through copying others or implementing more academic solutions as a means of counteracting the impact of change within and beyond the organization. He continues his argument by suggesting that

> new concepts and ideas are taken up by practitioners under pressure, who need to demonstrate their 'state of the art' knowledge and expertise, but who do not have the time to assess the practical utility of a concept for their own unique business environment. Often fads have not been properly evaluated empirically before they are touted as the latest 'cure-all' for every management problem.

The new models of industrial organization and their associated techniques can be classified into two major generic categories: those dealing with the internal restructuring of the organization and its resources; and those dealing with the development of new working relationships within the supply chain. The former group of models include such concepts as Business Process Re-engineering (BPR) (Hammer and Champy, 1993), 'de-layering' or 'right sizing' of the organization (Kanter, 1989; Keuning and Opheij, 1994), employee empowerment (Belcher, 1987) and continuous improvement (Imai, 1986). The latter, supply-chain-focused models, have included the concept of the 'value chain' (Porter, 1980; Johnson and Scholes, 1988), time-based competitive strategies (Stalk and Hout, 1990), and supply base rationalization (Hanan, 1992).

However, few authors have combined the internal strategies and structures with the external elements of the market change and the customer service equation. The authors who have adopted this holistic approach include: Womack and Jones (1996), who provide the 'lean model' of supply chain and organizational management; Merli (1991), who proposes the 'co-makership' model; and Stevens (1989), who describes the evolutionary 'supply chain' model.

Few authors have combined the internal strategies and structures with the external elements of the market change and the customer service equation.

Within this category of authors, these models have very different practical roots. The 'supply chain model' of Stevens (1989) is prescriptive and conceptual in nature and has been included in the work of Merli (1991), who draws his arguments from case material of high-performing companies. The 'lean approach' also adopts a case approach, uniting the different contexts and contingencies of the cases, through a concern for supply chain management including the central tenet that companies must seek to eliminate 'waste' and costs by radically and continuously improving the 'value added' ratio within and beyond the focal business. In many respects, the arguments forwarded by these authors are similar and underpinned by the concepts of integration and alignment within and beyond the organization.

Tracing Supply Chain Management Thought

A model that synthesizes the issues of the supply chain and organizational structure has been proposed by Stevens (1989). The model can be summarized as a four-stage process of 'backward integration' from the customer-facing departments within a single business to those with an indirect impact on the day-to-day generation of customer satisfaction. Stevens (1989) identifies the following organizational arrangements that mature and develop into a supply chain competence in the fourth evolution:

1. *The Baseline Organization* – focus rests on short-term *distribution* efficiency, with reactive management and preoccupation with cost management.

2. *Functional Integration* – short-term budget focus and management of finished goods customer service. *Order processing* and service characterize this format.

3. *Internal Integration* – medium-term focus and measurement against annual goals with management attention resting with productivity improvements. The management of *sourcing and production planning* are paramount to the competitive strategy of this format.

4. *External Integration* – long-term attention to integrating corporate strategies and policies. Flow management techniques are adopted to provide a platform for world-class competitive position. *Cross-functional management*, integration and capability management are key elements of this class of *fully integrated organization*.

This model suggests that the traditional business functions within organizations will rise to gain 'power' within the long-range planning processes until all departments have reached a level of elevation to create a democratic and holistic 'systems' approach to the management of the organization and its supply chain dependencies. In parallel, Merli (1991) provides a similar model which is grounded in a retrospective analysis of the historical development of the supply chain concept. He also identifies four distinct forms of evolution in the business and supply chain activities of companies. However, in the Merli model, the embryonic integration of the supply chain occurs in the third stage of evolution and became a prevalent force during the 1970s in Japan, but has yet to become fully developed in the West. The *four* stages of evolution proposed by Merli are as follows.

1. The Early Myopia of Mass Production Efficiency

The early theories of industrial organization were dominated by economic principles, and during this period, the 1920s to the 1950s, large-scale industrial organizations began to create mass production systems to meet the needs of mass consumption within domestic markets. Business strategies during this period were underpinned by 'expansionism', with companies offering a limited product range to a growing and predictable market environment. These companies were often pioneers of technology and manufacturing systems, exemplified by the Ford Motor Company, and managed by charismatic and dynastic families. Indeed, the importance of large volume manufacturing is captured in the writings of Henry Ford himself, who proposes that 'the true end of industry is to liberate mind and body from the drudgery of existence by filling the world with well-made, low-priced products' (Ford Motor Company, 1995).

Merli (1991) reinforces this 'technology' perspective by contending that this early period of industrialization included

> the application of operations-oriented strategic principles and organisational principles of a mechanistic type (Bureaucracy). ... The bureaucratic / product out company believes that business is carried out only with products and technology. Technology know-how and product know-how are thus considered the most important factors in business.

The rationale for factory activities during this era of development was volume efficiency and principally that of internal cost containment through the use of standard procedures or the routinization of work to gain processing efficiencies in both the administrative and factory activities.

The internal manufacturing system operated by these early industrialists was reinforced and supported by the concentration of all planning activities on the most senior managers within the organization and the development of an administrative system which contained departments of functional specialisms (such as quality control, purchasing, manufacturing, scheduling and expediting). The factory administrative structure was therefore established to create efficiencies that were not available under the earlier and discrete system of craft production. These administrative structures were further divided into levels of responsibility and authority based on a hierarchical structure of organizational positions which created a scalar chain of superiors and subordinates. Within this structure, managers controlled the work of direct subordinates who, in turn, controlled the work of their subordinates. At this point, the value-adding process was the responsibility of the organizational administrators and technical specialists in the factory, which in later development created functional professionalisms (including the defining of educational and career paths in the organization). To cement the strategy of growth and efficiency with a functional business structure, the system was encapsulated in formal lines of demarcation between departments and formal rules relating to the conduct of activities by each department and individual.

The division of the human resources in the factory, through the use of the functional hierarchy within the support departments and at the conversion process, served as the skeletal framework with which corporate management and government could be exercised, through practices of 'command and control' and work regulation. This logical fragmentation of roles and responsibilities within the factory became an implicit part of factory life and created the 'scientific' management school of academic thought (Taylor, 1911). At the very heart of the 'scientific' school of thought was a concern for the rational application of economic techniques to maximize profits by minimizing costs in the factory. To achieve these ends, all business procedures reflected a concern for efficiency and output including the remuneration of workers through piece rate systems and the control of management activities through the process of management-by-objectives (MBO). The company was focused on the movement of materials in volume through the factory processes, and the management of the factory provided the leadership, with unilateral control, to redirect the resources of the factory to ensure that production volumes could be achieved. This attention to the workings of the internal organization, little influenced by external change or dependency in either the customer or supply markets, generated the academic term 'closed' systems management.

From a supply chain perspective, these closed and insular organizations showed little interest in the management of suppliers, preferring where possible, to 'make' rather than to 'buy' (vertical integration). In this respect, the management of suppliers to the organization were of low priority and supply agreements were entered into with reluctance. Where such contracts existed, the prevailing concept of cost economics was deployed by the purchasing department through procurement activities which were dominated by a concern to secure the lowest piece-part price from the vendor. To achieve the lowest price of commodities supplied, the purchasing department engaged in adversarial methods of bargaining and contracting as a means of exerting the power and economic leverage of the mass-producing customer, often engaging in contracting such high volumes of the capacity of the supplier as to create a form of quasi-vertical integration through domination, but without incurring the cost of owning the facility itself (Blois, 1971).

In summary, these early management strategies and structures presented by Merli (1991) represent 'closed' systems of operations which were little affected by the environment in which they operated and in many respects these organizations determined the rate of change themselves. The low level of uncertainty created by mass consumption and low levels of domestic competition created a strategic perspective which was inwardly-facing and preoccupied with the volume and costs of everything under its control.

2. Competition and Internationalization

The second evolution of management thinking, identified by Merli (1991) occurred during the 1960s when companies began to experience increasing levels of market and environmental turbulence. In this new scenario the dominance of technological and the corporate perception of the importance of manufacturing had declined and been replaced with a concern for 'marketing'. This period of evolution also witnessed many dysfunctions of the 'classical' system under conditions of uncertainty and an increase in domestic competition. Such dysfunctions included the inability of the rigidly structured organization to cope with rapid market changes, problems with purchasing regimes which were based on 'price-alone', the inability to define clearly a long-term strategy for the business with any degree of certainty that the strategy could be achieved, and a myriad of other signs of weakness in the 'closed' system of scientific management. Merli (1991) proposes that companies during this period of evolution had begun to change from the base level of the classical organization, replacing the 'technology' bias with a concern for the 'market' and the development of new capabilities to seek out opportunities. He contends that ' ... on this basis, a company might suspend consideration of its technological capabilities. Should the opportunity arise, it could initiative new enterprises, or it might stick to marketing existing products or have goods produced by other firms' (Merli, 1991).

The change in the market environment from the relative stability of the early period of the industrial organization to a new competitive environment, characterized by instability, created pressure on such companies to decentralize decision-making routines in order to provide an adequate response to change. The decentralization of decision-making, away from a central core in the functional hierarchy, was paralleled by an entrepreneurial interest in exploiting market opportunities as they occurred. The rationale for these activities was to sell the productive capacity of the manufacturing organization and to maintain a full order book. The technological focus remained an aspect of organizational behaviour but in a modified format, superseded by the need to 'sell' against other market competitors.

The turbulence in the 'output' element of the conversion process stimulated management to pay more attention to the 'inputs' to the business the treatment of suppliers. The response of the purchasing and supply departments was to dismantle any form of dependency relationship with suppliers by creating competition amongst the rival suppliers, but to remain with the adversarial processes of negotiation which had been employed effectively in the 'classical' system. The result of this activity was to increase the numbers of direct suppliers to the company (in order to maintain the lowest prices of materials through such means as competitive tendering) and to engage in short-term contracts which matured quickly and ensured that frequent tendering cycles were used to manipulate the power of the customer against the supplier in a zero sum game. In addition, the use of 'arm's-length' contracting reinforced the dislocation of customer and supplier by preventing any form of information exchange for fear that this information would be used by either side to gain or exploit advantage during the many rounds of tendering and contracting.

> *The turbulence in the 'output' element of the conversion process stimulated management to pay more attention to the 'inputs' to the business and the treatment of suppliers.*

The input element of the supply chain equation was therefore dominated by policies to disengage the organization from any form of dependency or long-term relationship with the companies which provided the materials for conversion. The relationship between the customer and supplier were effectively encased in a vacuum, and the purchasing department remained a tactical weapon as the customer organization focused firmly on the exploitation of the 'outputs' from the supply chain. At this point in the evolution of industrial organizations, the traditional 'closed' systems of management had begun to erode in favour of developing advantage in the marketplace through understanding the demands of consumers. The importance of suppliers to the strategic management of the business, which was dominated by the marketing function, was seen as unimportant and unrelated to the consumer. The concept of supply chain management remained undeveloped, even under conditions of higher levels of subcontracting, and was considered to be an area of cost management rather than creating any form of supplier integration.

3. The 'Involvement' Stage

Merli (1991) continues his analysis of industrial evolution to suggest that the trend of market uncertainty, competition and the decentralization of decision-making continued and formed the third evolution of organizational development during the 1970s. In this period, companies began to refine the previous opportunistic strategies by focusing on customer retention and the continuous improvement of 'outputs' from the company in terms of the quality 'customer service'. This period of development included the strategic management of the capability of the manufacturing operations and the development of standard working methods used to create products of 'value' to consumers. These values draw from the influence of the 'total quality' movement and grew to dominate the strategic policies adopted by Japanese manufacturers becoming manifest in the post-war period. During this time, the limited number of Japanese industries that remained were faced with making the most of the materials they could secure (a position of supply dependency). As these Japanese organizations emerged from the post-war period, these concepts remained an implicit part of the management strategy and, as the availability of material inputs was restored, the competitive challenge was to ensure the flow of quality materials to, through and from the organization to its customers. This holistic approach marks the beginnings of supply chain management and was focused on the concept of internal and external 'customer service'.

The evolution from the Western concept of 'selling' towards one of 'marketing' and the marketing of relationships between customers and suppliers marks a major watershed in the development of industrial organizations. This advance displaced the earlier concepts of technology and selling to include the management of key processes that yielded customer service. Merli (1991) contends that these companies focused on the company-wide management of quality, delivery and cost. Traditionally, the classical departmental structure of the organization created specialisms that maintained responsibility for elements of each of these processes (for example, the quality control department was responsible for in-process quality but the quality of despatched goods was the responsibility of the transportation department, and the quality of input materials was the responsibility of the purchasing department). However, these Japanese companies had begun to create a holistic approach to the organization that was lateral (crossing departments) rather than vertical (the formal accountability of a single department). By redefining the business as a process of hand-offs and responsibilities that needed to be optimized in their totality in order to increase the level of service provided to the customer, the traditional 'efficiency' structure of the organization became modified to include an 'effectiveness' structure (lateral management).

> *The evolution from the Western concept of 'selling' towards one of 'marketing' and the marketing of relationships between customers and suppliers marks a major watershed in the development of industrial organizations.*

In parallel to this redefinition of business management, the trend towards the decentralization of decision-making continued and was accelerated by the concepts of the 'total quality' movement which promoted the development of autonomous teams of employees in the factory (Ishikawa, 1976). The process of decentralization marked another turning point in the development of the organization in that it was the first real attempt to harness the intellectual capital of employees rather than reserving all leadership and control to the management prerogative. The focusing of team efforts within the factory shared the 'customer service' concept with the managers that remained in the formal organizational hierarchy. The performance measures of the factory reflected the values of quality, cost and delivery and formed the link that bound together internal operations and administrative processes within the organization. The deployment of these measures served to qualify the 'output' thinking that had dominated earlier organizations by integrating the concept of 'time' for delivery, the production of 'saleable' output, and the substitution of 'price' with 'cost'. This three-dimensional measure of customer service also served as a basis on which to focus the continuous improvement of each element of the organization in generating products that provided maximum value to customers.

During this evolution in organizational strategy and form, these measures, the concept of customer service, and the need for continuous improvement in the levels of customer service outputted by the business, transformed the management of procurement activities. The purchasing department, measured in this new way and having already established close working relationships with suppliers (including patterns of inter-locking ownership during the post-war period), began to develop an 'integrated' approach to the management of the 'inputs' to the customer service equation. The internal principles of the 'high involvement' company were therefore extended to include those organizations which represented indirect influences on the performance achieved by the purchasing organization. The internal measures of quality, cost and delivery were externalized and used as a means of prioritizing the efforts of the supply base as a collective and also as individual suppliers.

This approach to the management of the 'supply chain' from indirect supplier to the consumer, over which the focal company had a limited degree of control, could no longer be conducted using the traditional adversarial tactics adopted in the West and traditionally used in Japan (Hines, 1994). The development of an integrated approach to the supply base therefore rejected the adversarial model of relationship management and, in the process of integrating suppliers with the strategic aims and performance required by the focal organization, the role of the purchasing department changed. The new model of purchasing behaviour required a more proactive and elevated role in the business, rather than that of a tactical business function that was tasked with efficiency rather than the effectiveness of the supply base. Imai (1986) contends that the new role of the purchasing agent therefore encompassed the development of 'criteria for checking the relative strengths of the suppliers in terms of price, co-operation, quality, delivery, technology and overall management competence' of the supplier. These processes created a holistic view of the supplier and the capability of that supplier to integrate with the purchasing organization.

The proactive management of the inputs to the business, over the long term, stabilized the number of suppliers to the purchasing department and allowed the development of relationships and the sharing of information and working practices across a number of organizations. The collaborative and integrated approach to the supply chain therefore served to stabilize the numbers of suppliers and also created an elevated role for the purchasing department in terms of the new levels of competitive advantage that could be achieved by controlling the capabilities and capacity of the external resources to the business, not least in aligning the activities of the supply base in reducing 'waste', 'cost' and 'time' in the supply chain (Ohno, 1988). During the development of the 'involvement' company, suppliers were regarded as key elements of the competitive strategy generation process and extensions of the customer's factory itself.

4. The 'Market In' Stage

The final evolution of strategic management of the manufacturing organization is termed the 'Market In' company by Merli (1991) and has developed since the 1980s. These companies represent the amalgamation of the Western preoccupation with 'marketing' and the predominantly Japanese approach to managing the factory for maximum customer service by eliminating 'waste' in the entire supply chain. As such, these organizations adopted structures that were highly integrated and consisted of both formal vertical (functional specialisms) and formal lateral (cross-functional management) processes. The latter activity involves the development of management teams from the vertical functions in the business, who influence the performance of key processes such as quality, cost and delivery rather than the traditional management method of assigning the responsibility for quality to the quality control department, cost to the management accounting function and delivery to the logistics department. Instead, lateral management comprises all the relevant business functions through which the process 'flows', so that the 'cost' process may well include the cost of purchases (purchasing department), the cost of production (manufacturing and maintenance department), the product cost (design and management cost accounting) and the shipment costs (distribution department).

The decision-making processes operated by this form of organization retains the decentralization of authority and responsibility of the Japanese system, but this time includes greater levels of autonomy and self-management within the lower 'team' levels of the organization. Merli (1991) contends that the strategies of these companies had also changed from the classical approach to strategy generation (a logical and incremental process) towards a more fluid and 'policy-based' approach within and beyond the organization. This holistic approach to the management of the enterprise within its context is termed an 'open system' of management planning and includes an integrated analysis of the consumer market, the organization and its structures, and the supply market to find new means of generating competitive advantage and 'fit' with the customers and their changing needs.

Merli (1991) proposes that the main characteristics of these 'high performance' companies result from the optimization of the key business processes (quality, cost, and delivery) by 'optimising the entire supplier-client chain of a business ... [and] that the potential of a business is heavily affected by the strength of all links in the chain involved in that business ... Therefore it is important to be in the right chain, with efficient and highly competitive partners'. He proposes that the central coordination of this process of innovation and continuous performance improvement results from the decentralization of all decision-making to inter-functional teams that 'prevail over specialised management functions' (1991). The control mechanism which prioritizes the efforts with the business operations is therefore the continuous improvement of business performance against a priority list of 'process-based' improvements such as the quality, cost and delivery performance of the business. These processes are not the responsibility of a single business function but cross traditional demarcations to form a holistic view of 'output'-measured customer service. As such, the quality, cost and delivery of the linked processes between departments created a desire to engage in cross-functional management activities (as identified by Stevens, 1989).

The strategic integration of the two companies is a function of the level of 'trust' created between the strategists of the two organizations and the integration of information systems.

These new working structures and the issuing of policy goals attempt to improve the capabilities of the company at a faster rate than the demands of the customer market (and thereby determine the level of competition within a product or service segment). In the new evolution of the organization, the key competitive dimension is therefore 'time' and 'time-based' competitive advantage. This focus does not replace the key processes of quality, cost and delivery, but represents a 'higher level' motivation for the company that builds from a basis of customer service. New product introduction and other key processes emerge as 'time-based' competitive capabilities to counter reductions in the life cycles of products, the development of personalized products and the timely movement of materials from the factory to the hands of the consumer (the tightening of the 'delivery' process). A major consideration in the generation of competitive advantage from 'time' compression is the integration of the supply base, so that concurrent engineering can take place, and the levels of supplier collaboration as well as the importance of the purchasing department become an elevated concern within the strategy process for the entire supply chain.

Merli (1991) proposes that the supply strategy adopted to support this form of 'market in' organization must reflect the creation of long-term trading partnerships of a global nature, and the integration of customer-supplier in a seamless flow of information, strategies and capabilities. The

The strategic integration of tghe two companies is a function of the level of 'trust' created between the strategists of the two organizations and the integration of information systems.

strategic integration of the two companies is a function of the level of 'trust' created between the strategists of the two organizations and the integration of information systems. Merli (1991) describes these relationships as 'partnerships' that include a high level of dependency and integration founded on the concept of customer service, pro-activity, concurrency and synchronous operations that are bound by the policies deployed by the head of the supply chain – the company that services the customer most directly and therefore the one with the greatest market intelligence regarding future anticipated and known changes in the competitive performance criteria needed to meet the needs of the customer.

The 'Co-Makership' and Lean Models

The concepts and historical analysis developed by Merli (1991) identify many dimensions of long-standing academic debates relating to the management of industrial organizations under conditions of environmental uncertainty including the centralization–decentralization of decision-making, the reduction of bureaucracy within the organization, and the reduction of command and control structures (Quinn, 1992). Also, the Merli model encompasses many of the 'internally focused' models of management behaviour. However the descriptive nature of the analysis does not explain how the stage three and stage four evolutions can be achieved and managed in terms of the arrangement and processes which underpin the new working relationships of the organization and its dependencies in the customer and supply markets.

The Merli (1991) and Stevens (1989) models display a strong correlation with the 'lean' school of academic thought. The origins of the 'lean' approach can be traced to empirical and comparative studies of industrial performance by academics (Womack, Jones and Roos, 1990). The early studies that characterize this school of thought were drawn from the 'benchmarking' of automotive assembly and component supply sectors and have recently been translated into more general applications in terms of warehousing, the service sector, and general industry (Womack and Jones, 1996). The impact of the early empirical work undertaken has been profound and draws from evidence that highlights the efficiency and effectiveness of the Japanese manufacturing systems, and the systems that have been developed by Toyota Motor Corporation supply chain, in particular.

The first comparative study, comprising the world's leading vehicle assemblers, demonstrated an enormous gap between the productivity and quality achieved by the Japanese over their Western counterparts

(Womack, Jones and Roos, 1990; Lamming, 1993). These figures were then tested by comparing the performance of British and Japanese automotive component suppliers (Andersen Consulting, 1992) to find results that demonstrated a 2:1 gap in supplier productivity and a 100:1 gap in favour of the Japanese. These studies were then extended to include the British and Japanese sample of suppliers in a worldwide survey of suppliers to find similar patterns of industrial performance concentrated in Japan (although this time other European factories were found to exhibit Japanese levels of performance). Throughout these studies, the concepts of the 'lean' school were developed and included analyses of the social arrangements of work, the impact of the product design process, and also the developed of integrated supply chains to support high-performance customers. These empirical studies confirm the work of Merli (1991) and the companies studied exhibit a similar approach to the latter two evolutions of the 'co-makership' model.

Jones (1990), cited in Hines (1994), proposes that the 'lean' model is characterized by the following activities:

1. It is customer-driven – not driven by the needs of manufacturing.
2. All activities are organized and focused on a product line basis led by a product champion, with functional departments playing a secondary, servicing role.
3. All activities are team-based and the organization is horizontally, not vertically, oriented.
4. The whole system involves fewer actors, all of whom are integrated with each other – 330 engineers in the product development team versus 1400, 340 suppliers versus 1500, about 300 dealer principals versus 3600, and 2000 assembly employees versus between 3000 and 5500.
5. There is a high level of information exchanged between all the actors and a transparent and real cost structure.
6. The activities are coordinated and evaluated by the flow through the team or plant, rather than by each department meeting its plan targets in isolation.
7. The discipline necessary for the system to function and expose problems is provided by JIT and Total Quality in the plant and supplier and dealer performance evaluation.
8. Wherever possible, responsibility is devolved to the lowest practical level in the plant or the suppliers.
9. The system is based on stable production volumes but with a great deal of flexibility.
10. Relations with employees, suppliers and dealers are based on reciprocal obligations that are the result of treating them as fixed costs.

The 'lean' models of organizational and supply chain behaviour are underpinned by the concept of internal (within the business) and external (within the supply chain) integration. The key elements of these 'high performance' and 'open' systems of management involve participative management techniques that are decentralized, concepts of worker empowerment, the development of the supply base to reduce the exposure of the entire supply chain to disruption, the alignment and transparency of strategies and operations throughout the supply chain and a constant reinforcement of the continuous need to improve the output of the entire supply chain as a competitive weapon in raising customer service expectations.

The 'lean' models of organizational and supply chain behaviour are underpinned by the concept of internal (within the business) and external (within the supply chain) integration.

In later, cross-sectorial case analyses of high performance organizations, Womack and Jones (1996) have encapsulated how these 'Toyota production system' concepts can be transferred to non-automotive contexts. The authors contend that the application of these 'lean' ideas will be specific to each company, their culture and their unique circumstances (a contingent approach), but that there are *five* basic elements of the 'lean' system that are ingrained in all 'lean' businesses wherever they may be found:

1. The specification of value (the definition of 'customer service').

2. The identification of the value stream which needs to be developed in order to improve the level of customer service provided to the consumer (the definition of the key processes in creating valued products which ranges across many customer–supplier nodes in the supply stream).

3. The creation of 'flow' so that materials move in a timely and smooth manner between internal operations and between the different elements of the supply chain that create value (eliminating waste and time from the supply stream to create synchronous operations and administrative activities).

4. The introduction of a system of 'pull' triggers in the company and supply chain so that materials are consumed by internal or external 'customers' that provide the signal for the internal or external 'supplier' to replenish (this reinforces the concept of 'flow' by providing the stimulus for replenishment throughout the entire supply chain as internal replenishments cause a reduction of in-bound materials and therefore the sequencing of replenishments from suppliers. This feature also serves to maintain the focus of all managers in the system on the demands of the customer).

5. Finally, the authors propose that the 'lean' organizations are highly motivated and focused on the development of productivity through the removal of all wastes in the system and the attainment of 'per-

fection' or 'perfect quality' of materials and services (this process includes the assignment of company resources, especially human capital, towards the improvement of the supply chain so that there is no waste and 'zero losses' in servicing the ultimate consumer of the supply chain product or service).

Examining the External Validity of the Supply Chain Management Models

The summary of the key models in the supply chain management field of study is by no means an exhaustive list of the assumptions and arguments that seek to provide a 'lean' frame of reference for managers seeking to reduce the impact of environmental uncertainty. The key arguments contained in this chapter were included in order to provide only a broad overview of the modern 'strategy and structure' debate. However, despite the emergence of distinct themes within industry, most of the models remain at a conceptual stage, drawing from limited case material, and therefore the localization and realization of the concepts has been difficult to achieve and involves large-scale organizational changes that can only occur over a relatively long period of strategic restructuring and alignment. Inevitably, many of the proposed models answer questions that relate to 'why' organizations have changed but few have tendered the means, or sought to develop models of 'how' these changes can take place while remaining aligned with the 'strategy' of the business. These problems are compounded by the fragmentation of organizations into functional departments, the way in which these sub-units are controlled and aligned, and how a fit can be made between dependencies in the output and input markets. The key element of this three-dimensional puzzle concerns the management of individual and organizational relationships.

The Supply Chain Development Programme and the Four-Pillar Model

The stimulus for the empirical research work undertaken on behalf of the Supply Chain Development Programme (SCDP) was the need to create a bridge between the macro-level models of the supply chain and a more detailed understanding and model of the mechanisms through which high-performing companies created such internal and external structures. The research was conducted during the period 1994–6 and focused on the analysis of high-performance companies drawn from a number of industrial and service sectors in Japan, UK and North America. The research adopted a case study approach to gain qualitative data relating to the operations of the company and also quantitative material drawn from questionnaire and secondary materials. The resulting model has been termed the 'four-pillar model' of 'how' lean organizations are structured and 'how' the supply chain forms an integral element of operational and strategic competitive advantage in the consumer market.

In overview, the four pillars of the model developed by Rich and Hines (1998) consists of:

1. The cascading of strategic management direction to the daily improvement activities of shopfloor employees through a process that has become 'westernised' as *Policy Deployment*'.

2. The formalization of *Cross Functional Management (CFM)* to create an improvement activity of lateral integration between vertical functional specialisms. This activity is conducted by management within the business, because this grade of employee has the ability to undertake decisions which can make wholesale changes to the operating systems of the company and the assignment of resources within the organizational structure.

3. The development of a *Standardized Production System* that involves a routinized and efficient means of controlling the production system (and administrative processes) within highly defined and visual standards. Any deviation from these standards becomes instantly obvious and a stimulus for correction, improvement or the elimination of the source of failure that has caused the abnormality in the operation or system.

4. The integration of the supply base, and the productive capacity held by suppliers, through the use of supplier integration techniques, including the use of a *Supplier Association*.

For convenience, the model is divided into the distinct 'themes' of management, however, it should be noted that all elements of the system have two key dimensions: first, an internal one (forming a closed system) whereby the company establishes its own policies or activities based on information supplied to it by customers and suppliers, such as the establishment of an 'internal' cross-functional team drawn from personnel in different business specialisms; second, one that concerns the externalization and integration of key stakeholders who operate outside the direct control of the focal company – so, for example, the internal members of a cross-functional team may be joined by personnel from key suppliers or customers. Also, for ease of explanation, the four elements of the system will be analyzed in isolation, although the behavioural patterns and operationalization of each technique has obvious overlaps and relationships with other 'pillars' within the system so that all the pillars are mutually reinforcing.

Pillar 1: Hoshin Kanri (Policy Deployment)

Hoshin Kanri is the Japanese term for 'directional control' or 'directional management' – which has become translated as 'policy deployment' in the West – but which can be traced to a literal translation of 'shining needle' (the needle being a means of navigation and direction). In Japan, these two words have been commonly accepted as *hoshin*, representing 'policy' or 'the selection of targets and means', which, combined with the *kanri*, can be translated as 'control' or 'management'. Combining these two elements creates a strategic management system that involves the setting of business direction and key targets for the provision of customer service, product mixes, financial considerations and so on.

Womack and Jones (1996) propose that this concept can be defined as

> a strategic decision-making tool that focuses resources on the critical initiatives necessary to accomplish the business objectives of the firm. By using visual matrices ... three to five key objectives are selected while all others are clearly deselected. The selected objectives are translated into specific projects and deployed down to the implementation level in the firm. Hoshin Kanri unifies and aligns resources and establishes clearly measurable targets against which progress toward the key objectives is measured on a regular basis.

However, the policy deployment method of management is a comparatively new technique, originating in Japan during the late 1960s and early 1970s at the time when Merli (1991) proposes that the 'involvement' phase of organizational development had crystallized. The approach is inextricably linked to the concepts of 'total quality management' and the impact of Drs Deming and Juran who had already gained fashionable support amongst the leading Japanese companies in the early 1960s (Bicheno, 1991). These leading quality gurus emphasized the need to gain control of the factory through the application of statistical process controls and also the proactive strategic management and promotion of quality on a company-wide scale. In order to experiment with 'total quality' within strategic management, the companies were drawn from a broad cross-section of industrial manufacturing companies, some of whom were 'close' to the consumer but also many 'pioneers' that were lower in the supply chains and had only indirect relationships with the consumer. These companies included the Toyota Motor Corporation, Komatsu and the Bridgestone Tire Company (Shiba *et al.*, 1993). Since these early beginnings, policy deployment has become widely diffused amongst the suppliers to these companies and also across industrial sectors (in terms of the promotion of the policy deployment approach by professional bodies including the Japan Union of Scientists and Engineers (JUSE)).

Nevertheless, the policy deployment approach has rarely gained international support in the West despite a wholesale acceptance that Japanese production systems can be localized successfully and emulated. However, of all the Japanese management techniques, the policy deployment system is the one most 'invisible' within the factory and less easy to distinguish or emulate than those 'visible' elements of the Japanese production systems such as *kanban*, material control (Ackroyd *et al.*, 1988). However, the visible elements of the Japanese systems are not strategic in nature, but represent the manifestation of strategy – in short these techniques are 'hows' to achieve other business 'wants'. As such, the visual techniques involved in a 'Total Productive Maintenance' (TPM) system are comparatively easy to emulate with certain benefits for the emulator, but the TPM techniques are reflections of 'how' the maintenance and production departments have allocated resources to meet other goals. These other goals are strategic in nature and represent the manner in which these departments will make a contribution to the quality, cost and delivery of products to the next customer in the supply chain.

The concept of policy deployment is therefore the application of the 'total quality' philosophy to the strategic management of the business and also the re-definition of the senior management role within it. In terms of these new roles for the senior managers, the value of such a position lies in activities concerning the preparation of the business to manage increasingly demanding customers over a long time horizon (over five years) and to determine within this period the key competitive measures (and targets for these measures over each time period) that must be achieved in terms of outputted customer service in its broadest context. Customer service therefore includes the development of product ranges, the allocation of work to factory sites, the planning of financial returns,

FIGURE 6.1 The Four-Pillar Model

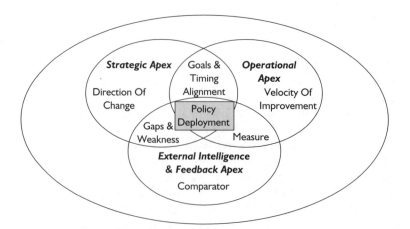

the compliance of the factory to external regulations, as well as the quality, cost and delivery issues that represent customer service transactions. These activities are 'directional' and establish static targets for each year of business operation that can be measured and compared. As such, the senior managers do not engage in day-to-day activities or work that distracts them from this long-range planning priority.

> *The concept of policy deployment is the application of the 'total quality' philosophy to the strategic management of the business.*

The senior managers within a business are concerned with information processing and the establishment of goals to be achieved by others in the business. The nature of change and turbulence in the marketplace makes extended long-range planning difficult and subject to error or random 'chance' factors in the environment, and therefore the planning activities are deliberately limited to within five years (during this period the enactment of legislation can be identified, trends in key inputs to the organization and other planning variables can be established within a tolerance of accuracy). However, in parallel with these basic information-processing activities, the senior managers must also be aware of the performance of the factory against its current targets, in order to track the accommodation and implementation of key business initiatives aimed at generating competitive advantage. Senior managers must, therefore, receive a second stream of 'comparative' information relating to the trends and rate of organizational improvement. This information can only be derived from the lowest levels in the organization in terms of data which must be accumulated and summarized by the middle management of the business so that it holds meaning for the strategists concerned. In this respect, the planning 'loop' is closed and the role of the senior management team, other than that of leading the middle managers, is completed.

The policy deployment approach to the strategic management of the business therefore contains the main environmental scanning routines of the business as well as the feedback of information on a routinized and formal (typically monthly) basis. This approach differs from the traditional Western methods of logical incrementalism and the use of specialists to conduct these planning activities and their associated dysfunctions, including the development of plans that are 'ideally' what should be done, the definition of unachievable business goals (Quinn, 1992) and the problems of individual decision-making under conditions of complexity (Simon, 1947). The policy deployment approach is therefore a group activity, based on business facts, and utilizing a 'process' or holistic approach to the 'output' requirements from the business. Traditionally, the long-range planning activities of the business are then translated, in a top-down fashion, into functional goals with poor levels of review (Hill, 1995) as the functions develop, independently, their own functional strategies.

The policy deployment philosophy does not operate using the long time frames and the difficult-to-reverse commitments of the traditional approach, nor does it acknowledge the business functions as the key method of organizational control. Instead, the concept of customer service promotes the measures of quality, cost, delivery, customer partnerships, supply partnerships, specific competences and new product introduction. These processes 'flow' throughout the organization irrespective of functional boundaries, and therefore the statement of goals in these terms provides a common frame of reference for all departments because each has a relationship with almost all of these processes. For example, the quality of products is a function of quality supplies (the supplier and purchasing department), the process quality (engineering, production and quality assurance departments) and the outbound goods quality (logistics department). As such, these measures hold validity for each department, differentiated only by the contribution that can be made by each department individually, and allows improvement targets to be deployed to each area of the factory and its administrative structures. The 'portfolio' approach encapsulated in process-based measures rather than strictly functional ones provides the motivation for departments to work together as cross-functional teams (the second pillar in the system).

The Process of Policy Deployment

The policy deployment process is iterative as the goals of the company are decomposed into performance targets, but this process is not one of strictly top-down (command and control) planning but represents a process of integration, participation and conflict resolution. To explain the process of implementing policy deployment, the following characterization is provided (Rich and Armitage, 1998):

1. The senior management of the business conduct a diagnosis of company performance and establish the current performance levels of the factory in terms of the key processes that make up customer service.

2. The senior management of the business conduct environmental audits (in terms of markets, regulations, customers, products and competitors) and establish the weaknesses and negative current performance gaps in the company over the next three to five years. This establishes the priorities or themes for change within the business as a focusing exercise.

3. The senior management team use quality techniques to establish the causes of problems and the priorities, using facts taken from the business and the long-range planning activities. This process confirms the measurements of success by targeting issues such as the measure

of output customer service (a zero-defect requirement over five years) that must be achieved and as a result the rate of improvement needed over time (a 50 per cent reduction in defect levels in Year 1, etc. until the zero goal is achieved by Year 5).

4. The senior management create a policy document explaining the strategy and its purpose. A joint meeting is called with the middle managers to discuss the reasons and promote the new strategy. At the end of the meeting, the middle managers provide a critique of the plan and assess its feasibility, and implications it contains for success and the conduct of operations in the factory. This activity also includes the determination of 'contributions' to be made by each department in achieving the goal. For example, the source of quality problems may lie with the suppliers to the business and, therefore, through the use of analytical quality methods the suppliers will be targeted for a greater contribution than the manufacturing departments. This process is known as 'catch-ball' as it mimics the throwing of a ball (business problems) around the various departmental representatives until a solution can be achieved, including the re-assignment of resources between departments. After several iterations, the plan will be accepted and will come into force (amending and replacing the existing plan to maintain a five-year planning horizon) during the development of financial budgets for the coming year onwards.

5. The middle management, drawn from the functional specialisms, with a known contribution rate to return to the business, go back to their functional structures to engage in a process of promotion, communication and catch-ball. However, this level of the business is focused on the achievement of the annual goals with the functional subordinates. This process again uses quality tools and techniques to assess the 'sources' of problems in the factory including those that lie in the activities of other departments. At this stage, the 'project plans' are developed to become the 'means' of realizing the emergent strategy of the business.

6. The middle managers also engage in lateral-management or cross-functional management promotional activities to ensure that the interfaces between departments, through which the key processes pass, provide a contribution to the business.

7. Once all the improvement 'means' are known, the functional and cross-functional teams again deploy the strategy by devising implementation plans and timings for their subordinates. Once again, this process involves discussion and promotion of 'why' the senior management request is important to the future of the business and that the day-to-day actions of the teams involved will realize meaningful business benefits. The implementation plans are then collated and agreed before planning the departmental budgets for the business

involving the middle managers (who are best placed to know the constraints of the business and also the 'best practices' to implement).

8. Following this stage, the standard project reporting documents are established. For the shopfloor teams this includes the 'project plan' and the creation of graphs to track (against the known target measures for quality, cost and delivery) the trend of the business area on a week-by-week basis. This report is sent to the middle manager responsible, who in turn collates the information into a statement of monthly achievement against plan (trend information which in turn is presented to the senior management team for analysis and the reappropriation of resources to ensure that the direction of change in the business is aligned with that of the strategy).

9. Finally, on a half-yearly basis two senior management reports are communicated throughout the organization – the first, an interim statement of progress which identifies the key priorities for the business until the financial year end, and the second, the final report of success and failures. At the annual diagnosis meeting, the senior managers promote the key themes for the coming year which have been drawn from the steps 1–4 that occur prior to the close of the trading year.

The policy deployment process attempts to synthesize the rate of change and environmental constraints through a process of evaluations and analysis, from which the strategy emerges after iterations of promotion and conflict reduction in the business. This means that the policy is based on the known and anticipated weaknesses of the company rather than on unrealistic 'ideal' concepts. This process ensures participation and understanding within the company rather than the traditional attitude that the business strategy should be shrouded in secrecy and should be a function of the senior management team only. The approach is therefore holistic and considers the business, and its supply chain, in the context of market change.

The traditional means of reinforcing the motivation of the individual is replaced by the concern to manage processes through management and operational-level team working. The use of the team concept, a central tenet of the 'total quality' approach, is deliberate in that the accommodation of change by the organization will require the focusing of many people to conduct discrete tasks to achieve a goal rather than the traditional approach of top-down planning through 'command and control' directives. The policy deployment system is also unrelated to the career management of the individual, in terms of the management-by-objectives form of motivation that is typical of the 'classical' approach to management. Instead, the cultural specificity of the

The use of the team concept, a central tenet of the 'total quality' approach, is deliberate.

'lifetime employment', seniority-based pay and the frequent rotation of managers between departments removes the promotion of 'individualism' over the objectives of the group or company. Instead of specific task objectives, the approach of 'management-by-policy' requires that the limited control that can be applied by an individual manager over a key process-based target creates the need to work with other business departments, the generation of consensus and the alignment of 'means' across the business.

Policy Deployment: Summary

The strategy process, created by policy deployment, is a means of achieving the internal integration proposed by Stevens (1989) and also of developing the 'involvement' company suggested by Merli (1991). The 'fluid' nature of this emergent strategy process will cause the emphasis of 'control' within the business to change with changes in the external environment – for example, from the management of quality to achieve perfect products, to the competition based on time and deployed through the tightening of the 'delivery' or 'new product introduction' measures. The result of this approach to the business is to release the intellectual capital of the many layers in the business of which the most important is the use of cross-functional management not, as typically portrayed, the shopfloor quality circles (Suzaki, 1987). It is the collective of managers who, in a single decision, can overturn business systems which institutionalize 'waste' in the business or remove demarcation that stagnates 'flow'. It is also this level of management in the business where strategy and practice meet with individuals who have knowledge of functional 'best practice' or specialist skills or analytical techniques that can be employed to solve problems in other elements of the business. Policy deployment, and the challenges it creates, is thus a key process in energizing the middle management teams by changing the constitution of their roles towards work of an 'improvement' nature.

The policy deployment process is, therefore, the central link that unites the vertical and lateral communication channels in the business by prioritizing what must be done in the short term with the future requirements of the business strategy (including the ability to assess investments that realize a longer-term 'pay-back'). However, the policy deployment process has another dimension – through the allocation of improvement targets to the purchasing department the process of prioritization can become externalized. The development of supply strategies that are underpinned by the concept of customer service, the relationships with suppliers and the supplier evaluation systems used to measure performance can be adjusted to accommodate changes in business emphasis. The traditional practices of classical organizations were limited in this respect, concentrating on 'price' rather than the quality, total cost and delivery of products to be converted. The externalization of policy generates an awareness of the 'gaps' and 'weaknesses' in the broader supply chain that cannot be overcome by adversarial means, but must involve a high level of coordinated integration of suppliers as individual nodes in the chain, as well as collectives which need to become aligned and coordinated if the efficiency of each supplier is to be translated into supply chain effectiveness or a capability for competitive advantage. The externalization of policy throughout the chain, through the strategic and operational integration of activities, creates a central nervous system of synaptic relays of information from the consumer market that is focused on continuous improvement as well as 'breakthroughs'. In this manner, suppliers become 'associates' to the focal business when they provide quality, cost and delivery to the levels required by the policy of the customer and represent extensions of the factory that yield a 'return on investment' for the supply chain. However, as higher levels of integration occur and companies begin to reinforce the formal working relationships with informal channels and the strategies of the businesses align, then companies engage in 'partnerships' of greater dependency. This dependency involves the complete alignment of the strategies between companies and also the reduction of individual risk by sharing issues of commercial sensitivity and by engaging in broad human and technological investment programmes that support the customer organization, but whose financial return is long term or not quantifiable. The policy deployment process, and its focus on the creativity of teams, is thus a medium through which the concurrent improvement efforts within the supply chain can remain fixed on the needs of the consumer.

Pillar 2: Cross-Functional Management

The second pillar of the 'lean enterprise' model consists of lateral processes of management that are often termed 'cross-functional management' (Dimancescu et al., 1997). This 'pillar' is inextricably linked to the concept of policy deployment and is the 'enabling mechanism' that harnesses the efforts of internal and external collectives of operational decision-makers. Under conditions of environmental turbulence decision-making becomes devolved, but the difficulties associated with the coordination of such 'remote' activities increases in the absence of common targets and means. Cross-functional management is therefore a vital structural response to the decentralization and coordination of resources in the factory. The concept of cross-functional management can be defined as

> a management process designed to encourage and support interdepartmental communication and co-operation throughout a company – as opposed to command and control through narrow departments or divisions. The purpose is to attain such company-wide targets as

quality, cost and delivery of products by optimising the sharing of work (JUSE, 1988).

Cross-functional management, or the management of customer service by optimizing the quality, cost and delivery of activities across the business, represents a coalition of interest groups that share the same targets. However, these structures are not permanent features of the organization, as in the case of the vertical functions from which the managers are drawn, but are teams of managers and departmental staff drawn together to enact changes in the systems and structures of the organization. The permanent nature of the key business processes of quality, cost and delivery ensures that this form of management team structure will continue to exist but that the individuals involved in the cross-functional team may change. The purpose of creating a 'committee-style' management group is important and ensures that individuals with decision-making power interact as a collective response to the deployed business policy. These individuals control resources and also have the responsibility of internalizing cross-functional decisions by changing the way in which the vertical functions operate.

The establishment of these key process teams based on two key criteria, the first related to the operational contribution of the functional departments, and the second being the secondment of technical expertise and experience of individuals within the business. In this respect, this forum is drawn from the key business departments that are expected to yield the greatest returns to the policy deployment process. In the case of cost management this may include representatives from the product design department (design cost), the purchasing department (cost of

FIGURE 6.2   The Cross-Functional Nature of Key Processes

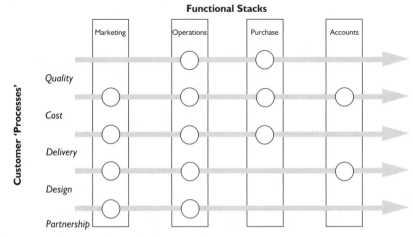

Note: The circles show the main areas of contribution to goal.

SOURCE: Rich (1998).

material supply) and the engineering department (the design of equipment to process the product) as the key 'players' in the team, but also additional members such as the production planning department (the cost of production process and batch size considerations).

The number and exact structure of these cross-functional management teams will represent the complexity of the business and how the activities of the organization can be decomposed into 'manageable' elements either through the use of a site-specific, product-specific, single-key process orientation or a mixed approach. Regardless of the exact definition of this scope, the activity of reducing the 'waste' at the interfaces within the organization as a means of improving 'outputted' customer service remains the rational for this lateral approach to business management. As previously discussed, the cross-functional management activities cause internal adjustments in the operating systems of the organization by highlighting and then eroding internal conflict, but equally the process can be externalized to incorporate the customer, the supplier or the entire supply chain. Customer representatives may be asked to participate in the improvement process directly as regular and formal team members. An example of this type of 'involvement process' might be where a member of the customer's scheduling staff may engage in the 'delivery' process team initiatives as a means of solving the problems of demand amplification at its source (Senge, 1990) or a representative of the logistics department in a strategically important supplier may join the process to ensure that the benefits of change can be implemented quickly with known quantifiable improvements in the short term. Cross-functional management is a means of decreasing the uncertainty of 'dependency' between the focal company and its immediate relationships in the supply chain.

Cross-functional teams, motivated and guided by customer service and performance targets alone, constitute a decentralized form of decision-making structure but lack a form of 'leadership' and 'co-ordinating' link back to the 'directional' senior managers of the business. This 'loop' is important and serves as a means of resolving conflict and also as a source of funds acquisition. To counteract this weakness, the cross-functional teams operate with leaders who are drawn from the senior management group. These senior managers may or may not have a direct functional responsibility for the cross-functional team they lead (for example, the engineering director responsible for the cost improvement process rather than the financial director) and this is not important. The participation of the senior manager serves as a conduit to business strategy, provides clarity of the business strategy, removes confusion and serves to maintain a balance between the objectives of the team and the holistic view of the business. The cross-functional management is therefore similar to the concept of 'linking pins' developed by Likert (1967). In this respect, the senior manager is one member of the executive team,

FIGURE 6.3   The Linking Pin Structure

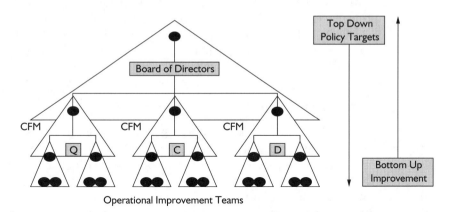

Operational Improvement Teams

but a leader of a cross-functional team, who in turn may lead the implementation projects of sub-teams and the day-to-day customer service improvement activities.

Cross-Functional Management: Summary

The use of cross-functional management techniques to optimize the customer-service exchange activities of quality, cost and delivery creates the return on investment for the factory. These activities can only be undertaken by the middle managers in the factory, since it is this level of personnel that control resources, has the power to implement decisions quickly, has a good appreciation of the capabilities of the people and processes under its direct control and is the most 'innovative' level of management in the factory. The view of management as key innovators in the factory is not common; instead, the popular image is that of team leaders and shopfloor employees, but the management level has the ability to undertake 'breakthroughs' in organizational systems (that lie beyond the authority of team leaders) as well as engaging in the continuous improvement of processes. The existence of formalized cross-functional management would therefore confirm the assertions of Merli (1991) and conclude the model proposed by Stevens (1989). Once again, this element of organizational practice is rarely visible in the factories of 'world-class' companies and has not gained widespread support in the West (Dimancescu *et al.*, 1997) in the same manner as the cross-functional activities which result from the policy deployment methodology.

> *The use of cross-functional management is key to the 'health' of the organizational improvement programme.*

The policy-guided teams are not reactive (as in the case of management teaming in the West) and they are not social groupings used to control discrete projects. The use of cross-functional management is therefore key to the 'health' of the organizational improvement programme and it is an element which is 'reincarnated' annually as the new targets are deployed and personnel change.

Pillar 3: Standardized Production and Operations

The third pillar that unites the strategy and structure of the business is the conversion process itself and the control of the daily management of customer service. The strict control of the conversion process is an essential ingredient in the strategic planning process, and ensures that the resultant policies are founded on a fact-based approach matched to the capabilities of the business operations, and that the strategies have validity for those personnel tasked with operating and controlling the level of 'output efficiency' throughout the factory. In this respect, the management of the day-to-day operations forms a stable base on which the long-range plans of the factory, and key weaknesses in factory performance can be quantified objectively. The management of the daily activities in the factory must therefore be standardized for two purposes: the first to gain efficiencies in the production process that yields transactional customer service (quality, cost and delivery measures); and the second to create a basis on which to monitor and improve the production system. These two activities are the responsibility (and a value-adding role) of the team leaders and supervisory staff. Their purpose is to provide the 'front line' management with control of the production process (if they are responsible for the efficiency of the factory not its effectiveness, which remains a middle management task).

The development of a common 'way of doing things' or approach to the management of the operations provides a frame of reference (and factory language) that is shared between all the elements of the production process and the administrative activities. The process of standardizing the procedures that govern the operation of the production system is a means of creating discipline and 'self-regulatory' control. In this respect, these procedures create discipline by establishing 'checklists' of activities that must be conducted in order to ensure that the process of manufacturing is efficient as possible. The standards are therefore documentary evidence of the 'internal' level of customer service expected by those employees who work in the factory.

These standard controls affect every area of the operations within the facility and provide the basis for the conduct of all activities related to the management of the conversion process and the technology itself (Ohno, 1988). The controls themselves can be divided into several identifiable elements which would typically include:

- The auditing/appraisal of the environmental conditions in the factory including the safety and 'housekeeping' of the factory (Environmental Issues).
- The auditing of employee 'skills' and abilities in terms of operating the production process to a high level of competence and the ability of the individual to engage in problem-solving and continuous improvement activities (Employee Issues).
- The auditing of the inventory system to ensure that all materials are presented in standard containers holding an exact amount of material (Buffering Issues).
- The auditing of the production process (Quality, Cost and Delivery Issues) in such a way that the process does not drift from predetermined tolerances during its operation, and the monitoring of 'losses' in the efficiency of the conversion process as a means of focusing the improvement activity of the teams (through the elimination of quality or time losses from existing procedures).
- The development of machine maintenance standards, that are conducted on a periodic cycle, to ensure that the production process is always available for the conversion of products (Availability and Performance Efficiency Issues).

The development of a production system which is supported by written and formalized standards creates a 'web' of discipline and control in the workplace. These 'control' measures create a 'one best way' principle so that any activity undertaken within the production facility, from taking an order, monitoring inventory levels or setting a die, has a common and standard method. These principles are not new and can be traced to the prowess of the industrial engineering departments of the classical enterprise. However, these standards are not developed by professionals or 'craft' employees but are the responsibility of the team and the team leader in each area of the factory. The approach to the standardization of activities is a means of creating 'quality control' in the factory, and the development of standards ensures that there is a common method that can be improved by team-based problem-solving or efforts to reduce 'waste' and time losses in the factory. These standards are therefore 'yardsticks', and many of the time standards used by the shopfloor personnel are the basic data, converted into meaningful information by the middle managers, for the policy deployment process.

In summary, the use of a well-documented and proceduralized approach to the factory creates 'stability' and 'uniformity' in the management of the input–conversion–output equation. This 'stability' is the means of controlling the production process and improving it through incremental and 'creeping' improvements by the shopfloor teams to address areas of 'abnormality' that have become identifiable. These procedures are thus the basis on which the 'high performance' factories create and sustain increasingly higher levels of efficiency using the 'total quality' approach to the elimination of cost and the prevention of failures (Rich, 1998).

Pillar 4 : Supplier Integration

The final element of the four-pillar system is the development of a mechanism which incorporates the many suppliers to the factory in a manner that allows individual suppliers and collectives of suppliers to become integrated into the strategy process of the focal company (through the policy deployment process). The fourth pillar is therefore an attempt to reduce the uncertainty associated with 'supply-side' dependency and to develop a supply base with the same skills, characteristics, terminology and standard procedures of that operated by the focal purchasing organization. The concept of supply integration is integral to the models of supply chain management discussed previously (Stevens, 1989; Merli, 1991) but neither model addresses the mechanism through which dependency relationships can be aligned and maintained. Another drawback of these abstract models is the concept of 'partnering' relationships between high-performance companies and their direct supplier populations. This concept suggests that suppliers, faced with a dependency relationship with their customer, can be motivated to engage in joint activities and a transparency in the operations of both factories in the absence of vertical integration.

A further problem with the supply chain models is the implicit assumption and rationale that the focal purchasing organization has or operates a much smaller direct supplier population than the number of suppliers that provided materials and services to the traditional organizations. In this respect, the companies have reverted the traditional adversarial purchasing policies and engaged in the development of dependency between the organizations to the point of 'partnering' (Merli, 1991). The evidence discovered by the SCDP research programme and previous studies (Lamming, 1993) would support this view, but would also suggest that, whilst the number of suppliers was comparatively reduced, the focal companies had engaged in a tiering of the suppliers (restructuring of the logistics routes) as well as expanding the scope of activities undertaken by the remaining direct suppliers (these suppliers provided semi-built systems as opposed to individual elements of the system which would traditionally have been assembled by the customer organization). For the Japanese companies in the research sample, this did include patterns of interlocking ownership, but this was not typical and was rarely the case for Western companies.

Instead, the high-performance companies had undergone several iterations of supply chain restructuring over many years, to improve the 'flow' of materials to the conversion process and to develop 'areas' of technical core competence with the remaining strategic suppliers to the business (based on the provision of 'system' solutions rather than material component supply). In short, the supply chain structure operated by the high performance factories was streamlined to create a 'network' of supplier communities which were led by a focal 'systems' organization and it was this company which held the direct relationship with the customer organization. This pattern of material flow is identical to the structural form of Likert's linking pin concept, but this time, the focal purchasing organization is the head of the network and each direct supplier is a member of the team and also the head of a secondary level of suppliers.

The Supplier Association

The restructuring of the supply base also included the development of supplier integration programmes, through policies to coordinate and develop suppliers (Hines, 1994; Andersen Consulting, 1992 and 1994), by the transfer of 'hard' and 'soft' technology, demand information and strategies to the direct level in the 'linking pin' supply structure. In this way the restructuring of the supply chain created opportunities for the limited numbers of purchasing agents to engage in 'one-to-one' supplier initiatives (focused by the need for constant improvement to the quality performance of all suppliers, a mainstay of every policy deployment iteration due to the relationship of quality improvement to cost reduction). However, the new supply structure and individual supplier development programmes were only one part of a broader strategy operated by the purchasing agents within the high-performance factories. The disadvantage of individual programmes is the consumption of time and the constant need to monitor suppliers, and so the development of relationships within the supply base was facilitated by a secondary mechanism, the supplier association.

The concept of the supplier association can be defined as

> a mutually benefiting group of a company's most important subcontractors brought together on a regular basis for the purpose of co-ordination and co-operation as well as to assist all the members benefit from the type of development associated with large Japanese assemblers; such as kaizen, just in time, kanban, U-cell production and the achievement of zero defects (Hines, 1994).

This structure is similar to the externalization of the cross-functional management concept by creating a forum for exchange and relationship building between the focal organization and a collective of suppliers. This mechanism offered many significant advantages in practical terms, and creating a network of regular and formalized opportunities for the customer to meet with a cross-section of suppliers and allowing the development of a three-dimensional 'linking pin' structure. Therefore, the 'cycle' or regularity of meetings with suppliers could be used to incorporate the

policy deployment process and the senior managers of supplier organizations could be addressed by the senior management of the focal organization every six months to exchange market information, business
strategies and the key objectives for the improvement of the entire supply
chain (to gain alignment and concurrency in the policies adopted by the
suppliers *en masse*). However, in parallel with this activity, the operational staff at the suppliers could also use the forum to exchange operational and tactical information within a shorter cycle of meetings
(typically monthly). The combination of the restructured supply base
(externalized cross-functional management) and the development of
long-range planning and tactical planning with suppliers (the externalization of the policy deployment process) were key features of the 'lean
supply' network created to support the focal customer.

The 'lean supply' system of regularized interaction between suppliers
permitted the exchange and relationship-building processes to be developed by the coordination of activities in the supply base and also
through the exchange of improvements or supplier development activities. Hines (1994) defines supplier coordination as

> the activities made by a customer to mould their suppliers into a
> common way of working, so that competitive advantage can be
> gained, particularly by removing inter-company waste. This type of
> co-ordination would involve areas such as: working to common

FIGURE 6.4 The Supplier Association Network Model

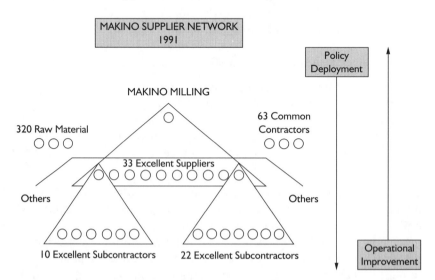

Note: KK is the Japanese abbreviation of 'supplier circle'.

SOURCE: Hines (1994).

quality standards, using the same paperwork system, shared transport and employing inter-company communication methods such as EDI … (whereas). … Supplier Development refers to the activities made by a customer to help improve the strategies, tools and techniques employed by suppliers to improve their competitive advantage, particularly by removing intra-company waste. This type of development would include the dissemination of customer strategies, so that suppliers could plan their processes more effectively, as well as the customer offering specific assistance to the suppliers in areas such as factory layout, set-up time reduction and the operation of internal kanban systems.

The supplier association, adopting a process of coordination amongst companies, serves to externalize the 'standard production' system concept and the externalization of controls which regulate the conduct and improvement of activities within the supplier factories. The focal organization, typically with much greater levels of human and financial resources, is a 'provider' to the association in terms of generating value for suppliers by exchanging resources and strategies, but the customer also receives a regular feedback and performance update regarding the rate of change and improvement in the supply base (a second key source of data for the monitoring of the current policies of the customer organization). The forum is therefore a two-way exchange and risk-minimization process by means of which the many supply chain organizations effect transactions and share the common approach to turbulence in the consumer market.

Unlike the internal cross-functional management teams, the supplier association is a permanent structure appropriate to the close long-term integration and working agreements between the supplier and the customer. The low levels of employee turnover or substitution of supplier representatives is therefore a basis on which individual and corporate relationships can be founded. The structure of the company and the organizational positions held by the representatives also serves to compress time in the same manner as the internal cross-functional system in which the authority held by the individual improves the decision-making cycle. The supplier association is a forum at which the broad 'customer service' equation of the quality, cost, delivery and design of new products can be focused.

The supplier association is a permanent structure appropriate to the close long-term integration and working agreements between the supplier and the customer.

In summary, the final pillar of the model is a process of integration and socialization by which the focal organization seeks to harness the total resources of the supply chain, in a climate of mutual benefit rather than adversarialism, to localize the pressures of the consumer market (through the externalization of the policy deployment targets) and to create competitive advantage by sharing resources and practices between suppliers in a lateral fashion. The combination of these two activities is the alignment and focused improvement of the supply chain and the ability to engage in concurrent activities to compress the amount of time associated with 'learning curves', as well as providing a comparatively quick reaction to changes in the consumer market.

Conclusions

This chapter has developed a 'micro' model of supply chain management, focused on the causal factors that underpin high performance organizations and the competitive advantage that can be gained by adopting a proactive approach to a supply chain strategy and structure. The four-pillar model has been drawn from quantitative and qualitative research methods employed with a number of companies, including SCDP sponsors, who have achieved a dominant status in their industrial sector. The chapter presented here represents the generic lessons from almost five years of study and a research agenda that is still ongoing. However, the model poses many interesting questions, not least questioning the application of recent management 'fads' and the limited impact of such activities as 'business process re-engineering' or 'supply base rationalization' when they are employed on a piecemeal basis and without reference to the organization and its particular context.

The research has also provided evidence to suggest that the 'threatened longevity' of organizational functions and the dissolution of internal functional departments (Kanter, 1989; Peters and Waterman, 1982) are not necessarily the case. Instead, those companies studied had supplemented these structures with cross-functional management, but maintained the business functions as a means of maintaining the formal structure of the business and as a key element in maintaining efficiency. However, the scalar chains, particularly in administrative departments, were smaller and those organizations studied often adopted policies of co-location of departmental personnel and the rotation of employees between functional roles. In this respect, the concept of professionalism and the traditionally-defined career routes may be challenged. These questions concern the 'value' role of the individual in the enterprise, a role which is cross-functional in nature rather than departmental, due to the inability of any department to exert exclusive control over the organizational processes for which they are accountable.

In parallel, the traditional scenario of the logical incrementalism of generating strategies may also be questioned in terms of the validity such methods have in the current climate of continuous change. These very long-range plans cannot account for every eventuality and therefore a shorter planning horizon, where greater levels of certainty exist, may well be a more effective means of aligning the resources of the business. However, the constant changing of priorities will generate confusion and misalignment of activities in the absence of 'process'-based management methods that are united by the concepts of 'total quality' and customer service improvement. Therefore, common measures, that unite every department and create the need to work cross-functionally will need to be generated rather than traditional budgetary control and functional autonomy.

A final question raised by the model is the nature of buyer–supplier relationships and the development of models for the integration of the resources that lie outside the direct control of the purchasing organization. In recent times, the concept of 'partnering' has gained fashionable support, but once again as a piecemeal solution to problems in the supply chain. To construct a tiered supply chain is a lengthy process involving new skills and competences on the part of the purchasing agent (Cox, 1995) and also an equally long period of relationship development between the organizations. The opportunity to gain, in the short term, by overturning traditional purchasing regimes are limited and require strategic endorsement as well as the cooperation of the supply base if the benefits of such integration are to be realized fully.

The four-pillar model has been presented as a means through which high performance organizations have evolved new working practices and structures to generate competitive advantage in the context of rapid changes in the consumer market. The model is an attempt to reduce the current level of abstraction concerning the concept of the supply chain by providing a synopsis of the research evidence collected by the SCDP research programme and as a means of generating debate to fill the vacuum between prescription and the contingent nature of supply chain management in practice. As such, it is hoped that the model reduces some of the gap between the academic world and what is happening in progressive and high-performance businesses.

CHAPTER 7

Management Key Processes[1]

Introduction

Contemporary literature in the 'supply chain management' field of study is dominated with the, explicit or implicit, concern to manage organizational change. In particular, it is concerned with the management of the speed of change by the organization as a means of maintaining the profitable 'fit' between the business and its provision of 'value' (Dimancescu *et al.*, 1997). The concept of 'value' and the optimization of the 'value stream' (Womack & Jones, 1996) is a direct attempt to create the highest levels of customer service as a competitive weapon, but also as a defensive 'barrier to entry' (Merli, 1990) in an ever-changing market. These external pressures, of change and increasingly demanding expectations for customer service, have a direct impact on the strategic 'direction' and support structure of the business within this type of environment.

The ability to match the environment, business strategy and business structure is at the heart of all issues and concepts of organizational design. A mismatch in any of these aspects will create a sub-optimized perform-ance by the company or an inflexibility to accommodate change. The strategy of the business must therefore provide a means of creating focus within the many different administrative and operational departments and, through the structure, create a conduit through which the roles and responsibilities of individuals within the organization are aligned to support customer

> *The ability to match the environment, business strategy and business structure is at the heart of all issues and concepts of organizational design.*

---

[1] Prepared by Nick Rich and Peter Hines.

service throughout the business. Dimancescu *et al.* (1997) offer the warning that traditional organisations and traditional approaches to organizational design create distance between the structure of the business and its ability to generate customer service, and that there is often dissonance between the departments themselves. According to Dimancescu *et al.* 'organisations are not built to serve customers; they are built to preserve internal order. To customers, the internal structure may not only mean very little, it may serve as a barrier. Organisation charts are vertical, and serving the customer is horizontal' (Dimancescu *et al.*, 1997).

The pursuit of customer service within the context of the functionally specialized organization and its reliance on central planning and control may thus serve to diminish the value and utility sought by both customers and consumers of the product or service provided by the or-ganisation. The objective of this chapter is to provide the reader with an overview of the current problems facing the organizational strategist when considering the 'fit' between the organization, its market and the management of change. The chapter will deal with key 'design' issues, such as the weaknesses of the traditional approaches to organizational design, the concept of customer service and the rate of change in 'order qualifiers' and 'order winners' (Hill, 1995). It will also provide an analysis of lateral (cross-functional) 'process' management as a means of cementing the power of the vertical organizational structure with the need to optimize the horizontal flux of organizational relationships and activities which enable and inhibit the flow of 'value' from the organization to its customers.

Customer Value and Organizational Management

The discussion conducted in previous chapters of this text has highlighted the deficiencies of the traditional 'stove pipe' or functional business structure, and provided many arguments that suggest these structures cannot accommodate the turbulence in modern market environments (Kanter, 1989; Peters and Waterman, 1982; Womack and Jones, 1996). However, for most companies this vertical and functional orientation is the structure through which the business is currently controlled and represents the means through which it has evolved over many years. These structures are therefore ingrained in the explicit control procedures of the organization and also implicitly accepted within the culture and customary practice of the business.

The modern trends and arguments proposed by leading business authors, focused almost exclusively on the notion of 'customer service', and are premised upon the decline of the functional business structure and the need to modify such structures in order to 'enable' customer service to 'flow' throughout the many departments within the business. The central arguments of this 'post mass-production' school of thought include:

- The need to reduce the administration hierarchy that supports the business (Kanter, 1989; Keuning & Opheij, 1994).
- The need to decentralize decision-making within turbulent environments (Lawrence and Lorsch, 1967).
- The removal of 'waste' from the organization through the adoption of 'lean thinking' (Womack and Jones, 1996).
- The use of cross-functional management as a means of improving the operations of the business by greater levels of organizational integration (Dimancescu *et al.*, 1997).
- The development of the supply and value chain concepts (Porter, 1980).
- The increasing sophistication and demands of customers and consumers (Stalk and Hout, 1990).
- The globalization of competition (Womack, Jones and Roos, 1990).
- The need to compete on the basis of 'time' compression in addition to the other elements of the customer 'utility' equation (Stalk and Hout, 1990).
- The need to align the strategies adopted by the various functional departments within the business in such a manner as to create a single 'customer service' focus (Dimancescu *et al.*, 1997).
- The availability of sophisticated processing equipment including information processing technology (Kurt Salmon, 1993).
- The need to embrace a 'total' quality approach to the business (Harrison, 1992).
- The need to 're-define' and remove bureaucracy from the administrative procedures within the factory (Hammer and Champy, 1993).
- The development of employee integration and involvement strategies through the use of 'empowerment' (Harrison, 1992).

These trends, towards a flatter and more responsive organizational structure, all impact on the roles and responsibilities of individuals and departments that make up the skeletal structure of the organization and raise the question how best to align these traditional building blocks to enhance the performance of the enterprise within its chosen markets. The problems associated with this form of 'structural' analysis are many and include several important elements:

1. The first problem is the need to modify the structures of the business to support the strategy rather than to 'fit' the business strategy to the structure of the organization as a means of improving the likelihood that the strategy will be successful (the 'chicken and egg' dilemma).

2. The second problem originates from the need to combine the efficiency and effectiveness of the business in an optimal manner. Traditionally, organizational functions improve control and efficiency but the myopic attention of business departments and the dominance of functional strategies can limit the effectiveness of the enterprise in

terms of customer service-generation. However, flatter structures with decentralized decision-making pose problems to do with the efficient control of the business and the coordination of activities.

These two key aspects of the 'design' puzzle represent major dilemmas for the strategist in that the market turbulence requires the structure of the business to be modified, necessitating a dynamic set of measures of customer service.

The Rise of Customer Service

The Merli model (1990), which featured as a key element of the previous chapter is worth reconsidering when analyzing the rise of the 'customer service' concept over time. Merli (1990) identified four stages of organizational configurations that can be distinguished since the early period of industrialization. These can be characterized as:

1. the Volume Producer Stage;
2. the Aggressive Marketeer Stage;
3. the High Involvement Company Stage;
4. The 'Market In' Organization.

Customer Service and the Volume Producer

The 'volume producer' represents the earliest form of mass production organization that developed through a passion for 'technology', 'utilization' and 'efficiency'. These organizations began to dominate national markets in the early 1920s and serviced a comparatively unsophisticated domestic consumer. The basis building block of this organization was the functional department. These departments formed the skeletal structure and served as a managerial control mechanism. The 'marketing' of products was also relatively underdeveloped due to the existence of mass consumption and an eager and growing market. Within this organization, the power balance favoured the engineering and technical departments.

The primary goal of the organization was to maximize profits by minimizing the costs of the operation, and in doing so, to pass these economies of scale to the customer in terms of low prices. Accordingly, the marketing effort was invested in convincing potential customers that these products were within their personal budget. The marketing department, still in its embryonic stage of development, was therefore subservient to the requirements of the manufacturing department and its job included the generation of high levels of demand and orders for the manufacturing order bank.

Customer Service and the Aggressive Marketeer

The second evolution of organizational strategy and structure occurred during a period of intense domestic competition when markets began to fragment and the levels of market uncertainty began to accelerate. Within this context, the ability to attract and retain customers became increasingly more difficult and the company began to rely on the marketing department. As a direct consequence of market turbulence the information and intelligence about consumers and their buying behaviour began to fall within the functional responsibility of the marketing department. The 'power' dominance of the engineering departments began to wane, and it was the marketing department which led the pursuit of profitability. The reversal in market conditions away from the 'producer' to the 'customer' stimulated competition and the need to attract sales volumes aggressively.

> *The marketing department led the pursuit of profitability.*

Customer Service and the High Involvement Company

The next evolution of the organization originated in Japan and adopted the concept of 'customer service' as the main motivation for competitive manufacturing. The developments in Japan represented a parallel to the 'Aggressive Marketeer' stage in the West but shared the same market circumstances. In Japan, market competition had begun to threaten the profit streams of organizations but, in these unique circumstances, the 'management profession' and its many professional representative bodies had accepted the concepts of 'Total Quality Management'. The company-wide philosophy of TQM served to focus factory efforts on the continuous improvement of factory performance through the creative potential of all employees, including managers and operators.

The 'high involvement' organization was thus a means of creating new factory relationships and the development of organizational coalitions to improve products, processes and technologies so that customers could be attracted and retained through the provision of high levels of customer service. For the Japanese, the management of the quality, cost and delivery of products and services held the key to the market share, profitability and the longevity of the organization.

Customer Service and the 'Co-Maker'

The final evolution of the organization has been termed 'Co-makership' and represents a hybrid of the 'marketing' prowess of the Western organizations with the 'adaptive' power of the Japanese system. The underlying rationale for this process of combination is the unification and focusing of the organization as a means of providing a flexible response to market demands. In addition to internal integration, these forms of enterprise seek to develop external relationships by the direct integration of the customers and suppliers through the development of 'partnerships' of 'dependency' relations as a means of protectionism and mutual benefit. The marketing element of this type of organization is therefore focused on a 'two-way' process of 'relationship marketing' as a means of seeking the integration of the supplier and customer whilst the manufacturing department continues to refine and improve the actual 'customer service' transactions that take place within the supply chain.

The Merli model provides a succinct analysis of the trends that have combined to create the new interest in the modern responsive organization. This form of organization Merli (1990) terms 'co-makership' but may also be described as 'lean' or 'agile', which are all terms that describe elements of each of the models and can be applied almost interchangeably.

The Concept of Customer Service: The Functional Perspective

The term 'customer service' originates from the 'marketing' field of study and profession. This single business function, heralded as the 'closest' internal department to the 'customer' (Peters and Waterman, 1982) has dominated the strategy formulation of the business for the bulk of industrial history since the 'aggressive marketeer' stage of the 1950s.

The marketing function, like many other business functions, has a distinct professional language which is dominated by the concept of 'customer service'. Indeed, one of the leading authors in the marketing field (and the author of the best-selling marketing textbook) reinforces the 'rights' of the marketing department to dominate exclusively the management of customer service and to make the other business departments subservient to the needs of the marketing department (Kotler, 1988). Kotler suggests that these basic elements of departmental business include the following concepts:

- *The production concept.* Kotler suggests that consumers will favour those products that are widely available and offered at a low cost. The implication for the organization is that managers of manufacturing companies should focus on achieving high production efficiency and offer a wide distribution coverage for their products, so that manufacturing becomes an instrument through which the company creates efficiency which can be translated into market share through the medium of the marketing department.
- *The product concept.* Kotler contends that this concept involves the hypothesis that consumers will be attracted to products that offer the

highest quality or performance. As such, managers in companies where the product features are a key means of creating 'utility' should concentrate on the development and improvement of attractive products. In this respect, Kotler emphasizes the role of the design department as a secondary process that interprets the market intelligence gleaned and translates it into products of high utility.

- *The selling concept.* For this concept, Kotler is keen to distinguish 'selling' from 'marketing' of which the former is merely a transaction and the latter a strategic and centralized function. He contends that consumers will tend to select products from a variety of organizations if they are not convinced, through aggressive 'selling' policies, to consume more of the output of the organization. In this manner, companies must engage in aggressive selling and promotional efforts.
- *The marketing concept.* As Kotler defines it, this is the hypothesis that the key to achieving the goals of the organization is the correct definition and satisfaction of the 'needs and wants' of target markets for the products of the company. Only by providing the correct level of satisfaction for these consumer 'desires' in a more effective manner than its market competitors will the company gain market share.

The preceding definitions, as proposed by Kotler, reinforce the legitimacy of the 'departmentalized' organization, using this notion to elevate the 'marketing' department above that of all other departments within the organization rather than sharing 'power' with them. The unfortunate outcome of this form of argument is the creation of a dissonance between every other department and the ambitions of the marketing department, so that the marketing process is sub-optimized as perceived customer requirements cannot be manufactured at a realistic cost or entail unfeasible technical requirements.

The result is that the effectiveness of the marketing department is reduced. The insularity of this functional view excludes the manufacturing management from full integration in the strategy formulation process, which is 'unhealthy' in the same way that dominance of the strategy process by manufacturing (during the mass production era) was also 'unhealthy' and played a part in the decline of the organization. However, for Kotler (1988), manufacturing should be concerned with economies of scale rather than scope and cost efficiency – a view not shared by the leading authors concerned with the production and operations management field of study.

The Manufacturing Environment: The Secular Mantras of Customer Service

Only since the 1960s, when the operations and production management field of study began to overlap and integrate with the philosophy of 'Total Quality Management' (TQM), has the concept and language of 'customer service' been transferred from the functional 'marketing dialect' to gain paramount importance for the manufacturing department. Traditionally, manufacturing strategies have involved indirect analyses of 'customer service' – most typically the benefits of 'capacity' (through which volumes can be leveraged for unit costs and availability of products) and 'technology' (through which new products can be introduced). Indeed, Hill (1995) proposes that the language and understanding of 'customer service' is often poorly understood by manufacturing managers as a result of a lack of integration with the marketing department and also as a result of the 'education' process for engineers (that serves to promote the 'technical' profession but does not often include 'commercial' or 'marketing' subjects within the educational syllabus).

The 1990s have witnessed an explosion in the academic and practitioner interest in the operations management field of study and a rejuvenation of interest in the manufacturing of products. This rejuvenation follows a reign of 'total quality' and 'marketing' dominance throughout the 1980s and has been fuelled by the acclaimed performance of the Japanese production systems. To date, the operations management literature is littered with secular mantras that 'will' forward the importance of manufacturing in order to achieve competitive advantage for the organization (Womack and Jones, 1996; Hayes and Wheelwright, 1984; Skinner, 1985). This reformation movement has often included 'calls' for the elevation of the manufacturing function within the business and the use of manufacturing as 'a competitive 'weapon'. The movement itself has many different individual 'schools' of thought but has been given the generic label of 'new wave manufacturing' (Storey, 1994). The different internal divisions within the 'new wave manufacturing' movement place greater emphases on different elements of the manufacturing equation, some advocating the development of human resources, whilst others expound the importance of the overall system of control in the factory.

The 'new wave manufacturing' advocates have also developed and disseminated new concepts and techniques to support the rejuvenation of the manufacturing department. These techniques tend to reflect the management of the manufacturing function within a greater holistic understanding of the organization, with the implicit understanding that the manufacturing department must act as an integrated part of the wider organization, regardless of the traditional functional boundaries that have served to constrain it.

The plethora of new concepts, languages and techniques that are promoted with the aim of elevating manufacturing has served to create a 'fashion-like' status for manufacturing companies in which managers are keen to implement the latest techniques despite the absence of academic testing and with only minor analyses of the disadvantages of such an approach (Cox, 1995; Slack, 1991). The common denominator that links these techniques, and the 'haste' to implement them, is the desire to improve customer service. Also, in parallel, is manufacturing's desire to accommodate changes in customer service from the traditional system of economies of scale to that of economies of scope. Indeed, Slack proposes that the 'new wave' movement has provided a

> *Managers are keen to implement the latest techniques despite the absence of academic testing.*

> regular deluge of ideas, techniques, theories and concepts ... (that) ... have showered down on the manufacturing function. Many of them come pre-packaged. Total Quality Management (TQM), Just In Time (JIT), Optimum Production Technology (OPT), Computer Integrated Manufacturing (CIM), Total Productive Maintenance (TPM), the list seems to grow monthly. (Slack, 1991)

In this mêlée the pressure to adopt new techniques quickly has often led to blind emulation and industrial absurdity, with companies accepting the legitimacy of these techniques as a means of improving customer service performance, without any form of true analysis of 'why?' or 'how?' or what is involved in changing the manner in which the traditional system must evolve to exploit fully these new ideas. In fact, the adoption of these new techniques can only happen at the most senior level if it is to ensure that all other internal customers and internal suppliers dealing with the manufacturing department are aligned with the objectives and implementation plan. To compound these problems, the number of 'new wave' techniques is expanding and the selective adoption of individual practices, without a solid support structure, or the development of a portfolio of other techniques to support a key initiative, creates a sub-optimization of the benefits sought (customer service), often bringing disillusionment. The net result is that the production process becomes a 'laboratory', instead of the process that generates value through efficient and effective conversion of materials into customer service.

The 'new wave' school has simply promoted the manufacturing cause and served to develop 'awareness' of new methods of managing the manufacturing function for improved customer service rather than providing a holistic model of how to structure and integrate the manufacturing function within the organization. The seductive rationality of the many models and techniques causes many problems both through the adoption of new techniques by the manufacturing department in isolation from the rest of the factory administration and also as a result of decisions taken by other departments that affect the performance of the manufacturing department. This form of conflict results from a lack of integration and alignment, particularly the alignment of performance measures, so that the company-wide impact of decisions is ignored or, at best, not quantified. As such, the concept of customer service, the motivation for the implementation of techniques to accommodate change or improve business performance, is lost and the secular mantras within manufacturing and academia have little effect. A practice that creates a secondary 'myopia' – the myopia of manufacturing managers focused on the production process itself and not the outputs of the process.

Understanding Customer Service: The Manufacturing Perspective

For the management of the manufacturing department, the notion of customer service is neatly summarized as the 'six rights' or simply, 'the right product, at the right place, at the right time, in the right quantity, at the right quality and at the right cost' (Dobler *et al.*, 1990). These six objectives represent the ability both to 'qualify for orders' with customers and also to 'win orders' through superior performance by the manufacturing organization relative to its competitors. One author to have bridged this gap between the 'marketing' and 'manufacturing' perspectives is Hill (1995) who proposes the concepts of 'order qualification' and 'order winning' outputs from the manufacturing system. He argues that these levels of performance determine the ability of the company to engage in the 'marketing' and 'selling' of factory outputs and also as a means of focusing the activities of the manufacturing managers on these key areas of customer service.

Hill (1995) defines 'order qualifiers' as the key elements of customer service provided by the organization which allow the marketing and sales function to enter into negotiations with any particular customer. He suggests that 'order qualifiers' are 'those criteria that a company must meet for a customer even to consider it a possible supplier. ... Furthermore they will need to retain the qualification in order to stay on the short list or be considered as a competitor in a given market. However, simply providing or attaining these criteria does not win orders' (Hill, 1995).

In this respect, order qualifiers reflect the 'baseline' of customer service which must be generated through the production system in order to form a 'marketing relationship' and enable sales transactions to take place. For many aspects of customer service, these qualifiers will represent implicit parts of the relationship between the buyer and seller. Such order-qualifying criteria as product quality, availability, price, performance and availability are a means of evaluating between the performances of competitor manufacturers. Hill (1995) extends his analysis by identifying 'order winners' or those features that cement the marketing relationship by providing manufacturing outputs which go beyond the baseline level of performance and differentiate the company from its rivals. This differentiation, or the use of the manufacturing system as a competitive weapon, creates high levels of satisfaction for the customer and provide the platform upon which marketing and sales efforts create a return for the business. The implications of the model proposed by Hill (1995) are that manufacturing and marketing departments must be closely aligned in order to exploit fully the direction and performance of the manufacturing processes, so that the company always has the capability to exceed the changing order-qualifying requirements and to exploit the comparative shortcomings of other manufacturers. Indeed, Slack (1991) provides a commonsense approach to the subject of competitive manufacturing as a means of generating customer service and the alignment of the direction with the performance of the manufacturing company by suggesting that a

> ... sensible strategic direction is more than just important, it is a prerequisite for success. But it is not enough on its own. At the most basic level there is no better guarantee of long term business success, nor is there a better defence against competitors, than simply making products better than anyone else.

The 'Baseline' Elements of Customer Service: Quality, Cost and Delivery (QCD)

The analysis of 'order qualifiers' and 'order winners' by Hill (1995) offers some very interesting points for marketing executives seeking to compete on 'customer service' as well as for manufacturing managers seeking to use the production system for competitive advantage. Obviously, order qualifiers and winners are subject to change (and therefore the effects of time and increasingly sophisticated customers) but they are also contingent on the unique product and market characteristics of the company so that the 'qualifiers' will differ between products and markets. At the detailed measurement level this may well hold true, but at the generic level there is a form of 'permanency' amongst the generic elements of customer service from both the manufacturing and marketing perspectives. These elements are:

- The quality of the output.
- The cost of the output.
- The delivery of the output.

These key features will vary over time in the measurements applied to them as controls within the customer service equation, but their permanent nature allows the rate of change in customer service to be plotted graphically and also extrapolated to form a competitive 'change' curve (Rich, 1995). These curves represent 'industry curves' (Figure 7.1) and allow an analysis of the performance of the company to be focused and tracked over time and constitute a form of 'customer service' benchmarking.

The curve plotted for the quality, cost and delivery of products represents the 'hurdle' that must be negotiated in order to 'qualify' for continued business with an existing customer or a target one. To provide a level of performance that is better than the customer expectation is therefore a source of differentiation and 'order winning' ability. These customer service curves can be used to direct effort into either the improvement of a single generic process or as a planning technique.

To explain this form of analysis, Figure 7.1 below demonstrates the 'curve' of performance that is historical, current and extrapolated for a market segment (using the existing and potential customers in that market). Taking just the quality measure, calibrated in the number of parts per million defects, in the 'current' year of 1996 the manufacturing company must meet or improve upon a target of 10 parts per million (PPM). If, in 1996, the company manages to achieve only 50 PPM, then the company is failing to meet the target and will be re-sourced to another supplier following an analysis of alternative vendors and their performance (the ability of the customer to compare between alternative product sources). However, if the current level was 5 PPM, then the company has performed at a better level than was targeted and gives the customer no reason to re-allocate their buying patterns or to perceive the company as offering anything less than 'good' customer service for the quality of products that are supplied (Rich, 1995).

FIGURE 7.1 Permanent Order Qualifiers and Time (Quality, Cost and Delivery)

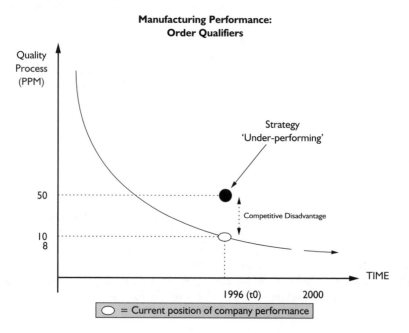

**Manufacturing Performance:
Order Qualifiers**

By plotting the traditional measures of customer service applied (say 250 PPM for 1994 and 80 PPM for 1995) a historical change curve can be identified, and with extrapolation this can be used to inform the rate of change over the coming periods. In the same manner, the delivery performance can be measured and also the relative costs of transacting business with the customer (rather than simply the purchase price of the products which is determined by either the market price or through negotiations during selling).

The use of a 'permanent' focus on the 'order qualifiers' for a market segment provides the means of interpreting 'customer service' in operational terms for both the manufacturing and marketing departments. However, as the previous discussions have indicated, the use of such a means of 'qualification' has created an interface between the marketing and manufacturing departments within the traditional functional business structure, but the alignment of the actions of all other departments is critical to the successful exploitation of customer service for competitive advantage.[2]

Customer Service: Influenced by All and the Accountability of One

The alignment of the goals and operating practices of business departments is a recognition of *three* important issues:

1. The enterprise is a 'system' whereby changes in one element of the administrative structure need to be supported with changes, adjustments and accommodations by all other departments in order to exploit the benefits for the company as a whole.

2. The key elements of customer service are the responsibility of all departments in the factory and cannot be assigned to a single department.

3. The basic building block of the enterprise and its structure is team work rather than just departments. The departments serve to maintain control in complex environments, but the ability to align and coordinate the business is a lateral process.

To provide a simplistic illustration of these points, it is possible to discern three key 'customer service' processes that are 'bought' from the organization and every department within it – namely, the quality, cost and

---

[2] Recent research evidence collected by De Meyer *et al.* (1994) suggests that European companies are developing strategies to compete using their known strengths in current levels of customer service, such as delivery, rather than identifying weaknesses and correcting these as a means of improving the total portfolio of customer service provided to the market.

delivery processes. These processes are horizontal, and the interaction of many different departments is required in order to maximize the value outputted by aligning the actions of each department around the improvement of 'product flow'. Customers buy processes that cross the organization horizontally, whereas the business itself is structured vertically by department. Thus the quality assurance department may be held responsible and accountable for the 'quality' performance of the company under the traditional system, but, in reality, the procurement of 'quality' materials from vendors will impact on the customer service of the factory as much as the care taken to protect the product during transit to the customer and the manufacturing process. In this respect there is a conflict between those with accountability in the traditional organization and the ability to influence the customer service which travels horizontally through each and every department.

> *Customers buy processes that cross the organization horizontally, whereas the business itself is structured vertically by department.*

The only means of exerting influence over the customer service offered by an enterprise is through the use of lateral or cross-functional management teams to align measures and focus on 'key business processes' (Dimancescu *et al.*, 1997). These lateral management practices represent the alignment of activities between internal business departments in such a manner that the output of the *series* of departments is optimized instead of each department individually (the traditional means of generating 'efficiency' under the conditions of mass production). These key business processes therefore include:

1. The quality, cost and delivery of existing products or the 'Order Fulfilment' process.[3]

2. The quality, cost and delivery of new products or the 'Time To Market' or 'Design Fulfilment' process.

3. The quality, cost and delivery of servicing a customer account or the 'Customer Partnership' process.

4. The quality, cost and delivery of managing the supply base or the 'Supplier Partnership' process.

5. Other processes relevant to the industrial sector and product include: 'Environmentalism', 'Reliability', 'Employee Integration' and 'Corporate Citizenship'.

The most relevant and important of these processes are those related to the existing products and the maintenance of high service levels with

---

[3] It should be little surprise that the Nissan (NMUK) site in Sunderland selected five generic supplier-evaluation criteria for its European suppliers that included Quality, Cost, Delivery, Design and Partnership measures of performance (Rich, 1995).

existing customers. The latter processes represent competitive capabilities which impact on the future trading position of the organization in its markets. The concepts of quality, cost and delivery represent key areas of management for each department and are the main ways of analyzing the effectiveness of the department and the business in its totality. The improvement of each of these three common traded elements, across the business, depends on the elimination of costs and 'waste' (Womack and Jones, 1996). In this respect, customer service holds a functional and corporate 'meaning' – that of the continuous improvement of quality, cost and delivery performance. At the functional level, these improvement targets may take one of *two* forms:

1. The departmental initiatives to improve performance and the flow of products.
2. The company-wide improvement of performance by cross-functional adjustments in roles, responsibilities, systems and practices.

In this manner, departments that are indirectly related to customer service can be integrated into the drive for effectiveness which would include a focus on the quality, cost and delivery of maintenance engineering support, or purchasing or cost accounting. The lateral processes, which impact on the utility transacted through selling and marketing, are therefore united to align the entire system, termed 'the enterprise', that includes the physical conversion processes and all the administrative functions. The process involves the sharing and internalization of 'order qualifiers', 'order winners' and the rate of change in these measures of customer service. The techniques promoted by the 'new wave' school of manufacturing management are therefore reduced as each technique can be related to the benefits to be achieved by implementation using a cross-functional or 'total approach'.

Process and Management: The Structural Debate

For many leading business authors, this 'process thinking' has been the basis upon which arguments have formulated to advocate the 'de-layering' of administrative functions and the 'right sizing' of the organization through the elimination of the business hierarchies. However, this approach is 'foolhardy' and denies the need to forge greater levels of alignment and integration between current functional departments before any form of streamlining can occur. To simply remove levels of management is neither a 'cure-all' nor source of business effectiveness nor improvement in itself. In short, the reduction in administrative staff is not the means of achieving customer focus. However, that is not to argue that the roles and responsibilities in the enterprise will continue without modification.

Kotler (1988) proposes that the interaction between customers, feeding information back to the company that relates to the perception and quantification of the customer service provided, should be conducted through the management levels of the business – or the levels that are targeted for reduction by some of the 'downsizing' approaches (Kanter, 1989). He proposes that the traditional organizational approach regarded the customer as a point of integration with those employees who converted the products. As such, process management, which relies on the calibre and integration of the middle managers in the factory, will have an impact on the role of these individuals as 'information processors' and 'facilitators' of the 'response' provided by the factory to improve continuously the levels of customer service offered. The traditional notion of the shopfloor employees as the source of continuous improvement is too restrictive, because these individuals, whilst affecting the quality, cost and delivery of their own actions, do not hold the necessary 'position' in the organization to amend the processes of the departments or the wider administrative systems. Instead, the middle management level in the business is the most potent source of 'holistic' innovation and improvement. This management level is also the most familiar with 'best practice' from a functional perspective.

The cross-functional process-oriented approach is a model of consensus management based on the use of a forum or committee for the exchange of these ideas for individual improvement and coordination of

FIGURE 7.2 The Role of Middle Management

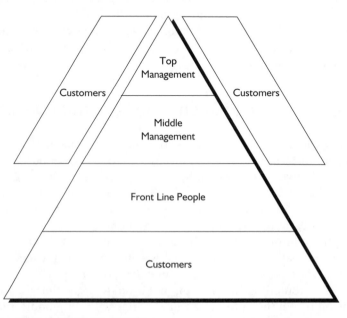

SOURCE: Adapted from Kotler (1988).

activities on a company-wide scale. These managers are accountable for performance only in the short term, whereas the directors of the business share accountability for the long term and the shopfloor personnel maintain responsibility for tactical and daily adjustments to performance. It is ironic that the middle managers are therefore targeted for reduction through re-engineering existing processes (Keuning and Opheij, 1994).

The middle management hierarchy is therefore an important level in the organization and is responsible for the assignment of resources. It stands to gain the most from cross-functional integration as well as being the most disadvantaged form of worker under the traditional functional business with its rigid boundaries. According to Imai (1986), cross-functional activities designed to improve customer service 'generates process-oriented thinking, since processes must be improved before we get improved results. ... This contrasts sharply with the result-oriented thinking of most Western managers'. The middle managers must therefore share the same measures of internal performance evaluation, those of quality, cost and delivery, in such a way that the motivation to create coalitions of managers to improve the performance of each area and the optimization of the key business processes forms a mutually reinforcing system of practices and decision-making. The latter activity has been highlighted as a major source of organizational 'adaptiveness', through the decentralization of decision-making, within turbulent environments. The arguments that suggest a radical reversal and displacement of the vertical business functions have missed the opportunities available to companies that maintain these forms of control but enhance the levels of cross-functional integration within the business.

> *The middle management hierarchy is an important level in the organization.*

The Customer Service Multiplier and Management Responsibility

The alignment and common focus of business departments on the lateral key processes of the customer service equation also serves to improve the flow of materials within the enterprise by 'de-bottlenecking' each element of the physical and administrative process. In this respect, the common portfolio of quality, cost and delivery represent internal dependencies between departments as well as functional measures of performance. The customer service generated by a single node (department) in the business can be calculated by multiplying the quality and delivery performance of each section (Rich and Francis, 1998). If the quality performance of the purchasing department is 90 per cent and the delivery performance of the suppliers is 50 per cent then the overall effectiveness of the inbound materials process is only 45 per cent. Faced with this situation, the purchasing department would concentrate its 'de-bottlenecking' effort on the improvement of supplier delivery performance. Only when the combined quality and delivery performance of the supply base is near 100 per cent can costs be reduced by eliminating levels of inventory and such like. The other business departments that each share these measures can therefore assign their human and financial resources in the same manner, and with each incremental improvement in these 'point' measures the overall customer service of the factory is improved.

This form of cross-functional management and the selection of meaningful measures allows the unification of effort and focus on 'customer service' by the vertical departments and therefore permits a truly holistic and 'total' perception to be created. It is this ability to provide a systemic response by the organization, seen in terms of quality, delivery and the costs of products, that informs the supplier selection evaluation of the purchaser either subjectively or through quantifiable means (such as a formal supplier evaluation and ranking system).

The Product-Focused Organization

An extension of this 'process' view is the development of an organization, explicitly focused on the management of customers or product families, which is the idea of the 'focused factory' approach which has originated in Japan. This system disbands the traditional functional departments and forms them into a microcosm of the factory. A member of each of the administrative departments joins and co-locates with other specialists to become dedicated to a certain product range or customer account. This form of management creates a 'business within a business' or 'focused factory' wherein all the support functions necessary to ensure the smooth flow of materials and services are provided by one team. This form of structural review and adjustment, like the process of cross-functional management, marks a deviation from the department as the fundamental building block of the organization towards that of the 'team'. In this sense, the organizational hierarchy does become 'flattened' and more responsive, not through the wholesale de-layering of the organization, but by changes in the roles, responsibilities and reporting structure of the administrative staff. To a certain extent this would confirm the arguments of Hammer and Champy (1993) who propose that 'companies that try to improve their performance by working on the pieces miss the point. ... Yet in company after company management works at fixing the pieces instead of redesigning the processes by which the companies get work done'.

The Importance of Process Management for World Class Manufacturing

To finalize the arguments for cross-functional measures of customer service and the role of process management as an alternative to the traditional approach to organizational design, there is a growing amount of empirical evidence, of both a comparative and case nature, which has been identified in recent surveys and studies. These studies tend to feature Japanese manufacturers and in particular the power of the Toyota Production System or TPS (Womack and Jones, 1996; Andersen Consulting, 1992 and 1994). The concern for customer satisfaction, and the rationale for the development of TPS, is demonstrated by Shigeru Aoki, a senior managing director at Toyota Motor Corporation. Aoki contends that the foundation upon which Toyota has gained global market share and profitability results from a basic understanding that

> the ultimate goal of a company is to make profits. Assuming that this is self-evident, then the 'superordinate' goal of the company should be such cross-functional goals as quality, cost and scheduling (quantity and delivery). Without achieving these goals, the company will be left behind by the competition because of inferior quality, higher costs, and will be unable to deliver the products in time for the customers. If these cross functional goals are realised, profits will follow. (Imai, 1986)

In this manner, the internal processes are promoted to assume a strategic and operational importance, a point of elevation that, as we have discussed, has eluded most departments in Western companies. However, in Japan the administrative and management functions within businesses exist 'to serve the three superordinate goals of QCS (Quality, Cost and Scheduling). These auxiliary management functions include product planning, design, production, purchasing, and marketing, and they should be regarded as secondary means to achieve QCS' (Imai, 1986). The key processes are the means of creating internal management teams of personnel who are drawn from the relevant internal departments. The objective of these teams is to modify the roles and activities of departments and individuals in such a manner that the flow of 'value adding' is optimized as is the product or service provided when measured by the consumer (the concept of 'value' promoted by Womack and Jones (1996). This process is therefore a powerful form of innovation and discontinuous improvement which, when compared to the efforts of continuous improvement teams on the shopfloor, has a much deeper and profound impact on the performance of the organization.

Indeed, cross-functional management, or lateral process management, features as a major element in the promotion and dissemination of 'best practice' manufacturing in Japan. The Japan Union of Scientists and Engineers, the Japanese professional body which regulates industry and is a powerful lobbying force for the education of professional engineers, offers the following definition of cross-functional management:

> a management process designed to encourage and support interdepartmental communication and co-operation throughout a company – as opposed to command and control through narrow departments or divisions. The purpose is to attain such company-wide targets as quality, cost and delivery of products by optimising the sharing of work. (JUSE, 1988)

It is therefore quite perverse, given the earlier arguments that companies must create a unified response to turbulent markets, for the first initiative taken by companies to be to reduce, rather than to integrate, the existing administrative structure (a less traumatic and chaotic means of generating change).

In modern accounts of 'world-class' performance and the role of middle managers – who have already spent many years working together as a group – would suggest that these structures themselves are undergoing a refinement process that reflects the constant improvement in the measures of customer service, so that world-class competitors have demonstrated that establishing a hierarchical list of competitive priorities and focusing exclusively on the top of the list is short-sighted. These competitors have mastered quality, delivery, cost and flexibility. Indeed for them this mastery is merely a necessary although not a sufficient condition for their competitiveness. Furthermore, frequently the best performing plants are not single-purpose, but share a variety of competitive priorities. Integration is often correlated with improved performance, and the evolutionary process of integration would appear to generate a new capacity for the organization to respond and compete successfully. In turn, the management teams have the ability to quickly reassign resources to meet changes, both real and anticipated, in the environment and thereby 'switch gears' to meet new order qualifying and winning criteria. At this point, '... the goals of the strategy becomes strategic flexibility. Being world class is not enough; a company also has to have the capability to switch gears – from, for example, rapid product development to low cost ... The job of manufacturing is to provide that capability' (Hayes and Pisano, 1994).

Cross-functional management, or lateral process management, features as a major element in the promotion and dissemination of 'best practice' manufacturing in Japan.

In this respect, it is the integration of the managers in a business rather than the promotion of the shopfloor production operators that is a fundamental determinant of 'customer service'. The new arrangements of formal management working groups relies less on the chant of secular mantras and more on the development of a common language and frame of reference within the business. It is only when managers form teams that the concept of 'manufacturing as a competitive weapon' holds validity both internally (amongst all business departments) and externally (with customers and suppliers).

Conclusions

This chapter has sought to provide an overview of the current trends and 'schools' of thought that relate to the management of the enterprise within a turbulent and uncertain market. The chapter offers caution against accepting the legitimacy of some of the modern authors, whose models appear rational but may prove disappointing in application. Those authors who attack the functional organization for its deficiencies without proposing new structures and accommodations to it do little to assist the practitioners – who are themselves deluged with new 'cure-alls' touted by consultants and academics alike.

The modern approach, reinforced by research evidence, is not that the departmental organization is dead, but that the 'edges' of traditional demarcation have become blurred to the point of being almost indistinguishable. The convergence of departments is a deliberate attempt to focus the attention of managers on key business processes that generate the customer-service equation and, as such, the ultimate survival of the organization. The modern approach of 'world-class' companies is not to allow the dominance of a single departmental 'power player', as this is short-sighted and decisions taken using a dominant departmental perspective (such as marketing) are difficult to 'sell' within the enterprise.

Instead, the 'elevation' debate is redundant under cross-functional management – all key business departments should be integrated in the formal business planning processes, share the key measures and adapt internally to new innovations and external change. It would seem ironic that the 'total' element of 'Total Quality Management' or 'Total Productive Maintenance' is neither seen as a 'cross-functional', 'managerial' nor 'shared' organizational initiative, but is deemed to be limited to the manufacturing or maintenance departments alone in the West (Rich, 1998). In reality, and in Japan, these initiatives are only two of the vital processes that have been chosen as 'hows', or simply 'what' the business in its totality, has agreed to be implemented.

This chapter opened with an analysis of the general trends of enterprises that find themselves in turbulent markets. Within this context, the paper has promoted several very strong themes including:

- the decentralization of decision-making;
- the need to integrate the business;
- the development of 'empowerment' and a team-based approach;
- the development of an 'open organizational system' that interfaces

with the environment and is adaptive to prevailing conditions – capable of changing competitive priorities quickly;

● the concept of customer service.

For traditional enterprises, where lines of demarcation are maintained, the ability of the organization to maintain high levels of 'customer service' represents the fragile and volatile combination of efforts and good fortune. However, with each incremental step towards 'company-wide' lateral management practices the ability of the organization to enhance customer service levels and compete successfully is released. The new organizational structure is a weave of vertical control (and independent autonomy) supported by a horizontal process of integration (and the development of explicit dependency relationships between departments). Only when these two systems are combined, the 'efficiency' strength of the departmental structure with the informational processing strength of process management, does the organization act as a single entity and possess the ability to use manufacturing as a competitive weapon.

Finally, the managerial 'fad' culture that has been responsible for the rapid introduction, emulation and often the failure of key business initiatives such as the 'total' programmes mentioned earlier may well have been proposed with the genuine intent of improving effectiveness or they are seen to work within the Japanese context. However, cross-functional management is an intangible process that forms the 'invisible guiding hand' of organizational control. Through complete alignment of all the business departments it ensures that each corporate programme is optimized.

Unfortunately, cross-functional management has often been neglected or not made explicit within Western companies. Without a proper management infrastructure many of these good ideas fail to become realized or to sustain benefits over time. In short, these initiatives represent the 'chosen' improvement initiatives of the cross-functional management teams as a result of the ongoing pressure to improve quality and delivery whilst continuously reducing the costs of servicing business with customers. With this in mind, there is '... no universal cure-all in manufacturing. We should look on JIT, TQM, et al, not as panaceas, but for what they are; interesting and stimulating ways of seeing operational issues, which can reshape the way we view the operation and, if we are lucky, provide the spark for creative and novel solutions to old problems' (Slack, 1991).

> **Unfortunately, cross-functional management has often been neglected or not made explicit within Western companies.**

CHAPTER 8

Developing Standard Operations in the Factory[1]

Introduction

This chapter continues the strategic analysis of the enterprise and supply chain by concentrating on the issue of organizational 'control' as a means of generating both efficiency and effectiveness. This issue lies at the very heart of all notions that manufacturing can be used as a competitive weapon and, in its many guises, is the central concern of all researchers in the operations management field of study. In contemporary times, this concern has focused management attention, and research activities, on the development of a 'standardized production system'. The interest in standardized production systems has been fuelled by the widespread dissemination of Japanese manufacturing systems and the Toyota Production System (TPS) in particular. These analyses have taken many different forms but are unified by the title 'new wave manufacturing' practice.

The use of 'a standardized production' system is neither new nor original but derives from the development of mass production itself, exemplified by the principles of the Ford Motor Company, where standards were created as the main operational controls on which large scale economic efficiency was achieved. Since this period of industrial history, the importance of 'control' through the use of factory 'standards' has increased, initially reinvigorated by the war effort, and then as a result of the adoption of the 'Total Quality Management' (TQM) school of thought. More recently, the issue of 'control' has, once again, been brought into sharp focus through many comparative analyses of performance between Japanese and Western manufacturers (Womack *et al.*, 1990; Andersen

[1] Prepared by Nick Rich.

Consulting, 1992, 1994). This research and body of evidence demonstrated the huge rift in performance, measured in terms of the productivity and quality of the factory, in favour of the Japanese, citing figures of 2:1 in productivity and 100:1 in quality (Womack *et al.*, 1990).

A History of 'Control' Thinking in the Factory

The concept of standardized production systems, and the role of control in the factory, can be traced back to the development of mass production and the 'classical' management practices adopted to satisfy mass consumerism. These early approaches to the control of factory operations, developed during the early 1900s, represented a means of creating factory efficiency through the use of de-skilled traditional 'craft' practices for the basic task elements of the job so that these responsibilities could be shared amongst many different, and less 'professional', employees. The intellectual knowledge and time-served apprenticeships, needed to become recognized as a craftsman in the earlier period of production, were no longer prerequisites for employment within the new mass production factories. The basic tasks needed to produce one element of a finished product, repeated continuously throughout the working day, was the basis on which an individual was employed. These tasks and routines were designed, calibrated and monitored by departmental industrial engineers with the objective of maximizing the output of the factory.

> *The concept of standardized production systems can be traced back to the development of mass production.*

Employees tended to the needs of the equipment at a rate determined by engineering staff and in accordance with the written standard operating procedures issued to them. The control standards operated by these factories have been characterized as 'the one best way' approach, and any behaviour in the factory that was not encapsulated in the stand-ard procedures, was regarded as 'deviant' or 'non-conformist' (Taylor, 1947).

Henri Fayol, one of the leading authors to emerge during the development of mass production organizations, demonstrates the concern to find the 'one best way' to 'standardize' operations in the factory by proposing that 'in an undertaking, control consists in verifying whether everything occurs in conformity with the plan adopted, the instructions issued and the principles established. It ... operates on everything, things, people, actions' (Fayol, 1949). In parallel, Frederick Winslow Taylor (1947), another key influence on the development of the industrial engineering-led factory system, goes further to suggest that the employees in the factory system should be highly supervised and coerced by management to prevent the opportunities for workers to engage in the 'systematic soldiering' against the time standards and control measures. In short, workers were perceived as lazy, unintelligent and expendable (both in terms of the economic ability to remove labour from the production process and also the level of 'deaths' in these factories as a result of the desire to cut corners and improve the remuneration of the employee) as inputs to the manufacturing process.

The concepts promoted by Taylor (1947) gained widespread and fashionable support by industry, from the 1930s onwards, and he has been dubbed the 'father of scientific management'. His main arguments included the 'scientific selection' and training of workers so that the physical characteristics of the worker could be used to improve efficiency, the use of engineering specialists as mediators to convince workers to adopt the 'one best way', time and motion study, output-based remuneration and 'functional foremanship'. Taylor believed that the worker should be guided by two key forms of specialist controls: the *'planning'* of work for the employee; and the measurement of the *'performance'* achieved. These two activities were the responsibility of *eight* different foremen, with each individual foreman responsible for (or for being):

1. the planning of the order of work (Planning);
2. the issuance of job instruction cards (Planning);
3. the assessment of time and costing (Planning);
4. the control of discipline (Planning);
5. the 'gang' boss;
6. the 'speed' boss;
7. the 'repair' boss;
8. the inspector.

The early generations of factory standards can be summarized as a 'mechanistic' approach to the control of activities in the factory which was to support the dominant ideology of close and direct employee supervision through overt surveillance procedures. In this manner, 'control' was formal, restrictive and served no purpose as a means of integrating the employee or permitting 'self-direction'. The early approach to the organization of work, adopted by the classical mass production corporations, therefore emphasized the technical specialization of the factory above all other inputs to the process – especially that of labour.

Later academic studies, although once again focused on the industrial productivity of the factory environment, this time rejected the inhumanity of the 'scientific management' approach, and began to analyze the impact of the social systems within the workplace (Maslow, 1943; Trist, 1963; Crozier, 1964; Argyris, 1964). These authors, generically termed the 'human relations' school, advocated a much greater level of individual freedom and self-control in the setting of factory standards. This school also identified the need to harness the intellectual capabilities of the employee in managing the day-to-day production activities and this approach to the management of the factory advocated a much greater understanding of the human element of the production system.

The study which gave rise to this 'ethnocentric' school is the renowned 'Hawthorne experiments'. This research comprised a series of sociological analyses of working conditions as a means of understanding the 'informality' of the workplace and the group dynamics that create the social element of the factory (Roethlisberger and Dickson, 1939). The findings of the study suggested that a higher level of integration of the manager with the team in the factory setting was the primary causal factor of increased productivity. The study, albeit with problems associated with academic rigour (Silverman, 1970), provided a new interest in issues such as the leadership of teams in the factory, self-management, the motivation of individuals at work, informal factory 'norms', job design, communication and the role of personnel management. The study provided some evidence that employees were motivated by a wide variety of 'social needs' and not simply by the remuneration achieved by productivity. For these authors, job satisfaction resulted from 'involvement' in decision-making and jobs designed for the worker.

A key concern for this 'behaviouralist' approach was the development of the concept of 'consensus' between the individual, their work group and the objectives of the company. However, the impact of these studies was poor compared with the dominance of the 'classical scientific' approach which was already deeply embedded in the operating culture of industrial organizations. Nevertheless, the combined effort of these 'human relations' authors provided a new dimension to the control puzzle, that of 'social control' and the role of the team.

The importance of the informal and 'social' element of the production system increased during the 1960s when technological advances and environmental turbulence began to affect the 'socio-technical systems' in industry and displaced many manual grades of labour, as well as creating a demand for 'educated' workers to operate this form of new technology (Trist, 1963). These turbulent times generated many studies that focused on the 'fit' between the human and technological elements of production. From the early 1970s onwards, the generalized theories of the 'behaviouralist' approach gave way to the study of organizational structures as an explanator of performance, employee roles and departmental integration. This new school was termed the 'contingency school' of thought and rejected the concept of 'universal' management or 'the one best way' of the previous regime.

The 'contingency school' typified by studies conducted by Woodward (1980), Burns and Stalker (1966), and Lawrence and Lorsch (1969) promoted the concept that the earlier 'human systems' approaches were too introspective and that the use of control within the socio-technical system was related to the wider business environment. As such, the organizational structure, the formal working relationships, and the informal elements of the production system (all of which represent forms of control) will differ between contexts. The 'contingency school' proposed that the 'one best way' sought by managers may not actually exist, or will vary between companies as would the principles of 'control' adopted. The models and frameworks developed by the contingency school add a further dimension to the previous work that concentrated on the development of bureaucratic formal standards and informal social standards, by emphasizing the need to 'fit' the holistic production system with the operating environment of the company. This 'fit' is therefore a continuous process of internal adjustment to such variables as the turbulence in external customer markets. As a result, the selection and amendment of control standards is a reflection of the competitive advantage and efficiency sought by the business.

Modern Studies of Industrial Performance and Factory Control

Modern studies of industrial performance and the control standards applied to the production process have focused on comparative studies of organizations and the application of Japanese manufacturing systems in particular. The common denominator that unites these studies is the perception of 'control standards' as measures to assess the performance of the conversion process. This current focus is once again a concern to manage the factory to ultimate levels of production 'efficiency' and to generate the highest levels of customer service. The current studies tend to emphasize ratios that evaluate the 'input-conversion–output' performance of factories through the analysis of companies operating in the same product markets but employing different approaches to 'control'.

The common denominator that unites these studies is the perception of 'control standards' as measures to assess the performance of the conversion process.

The primary focus of the modern comparative studies, that of 'efficiency', is supported by a secondary level of analysis which tends to focus on the socio-technical elements of the conversion process. These 'secondary elements' are often used to evaluate the way in which employees act as 'enablers' or 'inhibitors' to the performance of the factory, and also the manner in which the employees are autonomous in the procedural management of their element of the entire system. This analysis of procedural and self-empowered 'control' focuses on the interface between the formal and informal operating systems adopted by the company, and recent studies of comparative industrial performance suggest that this is a causal factor that underpins higher levels of operational performance (Womack *et al.*, 1990; Andersen Consulting, 1992 and 1994).

Understanding the Foundations of 'World-Class' Industrial Performance

Three of the most influential studies of manufacturing performance in recent times have concentrated on the automotive sector. These studies include one longitudinal analysis of the automotive assembly sector, conducted by the IMVP research programme (Womack *et al.*, 1990) and two research programmes that have evaluated the performance and practices adopted by automotive component suppliers (Andersen Consulting, 1992 and 1994). These studies have each identified the existence of wide gaps in operational performance that exist between typical manufacturers and their 'world-class' competitors. These 'world-class' companies, defined in terms of the ability to maintain near-perfect levels of productivity and quality simultaneously, were found to operate with a '2:1 difference in performance between the world class plants and the rest ... This 2:1 difference appeared over a wide range of measures including productivity, inventories and schedule variation ... the gap in quality was wider 9:1 in seats, 170:1 in exhausts and 16:1 in brakes' (Andersen, 1992) and were dominated by Japanese manufacturers – although not all the Japanese companies in the sample managed to achieve this level of performance. Similar findings in this order of magnitude were discovered by the studies which focused on the performance of the global vehicle assemblers, once again demonstrating a distinct advantage for the Japanese (Womack *et al.*, 1990).

The secondary analyses conducted by the research teams uncovered a new set of management practices in the workplace which permitted the control of the production process to be delegated to 'empowered' factory teams and revealed the core role of the team leader in this process. In addition, the standards adopted to create the production system were also deployed to these workplace teams, who drew upon technical support provided by specialists in the formal administrative hierarchy. The Andersen research concluded that the source of the competitive differential originated from the maintenance of 'tight discipline and control over their internal processes. This rigour extends to the whole supply chain, including second tier suppliers and the car assemblers' (1994).

These control standards were used to create a foundation on which the continuous reduction of 'losses' to the production process could be eliminated by the teams in each area and between factories. The key variable in this supply chain puzzle was the use of standardized production systems and the role of the teams in improving the productivity of the process. The difference between the discipline of the 'world-class' plants is displayed by the following table that compares the performance of a traditional Western factory (GM Framingham), a typical Japanese Toyota factory (Takaoka) and a recent joint venture located in America (NUMMI):

TABLE 8.1 The Comparative Performance Standards of Vehicle Assembly Factories

Performance Indicator	GM Framingham	Toyota Takaoka	NUMMI Fremont
Assembly Hours Per Car	31	16	19
Assembly Defects Per 100 Cars	135	45	45
Assembly Space Per Car	8.1	4.8	7.0
Inventories of Parts (Average)	2 Weeks	2 Hours	2 Days

SOURCE: Womack *et al.* (1990).

The most interesting conclusion of this analysis is the performance of the 'fledgling' NUMMI assembly site.

> NUMMI uses an old General Motors plant built in the 1960s to assemble GM cars and pickup trucks for the U.S. West Coast ... it convinced Toyota to provide the management for the re-opened plant, which would produce small Toyota-designed passenger cars for the U.S. market ... NUMMI was to make no compromises on lean production. The senior managers were all from Toyota and quickly implemented an exact copy of the Toyota Production System. (Womack *et al.*, 1990)

The NUMMI site, disadvantaged by a long supply chain, a 'brown field' operation and attempting to employ Toyota working standards in a Western culture, demonstrated that the 'Japanese' socio-technical systems could be transferred between countries.

However, even though there was clear evidence to support the view that the performance of Japanese assembly operations held a superior performance advantage over their Western counterparts, the same did not hold true of the Andersen Consulting studies (1992 and 1994). The initial 1992 study found that all the companies determined to be 'world-class' were Japanese, but that not all of the Japanese survey had achieved this position. In the 1994 study, the 'world-class' Japanese component manufacturers were joined by other Western companies. The common denominator between these factories, operating in different regions and with different ownership, was the use of the Just In Time production systems. These systems originate from the principles developed by the Toyota Motor Corporation and have become generically termed the 'lean system' in recent times (Womack and Jones, 1996).

The Toyota Production System Approach to Factory Standards

The Toyota Production System is both a philosophy and suite of practices that have been developed since the 1950s. The initial concept for the design of the production system was conceived by Kiichiro Toyoda (Chairman of the company) and the enactment of the system was led by a charismatic engineer Taiichi Ohno. The basic philosophy of TPS is to eliminate all sources of 'waste' in the factory and its conversion processes as a means of continuously improving the 'value added' achieved. TPS is therefore a holistic approach to the management of quality and productivity in its broadest sense, not simply an approach to the shopfloor. The TPS system provides a frame of reference for all employees in the factory, regardless of whether these employees conduct administrative or manufacturing tasks, and as such the Toyota principles operate across different environments.

At the very core of the value system of TPS is a belief in continuous, people-based improvements and the development of 'evolving' standards in the workplace.

At the very core of the value system of TPS is a belief in continuous, people-based improvements and the development of 'evolving' standards in the workplace. Indeed, the foreword to the TPS information booklet produced by Toyota states that

> … we are eager for readers to bear in mind that the Toyota Production System is a continuously evolving system. The methods and practices described … are representative of the system at the time of writing. But we continue to modify them in response to changes in circumstances, while remaining faithful to the fundamental principles of the Toyota Production System. (Toyota Motor Corporation, 1992).

The internationalization and transferability of the TPS approach is also recognized by Toyota in that

> today, the production system that we have worked so hard to build at Toyota has become the subject of attention in industries besides automobiles and in nations besides Japan. We and our many suppliers have implemented the system successfully around the world … The Toyota Production System, we believe, has a contribution to make to industrial vitality in every country, if companies make the effort to adapt it to local circumstances and values. (Toyota Motor Corporation, 1992)

The latter statement represents an acknowledgement that the TPS system is contingent and offers many 'best ways' that are dependent on circumstances, people, products and the markets serviced by the manufacturer.

The TPS approach is, therefore, a 'systems' approach to the manufacturing business which adopts continuously improving standards as a means of 'waste' elimination and involves the actions of all employees in the socio-technical system. As such, TPS has many different 'guises' and the general principles of TPS manifest themselves in different ways according to these 'constraints', so that a 'fit' is achieved. This 'fit', between the social elements of work and the technology employed, is achieved through the development of a standardized production system that serves to differentiate 'normality' from 'abnormality' in operations throughout the factory. In the process of eliminating 'waste', the standards adopted will therefore change and become incrementally redefined until 'zero loss' process performance has been achieved (Rich, 1998). The production system is therefore a means of regulation that is administered by those teams of employees who work at each process.

Losses and Waste in the Factory

The TPS system is supported by an evaluation system, developed by Ohno (1988a), to rank 'waste' in the factory which included:

1. *Overproduction* – the conversion of materials that was in excess of the actual quantities required by the customer.

2. *Defects* – the use of manufacturing product conversion time unproductively absorbed in making unsaleable goods.

3. *Unnecessary inventory* – the use of high levels of buffer stocks.

4. *Inappropriate processing* – the routing of materials to assets within the conversion process that were either incapable of holding the tolerances required by the customer or assets that were comparatively over-complicated when a much simpler technology could have been employed.

5. *Unnecessary transport* – the great distances involved in the movement of materials through the production process stages.

6. *Unnecessary motion* – the poor design and ergonomics of the conversion process which entailed the exposure of the operator to risk and strain.

7. *Unnecessary delay* – the constant interruption to the flow of products through the many stages of the production process as a result of untimely delivery of products to the process stage or the stagnation of materials that were forced to wait for the conversion process to be cleared of the current batch of work being converted.

The seven key losses to the factory represent physical (defects) and procedural (delays and over-production created through the setting of large batch sizes) wastes. To counter these forms of factory loss, the TPS approach developed by Ohno (then a machine shop manager at Toyota) began to emphasize the need to exploit the most value from the material inputs to the process, the technology employed and the labour that supported the movement and conversion of products. Initially, and with limited resources, Ohno focused on the improvement of productivity through upgrading the quality levels achieved by each element of the factory system using such techniques as 'mistake proofing'.[2] Then, as factory losses began to decline, Ohno switched his attention to the development of 'flexibility' in the production system by reducing the lot size of production and introducing the quick changeover of technology from one product to the next as a means of creating economies of scope without interruption to the flow of materials to be assembled. As a result, the technology employed by the factory began to be modified to remove the wastes associated with over-production, inventories, delay and storage.

'The third and most radical change Mr. Ohno made was also born out of necessity. Since Toyota had not got the money to stock pile parts and materials, he evolved the kanban system by which products are pulled through by market demand, rather than being driven by the supply of raw materials' (Grimsdale, 1990). During this evolution stage, parts were produced by the internal supplier within the factory only when they were required by the next production process. This was accomplished by sending 'cards' detailing the products required from the internal consumer back to the source of the parts. In this system, the internal customer consumed materials that were held at the customer process and, as these inventory levels dropped, the cards were returned to the internal supplier for replenishment. By this means Ohno had created a system that reflected true customer demand without the need to compute production schedules for each area of the factory – termed a 'pull' system.

The 'pull' system allowed the factory environment to stabilize and Ohno switched his attention to the 'human' wastes in the factory and the redefinition of the 'informal contract of employment' with employees. In this effort to reduce waste, Ohno attempted to reverse the traditional workplace control routines which had developed during the dominance of the 'scientific management' approach in which employees were expendable and treated as 'slaves to the production process'. The traditional system of de-skilled workers performing routine tasks did not 'fit' with the pressures facing Toyota. These pressures included the need to manufacture in small batches and to optimize the deployment of human resources in the factory as a means of controlling costs and maintaining a high level of defect-free production. In this environment the division of roles and responsibilities in the traditional factory was not conducive to employee integration and self-management.

---

[2] The philosophy of 'mistake proofing' and the 'intelligent automation' of equipment originates from the Toyoda family and the interests of the family in manufacturing industrial textile looms.

During this re-invention of the TPS Ohno began to conceive of ways in which the intellectual capabilities of the worker could be harnessed in such a way that many machines could be operated through job enlargement. Ohno states that 'I called my men together and I told them "you are only working two hours a day. The rest of the time you are standing over a machine, watching it work". I told them to go away and try each process with half the number of men ... in time they came back to me ... so I would say half the number again' (Grimsdale, 1990). In redefining the 'human' configuration of the factory, Ohno created a system in which the role and skills (including the diagnostic skills) of the worker were enriched and, to cement this form of lean manufacturing system, Ohno then began to seek ways of integrating the workforce through a direct participation in the improvement of working conditions and factory performance. This new thrust involved the development of problem-solving and new social groups, known as quality circles, to formalize this 'rejuvenation' process. At this point, Ohno had created a system wherein roles and responsibilities could be deployed across the factory and one where process management, process improvement, and rate of improvement became the responsibility of the team. To facilitate this 'software' approach to operational efficiency, the factory procedures were standardized into a visible manufacturing system – this represented the coding of knowledge and practices in such a way as it could be transferred to other company factories and also to suppliers. They note that 'after a lot of effort and a lot of trial and error, they (the codified practices) became standard procedure at all Toyota plants, at plants throughout the Toyota Group, and at many of Toyota's independent suppliers' (Toyota Motor Corporation, 1992).

The Toyota Production System Logic

The underlying logic of the production system developed by Ohno is 'commercial' rather than 'technological' logic and is supported by the concept of customer service and the 'market'. This logic also creates a 'hierarchy' of priorities in the management of the factory that emphasizes the primary role of operational 'quality', then the 'delivery' of materials, and, finally, the continuous 'cost' reduction of the operation as a means of creating profit (Rich, 1998). In this respect, TPS provides a natural translation of the commercial realities of selling factory output into the 'internal' sales transactions which must be conducted between each stage of the production process.

This logic is also emphasized by the approach to servicing customers by Toyota today:

> market conditions determine a reasonable selling price, which becomes the constant in our equation; cost and the profit margin are the variables. We take responsibility for controlling costs internally. By keeping those costs below the reasonable selling price, we secure

a profit and retain control over our own destiny. (Toyota Motor Corporation, 1992)

The level of internal discipline and 'control' required to operate such an approach to manufacturing requires standards and procedures that will ensure that transformation in the factory processes are founded on a solid – and predictable – basis. The relentless pursuit of waste by all employees is formalized, has a stability in the costs of the business and provides the day-to-day procedures for optimizing the efficiency of the conversion process.

The relentless pursuit of waste by all employees is formalized.

Standards distinguish 'normality' from 'abnormality' in the production process and focus the improvement efforts of teams on the elimination of abnormality (Rich, 1998).

Standards and the Toyota Production System

The development of procedural and process standards that govern the manner in which the production system operates provides a source of 'certainty' for decision-making in the factory. In such a system many of the production variables are 'known', such as the amount of inventory at each point in the conversion process or the standard time required to process work (an element of the production system which was never truly developed under the conditions of mass production). The role of 'management' is, by consequence, simplified and less reactive when compared with the traditional models. As a result, the role of the manager is focused on more fruitful and rewarding activities in the elimination of administrative 'waste'. TPS managers are engaged in planning, controlling and facilitation activities rather than 'fire-fighting' to maintain a semblance of normality within the manufacturing process.

In addition, the involvement' and 'empowerment' of the front line supervision allows many of the traditional and routine management tasks to be delegated completely (improving the span of control that can be exercised). For shopfloor teams, the standardized production system offers the opportunity to engage in continuous improvement (termed *kaizen*) and problem-solving activities (Imai, 1986). This aspect of the socio-technical and standardized production system is reinforced by Ohno himself who contends that 'standard work is the origin of shopfloor improvement. There is no improvement where there is no standard work' (Ohno, 1988b).

The TPS system is mutually reinforcing in that improvement efforts are both planned and 'standardized' on completion of the planned project and each activity results in a new standard 'way'. In this sense labour is no longer regarded as a variable cost but an asset within the business and a further deviation from the traditional approach to manufacturing. Indeed,

... for people accustomed to the regimented work of traditional production formats, the Toyota Production System and the broad-ranging responsibilities it assigns to employees can come as a shock. In place of the rigid job designations of conventional systems, the Toyota Production System is predicated on employee flexibility in acquiring multiple skills ... employees can translate their own ideas into visible improvements in production flow and in product quality, take pride in their work, in their jobs and in their companies. ... The overall result ... is a stimulating workplace. A workplace where employees can take charge of their own destinies. (Toyota Motor Corporation, 1992)

The development, constant refinement and 'ownership' of the production system by teams through the use of standards is the basis for the incremental improvement of each stage in the 'value-adding' process, involving modifications to both the 'hardware' and 'software' within the business.

The Application of the Toyota Production System Logic

The generic concepts of TPS have been condensed into *five* generic elements:

1. The specification of 'Value' in terms of benefit derived by the customer from the product or service offered to them.
2. The identification of the 'Value Stream' that creates the benefit for the customer in terms of the actual processes which must combine to create the product or service and provide customer satisfaction.
3. The development of standards which enable the 'Flow' of work throughout the organization in such a manner that the product or service does not stagnate or incur unnecessary costs.
4. The creation of a process and procedures which allow work to be 'Pulled' by the customer so that the product or service arrives at the right time and place for consumption.
5. The continuous improvement of the task, operation and the business to achieve 'Perfection' and the 'zero loss' environment in which all the actions which are required to create the product or service happen with minimal cost.

(Adapted from Womack and Jones, 1996.)

Part A) TPS in the Factory

The five 'lean' concepts provide a final summary of the 'background' to the development of standards within the factory. The chapter will focus now on the typical array of standards which combine, in a holistic manner, to create TPS in its many formats. These standards[3] can be sub-divided into the following key activities within the context of the factory:

1. Standardized Inventory and Material Flow.
2. Standardized Production Planning and Logistics.
3. Standardized Operations.
4. Standardized Supplies.

1. Standardized Inventory and Movement: The Concept of kanban

As mentioned previously, one of the techniques developed by Ohno was the use of *kanban* to disconnect all internal suppliers and customers through the use of standardized inventory buffers, offering the full range of outputs from one area as a means of guaranteeing the availability of inputs to the next process. The term *kanban* can be translated as 'sign-post' or 'card' and serves to provide 'authority' to move or manufacture materials. Within the TPS system there are three types of *kanban*, one for the 'logistics' associated with material movements and two for the production function.

The 'logistics' *kanban* is, typically, a laminated piece of paper which contains the product, location, quantities and storage of the materials that need to be moved. This card is kept by the 'internal customer' or despatch department permanently. When such a product is required, the card is issued to trigger the movement of materials. This is achieved by going to the point at which the product is manufactured and taking a quantity of products (fixed and displayed on the withdrawal *kanban*) from this point of storage and moving it to the point of consumption (despatch or further processing).

In this process, at the point of product manufacture there is a 'super-market' that contains a quantity of all the products made by that point in the manufacturing process, each product being stored in a standardized number (say four products) in a standardized container (say a blue returnable plastic bin) and each container having a standardized laminated *kanban* card attached to it (one of the two production *kanban* types). When attempting to collect materials and exercise the authority to move materials, the 'customer operation' must take a plastic bin of products, ensure that these are the correct products, remove the production *kanban* card and replace it with the withdrawal card before taking the materials away.

The production *kanban* card is also a visual sign of authorization, and once removed from the container instructs the manufacturing cell to

---

[3] It should be noted that this analysis of standard operations in the factory context refers to manufacturing as opposed to vehicle assembly.

replenish the standard amount of products taken. There are two forms of card: the first are regular ones that are in the system to form the standard buffer held between areas (say in this case 10 containers which equals 40 products) and the second, the 'safety' stocks held of say two containers (8 products) which serves to maintain the availability of products for withdrawal in the case of disruption such as machine breakdowns. The latter form of *kanban* tends to be coloured 'red' and requires the person withdrawing products to inform the manufacturing operation that the 'safety' level has been breached, creating an 'abnormality' in the flow of materials.

In the same manner, the entire production process is decoupled by these *kanban* areas which protect the inputs and outputs of each process stage. The 'abnormality' situation is a time when the amount of inventory held is lower than the demand placed on the particular production process – this is a fault with either the size of the inventory held (demand has risen without amending the size of the buffers in the system) or an indication that the 'customer' operation has 'rejected' materials as substandard and is therefore returning for more products from the internal 'supplier' (demand has risen artificially through the existence of defects). The safety stocks are therefore critical to all TPS systems and it is the management of these stocks that is the focus of all efforts by the teams in the factory – not the amount of working stock required to meet existing planned and known demand.

The production cards are the means of allowing the 'customer' to withdraw the product and 'pull' production rather than simply manufacturing goods in a sequence which is determined by a 'production schedule'. The management of these standard cards is a critical part of TPS so that more cards are injected into the system to cope with rises in customer demand, withdrawn during low periods and used to position inventory to protect the weakest links in the internal supply chain.[4]

2. Production Planning and Logistics: The Levelling of Demand

The use of *kanban* is the primary level of the TPS system, above which is a production planning system that manages the total amount of inventory held at each area of the factory to support customer service. The production planning department is responsible for the levelling of production demand by taking the known orders for the factory, thus ensuring that the factory has the capacity and inventory to support the level of demand at the aggregate level. The production control department tends to analyze

---

[4] The production cards can be sized to accommodate the need to manufacture small batches of product. In this case, the four products held in a container may not equal the batch size required of twelve pieces; therefore each production card will state that the card is worth only four products and, until three such cards have been withdrawn, the manufacturing cell cannot launch a batch to fill its finished goods *kanban* area

the short-term demand requirements – over say a period of a 'rolling' four weeks. The department represents a checking mechanism (which arbitrates production requirements at an aggregate level) but serves the purpose of planning rather than expediting. To achieve this, the forward orders for a product may be for 20,000 units a month – which means that over the 20-day working month for the factory products must be replenished at a rate of 1,000 per day. It is the responsibility of the production control department to ensure that demand can be met and to plan for the longer term to see whether demand is rising and whether *kanban* cards will need to be issued to raise inventory or overtime, and/or new shifts will have to be introduced to cope with such an increase.

At the operational level in the factory, it is the logistics and despatch operations that control the pull of materials throughout the entire factory. The despatch department receives 'shipping instructions' for the picking of materials for transit to the customer, using vehicles that leave the factory at known times throughout the day. To ensure that the materials are brought to the despatch bay at the right time, the order is broken into its constituent parts for picking and the movement of materials prior to the arrival of the vehicle. To achieve this, each order is converted into withdrawal *kanban* cards for each load – using the standard cards in the system – and the known shipping time serves as a position at which all the materials must be collated.

> *At the operational level in the factory, it is the logistics and despatch operations that control the pull of materials throughout the entire factory.*

However, if all these cards were simply issued for collection by a materials handler in one batch, all the *kanban* positions in the factory would witness a massive 'uplift' in demand in one withdrawal (possibly breaching the safety *kanbans* and causing panic). To avoid these self-induced 'peaks', the withdrawal cards are spread evenly throughout the time prior to the actual time of despatch. In this manner, a small quantity of products are brought at frequent intervals to the despatch bay and material movements (and their production) becomes levelled. In the illustration, the customer may require 12 products (3 containers) to be ready for a noon shipment. In turn, a container of the product may be collected at 9:30, 10:30 and 11:30. The means of controlling the *kanban* cards issued to the materials handler is achieved using a 'heijunka box' or simply a 'pigeon hole' system where an amount of cards can be placed in one hole (representing a 30-minute interval) throughout the working day. In this way, the integrity of the standards in the production system is maintained across the entire factory and beyond the factory to include the orders placed on the suppliers.

3. Standardized Operations

The standard amount of *kanban* inventory held to support each cell combined with the standardized routings and times of withdrawal in the factory are supported by standards adopted at the point of manufacture. These standards are maintained by the teams in the manufacturing area and tend to be manual analyses of the production process. The information collected and analyzed by the production control department provides the means to determine the rate of replenishment needed – as previously illustrated – and this information is used by the teams to check that the cell is capable of meeting these requirements as well as the deployment of the labour available in the cell. This concept is known as *takt* time[5] – in our illustration the cell needs to make 1,000 products a day in order to meet monthly demand, but this can also be conducted for the daily product requirements. In this case, if there are two shifts in the factory then 500 products should be made, on average, per shift per day (approximately 1.04 products per minute based on a full 8-hour shift). To know whether this indicator can be achieved, the cell teams must be able to determine the capacity and speed of the cell under a variety of different labour conditions.

The first standard analysis that is conducted by the team is therefore to understand the cycle time of the equipment in the cell. This comprises two elements – the first the time required to load the machine (2 seconds), and the second the automatic processing time required (40 seconds), making a total gross cycle time of 42 seconds. However, this figure assumes that the machine has already been set up, so an adjustment needs to be made to the gross cycle time to inflate it for the changeover (calculated by taking the set-up time and amortizing it by each piece in the batch of products). As illustration, this may add another 2 seconds per product, making a total net cycle time of 44 seconds (654 products can be made in a single shift with a requirement for 500).

The cell thus has the capacity to manufacture the demand placed upon it, assuming that the cell consists of a single machine. This analysis would be conducted for every machine if there was more than one. In the latter case, the output of the cell is determined by the machine with the slowest net speed and therefore the most capacity restrained – not, as in the traditional case, which is simply the slowest cycle time (ignoring the impact of long set-ups and changeovers). In the case of a multiple machine environment, the team must now determine the labour process involved in manufacturing to the *takt* rate and the optimum deployment of personnel in the cell.

In the case of a multiple machining cell, the deployment of labour is

---

[5] *Takt* is the German word for 'a measure of musical pace' and therefore the pace required by the manufacturing area to meet demand and this forms the first analysis in determining whether or not the cell can meet the 'pace' required.

important because of the 'automatic' element of the machine's cycle time. A worker has only to unload and load a machine before having nothing to do other than watch the machine cycle. Accordingly, the team conducts a second series of standard analyses to determine the ability of workers to unload and load several machines in a series – with the idea that the worker will return to the first machine at, or just before, it requires to be unloaded and loaded again. In our illustration above, the automatic time releases some 40 seconds for the person to conduct this activity (and walk between machines). The layout of the cell is also standardized – often in a 'U' cell format – to allow these plans to be created. Once this analysis has been conducted, the roles of each worker can be assigned.

The final element of the analyses is the use of standardized work charts. These are laminated work instruction documents that are displayed at the point in the physical layout of the cell where the task is conducted. The document usually displays a written description of each task (such as 'unload jig', 'check outer dimension', 'load jig', 'press start button', 'walk to next operation'). The chart also contains a picture of a raw material input to the process and a picture of a good product outputted by the process, including any critical dimensions, periodic checks and safety hazards which must be observed.

In this manner, the production area is stabilized through procedures and to cement the system, the TPS system reinforces the 'work rate' needed to be achieved by the cell through the use of 'andon' boards. These boards are illuminated displays that are located high above the cell so that each operator can view the board easily. The information on the board shows a running total of output against the target to be achieved for the day. In this manner, the team can determine whether they are at the right pace, slightly behind or above the rate required. The boards also serve a second purpose and are connected to signalling devices at each machine so that, in the event of quality or maintenance problems, the operator can call for assistance. In the event of such a warning, the problem is identified, corrected and noted for continuous improvement activities by the team at the next opportunity (with the focus on prevention of problem recurrence).

4. Standardized Supplies

The use of the *kanban* system and the pull production is typically translated into the manner in which the suppliers to the factory are controlled and the primary process areas in the factory directly linked to the finishing areas of the supplier factory. The TPS system is thereby extended deep into the supply chain. In parallel to this physical 'pull' system, the production planning department also issues 'directional' schedules for suppliers. In this manner, the suppliers can interrogate the known or anticipated future demand and can take action to increase the *kanban* levels held to support the customer, or run them down as required. This process allows decisions to be taken by suppliers quickly – for example, the establishment of a third shift so that personnel must be moved within the factory or the shutdown of the customer can be planned for.

In summary, the use of factory standards that are written, formalized, and allow the participation of all members of the team creates a mutually reinforcing system of manufacturing that is capable of continuous improvement. The standards create a platform upon which improvements can be made and quickly integrated into the 'customary practice' of all employees. The codification of this knowledge is critical as a means of generating a series of 'ratchets' that allow improvements to be made, stabilized and improved again. For example, an improvement in the ability to load a jig will reduce the cycle time of the equipment in the cell and therefore the amount of labour required, or an improvement in the changeover time required for a product will improve the net cycle time (and total output of the cell). These improvements can be captured quickly, through the continuous improvement process, and used to provide short-term savings before the improvement cycle happens again as the teams constantly seek the 'zero waste' or 'perfect' environment.

Conclusions

This chapter has provided an account of the TPS system of standardized production within the factory setting. It has sought to demonstrate how the social and technical systems of the factory are combined to create a stabilized production process that is continuously and iteratively improved by those who work and control the process itself. This system offers many advantages in terms of responsiveness and proactivity in the workplace, whereby the standards applied reflect 'commercial' rather than 'technological' logic.

This approach to the production system, sharing the same origin as the mass production system, is founded on an entirely different set of values – the manner in which roles and relationships are formed in the factory and the treatment of the 'human' element of the manufacturing equation. The empirical studies of the performance levels achieved by these two systems would suggest that the perpetual de-skilling and fragmentation of the organization within the mass production era has created inflexibility and instability of the conversion process (Womack *et al.*, 1990; Andersen, 1992 and 1994). The deployment of 'ownership' and responsibility – abhorrent to the 'classical' school of thought – has proved not to provide the fertile opportunity for 'systematic soldiering' within these conditions, although the majority of studies have involved Japanese companies operating these principles for many years and resident in Japan. It is perhaps a little ironic that the quality and productivity improvements to the standardized production systems are still in existence despite over fifty years of incremental perfection by companies like Toyota (and two generations of factory employees), whereas the 'command and control' approach of the classical organization, which sought to design the 'one best way', suffers in terms of productivity or quality and often both. The next section of this chapter will provide an overview of the 'warehouse' within the 'world-class' supply chain.

Part B) TPS in the Warehouse[6]

The concept of the warehouse, a point in the supply chain where products are stored and await shipment to customers, may seem contradictory to the principles of 'lean thinking' (Womack and Jones, 1996). The concepts of 'lean thinking' advocate the elimination of waste, highlighting inventory as a major source of business costs in particular; however, in reality and even within the supply chain of the Toyota Motor Corporation, warehouses exist. These two points are difficult to synthesize and would appear, at first sight, to be contradictory.

> *The sole purpose of lean production and supply is to maintain the highest levels of customer service.*

However, the key concern which unites the two points of view is that of using 'customer service' as a competitive weapon. The sole purpose of lean production and supply is to maintain the highest levels of customer service and therefore certain nodes in the supply chain represent points at which the global supply chain meets to service a local market. To simply remove all the warehouses from a supply chain is either a sign of ultimate lean production or the result of a myopic attention to cost reduction. In this respect, the 'value' of a warehouse results from its ability to maximize customer service and to provide a temporary staging point for the frequent and effective distribution of supplies to consumers.

Lean Thinking and TPS in the Warehouse Environment

The generic concepts that govern TPS and standardized operations have rarely been transferred between environments and have remained largely an automotive sector phenomena. However, the generic principles and TPS frame of reference can be localized to operations where little or no physical conversion takes place. Indeed, the Toyota Motor Corporation has successfully transferred these TPS concepts to auxiliary activities such as warehousing and parts distribution and has begun the process towards 'perfecting' these operations in the same manner that the manufacturing systems have evolved (Womack and Jones, 1996).

---

[6] Material for this section was also provided by Professor Daniel Jones.

Accordingly, the warehouse will exist, as a strategic 'service' point in the supply chain and continue to play an integral role in the dampening of order volatility throughout the different sub-contractors that supply to the warehouse. In the case of the warehouse, the localization of the Toyota Production System principles involves a modification in the terminology adopted, but very little modification of the techniques employed.

Wastes in the Warehouse

In the same manner that Ohno (1988a) developed the seven wastes in the factory environment, Toyota Motor Corporation have modified these wastes for application to their parts distribution operations. These new 'context-specific' wastes include:

1. doing things faster than the necessary pace, creating piles of inventory awaiting transportation to the customer and creating 'peaks' in the work load of employees;
2. unnecessary waiting as materials are not available or obstructed from picking;
3. unnecessary motion and searching for products;
4. conveyance;
5. inappropriate processing;
6. correction routines;
7. unnecessary inventory.

These 'wastes' reflect, once again, the physical, procedural and structural excesses that serve to add costs to the warehouse operation but add no value to the customer. To counter these sources of inefficiency the principles of the Just In Time (JIT) system are applied to the material flow within the warehouse. Central to this logic is the 'pull' demand from the customer, serving to trigger the distribution of that part, and the replenishment of the part for the warehouse.

Thus, material flows rather than stagnates through the use of batch ordering and infrequent shipments to the customer. The JIT distribution system, with each warehouse serving a local market, creates a 'stable' logistics route, serviced by low stocks, and offering high efficiency through the combination of customer demand, volume and speed. To operate such a system, the warehouse and distribution system are enveloped with 'control' standards in the same manner that the manufacturing processes are managed. Some of the major differences in the logic and approach taken by the Toyota JIT distribution system and the traditional system are shown in Table 8.2.

TABLE 8.2 Approaches to the Warehouse

Standard Activity	Traditional Warehousing Approach	Lean and Just In Time Approach
Ordering	Large batch ordering	Small batch ordering with frequent delivery
Inventory Policy	Large inventory creating customer service	Low inventory giving customer service and less space (safety)
Inventory Use	Duplication of stocks at each level in the distribution system	Minimal stock and limited duplication for customer service
Volatility of System	Efficient operations but large fluctuations in work loads for the individual and site	Small fluctuations in demand for the site and stable operations
Equipment Specification	Equipment in the warehouse is purchased for maximum work load requirements	Equipment purchases are based on level utilization
Shipments to Customers	Regular shipments based on post code and minimum orders	Very frequent shipments based on fixed routing. No constraints.
Operational Improvement	Operations are difficult to improve	Operations are easy to improve through procedures
Optimization Technique	Individual optimization of each activity	Optimization of the entire flow in the warehouse
Inventory Locations	Warehouse locations are electronic and random	Warehouse locations are manual and fixed
Picking and Put Away Routines	Routings and work load are determined by the computer	Work load and routings are stable and fixed

Explaining the Standardized Process of Distribution Control

To understand how Toyota applies standards to the operations of the warehouse, it is necessary to understand the activities undertaken by the warehouse operations at the tactical level. These activities can be broken into *three* key activities: receiving materials; storing them; and despatching them to meet customer orders. The following section of this chapter will analyze these activities separately so as to provide the reader with an understanding of the manner in which a 'lean warehouse' operates, but it should be noted that these activities are concurrent in actual practice.

1. Receiving Materials: Smoothing the Inbound Flow

The first activity that is undertaken by the warehouse management, using standard operations, is the receipt of products from the many 'channels' in the supply chain. The management analysis of the 'deliveries' is commenced on the evening before the physical arrival of the products into the facility and serves to identify the requirements for the 'unloading' and 'sorting' personnel to be assigned at the site. These personnel conduct a vital role in ensuring that products are 'put away' quickly and can be 'sold' whenever an order is taken by the warehouse. To enable a balanced 'flow' of labour and materials, these deliveries follow a standard pattern so that vehicles are received at set times during the day to avoid 'peaks' and 'troughs' in the operations at the site. These 'delivery slots' serve to balance effort and discipline the 'pace' of work at the site. Once the delivery profile is known and 'levelled', labour is assigned to the activities throughout the day, using simple manual planning boards which provide a visual display of all the activities undertaken by all employees during the working day (Figure 8.1).

When the vehicle arrives on site, at its fixed time, the relevant employee also arrives and begins to 'off-load' products using a standard method. This standard is a pre-sorting activity where the contents of the vehicle are placed on the floor according to their physical characteristics (this activity is important because the warehouse is divided into zones that reflect the product characteristics). The categories of materials are 'large', 'medium' and 'small', and also 'free pass' or 'emergency' items. Then, in strict accordance to standards, the 'free pass' materials – clearly labelled as 'urgent' items – are handled immediately, which answers the need to bypass the storage activity and satisfy the customer immediately by placing these items on the next available outbound despatch vehicle.

2. Put Away and Storage

The remaining materials, sorted by size, are put away using a standardized product-defined 'zone' system. The pre-sorted materials are then unpacked and placed onto materials-handling carts in such a manner that a cart holds a known number of 'put away' items that should take a standard time to complete each 'put away' cycle. The cycle itself is defined by the zone to which these products are destined. The use of the standard-

FIGURE 8.1 The Receiving Planning Board

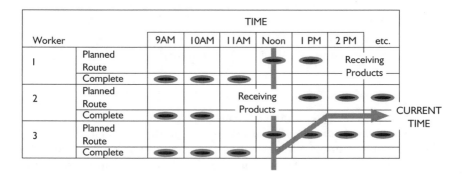

ized time for each cycle of put-away is equivalent to a machine cycle time and once again is predetermined. In this manner, the small-sized parts may take 15 minutes to put away 25 items, the medium parts may take 15 minutes to put away 18 items and 10 large items may take 15 minutes. These times are fixed planning slots and allow warehouse personnel to return to the point of receiving products at frequent and staggered intervals.

The physical routings for these products (to and from their zones) is also predetermined to ensure that the most efficient route is taken and, to cement the system, the 'andon' approach is also employed. However, instead of an illuminated board, the warehouse system uses a planning board and magnetic disks to display the number of cycles completed for each worker (Figure 8.1). Using these, the current time can be compared in a visual manner against the progress of 'putting away' products and therefore the 'pace' of the operation can be determined in the same way as *takt* time is calculated.

The team leaders in the warehouse are therefore involved in the calculation of *takt* time, in this case by taking the number of 'inbound' products and dividing by the working day to result in the 'pace'. As an illustration, this may require a 'put away' cycle every twenty minutes for small items – with a standard cycle for one person being only fifteen minutes – so the small zone area will be serviced by one employee throughout the working day.

To ensure that the warehouse 'put away' process is under control, and that the computerized sales-order processing system is updated quickly, the products entering the warehouse each display a tag containing all the relevant information (in a similar manner to the *kanban* cards). Once the sorting activity has taken place, these tags are removed and sent to be inputted to the computer as 'available for picking'. The small and frequent cycles of 'put away' activity thus prevent the situation of 'no sales' that results from products being delayed at the sorting area. As each cart is readied, the warehouse staff arrive from the last cycle, leave an empty cart for filling and take a full one (updating the control board by moving the magnetic disk from 'planned' to 'completed'). At some stage during the day, the sorting staff will have completed all the inbound loads and move to another operation in the warehouse, and so the product is 'flowed' to the storage point.

Visual management techniques are also used within the storage zones of the warehouse itself.

3. In-Warehouse Controls

Visual management techniques are also used within the storage zones of the warehouse itself, and the discipline of standards is maintained as a means of determining 'abnormality' instantaneously. The racks and the routes in the zones are often colour-coded with signs that are offset at the end of each aisle to make navigation easier. The logic of the warehouse layout is also standardized, so that the zone itself is set with 'one product per position' and the position of the stocks is determined by the frequency of sales. Ends-of-aisle racks are designated to hold the fastest moving stock to avoid picking cycles with long travel distances. Within each aisle a further logic is used which relates to the volume of 'medium selling' items, but this time based on the physical dimensions of the product. Slightly larger and bulkier items are placed within safe and ergonomic positions (typically at lower levels of the racking).

Under the TPS logic, no materials should be stored on the top position of any rack, as this is used to signal abnormalities discovered by the teams – such as incorrect products, products that have not 'moved' for quite a while, or over-flow materials. The positioning of a product at this level in the racks allows the team leader to begin to problem-solve during routine cycles through the store. The rare occasion when a product is close to being 'out of stock' is also captured by the 'put away' and 'picking teams' through the use of a card system (the similar principle to a 'safety stock' *kanban*) which is held at each stock point and used to trigger a quick response and problem-solving activities in the warehouse. Empty locations are monitored strictly and continuously, since these are also abnormalities and represent 'failures' in the system.

4. Despatch and Customer Service

The despatch operations of the warehouse have many similarities with those of the in-bound receiving process. The initial 'trigger' for the movement of materials from the warehouse is the receipt of a customer order and, in the case of Toyota, this is the dealer order requesting parts for car services and less routine appointments in the workshops. The primary standard activities which begins the process of 'pulling' materials is therefore unseen by the warehouse staff, but is nonetheless a part of the overall standardized system of operations.

In the Toyota dealer system, very low, and, typically, 'no parts' inventory is held at the actual dealership (as a result of the efficiency and reliability of the parts distribution system). In the dealership there is a visual progress board showing the appointments placed by customers and the work required – in the same manner that supplier vehicles are booked into the warehouse standardized 'slots'. These boards trigger the ordering of the service parts required to complete the work on the customer's vehicle. For servicing and pre-diagnosed remedial work all the relevant parts have been predetermined, leaving only 'discovered' defects as the chance 'order' variable for the system. Thus, the dealer can order a 'kit' of parts to complete the work, within a defined time standard, and to the highest level of customer service.

The appointment board serves a very important purpose, it is the central processing unit for the information exchanged with the warehouse and the orders placed upon it. The visual display of customer orders allows the requests for materials to be sequenced 'just in time' for the consumption by the technicians at the work bay. To achieve this level of customer service, the shipments from the warehouse follow a fixed and regular 'slot time' for each dealer (along a fixed route along which a number of dealers are serviced before the vehicle returns to the warehouse and begins its next route at a later time during the day). The constant deliveries of materials, or opportunities to receive parts from the warehouse, has the consequence that no materials need to be stored at the dealer's and all parts can be ordered 'just before' they are actually required. The planning board allows this information to be shipped to the warehouse in aggregate form and also allows for the products to be picked and marshalled for shipment by the warehouse when the parts are needed.

The level of precision and reliability offered by the despatch operations of the warehouse creates stability for the dealers and 'standards' of 'normality' to be applied (the translation of customer service for the warehouse). The placement of orders is subject to 'cut-off' times (which vary between the different logistics routes to avoid 'peaks' or activities at the warehouse). To illustrate this process, all parts that are required for the noon delivery at the dealer must be placed by ten o'clock in the morning and, say, by noon for the two o'clock delivery slot, and so on throughout the day. These orders are received and processed electronically (although this automation evolved from a manual system) through direct computer-to-computer data transfer. The 'speed' advantages of rapid processing is exploited by the warehouse and used to level the despatch and picking effort required at the warehouse, and the aggregate effect of small and frequent ordering by all dealers is absorbed by modifying the number of personnel involved in the picking and marshalling zones.

The system requires the staggering of order cut-off points for each different delivery route (the route being a collection of dealers) and serves to level the demand placed on the warehouse. For example, route 'A' may be set at 9am, 11am, 1pm and 3pm for despatch, whilst route 'B' commences at 9:45am, 11:45am, 1:45pm and 3:45pm and so on throughout the different delivery routes. The 'orders' therefore flow into the warehouse to create a 'smooth' and even 'demand'. On receipt of the orders they are sorted into standard batch cycles for the 'picking' staff to collect, and the cycles begin in the same manner as those products which are received. Any emergency orders are, once again, the priority for the picking operators and these are treated as special items for immediate despatch. The concept of *takt* time also applies to this area of the warehouse and requires the levelling of activities by the team leaders (once again using the monthly volume of orders and quantities to estimate the typical rates as a 'directional measure' of anticipated activity required from the warehouse). Inevitably, the time required (as a cycle) to meet the 'picking routines' tends to be smaller than those for 'put away' activities and the actual 'picking' notes are generated by the computer system.

The 'route cards' generated by the computer system conform to the same procedures as the inbound materials procedures and so the cards are levelled through the use of the 'planning board'. This planning board is used to offset the collection of all materials ready for the fixed despatch 'slot' of the vehicle and also as a measure of whether the 'picking activities' are at the right 'pace' to meet demand. The pickers select a cart and conduct a 'fixed cycle' of the storage zones before returning to the sorting area. On their return, the 'picking' progress control board is then updated, by moving the magnetic disk to show that the cycle has been completed and the next set of instructions are taken.

The levelling of the picking operations is a standard approach that allows the human element of the operations to be 'flexed' as a means of accommodating the customer demand, the cycles for products being set at no more than ten minutes. With a prevailing *takt* time of 2 minutes there is a conflict and the warehouse is too slow to respond – given the use of a single picking employee – so the system requires five employees to meet the demand. However, this is only one element of the system; after picking comes the checking and sorting of work (a standard time of 6 minutes) and therefore three people are required here to meet the *takt* time of 2 minutes. Within the standard cycle times there is also an element for in-operation checking within almost all tasks.

Once the products have been picked, using the standardized cycles, they are checked and sorted before being moved to the despatch area (the gate at which the products will be shipped). The products are now authorized to be shipped and the durable containers are marshalled in reverse order onto the truck (so that the products closest to the unloading doors of the vehicle represent the first dealer, and so on). The vehicle then arrives and is loaded within predetermined times that are monitored continuously to ensure that improvements are not missed in vehicle loading operations, and the vehicle is despatched.

The 'milk-round' of dealers levels movements and maintains a high level of vehicle loading utilization as well as customer service. For the dealer, the frequency of shipment means that the quantity of products delivered in any one 'drop' is small and can be handled by dealer staff rather than requiring a delay to be incurred before materials handling equipment can be found. The products received are sent directly to the workshop without stopping the continuous process of ordering and receiving parts throughout the entire supply chain.

The warehouse is also enveloped within the 'culture' of continuous improvements and the standard operations create the ability to correct permanently abnormalities as they are discovered. The warehouse is therefore a strategic position in the supply chain that allows products to flow through the distribution channel to yield the highest levels of customer service, but also to maintain an improvement drive to increase these levels continuously and support the dealers in attracting and maintaining a satisfied vehicle consumer for life.

Standard Operations: The Conclusions

The modern standardized production systems and the traditional business systems share a common concern – that is, the development of the 'one best way' to add value. Under the traditional system, this was the prerogative of the industrial engineer and an element of the job-planning process. Under TPS, the process is more flexible, less well-planned, and 'emergent' from the intellectual capabilities of employees rather than specialists. Thus, the improvement of factory performance results from the efforts of all employees rather than a management elite. The decentralization of decision-making, far from creating systematic soldiering, serves as the catalyst for self-regulation and meaningful empowerment.

The improvement of factory performance results from the efforts of all employees rather than a management elite.

Self-regulation itself is determined by the ability of employees to distinguish between the 'normality' and 'abnormality' of any given process and react to, address, or improve such situations. To this extent, the codification of the production system is also the codification of knowledge and the application of standardized activities is the cement that binds together high productivity and high quality operations. The standards that govern the operations of the business also provide an important frame of reference and the ability to select the appropriate problem-solving tools and techniques to address exposed and perceived imbalances, which creates a problem-solving activity that is responsive (reactive) and predictive (proactive) in nature.

The capacity to operate within a 'self-regulating' system at the business and task level reinforces the ability of the site to create the highest levels of customer service and therefore profitability by ensuring that the quality and delivery of parts is maximized (and as a result the decline of operational costs). To this extent, the use of standards is the only shared element that unites the early 'classical' management theories and the TPS concept. Within the early systems, the target for the development of standards was the processing 'speed' of the individual (known as job standards), regardless of the pace required by the holistic factory system, whereas the modern concern is for the pace of the system, regardless of the natural characteristics that allows one person to work faster than another. Instead, in the modern approach, the sub-optimization of the factory and the need to control this is recognized and is the origin of continuous improvement efforts by the operational teams. Under the classical systems, sub-optimization was greeted with punitive actions against the individual and the worker was excluded from any form of self-management, yet under the TPS system the worker is instrumental in the development of the company and suggestions from one element of the company can be translated into standards in another quickly and with immediate benefit.

The ability to determine 'abnormality' on a company-wide basis is therefore the power of operational systems such as TPS. In the manufacturing divisions the production process is treated as a system and not as a laboratory, as is the warehouse. These areas serve only one purpose, which is to optimize value for the customer and to create the highest levels of customer service possible.

PART THREE

Thinking Strategically About Supply

CHAPTER 9

The Management of Supply as a Strategic Process[1]

Overview

This chapter will discuss how purchasing can evolve from a tactical, re-active function towards a proactive process. The research developed a model to allow firms to benchmark their activities against a range of attributes. The model highlights what firms need to do in order to enhance their strategic position. Ironically, the key issue that arose from the research was that Purchasing needs to become better at selling – internally – in order to raise its profile and give it the recognition that the respondents felt it deserved.

> *Purchasing needs to become better at selling.*

The research was grounded in existing literature on the subject of strategic sourcing, and on existing models, specifically the Reck and Long (1988) positioning model. The model was tested on a range of sponsor companies for validity and applicability.

Respondents found the model helpful in benchmarking their current levels of performance and also in enabling them to formulate a strategy for the further development of the supply process.

The Literature Review

The need for purchasing to become more strategic has been called for by academics for around twenty years. However, it is only since the begin-ning of the 1990s that firms have taken this message seriously. The main

---

[1] Paul Cousins was the principal researcher and Donna Marshall the research officer for this chapter.

drive for this change was the worldwide recession of the late 1980s. Firms were unable to pass increased costs (due to, for example, either production inefficiencies and/or market trends) on to the final consumer. They either had to absorb the costs and therefore become less profitable or find other ways of reducing costs; the supply chain became the obvious target – focus on the business inputs.

During the late 1980s and onwards, companies also became fixated with implementing the 'Japanese' approach: concepts such as Just-In-Time (Schonberger, 1986), Lean Production (Womack *et al.*, 1990; Womack and Jones, 1996), Lean Supply (Lamming, 1993) and Total Quality Management were terms used in everyday parlance. Firms found that the problem was not a lack of concepts, but a naivety regarding implementation (Steudel and Desruelle, 1992). Furthermore, firms did not understand how to put these approaches into an overall strategic context. The development of the partnership approach and the drive to reduce cost and add greater value has led firms to reconsider the role of the purchasing department itself. Purchasing was traditionally seen as a service department performing no real 'strategic' role (Caddick and Dale, 1987). In fact, in most production organizations purchasing departments have traditionally reported directly to the Production Director. According to Ellram and Carr (1994: p. 13) the purchasing function is moving from a 'passive' or reactive role to a strategic role. Numerous studies have been conducted on the strategic importance of purchasing and supply to the organization, ranging from Farmer (1972, 1981), and Van Weele (1984) to Cavinato (1987). These studies have tended to be conceptual (Speckman, 1989; Burt and Soukup, 1985). However, recent studies have exhibited a large amount of empirical evidence supporting the argument that purchasing should be viewed as a strategic function (Laneros and Monczka, 1989; Carlson, 1990; St John and Young, 1991; Hines, 1994; Nishiguchi, 1994). These various studies can be summarized as shown in Table 9.1.

Farmer (1981) conducted longitudinal empirical research by observing strategy development in large companies over a period of ten years. The aim of his research was to increase the awareness of some of the problems involved in the development of strategy. His main findings were that few organizations involved purchasing in the strategic decision-making policy of the firm.

Speckman (1989: p. 99) concluded by stating that:

> Corporate managers can no longer afford to develop strategic alternatives that are based primarily on product/market considerations. [Supply issues must be considered, and purchasing strategies] must conform to the strategic plans of the firm and reflect consideration for the firm's present and future competitive posture.

Other authors (including Monczka, 1992) have developed various frame-

TABLE 9.1 Review of Strategic Purchasing Literature[2]

Author(s)	Methodology	Major Findings
Reck and Long (1988)	empirical	Methodology for understanding the level of strategic attainment of purchasing – Four-phase model.
Caddick and Dale (1987)	empirical – case study	Purchasing must develop strategies and link purchasing and corporate strategy
Spekman (1989)	conceptual	Purchasing needs to be integrated into corporate strategy. First, purchasing must think and develop strategically.
Burt and Soukup (1985)	conceptual	Purchasing can have an impact on achieving success in new product development if purchasing is involved early in the new product development process.
Laneros and Monczka (1989)	empirical – interviews	Purchasing can support the firm's strategic positioning using cooperative buyer–seller relationships.
Carlson (1990)	empirical – case study	Purchasing strategy is important to product development and long-term goals of the firm.
St John and Young (1991)	empirical – survey questionnaire	Purchasing, production, and production planning managers agree on long-range strategy. However, their daily activities are inconsistent with the long-range strategic plan.
Lamming (1993)	empirical	Four-phase model of supply. The concepts of lean–supply – post Japanese model.
Saunders (1994)	conceptual	Purchasing is no longer a service function. A discussion of practical approaches for strategic purchasing.
Macbeth and Ferguson (1994)	empirical – case study	Strategic relationship assessment and implementation. Development of internal and external relationships.
Burt and Doyle (1994)	conceptual	Purchasing should become part of the *keiretsu* culture. Implementation of the Japanese *keiretsu* approach to the supply chain activities of firms.
Hines (1994)	empirical – case study and interview	Strategic rationalization of the supply chain – particularly concerned with the development and application of Japanese supplier association management techniques on UK supply chains.
Nishiguchi (1994)	empirical – case study and interview	Study of Japanese coordination of the supply chain for competitive advantage.

works for the evaluation and implementation of strategic purchasing decisions. Reck and Long (1988) provide a four-stage development model of purchasing to evolve into a strategic function (see Table 9.2).

[2] Adapted from Ellram and Carr (1994).

TABLE 9.2 The Four Stages of Purchasing Development[3]

STAGE I	In the *passive stage*, purchasing normally begins as a reaction to requests from the other departments. Many of purchasing's legitimate activities are handled by other functions outside purchasing.
STAGE II	In the *independent stage*, purchasing departments spend considerable time attempting to professionalize the purchasing function by introducing such things as computerized information systems, formalized supplier programs, and communication links with the technical function.
STAGE III	In the *supportive stage*, purchasing departments are viewed by top management as essential business functions. Purchasing is expected to support and strengthen the firm's competitive advantage by providing timely information to all departments in the firm about potential changes in the price and availability of materials, which may impact the firm's strategic goals.
STAGE IV	In the *integrative stage*, the firm's competitive success rests significantly on the capabilities of the purchasing department's personnel. Purchasing's role within the firm changes from facilitator to functional peer. This development process must be implemented and guided by management over a period of time.

Ellram and Carr (1994: p. 17) pointed out that:

It is critical to understand that there is a difference between *purchasing strategy* and purchasing performing as a *strategic function* ... When purchasing is viewed as a strategic function, it is included as a key decision-maker and participant in the firms' strategic planning process ... In addition, purchasing will participate in strategy formulation and suggest ways that the purchasing function can help support and enhance the firm's strategic success.

It is clear from this literature that the role that purchasing plays within the organization is now changing: purchasing as a function is becoming more strategic with smaller numbers of highly qualified buyers, decentralized control of non-value-adding items, and greater planning activity horizons.[4] Currently, both academics and practitioners are debating the very nature of what constitutes the discipline of purchasing and supply, and indeed whether the title of 'purchasing and supply' is sufficient to describe what purchasing people will be doing in the future. Lamming notes that:

[3] Source: Robert F. Reck and Brian G. Long, 'Purchasing: A Competitive Weapon,' *Journal of Purchasing and Materials Management*, Fall 1988, vol. 24, no. 3.

[4] See footnote 3.

It is the matter of a title for the discipline. 'Purchasing and Supply' is relevant to some practitioners but not to others. 'Procurement' is favoured by some, 'Buying' by others. These arguments may almost be dismissed as academic niceties.

... If the new discipline is to establish a new strategic role for purchasing and supply perhaps an entirely new name is necessary?[5]

In addition to this change, the educational and demographic structure of the purchasing department is also changing. Purchasing personnel are now better qualified and more professional in their outlook and approach to the task.

Furthermore, the same research shows that the structure of the function is also changing. The size of purchasing departments has reduced significantly from an average of between 50 and 60 buying personnel (in medium to large organizations) in 1980, to approximately 15 in 1993. This change is often combined with a decentralized purchasing strategy approach, where strategically important contracts are centralized at headquarters, and non-strategic important procurement is devolved to the various satellite plants and divisions. As one purchasing director puts it:

> *Purchasing personnel are now better qualified and more professional in their outlook and approach to the task.*

At our company we only have ten buyers for the entire business, and in fact they are not called buyers, they are called 'Purchasing Programmes Managers'. They are all qualified to at least degree standard, and it is their job to oversee strategic policy making decisions for all purchases within the business ... Day to day procurement is handled by administrators at plant level, who 'call off' from blanket five year contracts which have been negotiated by us. We only handle contracts of a value greater than £125,000 ...[6]

In 'Improving Purchase Performance', Syson (1992) suggested that the most fundamental factor in influencing the purchasing strategy is the focus of the department. He believes it is from this starting point that the manager can then begin to evaluate the purchasing department. Similarly to Reck and Long's development stages, Syson believes that by having a different organizational view (or focus), the purchasing department will develop according to criticality of materials, and the attitude of top management towards purchasing (see Table 9.3 for stages of development).

Syson suggests that the role of purchasing is changing owing to the changing business environment. With the move from large-scale production to differentiation becoming the principal competitive thrust, so must

[5] PSERG Conference 9–10 April, 1992.

[6] Andrew Wilson, British Sugar, Peterborough, October, 1993.

TABLE 9.3   Purchase Focus

Focus Key Element	Clerical Procedures	Transactional Systems	Commercial Price/quality /delivery	Logistics Integration	Strategic Sustainable competitive advantage
Evolutionary	Reactive and service- driven				Proactive and market- driven
Orientation	Efficiency				Effectiveness

SOURCE: Syson (1992: p. xi).

the purchasing department be moulded according to the strategy of the business.

It is important to note that such strategic changes also cause distinct managerial problems. As Quinn and Mintzberg (1988) note, strategic movements take place in a step-by-step manner or, as they term it, 'logical incrementalism'. These stages take a good deal of time and must be managed carefully. It is therefore vitally important when considering the implementation of any new strategy that the internal infrastructure is firmly in place. This concerns both the internal resources, such as the correctly qualified personnel, and also the relevant management systems and philosophies. This thinking led Cousins (1998) to develop a four-phase approach to supply strategy formulation, see Figure 9.1. The model argues that you are only as good as the bottom box.

FIGURE 9.1   Strategic Alignment Model

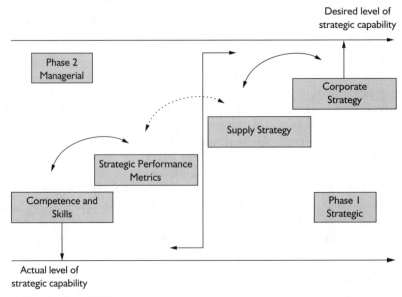

SOURCE: Cousins (1997).

The objective of the model is that a firm must have alignment of the four main mechanisms, that is: Corporate Strategy; Supply Strategy; Performance Measures (both internal and external); and finally Skill and Competence Sets. Without alignment, firms will not manage to effect any change. The principal driver in the model is the level of skills and competences of the individuals. If the appropriate skills are not in place the organization will not be able to move forward. In turn, these must be motivated with the appropriate measurement systems, which should align with the supply and corporate strategies. While this sounds conceptually very simple, the reality of the situation is that a great many purchasing functions have little perception of the overall corporate strategy, little to no development of supply strategy, unitary performance measures and a haphazard approach to skill and competence development (Cousins, 1999). With these findings in mind, this research project went on to generate a strategic transition model for the development of purchasing.

The Strategic Transition Model

The Transition model was based on research with ten of the Supply Chain Development Programme's sponsor companies. These companies were chosen from a wide range of sectors covering utilities, public sector, retail, engineering and chemicals. A series of focus groups and individual interview sessions were organized. The purpose of these was to support the findings from the literature and to test, iterate and validate the transition model so that a useable and realistic framework could be developed. Figure 9.2 shows the overview of the transition model, which consists of five phases.

FIGURE 9.2 The Transition Model

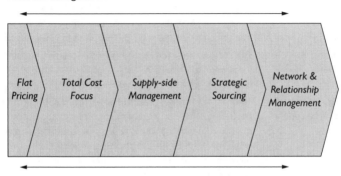

The model shows the movement from a purchasing focus on 'Flat Pricing' at one extreme towards 'Network and Relationship Management' at the other end of the spectrum. Our research clearly indicated that there were five distinct phases: Flat Pricing; Total Cost Focus; Supply-Side Management; Strategic Sourcing; and Network and Relationship Management. Each of these phases has a given output, and a set of characteristics that defines it. We identified nine key elements involved in purchasing strategy: key objectives, supply mechanism, supply structure, strategic approach, why fails, key issues, network structure, performance measurement and purchasing's perception within the organization (see Table 9.4).

TABLE 9.4   Purchasing Assessment Factors

Factor	Definition
Key Objectives	Refers to the main goal of the purchasing functions, i.e. price reduction, cost improvement, relationship development, etc.
Supply Mechanism	Shows how the purchasing function uses its position within the supply chain to achieve the key objectives, such as price leverage, cost transparency, benchmarking, etc.
Supply Structure	Refers to the structure of the supply market: for example, is it multi-sourced, single sourced, dominant supplier, buyers market, etc?
Strategic Approach	This is the focus of the purchasing organization: is it predominantly short-term, fire-fighting and tactical or longer-term, proactive and strategic?
Why Fails	This category was placed in the model as respondents felt that in order to move on to the next phase they needed to understand why their current approach was not sustainable. Reasons for failure could be that the focus of the approach was more on price than on cost, less on quality than on service, and so on.
Key Issues	Refers to common problem areas realized with these strategies, such as skill base requirements, resource development, technology infrastructure, etc.
Network Structure	This category was used to show the types of interfaces that are most prevalent, i.e. buyer–supplier, one-way, or two-way, customer–supplier–customer or indeed, network structure.
Relationship Type	Refers to the dominant relationships within the model such as traditional/adversarial through to long-term, close collaborative.
Performance Measurement	This is a key characteristic; it is essential to have the correct measurement systems in place. Measurement systems refer to internal as well as external measures.
Purchasing's Organization Perception	The final characteristic refers to how the rest of the firm sees purchasing. This is an extremely important factor and one which will directly influence the way in which purchasing can and does interact with the rest of the firm. The higher the perception within the organization, the greater the resource allocation and ability to effect change within the firm.

The factors were then mapped against the overall 'Transition Model'. This produced a matrix, which allows firms to see their relative positioning; the matrix is shown in Table 9.5.

TABLE 9.5   Transition Positioning Matrix

Stages of Excellence	Stage 1	Stage 2	Stage 3	Stage 4	Stage 5
Approach	*Flat Pricing*	*Total Cost Focus*	*Supply-side Management*	*Strategic Sourcing*	*Network & Relationship Management*
Description	Adversarial Tactical Focus on price Transactional	Focus on total cost Distant relationship with suppliers	Focus on supply service package Develop closer Relationships with suppliers	Cooperative Strategic focus on supply Commitment to single/few suppliers	Focus on supply, demand and mutual development Total commitment
Key Objectives	Contain Price	Contain cost over total product life	To gain from suppliers their specialist expertise and skills	Work jointly with suppliers to increase value in supply chain	Improve total understanding Mutual network development
Supply Mechanism	Volume leverage	Cost leverage	Total service leverage Benchmarking Supplier development	Leverage through cooperation	Network leverage
Supply Structure	Multi-supply Multi-relationship	Multi-supply Multi-relationship	Fewer suppliers	Single/few key suppliers	Network of key single supplier
Strategic Approach	Tactical	Tactical	Moving from tactical to strategic	Strategic	Strategic
Why Fails	Focus on price not cost	Focus on cost not on quality and service	Resistance or failure to share relevant information with suppliers Focus on competition not cooperation	Focus on cooperation not involvement	Too expensive Need high level of trust/dependency
Key Issues	Low skills Low information Low level decision-making	Relatively low-skilled Information-based	Less purchasing but greater 'management' skills required Greater information flow between firms	High level of information flow between firms High level of commitment	Highly skilled Complete information openness High level/complex decision-making
Network Structure	Buyer-competitive suppliers	Buyer-selected suppliers	Buyer and first and second tier suppliers	Supply chain	Network of relationships
Relationship Type	Adversarial	Distant	Involved	Committed	Trust
Performance Measures	Basic measurements based on price differences from year before	1. Process activity mapping 2. Production variety matrix 3. Decision point analysis 4. Cost transparency	1. Communications analysis 2. Supplier development matrix 3. Quality function deployment	1. Supply chain response matrix 2. Quality filter mapping 3. Performance measurement of purchasing	1. Value stream mapping 2. Advanced communications analysis
Purchasing's Organization Perception	*Passive*	*Supportive*	*Independent*	*Integrative*	*Differentiator*

Application of the Transition Model

In designing the model we identified three clear implementation stages: assessment; strategy development; and benchmarking. These are shown in Table 9.6.

Our research clearly showed that a generic benchmarking approach for the purchasing function would have been impossible. We found that the level of strategic focus was contingent upon the types of goods or services being purchased, i.e. commodity vs. specialized; and the relationship strategy being followed, i.e. traditional vs. collaborative. Therefore, in order for firms to be able to focus on strategic development they must first assess the types of goods that they purchase. This can be achieved by using the Kraljic (1983) matrix which positions against value/cost and market exposure.

> *Therefore, in order for firms to be able to focus on strategic development they must first assess the types of goods that they purchase.*

Each of these quadrants will require a level of strategic focus. For example, 'Tactical Acquisition' will need a Stage 1 level of maturity, whereas 'Strategic Critical', will require Level 4 or 5 in our 5-stage Transition Model. The various quadrants and stages are mapped in Figure 9.3.

Stage 1. Assessment

Stage 1 requires an assessment of the current resource capabilities and the strategic profile of the purchasing function within the organization against the commodity or service grouping. The purchasing function will need to examine systematically each of the assessment criteria and position themselves against them. This process will produce a profile effect, as shown in the example in Figure 9.4.

The respondents from this company said that they believed, according to the Kraljic matrix, that the IT purchasing activity would be positioned in the bottom right quadrant, with a low supply market complexity

TABLE 9.6 Stages of Implementation of the Transition Model

Stage	Purpose	Description
1	Assessment	The purchasing organization should benchmark where it currently sees itself against the characteristics and criteria listed within the model
2	Strategy Development	Purchasing should consider where it wants to be and examine the gaps in its approach *vis-à-vis* what the model is telling them. They should then develop a strategy to take the function forward
3	Benchmarking	The final stage is to use the model to review current progress and see how the function is developing

FIGURE 9.3   Assessment Matrix

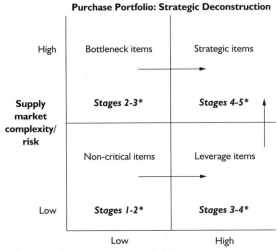

Purchase Portfolio: Strategic Deconstruction

NOTE: *From the Transition Model.
SOURCE: Adapted from Kraljic (1983).

FIGURE 9.4   Example of Purchasing Profile for IT Purchasing at a UK Pharmaceutical Company

Stages of Excellence	Stage 1	Stage 2	Stage 3	Stage 4	Stage 5
Approach	*Flat Pricing*	*Total Cost Focus*	*Supply-Side Management*	*Strategic Sourcing*	*Network & Relationship Management*
Description				X	
Key Objectives			X		
Supply Mechanism		X			
Supply Structure				X	
Strategic Approach			X		
Why Fails			X		
Key Issues			X		
Network Structure			X		
Relationship Type			X		
Performance Measures	X				
Purchasing's Organization Perception			X		

but a high impact on value added. Therefore, they should be aiming for a focus of Level 3 moving to Level 4. The majority of the factors were located in Level 3 with notable exceptions – supply mechanism which was located in Level 2, and 'performance measurement' which was located in Level 1. The profile gave the respondents a sense that the purchasing of IT had to be changed and adapted to reach the required level. Also, it was agreed that Stage 4 would be the optimal level to be reached and those factors which were situated in Stage 3 could be improved upon in order to reach the stage where IT products and services would be strategically sourced.

Stage 2. Strategy Development

The purchasing function needs to understand the overall goals and objectives of the organization, which can then be fed into the overall supply strategy. The strategy is then broken down into the various sourcing groups within the Kraljic matrix. For example, if the overall view of the purchasing activity is of a strategic sourcing focus, the factors which are not Level 3 or above need to be improved. There has to be a clear strategy, with resources allocated against the factor which needs the most attention. In the case of the pharmaceutical company, it was decided that performance measurement was in need of the most improvement, and therefore the management of this activity could deal with it effectively and did not waste time and energy on the factors that had achieved the desired level.

Stage 3. Benchmarking

The tool that was developed had to be uniform enough to enable the benchmarking of all activities within the purchasing department. This enables managers to focus their attention on the activities that are out of alignment with the strategic focus and provides a method for reaching a desired state for each of the activities. It could also provide a tool for persuading senior management of more efficient allocation of resources where it was needed most.

Conclusion

The research concluded that it would be impossible to give an overall strategic viewpoint, as this was dependent upon the product or service being purchased. Although the current trend is towards increased dependency on fewer suppliers, which implies that sourcing groups will tend towards a strategic role, it was found that certain purchasing activities will never be perceived as strategic. Activities which have low added value and low market uncertainty would therefore be better off competitively supplied, as time would be wasted on the management and building of closer supplier relationships.

Positioning purchasing on the 'Transition Model' provided motivation for change, as was shown in Figure 9.4. This type of benchmarking creates a tool for managers to improve the effectiveness of purchasing activities. This leads to the improvement of the overall focus of the purchasing department and also can improve the organization's perception of the function. Once activities have been positioned and assessed against the 'Transition Model', managers are then able to allocate time and resources most effectively to the activities under their control.

The use of the 'Transition Model' allows purchasing managers to understand clearly how the management of the purchasing activities needs to be changed, how resources can be distributed most effectively and can adjust the profile of the department within the organization.

CHAPTER 10

Purchasing in Complex Environments: Understanding Multi-Site Purchasing[1]

Introduction

The typical 'rule of thumb' within practitioner circles is that the purchasing department controls up to 80 per cent of the manufacturing costs (the purchased element) of products, yet operates with only 1 per cent of the employee headcount of the company. The deployment of human resources within the enterprise in this manner may seem surprising and somewhat inappropriate given the strong relationship between the performance of the purchasing department and the ability of the enterprise to convert products and services in a timely and cost-effective manner. However decades of 'calls' for the strategic elevation of the purchasing department by academics, professional bodies and purchasers themselves have fallen upon 'stony ground' and few companies have recognized the importance of supply chain management and positioned a purchasing representative at board level. Instead, the boards of directors in the public as well as the private sector remain dominated by marketing and financial professionals.

The boards of directors in the public as well as the private sector remain dominated by marketing and financial professionals.

The corporate context within which the purchasing department is set

---

[1] Prepared by Nick Rich and Owen Jones. The research scope, field work and source materials from which this paper is drawn was prepared by Mr Owen Jones. At the time of preparing this chapter, Owen and his wife Fiona were spending their first few days together following the arrival of their daughter Lawri. Owen must therefore accept full credit for this work and any omissions and mistakes are the result of the co-author.

is 'professional' in nature and this 'professionalism' is encapsulated within a language that reflects the 'customer' or the 'consumer' as opposed to the network of suppliers which must be brought together to add value and create customer service. As such, the strategic level of the business is neither supportive nor sufficiently 'externally focused' to understand and integrate the 'input' supplies part of the customer service equation (Stuart, 1996). In this respect, 'calls' for the elevation of the purchasing department, set in the specific 'language' of the purchasing profession and not in the commercial logic of 'return on investment' or 'market share', offer little credibility to the current 'power elite' at the board level. The justification for the integration of the 'reverse' market or supply chain must therefore originate from a proven performance, and a direct and unequivocal relationship between improved supplier performance and the trading position of the enterprise. For most companies with formalized administrative structures, this route represents a difficult blend of tasks involving direct attempts to influence the behaviour and perceptions of other managers in the business whilst adjusting the policies, role and structure of the purchasing department itself.

This chapter analyzes the role and structure of the purchasing department within the context of multi-site operations. These operations represent one of the most complex purchasing 'strategy and structure' puzzles involving the need to control and coordinate the efforts of a comparatively small number of purchasing staff in parallel with the need to extend these management policies between different and geographically separated operations. The objective of this chapter is to provide an analysis of the problems facing professional purchasing managers within such a complex environment and to create an overview of the types of activity that must be developed as a means of supporting performance improvement as well as elevation.

The Objectives of the Supply Chain Development Programme Research

The Supply Chain Development Programme of research involved many industrial sponsors that may be described as 'multi-site' purchasing operations, as well as organizations which were not sponsors but fell within the definition of the research scope or were perceived as 'highly performing' purchasing departments. Many of these sponsors and 'associate' organizations operated elongated or multi-site purchasing structures often with an international network of sites. The motivation for the research is encapsulated in the research objective which was 'to develop methods for identifying the optimum allocation of purchasing resources and competencies within multi site organisations in order to ensure the maximisation of the purchasing activity's contribution to business processes' (Jones, 1997).

The research team also investigated the tension between competing views relating to the strategy and structure of the purchasing department (and procurement activities) within these sites to establish the external validity of transferring approaches between different organizations and cultures. This chapter will focus on the general findings of the research project that relate to the management of multi-site purchasing as a means of supporting the corporate initiatives of each business as opposed to the detailed analysis of contextual issues which are specific to each company and its unique operating environment.

The research field work, employing a case study approach, included both formal individual interviews, panel interviews and exercises,[2] the 'diary' method, and observational techniques. The programme extended over a period of one calendar year. The companies involved with this research exercise, of which there were six active collaborators, were drawn from both public and private sector manufacturing and distribution industry segments.

Defining Multi-Site Operations

For the purpose of clarity and to 'ring fence' the research project boundaries, the term 'multi-site purchasing' has been adopted. This term can be defined as the management of purchasing activities within an organization that take place at different geographical locations. According to Jones (1997), 'these locations may be a few miles apart, a few hundred yards apart, or be in different continents'. The second dimension which relates to this 'definition' is that the term is equally applied to purchasing activities that are 'conducted at different levels within the organisation, for example at the operational and corporate level' (Jones, 1997) and as such includes an analysis of the centralization and/or decentralization of decisions and authority relating to purchasing.

> *'Multi-site purchasing' can be defined as the management of purchasing activities within an organization that take place at different geographical locations.*

The Constraints of Multi-Site Purchasing Operations

The problems associated with multi-site purchasing operations can be divided into two key groups of constraints; those that relate to 'internal' issues that affect the manager or person accountable for the management of the purchasing function at their specific site (Policy and Control

---

[2] The panel activities included such exercises as 'brown paper' activities, brainstorming, and the evaluation of internal company reports.

issues); and the 'external' constraints that affect the management of the supply base and the management of the 'dispersed' field purchasers (Task and Role issues).

The Major Internal Constraints

The 'internal' constraints include such issues as:

1. The level of representation of 'purchasing' within the organization and, importantly, at the directorial level. For many companies the purchasing department and its responsibilities, are subservient to another functional specialism and the strategies adopted by that department. This 'super-function' tends to be the accountancy function which participates in board-level decision-making whilst supposedly representing the interests of 'purchasing'.

2. The responsibility of the purchasing department in determining the strategies related to the materials, supplies and inputs to the enterprise. This point refers to the integration or 'closeness' of the purchasing manager within the strategic decision-making structures of the business and includes the participation, formalization, communication and review of policies that affect the purchasing and direction of improvement required of 'suppliers'. If the strategy process is dominated by the accountancy function, then the strategic integration refers to the closeness of the purchasing department to the accountancy function.

3. The responsibility of the purchasing department in determining its own measures of operational effectiveness as opposed to having these measures imposed from another source without negotiation.

4. The degree to which the organizational structure and management patterns of behaviour 'de-limit' or 'blur' the formal 'territory' of the purchasing process. In this respect the constraint identifies the extent to which the traditional 'ownership' and 'responsibility' of purchasing tasks and policies exist and to what extent these roles have become eroded by cross-functional management. Within this scenario is the dependency and performance measurement of the purchasing department on the actions of personnel within other functional specialisms. Accordingly, when the purchasing tasks become divided and re-assigned without a modification or transference of 'responsibility', then the purchasing department can become accountable without authority through this divorce in roles and role conflict.

5. The extent to which the personnel within the formal purchasing department are engaged in project management activities and therefore have a reduced resource with which to maintain the regular flow of supply to the enterprise. This includes the 'usurping' of activities

so that 'there is the likelihood that the demarcation lines separating functions in traditional organisations will become increasingly blurred. Observation ... shows that cross-functional project teams ... are usurping some functional roles' (Farmer, 1995). This activity constrains the purchasing department by limiting the amount of direct human resource whilst removing the ability to control those personnel tasked with 'purchasing'.

6. A further internal constraint is provided by the general rate of change and adjustment between the functional specialisms in the company, so that the purchasing department is engaged in a simultaneous 'gambit' of many different functional changes. Each change in the operations of other departments creates both opportunities and new constraints for the purchasing manager (especially where such activities encroach on the legal issues of 'capacity' and 'agency'). Indeed, the extent of change can also create frustration and open conflict as departmental strategies and default policies are misaligned, or the limited resources available to the company favour certain departments over the needs of others. These changes therefore require a 'dovetail' of company-wide planning and mutual functional adjustment.

The Major External Constraints

The 'external' constraints placed upon the purchasing manager are equally complex and interrelated and these include:

1. The need to structure the purchasing department in such a manner that control can be exerted without the opportunity to enforce strict supervision at the site. In this manner, the purchasing manager must use 'influence' to control staff for whom they are personally accountable. The decentralization process, therefore, creates the opportunity for sites to operate *de facto* policies and to 'double decentralize' from any form of control (the 'control' of external sites).

2. The constant improvement of supplier performance, either as an explicit objective of the company strategy or not, can only be achieve through supplier development activities which require human resources. These resources are not necessarily the skills possessed by the purchasing staff, but may include skills from the quality assurance department or production planning.

3. The lack of models developed by external agencies, such as the university system or through consultancy organizations related to the potential policies on offer to a purchasing manager given certain constraints and circumstances. 'Best practice' models tend to be case-specific and include a supportive senior management appreciation for the role of the purchasing department. The promotion of these 'best

practices' is often through the isolation of a specific technique rather than the portfolio of company-wide adjustments that were combined to create the superior performance achieved by the company. These 'best practices', when promoted with insufficient contingent analysis, have created a 'fad culture' amongst purchasers, who are keen to demonstrate their awareness of such techniques but fail to align these with the strategy or preconditions for their success (Cox, 1995).

4. The ability of the purchasing department to control and focus the improvement of the supply base in such a way that the average performance of supplier quality, cost and delivery measures continues to improve in line with the needs of the business strategy and with the cooperation of suppliers.

A Summary of the Generic Constraints: The Purchasing Landscape

The purchasing landscape has at least *five* key constraints according to Jones (1997):

- *Spatial Distribution* – in terms of the geographical locations of the operating sites and their respective purchasing staff.
- *Hierarchical Dimensions* – in terms of the access and participation in the strategy formulation process and the level of integration enjoyed by the purchasing department.
- *Functional Responsibilities* – in terms of those responsibilities that are conducted by the purchasing department within a changeable environment. This includes the amount of responsibility that has been re-assigned to other functions so that it is 'off' the organizational chart of the purchasing department.
- *Product Orientation* – in terms of the different policies and treatment of 'classes' of supplied products and services including their categorization.
- *Time Dimension* – which originates from environmental changes and internal restructuring and creates a constant pressure and requirement for all internal structures to become more flexible and 'fluid'. This includes the need to reassign human resources and secondments to internal project teams.

Aligning Purchasing and Competitive Advantage: The Reck and Long Model (1988)

The Reck and Long model (1988) has for a long time been used to validate the elevation of functional purchasing within the organization and create a new role for purchasing in the enterprise as a whole. This model underpins a great deal of the literature that surrounds the purchasing and supply chain fields of study, and has a band of dedicated academic and practising followers. Indeed, for some academics and practising managers, the model forms a 'mantra' and the means of justifying the elevation of purchasing, even though the model suffers some inherent weaknesses both in terms of the focus on purchasing in isolation to the wider business 'system', the behavioural changes which must happen in the business before the elevation of purchasing can take place, and also the links that form the cause and the effect (elevation). The model adopts a four-stage approach that is largely, although not necessarily, incremental in nature. The *four* stages are:

1. *The Passive Purchasing Department* The 'passive' stage is defined as a purchasing department that has no strategic direction and acts on the requests of other functional departments. This form of purchasing department is characterized as 'reactive', measured by efficiency (volume and cost) metrics, conducts business with suppliers on price and is not an integrated, or perceived as, a vital element of competitive advantage to the business.

2. *The Independent Purchasing Department* The 'independent' purchasing department is myopic and is motivated by the latest techniques for the management of procurement as a means of 'self-improvement'. It does not relate these activities to the broader corporate strategies. The purchasing department is characterized by a focus on cost reduction and efficiency, with a recognition that there is a link between purchasing and competitive advantage by senior management and the development of links between the department and internal 'stakeholders', such as manufacturing.

3. *The Supportive Purchasing Department* The 'supportive' purchasing department is an integrated and aligned series of activities that reinforce the selling and trading strategies of the business through the provision of high levels of internal customer service. The purchasing department is integrated with the sales activities and adopts a more professional attention to the development of staff, suppliers and internal interfaces. The department is also involved in the development of performance monitoring and greater levels of management analysis directed at the elimination of weaknesses within the department and the supply chain.

4. *The Integrative Purchasing Department* The 'Integrative' purchasing department is an active element of the firm's competitive strategy formulation and execution process. The department is engaged in extensive cross-functional management activities and is supported by strong communication channels within the business. The department is measured on the 'effective' contribution of the department to the realization of the business goals.

The Reck and Long model provides a logical development of the purchasing department by arguing a logic of 'convergence'. This 'convergence' proposition suggests that the traditional functional specialisms will become integrated, and that the interfaces which create the dependencies between functional specialisms will provide the opportunities to remove the bureaucratic rigidities that have prevented the historic integration of the department as an 'equal'. The model also includes a watershed point at the third stage where the traditional measures of 'efficiency' become displaced by measures of 'effectiveness' and as such reflect a radical change in the management of the enterprise away from the 'classical' design. The measures of effectiveness also elevate the contribution of the purchasing department and focus the organization on issues such as the quality, cost and delivery (cross-functional issues) of the activities within the business and each department. In this respect, the model presented by Reck and Long (1988) is sympathetic to the models forwarded by Merli (1991) in terms of 'co-makership' and Womack and Jones (1996) in terms of the 'lean' approach.

The Implications of the Reck and Long (1988) Model

The model of incremental integration proposed by Reck and Long (1988) is a seductively rational argument for the elevation of the 'purchasing cause'. However, as a practical 'route map' for managers, the model is somewhat superficial and limited. The most serious problems with this model are the relationship between 'cause and effect', and the internal business 'triggers' that create the environment within which the purchasing department can flourish whereby:

- there is a change to the internal perception of purchasing within the business;
- the precursors that allow the internal and 'backward integration' of the purchasing department to occur once the logistics and then manufacturing departments have been incorporated;
- there is a change to the allocation of 'performance' measures that reflect 'efficiency' to those that evaluate 'effectiveness'. The authority to change the measures of departmental evaluation lie at the strategic level of the enterprise;
- the skills needed to support the business are developed and bound by standard procedures to control the process of purchasing wherever it occurs (formal integration with the business systems);
- independence is a 'falsehood' in that most of the 'best practices' within the purchasing environment are simply extensions of company-wide or 'total' approaches (Total Quality Management). The semantics of the term 'independence' may therefore be wrong, and the term 'associated' would be closer to the truth in that the efficiency measures developed by the department will reflect the key

requirements for the operations of the enterprise including the improvement of the quality, cost and delivery of inputs.

Overall, the Reck and Long model is useful in terms of 'direction setting', 'positioning' and 'making sense' of changes to the strategy and structure of the purchasing department within its particular 'landscape', but provides limited assistance in making the changes that are necessary for elevation, many of which seem to appear as if by chance within the model. However, within the study of multi-site purchasing, the model does allow the constraints already identified to position the purchasing organization and its likely 'next steps'.

The Research Findings

The generic findings of the case-based research can be classified into the following sections:

1. The 'awareness' and importance of improved purchasing was accepted by the case organizations and their stakeholders but that 'acceptance' was subject to anomalies. These originated from the definition and perceived 'value' that would be gained from adopting a fully-integrated approach to purchasing.

2. The purchasing department did not necessarily control all the necessary activities (the purchasing process) associated with the management of the company inputs.

3. The proportion of purchasing activities that was devoted to internal integration with other business functions and to the development of supplier performance was comparatively very small when analyzed in the context of the activities conducted by purchasing agents.

4. The majority of tasks conducted by purchasing professionals and also 'non-professional' staff involved with purchasing activities was reactive in nature. These roles contained very little formalized appraisal activity, planning activity or preventative problem-solving work.

5. The purchasing department did not formally and systematically translate the performance requirements of the customer and consumer into common measures of supplier performance and evaluation.

The Awareness of the Importance of Purchasing: Strong Words Spoken Softly

The SCDP research found that most organizations 'explicitly' or 'implicitly' recognized the importance of the purchasing department. These internal stakeholders (internal 'customer' departments) understood that improvements in the 'input' element of the operations would bring benefits to the consumer and customer. Indeed, many external lobbying organizations had been instrumental in creating this awareness. However, there were many problems identified in the 'promotion' of the purchasing cause.

The SCDP research found that most organizations 'explicitly' or 'implicitly' recognized the importance of the purchasing department.

To draw from a public sector example, the audit commission (an external stakeholder) has explicitly identified the importance of professional purchasing by proposing that

> ... one quarter of a typical trust's expenditure is on supplies. There is a considerable variation between trusts in terms of prices paid, process costs, stock levels, and use of supplies. There is evidence of scope for cost savings in all of these areas. Almost all the scope for cost savings is in the non-pay expenditure, and would have no detrimental effect on patient care.

However, as with the generic research findings, this apparent sign of 'elevation' is a 'mirage' in that the commentary focuses on measures of 'efficiency' and the classical preoccupation with costs rather than the quality and delivery of inputs. The second dimension to this mirage is the use of the wording suggesting that the efforts of purchasing are 'not detrimental' to the customer rather than wording that forges a strong link between the efforts of the purchaser and the improvement of 'customer service' or the position of the enterprise. The research found that, whilst internal and external 'awareness' was high, the promotion of purchasing stressed issues which served to 'position' the purchasing organization as 'passive' and at best 'independent'.

Defining Purchasing: The Real Organization

The research team also discovered that the complexity of the purchasing landscape within multi-site organizations is three-dimensional, in that the deliberations which concerned the strategy and structure of the purchasing department were inevitably confused when placed within the context of 'time and distance'. The research discovered that a significant proportion of fundamental 'purchasing' procedures and the control of spend occurred 'off' the purchasing organization chart and that this scenario had caused a rift between control procedures and coordination activities.

This rift had resulted from the redeployment of activities, but also from the reassignment of staff to other functions so that the purchaser reported to the site management as opposed to acting within their professional function. In this respect, the fundamental purpose of a purchasing strategy, in setting the direction and controls for the department within the business were compromised by the need to mediate and influence procedures which were fundamental but not under effective control. Links, therefore, needed to be established between the management of the purchasing function and the conduct of purchasing processes – in terms of the Reck and Long model (1988) this compromises the ability of the purchasing department to reach the 'independence' stage. In this manner, decentralized purchasing structures were not under effective control and that the term 'purchasing process' is unhelpful, as it implies that there is a coherence between strategy, structure and operations.

Best Practice

The lack of central direction in governing the focus and improvement areas within the purchasing department created by the organization of purchasing activities and their control, also served as an inhibitor to the promotion of 'best practice' within the purchasing department (albeit that certain 'best practices' were subject to local laws relating to issues such as 'anti-trust' and 'partnering'). In this manner, the 'independence' stage was once again compromised, and minor *ad hoc* improvements to small elements of the purchasing organization did not realize the benefits that were sought, nor did they create a 'standard' approach or frame of reference for purchasing staff (due to the lack of a common policy). In this manner, any improvements resulted in localized gains in terms of efficiency, but not effectiveness.

Purchasing: Same Horse, Different Jockey

The research also highlighted a division between the purchasing process, the skills required by purchasers managing different elements of the process, and the resources required to manage different product or service types. When the research team analyzed the common 'process' elements they found that these included:

- supply market analysis;
- tender preparation;
- contract negotiation;
- tender negotiation;
- supplier performance improvement;
- dissemination of 'best practice';
- identification of internal customers Key Performance Requirements (KPRs);
- translation of KPRs into supplier evaluation system measures;
- the 'call off' of supplies in parallel to the demand for materials and services.

However, the research also found that there was 'often no differentiation' between these deconstructed activities and that the term 'purchasing' was perceived as 'elements' of this larger business process and as such the 'calling off' of material was deemed 'purchasing' by some internal departments, whereas for others only those activities that involved the use of professional skills and diagnostics, such as tendering, were so termed. In addition, the research team found that a number of these activities required, to a greater or lesser extent, different resources and competences and some of these tasks were more transferable to other functions and comparatively less skilled employees in the purchasing department.

The 'purchasing' activities were also poorly systematized and proceduralized so that the execution of the tendering process was time-consuming and treated as a 'bespoke' activity, whereas only a fraction of the information was specific to products and services. The study also found that there was a very low incidence of individuals referring to the continuous improvement activities as part of a 'total' and integrated approach to the management of the supply chain. The low level of correlation between the perceptions of purchasing and the role of continuous improvement originated from four sources:

- a lack of time and scope in the role definition of the 'purchaser' to engage in such activities;
- the 'pay back' period involved with such forms of development;
- the low impact that such activities have on the measurement of the individual;
- the absence of a standard approach (or policy) towards the integration of suppliers.

The 'absence' of continuous improvement activities also entailed an absence of such activities within the enterprise and between the purchasing department and other functional specialisms in the enterprise; this, once again, reinforces the distance between the 'passive' and 'independent' stages of the Reck and Long model. The understanding of the entire series of business processes served by the purchasing department, and the manner in which they were measured, was absent and rarely aligned. In short, the role definition and activities undertaken by the purchasing agents was insular, directed towards clerical efficiency and often involved low levels of professional diagnostic skills.

Failure to Manage the Deconstructed Purchasing Process

Another key finding from the research was the lack of a generic model of 'purchasing' within the specific context of the organization such that during the purchasing and functional strategy formulation adequate analyses can be made. This lack of strategic planning and of the employment of strategic tools and techniques with which to make sense of changes within the purchasing environment was, for purchasers and others, a major feature limiting the development of realistic plans and also the 'elevation' process. Analyses were not conducted in a comprehensive manner and often failed to recognize the following issues:

- The setting of the purchasing organization within the corporate structure.
- The development of an explicit structure for purchasing activities that enhanced communication and the formal participation of purchasers at the many operating sites.
- An analysis of the product portfolio procured by the company.
- An analysis of the current performance of suppliers and the type of suppliers that would be needed in the future.
- The structure of supply markets and the management of 'risk' to protect the company from exposure to increased material costs or disturbances (including inventory policies).
- The organizational culture and the precedence accorded to individual development and training. This aspect includes the grading of authority amongst purchasing staff and the activities that could be conducted by a person, of a specific grade at a specific site.

In Summary

The research conducted by the SCDP team provides some interesting evidence to suggest that the 'academic world' is somewhat dislocated from the reality of professional purchasing practice. The established textbooks and curricula tend to treat purchasing as a functional activity that is distinct and can be defined in strict terms, whereas Reck and Long (1988) acknowledge that it forms part of the business system. In reality, the textbook approach may provide an over-simplified account of 'purchasing', given the variety of different landscapes, stages of evolution and contingencies that affect the strategies and structures of purchasing departments especially those related to multi-site operations. Indeed, the academic world has been quick to publish accounts of 'best practice', with little credit given to such contingencies, which reinforce the 'independence' of the purchasing department and therefore does not serve to elevate the professional purchaser.

To compound the problems of purchasing strategy and structure further, the dissemination of the practices that underpin purchasing organizations and are perceived as 'successful' suggest that practice leads academic thought and that the current stage of academic thought remains embryonic (Humby, 1995; Cox, 1995). These weaknesses do little to further the 'elevation' debate and provide alternatives to the 'reactive' and myopic purchasing department.

Reactive Purchasing: Where Next?

Whilst the Reck and Long model (1988) is not without its weaknesses, the 'incrementalist' approach does highlight a common theme, that of the integration of the business functions through the use of a consensus management approach to the business as an 'open' system. In the context of the 'motivation' to elevate the role of the purchasing department within the modern enterprise and the incremental convergence model there would appear to be certain activities that could act as vehicles for 'supportive integration'. These vehicles, with which the purchasing manager can align the activities and direction of the purchasing department with the strategies of the business, can be used to create internal synergies (between departments and within the different levels of policy making in the enterprise) and therefore expedite the 'purchasing cause'.

The key questions that remain unanswered by the Reck and Long model (1988) and the case studies of the SCDP team include:

- How do you convince senior managers of the importance of purchasing and the need to include purchasing representatives in the strategy formulation process as equal and legitimate partners?
- How do you convince functional managers that the purchasing department would have a beneficial impact on their own performances if it is treated as an equal 'stakeholder' in the business?
- How do you 'upskill' the purchasing organization so that the technical and professional skills are complemented with the necessary 'cross-functional' skills and how is time to be found for such activities?

The following section was developed to provide some directions and potential opportunities for the management of the purchasing department to use to move towards a 'supportive' and integrated role within the business. It must be acknowledged that these practices are contingent and therefore adaptation will be required by the practising manager – there would appear that there is no 'one best way of purchasing' and potentially no single definition of purchasing itself.

The possible ways forward for the purchasing manager may include initiatives such as:

1: The Strategy Cascade from Top Down

The deployment of business strategy has traditionally involved the fragmentation of the strategy into 'manageable pieces' that are assigned, through a similar process of objective setting as management by objectives (MBO), to the basic building block of the traditional organization or the functional departments. However, the interdependencies between departments means that this process must ensure the alignment of functional goals. The detrimental impact of decisions taken in one department upon the performance of another and the optimization of the performance measures associated with a single business function over all others creates many opportunities to 'stagnate' or 'impede' the provision of customer service by the entire enterprise.

In this respect, the treatment of the purchasing department as a single, independent, and autonomous element of the enterprise does little to integrate the department with others and the overall strategy process. The development of purchasing strategies cannot take place within a vacuum, and purchasing managers must seek to align their policies not only with the business strategy but also with every other functional strategy in order to maximize their own resources. In this respect, a business strategy that concerns 'cost' competitiveness must be translated into purchasing policies that reflect the 'need' for efficiency and overall cost reductions in the supply chain. In the broader enterprise context, this activity can be accelerated through an integration with the quality assurance department (for the training of suppliers), the production planning department (in terms of the accuracy of forecast production requirements) and many other departments. If these 'stakeholders' are not integrated within the planning processes of the purchasing department, then shorter production batch sizes and the costs of poorly supplied products will not be addressed, and the purchasing department will return to a 'reactive' mode and will miss the opportunities of 'elevation' by 'integration' and 'alignment'.

> *The development of purchasing strategies cannot take place within a vacuum.*

Accordingly, the purchasing strategy must be cross-functional and make explicit its interrelationships with other functions in order to provide a meaningful and internally valid 'direction' for purchasing staff as well as other functional managers who use the professional service provided by the purchasing department.

2: The Purchasing CLAN (Structural Accommodation and Adjustments)

The alignment of the purchasing strategy in a vertical manner, so that the enterprise 'needs' are passed from the consumer market to the supply market, will affect the structure of the purchasing department. This structure is, to a large extent, within the control of the purchasing manager but, as the research has demonstrated, there are elements of the purchasing role which are conducted by other business functions and some which need to be deployed to others.

In this respect, the overriding principles of the structural design of the purchasing department should reflect the need for flexibility, but also for control. The structure and assignment of roles provides a formal allocation of effort and a skeleton, but this must be accompanied by a procedural structure of integration, participation, communication and formalization of interactions between direct and indirect 'purchasing' personnel. One approach to the structural design of the purchasing department to have gained fashionable support during the 1990s is the CLAN approach or the Central-Led Action Network (Humby, 1995).

The CLAN approach to the design of the purchasing structure is a model of consensus management which relies on the development of a federal network of employees. At the centre of this network lies the planning and policy setting (central core function), and through a series of 'linking pins' the direct and indirect purchasing staff are grouped by common interests. These interests could concern geography, key tasks, product orientation and so on. The reader will notice that the control and communication of policies within this structure is maintained by splitting the roles of certain employees so that they are members of a higher 'strategy' group, but leaders of a lower 'tactical' or 'implementation' team. The structure is shown in Figure 10.1.

The CLAN approach relies upon the regular interaction of teams, the building block of the contemporary organization, and substitutes 'command and control' bureaucracy with the deployment of 'bounded empowerment'. In this respect, the roles of the employees within the network of purchasers change to reflect the need to standardize the approaches and techniques employed within the department through an explicit, formalized and regular process of internal integration. The structure also permits the logical deployment of staff and the development of relationships, both formal and informal, which are important within the context of the flatter structures of the enterprise and the need for 'responsiveness' to changes in the wider business environment.

The Drawbacks of the CLAN Approach

The CLAN approach offers many advantages for the purchasing manager, not least to be able to deploy responsibilities to other members of the department and create a 'self-managing' and 'self-reinforcing' system within which the performance of the department can be controlled and coordinated. However, the CLAN approach has certain issues which must be recognized before this technique can be exploited to provide a meaningful return. The creation of the network requires that certain 'off structure' or indirect staff and their managers must be convinced that the exercise will prove a benefit in terms of the performance of their area of responsibility. Second, there are certain issues regarding the 'professionalism' of purchasing staff in that those staff at the 'centre' benefit from the ability to engage professional diagnostic skills, whereas those direct purchasers in the 'field' may feel that their personal development is somewhat limited or devalued (in terms of progression).

FIGURE 10.1   Likert's Linking Pin Model (1961)

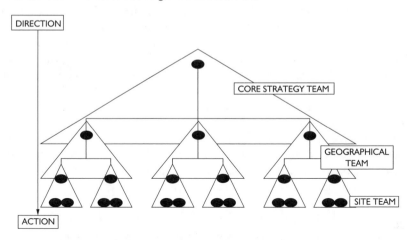

The ability to exploit the CLAN is therefore a test of the calibre of the purchasing managers themselves, their ability to promote the need to 'decentralize and coordinate' and also their ability to reconcile the commercial issues in the consumer marketplace, including product strategies, with purchasing policies in an aligned and supportive manner. To date, empirical evidence suggests that the level of commercial 'understanding' of functional purchasing managers may not yet be sufficiently developed to exploit these benefits fully (Stuart, 1996). Therefore, the fully integrated 'purchasing proposition' may provide more fruitful returns by seeking to integrate with the internal stakeholders of the process (horizontal integration) in parallel with seeking strategic elevation (vertical integration).

3: Sideways First (Horizontal) Elevation

One of the common denominators that unites the functional strategy and structure of the purchasing organization is the need to become a 'legitimate' and integral element of the cross-functional management team within the enterprise (Dimancescu *et al.*, 1997). In some respects, the dismantling of traditional functional boundaries through the use of 'de-layering' (Kanter, 1989; Keuning and Opheij, 1994) and the general re-engineering of business processes (Hammer and Champy, 1993) are a means through which the purchasing cause is gravitated towards such management activities, but to engage in cross-functional management without exploiting this activity as a platform on which to integrate the interests of the purchasing department would be short-sighted and foolhardy.

The purpose of these cross-functional management activities is to rejuvenate business performance by removing levels of bureaucracy and also the internal dysfunctions of a functionally-structured organization, including those rigidities which relate to the speed and accuracy of business decision-making. Farmer (1995) has already identified the 'usurping' nature of these efforts in terms of the traditional demarcation of roles in the company, and the SCDP research has identified several symptoms of organizations that are experiencing 'role conflict' within and beyond the purchasing department. Flatter and more responsive organizations call for new and 're-assigned' internal responsibilities including the deployment of purchasing activities to employees that are outside the formal control of the departmental management.

The adoption of cross-functional management, which is a threat to the stability of the traditional roles in the organization, brings with it new opportunities for the integration of the 'purchasing cause' and also facilitates a greater understanding of the wider business systems that surround the purchasing department. For the purchasing manager, this form of management does not threaten the professional 'agency' of the staff conducting 'policy decisions', but it does affect their integration in key business initiatives, especially those that relate to the development of new products and services (these are business capabilities that attract the attention of senior managers in the enterprise and are fundamental to the long-term future of the business).

Cross-functional management can thus be defined as

> a management process designed to encourage and support interdepartmental communication and co-operation throughout a company – as opposed to command and control through narrow departments or divisions. The purpose is to attain such company-wide targets as quality, cost and delivery of products by optimising the sharing of work. (JUSE, 1988 as quoted by Dimancescu, 1992)

As the quality, delivery and especially cost of the products and services of the enterprise cross the responsibilities of the purchasing department, this form of management integration may present itself as the first stage in the elevation process by which the performance of the department can be associated with 'success' within the consumer market.

Cross-functional management offers a means of integration for the purchasing manager and also an ability to engage in policy formulation with a significantly reduced level of risk. In addition, the process inevitably informs the purchasing strategy formulation process and the success of these strategies, so that the 'supportive' role played by the purchasing department can be used to gain greater involvement in business policy decisions. The latter activity calls for the adoption of a new company-wide perspective for the purchasing manager, and an acknowledgement that independence and myopic insulation are not the means with which elevation can be achieved and sustained. The cross-functional integration of the purchasing department does not guarantee elevation in itself, for a number of reasons, including the capability and skills of the purchasing

Cross-functional management offers a means of integration for the purchasing manager.

manager, but it does go some way to creating a 'level playing field' upon which the contribution of the purchasing department can be evaluated in terms of its effectiveness (rather than clerical efficiency).

4: Externalizing Measures of Horizontal and Vertical Requirements to Focus Supply Chain Improvement (Meaningful Appraisal)

The integration of the purchasing department within cross-functional management activities, deliberate attempts to gain a greater understanding of the internal business system and its measures of success, a greater awareness of consumer market requirements and attempts to create a new role and responsibility for the purchasing department are all worthy activities which go some way to alleviating current problems, as well as elevating the department itself. However, these actions must be directed towards a clear goal, which is supply chain performance improvement as measured by the quality, delivery and cost of inputs to the enterprise. The change from reactive to proactive management must include direct attempts to focus on the improvement of the suppliers to the business and to find means of sustaining this improvement drive so that it is economical (in terms of resources especially human resources) and tangible (in terms of measures that are shared as key performance indicators with other business functions).

To achieve this 'focusing' activity on the external resources to the enterprise, the suppliers, techniques such as supplier evaluation systems must be developed as control devices to monitor the rate and extent of improvement. These measurement systems monitor the performance of each and every supplier, as well as providing vital management information about the current weaknesses in the supply chain. To gain an alignment between the 'output' market and the 'input' market for the business, these measures need to be aligned. In this manner, the evaluation systems must be prioritized and must concern themselves with the quality, cost and delivery of purchases. The regular and formal appraisal of suppliers applies a degree of pressure on them to conform, to avoid being 're-sourced' and to maintain contractual relationships with the customer. In parallel, other techniques such as the supplier association concept, partnership sourcing, and similar measures can be employed to provide the long-term alignment of the supply base with the 'output' market needs of the company and the purchasing department (Hines, 1994).

5: Individuals and Individual Development

A final initiative which needs to be addressed explicitly during the policy formulation stage of the purchasing department is the assignment of the effort of the human resources within its control. For this, the tasks that form the role of each individual must be assessed to determine whether these activities are:

1. reactive and, as such, present a large human cost in correcting problems or mistakes and serve to constrain the individual by consuming time to correct a situation which should have been prevented in the first place;

2. appraisal activities that are undertaken to ensure that there is a degree of convergence between what is intended and actual events. This activity is a checking activity which has a business cost but should only be undertaken as a means of correcting the underlying source of the problem;

3. proactive activities which serve to improve the performance of the purchasing department or prevent the occurrence of problems.

The analysis of roles with the actual tasks to be carried out and the time allocated from purchasing resources allows the purchasing manager to determine which activities in the current 'task portfolio' consume the greatest amounts of human resources and whether these activities 'add value' to the efficiency and effectiveness of the business/purchasing department. In this manner, the movement of tasks from reactive to appraisal and then to the prevention/planning stage creates human resource with which new 'value adding' work can be found. In this process, the systems needed to control the purchasing department and supply chain become standardized and, when abnormality occurs, it is instantly obvious and provokes correction.

To achieve the new 'role' for the individual, the analyses of 'time spent' must be translated into a continuous improvement culture in which personnel, armed with the correct (but not necessarily 'best practice') skills, set about defining how the system should operate and where improvement efforts need to be directed. This in turn requires new skills and the addition of 'interpersonal' skills to complement the specialist and professional knowledge of the purchaser. For example, a major element of a 'successful' supplier association is how well the concept is 'sold' internally and with the suppliers – these are not traditional skills and require new forms of negotiation, including the use of informal channels of communication within and beyond the business (Hines, 1994).

Summary

In summary, the new purchasing agenda for the practitioner, the academic and the professional body is full of opportunities which did not exist in traditional times. The general level of turbulence in industry, the 'downsizing' of the organization, and the movement away from 'adversarial' relationships within and beyond the enterprise have created a new stage.

These forces for integration, when combined, provide a strong force to unite all elements of the business and serve as a medium with which the management of the purchasing department can begin to integrate with the business and relinquish the mistaken goal of independence. In reality, there is no such scenario as 'independence' and no purchasing department can make any significant, or sustained, improvement by remaining insular. If the purchasing department remains outside the structures of general (horizontal) management or remains in reactive mode, then the 'purchasing cause' has been lost altogether. Also, if the trilogy of practitioner, academic and professional body do not seize this opportunity, then several possible fates loom on the horizon.

The simple outcome is that the reactive purchasing department remains as it is, while the worst outcome is that the professional knowledge and potential contribution of the department to the business is 'decomposed' into a series of tasks that belong to others in the business and are conducted in the manner of an automaton – indeed advances in computer technology and new generations of service industry may well herald the outsourcing of the purchasing department itself. The new stage, and the unique combination of the pressures for change, cannot be paralleled with the traditional 'calls' for elevation *per se*, nor can the 'cost mantra' be used as the vehicle to convince others. The challenge facing purchasing professionals is, therefore, the management of their time and the use of this time in creating the necessary internal 'levers' that unite the business through the medium of purchasing.

In a similar manner, 'fashion' and generic models, although useful, lack the power to convince the senior managers of the business to admit that they could possibly be 'wrong' and should include the purchasing department. These models will remain of limited usefulness in the absence of 'hard' performance data that relates the activities of the input market to the consumer market unequivocally (couched in terms such as 'margin' and 'contribution' rather than 'costs'). The movement to the new 'challenge' for the purchaser is therefore daunting, and must include a degree of 'self-criticism' relating to the 'fit' between 'policy' and what is actually done (Joag and Scheuing, 1995). This requires 'up-skilling', new roles and the 'control' of activities which occur within the interfaces between the purchasing department and its internal stakeholders. The concepts of 'command and control' are almost meaningless for the new, flatter, organization and have come to be replaced with cooperation and coordination. The first tentative step towards elevation may therefore be to relinquish the quest and accept that 'houses must be put in order' for professionals, the professional bodies and for academics, and that the best vehicle for this corrective action is the aggressive 'selling' of what purchasing can offer to other managers in the business who themselves are in a state of adjustment and integration.

CHAPTER 11

Strategic Performance Measurement Systems[1]

Summary

Problems arise in measuring purchasing performance from the difficulties in quantifying and capturing the real value which purchasing can add. Traditionally, purchasing has been assessed on financial and/or efficiency-based measures which do not capture the full spread of purchasing activities. This can lead to major problems in assessing purchasing activities and their future direction, as measures communicate a very strong message regarding those areas which the organization perceives to be important; in essence, what you measure is what you get.

Measures need to be designed which track not only the outcome of the activities undertaken but also those processes which enable those outcomes to be met. Performance measures are often likened to the controls on a car dashboard, or in an aeroplane cockpit, in that there are a number of key factors in any activity that enable an organization to arrive at its proposed destination. As such, it is important that these indicators are interpreted in a comprehensive and balanced manner to avoid the danger of setting conflicting goals, which can result in the sub-optimization of key processes. This suggests the need for measurement to be recognized as a means of achieving goals which support corporate objectives.

The need for measurement to be recognized as a means of achieving goals which support corporate objectives.

In purchasing, however, problems arise because measures tend to concentrate on piecemeal efficiency activities which emphasis the reduc-

---

[1] Prepared by Paul Cousins and Jon Hampson. Paul Cousins was the principal investigator and Jon Hampson, the research officer. Jon now works as a consultant for Ernst and Young in London.

tion of cost, rather than the more significant areas of effectiveness against chosen plans of action. This has traditionally been because purchasing was viewed as an add-on cost, rather than a value-adding activity, and this has resulted in a great deal of data generated which at best provides decision-makers with the ability to deal reactively to events which have already taken place. Performance measures therefore need to be defined in the broader context of purchasing strategy and therefore, indirectly, of corporate strategy. This will often require the development of non-financial measures to complement the traditional ones, which should be attached to specific goals, and allow the tracking of performance against those goals. It is questionable, otherwise, whether it is worthwhile monitoring them.

The benefits of a well-planned purchasing performance measurement system which supports strategic objectives at every organizational level should include: improved decision-making; better communication across the organization; better visibility of activities, their consequences and any areas of waste or duplication; and improved workforce motivation in areas of critical importance to the purchasing strategy.

It is extremely difficult, however, to develop a menu of the 'right' purchasing measures to use across all organizations. If measures are indeed tailored to support strategic objectives, then it is unlikely that they will be transferable across industries, because strategies will differ from one organization to another. Since each will operate according to a different set of pressures from the external business environment, and differ in organizational structure, the way in which the measures are interpreted and used cannot be static.

It is up to the purchasing function, therefore, to develop its own measures in line with strategic objectives. A useful way to approach this task is to understand exactly who it serves and what the expectations of that service are. What is considered to be 'good' or 'bad' purchasing will be very much determined by internal expectations. It is therefore necessary to understand the 'internal customers' requirements of the purchasing function, which enable them to meet their own strategic objectives. This idea stems from the principle that the performance of one unit will depend very much on the performance of the preceding stage in the process.

Stakeholder analysis provides a means by which to break down the various internal requirements of a function. 'Stakeholders' are defined as 'those parties who either affect or who are affected by a corporations actions, behaviour and policies'. They are 'those groups on which an organisation depends – the people who can help it achieve its goals or can stop it dead in its tracks. They include customers, suppliers and employees.' Traditional stakeholder analysis deals with the stakeholders of an organization, and may be defined very broadly. It is possible, however, to focus more specifically on the stakeholders of the purchasing process.

This will allow a more internal focus, which should also include suppliers, as they may be considered to form part of the organization's 'external resources'. The breakdown of purchasing activities should reveal the various stakeholders of each activity, and allow a more focused and interactive understanding of internal customer requirements, a clearer definition of performance against these, and the appropriate channels along which to communicate them.

Given, then, that performance measurement needs to be aligned with strategy and focused on internal customer expectations, the Balanced Scorecard Approach provides a suitable context in which to structure these. Designed originally for measuring corporate performance, it is based on the idea that managers need measurement criteria that reflect not only the financial performance, but also the critical drivers of value. It attempts, therefore, to balance indicators of customer satisfaction, the internal business processes which enable customer satisfaction to be achieved, and the areas in which the organization needs to continuously improve in order to be competitive. These factors are the means by which financial performance can be achieved.

The scorecard can be developed to reflect the activities and expectations of purchasing, which is also responsible for performance across various financial, (internal) customer, internal processes and continuous learning criteria. Accordingly, a methodology for approaching performance measurement is suggested, based on the 'balanced purchasing scorecard', which synthesizes the analysis of both the external supply market and internal stakeholder expectations. This allows the organization to develop goals, aligned with strategic objectives, reflecting both internal performance and external capabilities. From this, a means by which appropriate purchasing performance measures may be designed is suggested, and performance against them collected and analyzed. The model has been designed and analyzed so far, and is now ready to be piloted among SCDP companies.

1. Introduction

1.1 Abstract

Measuring the performance of business activities is a familiar subject and a thorn in the side of many managers. The problem has been widely discussed and researched in a number of different forums over the years, but is gaining more prominence today, as businesses seek to understand how well they are doing in various critical activities, and to further improve processes, outputs and eventually competitiveness.

Measuring performance in purchasing and supply is no exception to this trend. Indeed, as companies increasingly recognize the crucial impact that purchasing and supply chain activities can have on their overall performance, the importance of measuring these activities has reached new levels. There are a number of problems and complexities in considering measurement in this area. This chapter attempts to identify some of these, and to pose a new approach to methods of measuring performance in purchasing and supply management.

1.2 Terms of Reference

The initial terms of reference which were discussed at length at the initial SCDP Group 2 sponsors' meeting in January 1995, and were eventually condensed into the following broad objectives:

1. To examine the organization of the procurement function as a basis for exploring various measurement systems.
2. To examine which types of measurement might apply to various types of commodity, parts and services that the organization purchases, and which of these need to be developed.
3. To determine the types of purchasing policies and procedures which need to be designed in order to ensure that the measurement systems operate in a motivating, rather than a demotivating manner.
4. To identify how relevant information should be communicated back through the organization to different stakeholders.
5. To develop a performance measurement system that can identify a portfolio of purchasing strategies.

1.3 Approach to the Research

Following the setting up of the terms of reference, and after having met with each of the participating companies, it was decided that the main issues faced by each manager concerned the lack of appropriate measures available to them to provide a legitimate indication of how well purchasing performs. A great deal of material in the purchasing supply field discusses the need to measure more effectively, but does not indicate the specific criteria to be measured, or the way in which this may be achieved. Accordingly, the decision was taken to try to synthesize current thoughts on purchasing activities and measurement, with the broader field of performance measurement in management generally in order to develop a generic approach to performance measurement in purchasing. This did indeed prove a more valuable base from which to proceed. Through the course of the literature analysis, and subsequent sponsor visits, various principles and models were adopted and discussed at workshop meetings to evaluate their usefulness and relevance to the project. This process culminated in an initial conceptual methodology being developed which, having undergone several iterations with the companies involved, and with academic counterparts, is discussed in the final stages of this chapter.

2. Performance Measurement

2.1 The Purpose

In the broadest sense, performance measurement of any activity should be designed to bring about improvement in that activity, highlighting variances over time, and enabling a more efficient allocation of resources. It is about establishing current performance levels, and improving the activities which are essential to the unit's success, while ensuring that important activities do not become neglected or slip out of control. As such it should be considered a strategic activity. If strategy is about understanding an organization's position and activities in relation to the environment in which it is operating, then 'without a thorough understanding of company processes and where the company adds value in those activities, it will have little success in developing appropriate measures' (Geanuracos and Meiklejohn, 1994: p. 123).

Performance measurement as a subject involves the development of goals and their related measures, as well as the appropriate mechanisms of feedback. It must therefore reflect the operating assumptions of the organization, in terms of culture, strategy and operational processes. This requires the identification of the pressures which the organization faces, both internal and external, and should consequently lead to a set of action plans for specific areas of the organization. Problems arise when conflicting messages are received by managers and operators about what is expected of them, or when measures are derived which are not directly related to the organization's purpose. Geanuracos and Meiklejohn (1994) quote a good example of this type of problem in describing the discrepancies between Glaxo's 1991 Annual Chapter, and the chairman's chapter. The former stated that Glaxo was 'an integrated research-based group of companies whose corporate purpose is the discovery, development, manufacture and marketing of safe, effective medicines of the highest quality'. The chairman, however, began his chapter, not with how well his company was making progress against these goals, but with, 'I am pleased to chapter on another successful year for the company. The total sales were … some … 7% higher than the year before … and earnings per share at 60.8p compares with 54p last year, an increase of 13%…' This is a classic example of how conflicting messages may be transmitted regarding the 'real' performance measures which an organization uses. Often, a piecemeal approach to performance measurement means that particular initiatives will be overrun by other corporate priorities which affect activities going on elsewhere. A fundamental problem is that many end up focusing on individual issues, rather than whole processes, so that they act in isolation.

> *Performance measurement as a subject involves the development of goals and their related measures, as well as the appropriate mechanisms of feedback.*

Problems also often arise because the measurement system in use was not originally designed as a measurement tool, but for operational requirements. Order processing or inventory tracking in purchasing might be examples of this. 'A common error has been to assume that the by-products of such systems provide suitable information for management chaptering and decision making' (Geanuracos and Meiklejohn, 1994: p. 279). This has traditionally been a widespread problem in purchasing. When measures are not related to specific organizational goals, they often end up either being misused or not used at all. As Meyer (1994) argues, measurement systems have traditionally been designed for senior managers to pull information up so that they can impose decisions, downwards. Business functions end up with their own measures, which are based on results, but which do not indicate to anyone either how they arrived at their current situation, or what to do differently. In some cases, this problem requires a total reappraisal of the types of measure which the organization is using in its different departments and processes. In others, what is needed is a system for interpreting the data generated in a useful manner – there is no point in measuring an activity unless the results inform the recipient of how well various goals are being met. This is an important point: it is often not so much the measures that are being used that make a difference, but actually *how* they are being used, and what they contribute to decision-making. This requires that they should be related to the strategic objectives of the organization, via the goals of the particular department or process. What is needed is a performance measurement system that is derived directly from corporate strategy, synthesizing an analysis of the external environment, with internal capabilities which reflect the purpose, technology available, and the nature of the activity (Lamming and Davis, 1995). The measures used should capture the essential nature of the business, and focus attention on long-term competitiveness rather than short-term considerations.

2.2 The 'Power' of Measurement

The nature of any performance measurement system will be extremely significant in determining what employees and functions do, and how they do it. Measurement therefore needs to be placed in a strategic context, because the way that individuals and teams are assessed will determine the nature of the activities which they undertake, and how they interpret their tasks. As Saunders (1994: p. 144) claims, 'what is measured not only provides data that can inform judgements about the standards of performance achieved, but also provides signals as regards what is important. Measurements have a motivational influence, therefore, and they help to shape perceptions of what is important and to concentrate energies on actions relevant to them.' It is commonly recognized that measurement influences behaviour in a certain direction, and this is often reflected in phrases such as:

What gets measured gets done;
What gets measured is *only* what gets done;
What gets measured gets managed;
What gets measured improves.

In view of this, it is essential that measures are carefully designed to suit the needs of the organization, in order to avoid resources being allocated in a sub-optimal way. Employees have been described as 'calculative receptors': 'The employee who is given a job to do and criteria to meet will not stop to evaluate the suitability of these criteria (even if they personally disagree with the criteria which have been set), but will seek to meet their own personal objectives, or maximise their own performance within the criteria identified, in the belief that personal rewards will be optimised as a result.' (Bleinkinsop and Burns, 1992: p. 21) Poorly determined systems, therefore, will encourage the wrong goals and reward the wrong achievements. Conversely, a well-balanced and structured stem should support and encourage performance in those areas which are critical to the firm's success.

2.3 Principles

As a means of exemplifying the way in which performance measures should be used, the literature is replete with parallels to driving a car. The most common example is that trying to manage a process without a good simple guidance system is like trying to drive a car without a dashboard, or whilst looking all the time in the rear-view mirror. To further the metaphor, measures are needed which indicate the smoothness of the ride, the ability to brake and accelerate as required, and potential hazards on the road. The implication is that measures which record outcomes to events which have already taken place are only of limited use to the manager. What is needed are indicators of what challenges are ahead of an organization, and the means with which to meet them successfully. Conversely, to simply monitor the number of times that things go wrong in a business is, 'the equivalent to tracking your personal automobile record by counting the number of tickets you have received. What this measures is not how well you drive, but how many times you've been caught!' (Hedstrom and McLean, 1993: p. 21).

Strategy and effective implementation are perhaps the most fundamental requirements for a successful performance measurement system.

Strategy and effective implementation are perhaps the most fundamental requirements for a successful performance measurement system. The requirement is for a process of comprehensive identification of all the different types of activities in which an organization is involved, in order to give them a coherent focus to ensure they are all driving in the same direction. Each top level objective should have a 'strategic staircase', represented by milestones, the achievement of which will lead to those objectives. The ultimate purpose behind the system should be to help employees improve their own performance (Ghorpade and Chen, 1995).

A number of checklists are available, which suggest 'principles' to be employed when designing performance measures. (Ghobadian and Ashworth, 1994; Meyer, 1994; Lynch and Cross, 1991). Most of these may be captured within the following list.

Measurement systems should:

- be linked to corporate objectives, and make 'fuzzy' strategic goals concrete ('goal congruence');
- combine different measures to meet the requirements of different organizational levels ('cascading goals' – i.e. the goals of one level are the means of another);
- capture the essence both of efficiency and effectiveness;
- allow the identification of trade-offs between different dimensions of performance;
- include a balanced mixture both of qualitative and quantitative measures, with common definitions of each;
- be recognized as an ongoing, evolving process;
- be incapable of manipulation;
- recognize that the measures should not become ends in themselves;
- enable management to plan as well as to control;
- not be entirely concerned with measuring in a 'negative' way, to facilitate correction;
- instil the confidence in managers to fully empower the teams;
- allow measures to be collected systematically and analyzed over time;
- permit the identification of critical situations, and generate a corresponding change in behaviour;
- differentiate between incremental/control measures, and radical objectives;
- track performance against customer expectations;
- encourage cross-functionalism;
- limit the amount of measures used, to a few key variables, in order maximize simplicity.

3. Measurement in Purchasing and Supply

3.1 The Need for Measurement

If performance measurement in general has proved to be a problem over the years, then finding common ways of measuring performance specifically in purchasing has been nearly impossible. This situation has become more pronounced as the potential contribution of purchasing's activities to overall corporate performance has increasingly become recognized. Indeed, as Dumond (1994: p. 16) argues,

> in the past, when raw materials were relatively cheap and simple, when manufacturing processes were straightforward, when engineering changes were few, when masses of stock was considered an asset, when the term 'quality' was reserved for engineers, the procurement function could survive as an island seeking to cut costs. Now that approach is not feasible.

The common difficulty across a number of industries is that, while the vital role that purchasing may play in the achievement of an organization's strategic goals has been recognized, there has generally not been a corresponding change in the types of measure used to support the more value-adding activities undertaken, which are generally less easy to quantify. The way in which many efficiency and financially-based measures are employed reflects the out-dated idea that purchasing is an add-on cost to the business. As purchasing has become more strategic, these traditional short-term efficiency measures have become less useful in assessing how well purchasing achieves its aims, and may also undermine the credibility of purchasing managers and their buyers, whose activities they should be designed to support.

3.2 Efficiency and Effectiveness

Traditionally, purchasing performance concentrated on achieving price savings in the supply market, and other efficiency-based measures. These, however, do not reflect the full extent of purchasing activities, and the pre-occupation with such measures may actually detract from the more useful indications of how purchasing performs across this range of activities. Van Weele (1994) argues that there are two dimensions to performance in any activity, which are efficiency *and* effectiveness (see Figure 11.1). He describes efficiency as the relationship between the planned and actual sacrifices which are made to achieve agreed goals – it is, in effect, an operating ratio of effort against results. This may depend on organizational factors such as the workload, certain procedures, the information system used, and headcount, often focusing on transactions. Effectiveness, however, is the extent to which a goal can be met, using a chosen course of action. As such, areas such as supplier development, value analysis, forward buying programmes and lead-time reduction, for example, may need to be examined. As Geanuracos and Meikelejohn (1994: p. 205) state, 'the efficiency of the process deals with how parsimoniously it uses company resources; the effectiveness of a process deals with the quality of its outputs.' Efficiency looks at competence and ability, while effectiveness influences strength, power, potency and validity. Clearly there is an important relationship between the two definitions – efficiency may be an important part of whether a function is effective in meeting its goals – but they remain distinct from each other. Price performance, therefore, which is a common expectation of purchasing, is one legitimate element of purchasing efficiency (and therefore of purchasing performance) but it is not the only one.

Syson (1995) identifies a number of reasons why price performance indicators may actually be misleading in themselves. Assessing buyers against the price they have paid is not as easy to assess as it may first appear. The real price may be blurred by quantity discounts, payment terms, credit and currency fluctuations. Also, the price paid in one period may be meaningless compared to the previous one, as the difference between the two may depend on the relative success of the buyer in securing price concessions on different occasions. The factors which contribute to this are unlikely to be constant. In the case of inflation indices, he argues that simply to be better than an index is no guarantee of profitability – competitive tenders only provide a 'snapshot' of a particular point in time, and inflation may not be passed on to customers consistently. Another problem might be in identifying who is actually 'responsible' if a fall in the market price occurs. Closer cross-functional cooperation may result in improved design specifications, but it is difficult to attribute the success in securing a lower price to any one function. To be meaningful, price savings should be considered in the light of 'those planned, predetermined actions undertaken by purchasing, or by purchasing and other departments, which result in measurable cost/price reductions, value improvements (through Value Analysis projects, quality control circles, etc.) or avoidance of higher costs'. In this sense, he claims that across-the-board price reductions by a supplier should not necessarily count as a measure of purchasing success. Similarly, savings which may result in an increased overall cost to the customer organization should be avoided – for example, volume discounts which lead to increased stockholding costs or quality failures: the danger of many price savings in an efficiency-orientated environment is that they may simply

FIGURE 11.1 Definitions

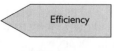

Effectiveness	Performance	Efficiency
Extent to which goals can be met using a chosen course of action	Extent to which purchasing achieves set goals sacrificing minimal resources	Difference between planned and actual sacrifices made in achieving goals

result in a cost being incurred elsewhere in the business. Again, attention is drawn to the effectiveness of such decisions in achieving a lowest total cost of acquisitions throughout the product life cycle.

3.3 Qualitative and Quantitative Measures

Butler (1995) has identified a number of broad ways in which purchasing can add value, as outlined in Table 11.1. As Table 11.1 shows, while a number of these areas may indeed be important to the final price obtained from a supplier, to focus entirely on price performance may be counter-productive, when other issues, such as product quality, or delivery reliability, for example, may be more immediately important to the well-being and smooth functioning of the organization, and the achievement of low costs overall. If these activities are not measured, then the traditional argument that you cannot control what you cannot measure means that important opportunities could be overlooked.

A further problem with an over-reliance on efficiency-based measures is that, in addition to focusing resources on only a limited part of purchasing activity, the nature of many quantitative data means that they may not be useful in decision-making when considered in isolation. Simple workload statistics, such as the number of purchasing employees, number of purchase orders raised, the number of requisitions received, and department costs, do not necessarily reflect the key areas of significance to the organization as a whole. It is therefore doubtful whether departments which are still primarily expected to deliver the best price savings or efficiency statistics, and which are measured on these criteria, will be effective in contributing to the organization's overall goals. As Geanuracos and Meiklejohn (1994: p. 56) reflect, 'financial accounting systems were never originally designed as a tool for business control. In consequence, performance measurement systems in many of today's

TABLE 11.1 Value-adding Activities Which Purchasing May Undertake

Strategic	Tactical
• Supplier relationship management	• Contract negotiation
• External resource management	• Contract management
• Customer satisfaction	• Improved utilization of money/getting better value.
• Product/range development	
• Process re-engineering	• Provision of commercial acumen
• Supply chain management	• Improved productivity
• Customer and supplier education	• Reduction of internal operating costs

SOURCE: Butler (1995).

companies focus on historic rather than future performance, financial rather than operational indicators, internal rather than external data, and numeric rather than qualitative results.' Financial data, for example, were originally designed to provide an auditable record of transactions for shareholders, rather than for encouraging the activities behind the transactions themselves. These results-based measures are naturally important, in that they allow organizations to 'keep score', but they do not enable managers to monitor the activities and capabilities that enable them to perform a given process. A survey undertaken by Business Intelligence (1992) shows that regarding performance measures in general, 88 per cent of senior executives were not satisfied with their performance measures, 63 per cent because they were too financially oriented, and 36 per cent because they focused too much on the short-term information. Too often they measure the value created, but not the processes which create that value. This provides them with information about results, but not about the means by which they are reached. As such, there is little basis for taking positive action about what factors to address, or at what level of intensity to pitch it.

As these types of issues have been recognized, various attempts have been made to integrate non-quantitative, and non-financial measures of performance into organizational measurement criteria, based on the belief that they may cause a shift in focus away from the short term, towards medium- and long-term goals as well, emphasizing causality: 'suitable non-financial measures are the cause, and successful financial performance the effect'. As the principle that 'what gets measured is what gets done' applies at all levels of an organization, it is important to create a measurement system which promotes such activities, as 'buyers behave not on what is expected of them but on what they are inspected'. While it is difficult to quantify such areas as supplier development, interdepartmental relationships, and negotiation skills, for example, these are often the types of activity which need to be monitored and stimulated, in order for purchasing to deliver the appropriate goods and services to internal users effectively. It would be pointless to continue to measure buyers on the price concessions that they may achieve with suppliers, through applying pressure, when the priority for a particular product or service might be to secure regular and reliable delivery, or a particular level of quality. Lip service may be paid to the stated priority, but actions will always be directed first towards achieving that target on which they are measured.

> *The principle that 'what gets measured is what gets done' applies at all levels of an organization.*

3.4 The Benefits of Measurement

The benefits of a well-directed and well-balanced performance measurement system for purchasing should be extensive. Van Weele (1984) cites *four* significant reasons for measuring in a way that focuses on the means by which purchasing can add value.

1. *Decision-Making*: focusing on the right types of measure will enable improved decision-making, through directing activity which is aligned to the needs of the organization, and identifying variances from planned results. In addition, the cause and effect relationship between processes and their outcomes will be more readily apparent, facilitating greater ease of planning and control, and coordination of activities across the organization.

2. *Communication*: the benefits of working towards targets which have more meaning or relevance to non-purchasing personnel, and which are tailored to their own requirements will enable an improved level of communication between different parts of an organization. It is important that other functions are aware of the contribution which purchasing can and does make, so they may draw on it to their own advantage. As van Weele says, 'to obtain the information required for a comprehensive evaluation, purchasing must leave its own comfortable niche in the organisation and interact effectively with key management people in other departments'.

3. *Visibility*: a well-structured set of objectives and targets will improve the visibility of activities both within the purchasing process and between other departments, and identify areas of waste in terms of defects, delays, surpluses and mistakes. It may also contribute to the status and profile of purchasing within the organization.

4. *Motivation*: as discussed above, measurement motivates people to act in certain ways. If targets can be seen to be related to the overall success of a particular objective, then employees will feel more motivated. This is related to the idea that people generally feel the need to contribute and, when they see an objective being fulfilled at least partially as a result of their actions, will find increased satisfaction in working to achieve those goals. If measures have no apparent purpose or link to the overall working of the company, there will be little attraction in achieving them. As Simons (1995: p. 83) says, often it is difficult for employees 'to understand the larger purpose of their efforts, or to see how they can add value in a way that can make a difference'.

3.5 The Importance of Strategy

Some managers may feel uncomfortable about assessing the performance of their purchasing department in ways which are not entirely financial, and in which there is perhaps greater potential for error in measuring soft activities. However, 'how many companies have found differences in how their various business units define apparently simple concepts such as gross margin, or even turnover?' (Geanuracos and Meiklejohn, 1994: p. 341). Often, efficiency-based measures continue to be used in purchasing, simply because managers do not feel they have an acceptable alternative or complement with which to chapter internally, although they recognize the limitations of the measures employed for reflecting the broad range of purchasing activities in which they are involved. However, when the rewards of activities which are difficult to quantify are linked to specific outputs, targets and quotas, they often promote behaviour which compromises the quality of their results. An example of this might be a police force which, although it has developed good working relationships with the local community, is not recognized for this, as it is measured on the number of arrests or convictions it manages to get (Johnson and Scholes, 1980). Again, it is being measured on how well it treats the symptoms of the problem, rather than tackling the cause, or the determinants of value; on efficiency rather than effectiveness.

In order to function effectively in contributing to the organization's goals, the activities of any process must be linked explicitly with the broader corporate strategy. The idea that objectives

Purchasing requires a clear alignment with corporate thrust.

must cascade from different levels of the organization into specific goals (i.e. the goals of one level are the means of the next) is fundamental to the success of any strategic activity. For purchasing to contribute to the success of the organization, therefore, it is crucial that it derives its strategy from the corporate strategy. Ellram and Carr (1994: p. 12) quote Caddick and Dale who claim that 'the objectives of the purchasing function need to be defined following the articulation of the corporate objectives, to support those objectives'. Similarly, Reck and Long (1988: p. 3) state that 'it is the role of the purchasing function within a firm to structure and manage itself to support and enhance the firm's ability to attain its desired competitive advantage. The philosophy of the purchasing system and its capabilities in terms of suppliers, personnel and information should focus on the elements of competitive strategy that management considers essential to the firm's success.' Purchasing therefore requires a clear alignment with corporate thrust: to operate according to any other criteria will mean that resources are being misallocated in terms of what the organization is trying to achieve. This implicitly requires that senior management should pass the information on which they base decisions regarding company operations on to each function, so enabling the credible measurement of purchasing contribution to the business. Lynch and Cross (1991) use the Performance Pyramid (Figure 11.2) to show how various activities can be shown to contribute to organizational strategy. The key here is that as the objectives are stated at each level of the Pyramid, so measures are derived at the respective level, which will support each set of objectives, in line with top-level strategy.

FIGURE 11.2   The Performance Pyramid

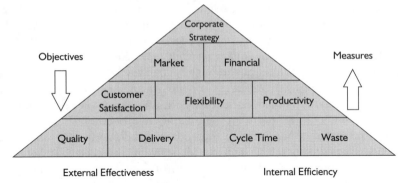

SOURCE: Lynch and Cross (1991).

Another important principle of performance measurement is that the measures designed at each organizational level should include specific input of the teams which will be responsible for delivering the progress against those goals. Managers will be required to set the strategic context, but should allow the teams to think about the most effective ways in which they can achieve them (to suit that strategic context). In this way, the measurement system will achieve a greater degree of credibility with employees than if the measures are imposed on them from the top downwards, and are less likely to fall into disuse, or be manipulated. As Meyer (1994) says, measures are too often imposed on employees by senior management, to pull information upwards so that they can manage downwards. This also ignores the likelihood that the people who do the job routinely, who are 'closest to the action', will know more about the nature of their work, and will be able to judge which measures will be relevant and effective. Johnson and Scholes (1980: p. 298) argue that the dominant purpose of performance measures should be to help the employees monitor their own performance: 'in this way it is more likely that objectives will be "owned" by those responsible for achieving them, and in turn, that they will regard them as useful measures against which to monitor their own performance'. It will also ensure that any 'hidden' or implied measures are exposed – for example, that while a goal of low inventory holdings may be pursued, the unstated priority might be not to be 'caught short'.

Simons (1995: pp. 84–87) introduces a strategic model for planning measurement systems which are designed to exercise control in environments which require flexibility and innovation, and which might be useful in establishing the types of measure needed for purchasing performance. It balances four 'levers of control', which he terms *Diagnostic, Boundary, Beliefs* and *Interactive* requirements (see Table 11.2).

Diagnostic systems track performance against goals and targets, enabling managers to scan for abnormal functioning and maintain critical performance levels within limits. Beliefs systems articulate the values and directions which managers want their employees to employ, to guide them towards the types of solution to seek in solving problems. They should be concise and value-laden, but designed to inspire 'the way we do things around here'. Boundary systems should 'employ the power of negative thinking' . Rather than telling employees how to do their jobs, through tightly-defined standard operating procedures, clear boundaries based on strategic directions should be established within which initiative and creativity are encouraged. As he says, 'the warm, positive, inspirational beliefs are a foil to the cold, dark constraints. The result is a dynamic tension between commitment and punishment. Together these systems transform limitless opportunity into a focused domain that employees and managers are encouraged to exploit actively.' Interactive systems are designed to share emerging information in the marketplace (which may have a strategic impact on the organization) between the disparate units of an organization. Interactive control systems 'track the strategic uncertainties that keep managers awake at night'.

Strategic direction is, therefore, of paramount importance when designing performance measures, through which the message of what is expected of a particular process and those involved in it is communicated. In purchasing, therefore, every measure should be assessed on its usefulness in helping purchasing to achieve its strategy. Again, it is not necessarily the measures which are used that are important, but how they are used. For example, Ringwald (1995) gives an example of measurement within her own purchasing department. The department received 35,000 requisitions in 1994, raised 28,000 purchase orders, and

TABLE 11.2 Levers of Control

Control lever	Potential	Organizational barriers	Managerial solution
Belief systems	To contribute to core values	Uncertainty about purpose	Communicate core values and mission
Boundary systems	To do right, and avoid major risks to the unit	Pressure of temptation	Specify and enforce rules of the game
Diagnostic control systems	To achieve against critical performance variables	Lack of focus or resources	Build and support clear targets
Interactive control systems	To create, and be able to meet strategic uncertainties	Lack of opportunity or fear of risk	Open dialogue and encourage learning

SOURCE: Simons (1995).

arranged and managed 26 contracts with a total value of £18 m. These are figures, however, are simply statistics – they do not give information about measures of efficiency or effectiveness. A more useful measure of efficiency measure might be that the average time from receipt of order requisitions to the placement of orders was 1.5 days. In this case, order turnaround time is a useful efficiency measure which indicates how well internal customer needs are being met. In addition, 75 per cent of deliveries on all orders placed were either early or on time. This gives a more meaningful indication of effectiveness against a particular criterion (delivery performance), and can be tracked over time.

> *In purchasing every measure should be assessed on its usefulness in helping purchasing to achieve its strategy.*

Purchasing strategy, however, will differ according to the way in which purchasing is perceived as contributing to corporate strategy. Reck and Long (1988) suggest that there are four strategic stages in the development of a purchasing function: *Passive, Independent, Supportive, Integrative* (see Appendix A). Each of these stages is characterized by the expectations of purchasing by senior management, and the nature of the tasks in which purchasing is involved, from a level where purchasing lacks strategic direction (Passive), to the other end of the continuum where the function is fully integrated into the firm's strategic planning process (Integrative). Once purchasing managers can position themselves on the continuum, they can begin to identify the changes in attitudes, managerial practices, policies and procedures required to 'propel purchasing to successively higher levels of competitive effectiveness'. They claim that it is not possible for a purchasing function to omit any one of these stages in order to get to another. It is also likely that the performance measurement criteria, against which purchasing is measured, will evolve as each of the stages are reached, and as senior management's expectations change. A significant feature of this model, however, is that it is improbable that purchasing will be operating any one 'box' alone. Most purchasing activities will be spread about the boxes simultaneously, according to the various requirements of the organization. As there is no clear delineation of where one stage begins and another ends, individual functions may exhibit the characteristics of more than one of the stages. The function will therefore have a 'portfolio' arrangement in terms of the roles that it will play in the overall business policy, and the measurement system will need to reflect the spread of these activities.

Syson (1995) builds on this idea, recognizing that each type of purchasing activity, clerical/tactical, commercial, or strategic, is appropriate to sustaining commercial advantage for different types of enterprise. The challenge is to concentrate in the 'correct' type of activity. As the role of purchasing changes over time, so the performance requirements must evolve in parallel: for example, a focus on price savings will shift towards a focus on whole life cost. This is depicted in Figures 11.3 and 11.4.

FIGURE 11.3 Positioning Graph for Strategies

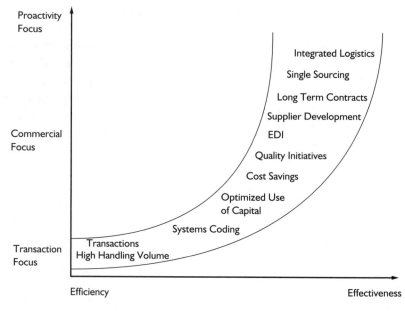

SOURCE: Syson (1995).

FIGURE 11.4 Positioning Graph for Performance Measures

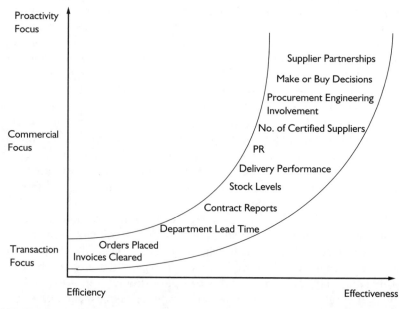

SOURCE: Syson (1995).

Strategy, then, is the starting point for any meaningful measurement of purchasing performance. Measures must support the goals of the purchasing strategy, which in turn should be developed in line with the corporate expectations of purchasing. These goals need to be translated into specific milestones which enable the function to plan activities and measure performance against the plan (Cannon, 1995). It follows, therefore, that no bespoke list of measures for purchasing can be applied across all organizations. Different organizations will have varying strategies and goals for success in their respective markets, based for example, on increasing market share, or improving market penetration. As such they will have different requirements and expectations of purchasing and how it can contribute to these overall goals. Any performance measurement system to be effective, therefore, needs to be flexible and dynamic, in order to adapt to the changing pressures on the organization. It should also be an iterative process, tracking performance against key indicators, and setting new objectives. Lamming and Davis (1995), in a survey of the purchasing performance measures used in 32 'blue chip' companies, found that there were no clear patterns of measures used for particular activities, or to which level these measures were chaptered.

A company located upstream in the production process is likely to focus on indicators which reflect standardisation, cost effectiveness, process innovation, capital budgets and technological lead time. A company which is located downstream in the business, on the other hand, is likely to search for indicators which emphasis customisation, high margins/niche positions, product innovation, research and development, the quality of its people and customer service. (Geanuracos and Meiklejohn, 1994: p. 120)

While it is likely that some of the activities required of purchasing may be similar across different organizations, the way in which they are interpreted or used can be radically different. Butler (1995: p. 2) found that, where comprehensive 'strategic' measurement systems existed for purchasing performance, 'they were usually tailor-made for a particular company's culture and processes, or for individual commodities or services'.

3.6 Structure and Culture

A further cause of the variation in performance measures used in purchasing is the differing nature of organizational structures. Stanley (1993) has developed a model which describes some of the influences on how purchasing measures are determined (see Figure 11.5).

Essentially, this model explains that the structure of the purchasing department will depend to a great extent on the variability of the environment in which the organization operates, the complexity of the marketplace, and how flexible it can be in responding to various market

FIGURE 11.5 Influences of Performance

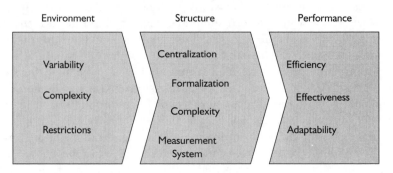

SOURCE: Stanley (1993).

pressures. These factors will determine the requirements of purchasing, and, therefore, the level of centralization–decentralization, and how formalized specified tasks are. The complexity of the activities undertaken, and of the supply market will also impact on the formalization of the tasks. These three broad factors, taken together in the context of the organization's environment will contribute to the nature of the performance measures employed. These, in turn, will affect the extent to which purchasing performs against efficiency and effectiveness criteria. In designing new performance measurement systems, the nature of the internal structure and expectations of purchasing will need to be understood, in addition to the overall corporate thrust. Indeed, as van Weele (1994: p. 198) suggests, as the scope of purchasing will vary between firms, and as few formal objectives and standards exist for purchasing in general, 'it is highly uncertain whether such a yardstick or method, of universal application, could be developed'. The key to successful performance measures is to design them according to the strategy, structure and culture of the organization, in order to ensure that they are directly relevant and useful to the needs of the users in that organization. 'The key to competitive advantage comes through innovation, not imitation' (Zenz, 1994: p. 23).

3.7 Problems with Implementation

The successful implementation of a new performance measurement system can be fraught with a variety of pitfalls which mainly relate to the context in which the system is introduced. As Ghorpade and Chen (1995: p. 35) say, 'the system that is used to appraise performance needs to be congruent with the culture and principles that guide the conduct of the organisation. Unless congruence is retained, anything that is developed is unlikely to be retained.' Too often, for example, the chaptering channels are devised before the formulation of strategy, based on organizational structure rather than on the activities or business processes which need the information.

Bleinkinsop and Burns (1992) chapter on the failure of a new performance measurement system in a company with which they worked, which illustrates some of the principles discussed up to this point. Although the system was designed to measure manufacturing performance, the principles behind the study are applicable to purchasing. They describe a company whose managers felt that they had understood the steps required for implementing the system – amongst others, that the measures should:

● be 'owned' by the group;
● be easy to calculate;
● be consistent and understood by all;
● shift the emphasis away from the short-termism of accounting drivers by introducing some non-quantitative measures.

In response, they anticipated that the benefits which would result would include:

● improved performance within the targeted areas;
● better employee motivation;
● an indication of how employees contributed to divisional performance.

However, a number of very basic organizational changes which were necessary for the success of the system were not implemented in parallel with the new measures. For example:

● there were no established mechanisms for data collection;
● the responsibility for analyzing and preparing the charts was not delegated to anyone specifically;
● as a result they suffered problems with the accuracy, availability and timeliness of the data.

The authors concluded that the reasons behind the breakdown of the system fell into *four* broad categories:

1. *Ownership*: the employees did not feel that problems in their area belonged to them. They were not invited to participate in designing measures, nor were they consulted about their implementation. Consequently, the employees had little commitment to them.

2. *Simplicity*: while the measures were easy to calculate, the data on which they were based was suspect and unreliable – and therefore had no credibility with workers or management.

3. *Consistency*: although the director had communicated his objectives well, they had no established feedback loop, and therefore no means of knowing whether they were understood by the employees. As a

result, the message was gradually diluted by daily operating pressures.

4. *Internal relationships*: the system reinforced the belief that performance is the sum of the performance of each individual or cell, not that of the network of interrelationships.

Behind this example lay some fundamental principles which were not considered in implementing the system. The managers failed to delegate the authority to allow their workers the necessary autonomy to make effective changes to processes, and largely ignored the information produced by shop floor. This manifested itself when the shop floor stopped producing the performance charts and no-one noticed. Not only had they failed to empower the workers, they were also communicating the message that they did not care about the measures, as they were obviously not using them in decision-making. The measures set also appeared to be arbitrary to the workers – no direct connection was made between individual cells and company performance. 'As the information displayed on the charts was not used by management as a measure of company performance, it was inferred that it was irrelevant.'

Bleinkinsop and Burns conclude that the changes introduced were not properly thought out in the context of the company structure and culture, and there was little commitment apparent from senior levels in the organization (for example, there was no project champion). 'In their hurry to find a solution to the problem, they failed to define accurately the *nature* of the problem.'

4. Focusing Internally

4.1 Internal Customers

In order to develop a coherent framework within which measures can be related systematically to the purposes which they are intended to serve, the purchasing function needs to look at the processes which are affected by its activities, on the basis of business need (Syson, 1995). Because procurement serves many customers in providing input to their processes, several goals are needed to improve decision-making, regarding all the vital responsibilities. These areas cover clerical matters, such as developing accurate, cost-effective systems, emphasizing value for money; the commercial focus, a business-orientated, selective management of the supply base; and strategic issues concerning the management of external resources. As such, any assessment of performance 'should be brought about with the active involvement of all those who are affected by the activity' (Ghorpade and Chen, 1995). Indeed, as Dumond (1991: p. 37) states: 'good or bad purchasing is largely determined by the perception of internal customers to whom purchasing provides its services ... purchasers will clearly be at their best when they fully appreciate that their performance will be evaluated in the light of its impact on the performance of their internal customers'.

Syson (1995) categorizes the major purchasing areas of responsibility as:

1. to assure short-term supply continuity;
2. to contribute to materials cost control;
3. to reduce company vulnerability to supply markets – long-term supply;
4. to contribute to product and process innovation;
5. to contribute to company image in outside world.

If the business units and functions within the organization have their own strategies aligned with the overall corporate goal, they will require that the relevant goods and services which they need are acquired in such a way as to enable them to meet their own objectives and to contribute effectively to corporate strategy overall. Purchasing performance, therefore, will not only be determined by the way in which top management perceives the role of purchasing, but also by how well purchasing reacts to the requirements of its internal customers. Cox (1995) argues that 'if the management of a supply and value chain is nothing more than seeking to make a sustainable margin (or profit) for the firm, then everyone in the company has to be involved in the process, not just purchasing'. However, purchasing should not operate purely as a service function, complying with internal customer requirements unquestioningly. 'A more realistic view is that purchasing should provide a healthy commercial opposition *vis-à-vis* its internal customers' (van Weele, 1994: p. 84), by looking for opportunities to improve cost awareness elsewhere in the company, or suggesting alternatives to product designs based on supply market knowledge and expertise.

The internal customer is an important element in assessing purchasing performance.

The internal customer is therefore an important element in assessing purchasing performance. As Geanuracos and Meiklejohn (1994: p. 135) reflect, managers often know how well a function is performing against a set plan, but not whether they are serving their internal customers' needs. Tracking the level of expenditure, for example, does not indicate how well the resources bought are used. The reason for learning about what internal customers perceive as important is that,

> the danger is you just pedal faster without understanding what it is your customer is trying to achieve. The classic example is deciding that speed of delivery is a key customer satisfaction criterion, when

customers would rather have certainty of delivery. Without verifying your strategic priorities with your customers, you may find that you are making investment decisions that have little value.

Chao *et al.* (1993) surveyed a number of purchasing managers, buyers and internal customers to assess their respective priorities on ten broad purchasing performance criteria, ranging from supplier development to levels of commodity knowledge. Their study found that the expectations of different parties regarding performance against these criteria were very different. For example, purchase order cycle time was the most important criterion for internal customers, who valued it nearly twice as much as the purchasing managers. Conversely, levels of purchasing professionalism were of far higher priority for buyers than they were for the internal customers.

Cannon (1995: p. 20) suggests the use of a purchasing audit in order to understand performance against internal customer's strategic requirements: 'in order to develop a mission statement which can be translated into achievable goals, the function should be involved in, or at least consulted during the determination of the mission statements of all of its internal customers'. If this is done successfully, then, he argues, the mission, goals and milestones, together with the function's structure, systems and processes, can be assessed.

The underlying principle of all ideas is the notion that 'we are all customers of each other', or as van Weele (1994: p. 24) puts it, 'the quality of the output of the preceding phase determines to a large extent, the quality of the output of the subsequent stage'. The objective should be to establish a 'chain of customers' which, directly or indirectly, links all the processes in the organization to the marketplace (Christopher, 1992). Each department must focus on the next department's needs, as the operating system only performs as well as the department next to the customer. In any process the customer is the next person or function for whom purchasing provides goods, materials, products or services. However, identifying exactly who internal customers are, and extracting what information they actually need to gauge performance can be a frustrating step in the performance measurement exercise.

4.2 Stakeholder Analysis

The 'stakeholder' concept can provide a useful input to the process of identifying internal customers. The stakeholders of an organization can be defined as 'all those interested groups, parties actors, claimants and institutions – both internal and external – that exert a hold on it. That is, stakeholders are all those parties who either affect or who are affected by a corporation's actions, behaviour and policies (Mitroff, 1982: p. 4). A generic description of an organization's potential stakeholders is shown in Figure 11.6.

FIGURE 11.6   Stakeholders – the Concept

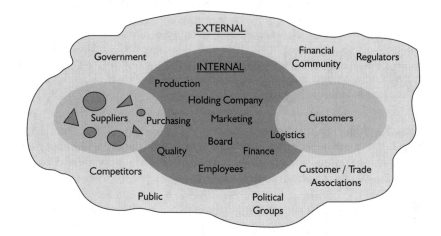

Kanter (1989: p. 127) describes stakeholder alliances as 'complementary coalitions between a number of stakeholders in a business process who are involved in different stages of the value-creation chain. Stakeholders are those groups on which an organisation depends – the people who can help it achieve its goals or can stop it dead in its tracks. They include customers, suppliers and employees.' The goal of every organization, therefore, should be to meet its stakeholder needs. However, as Poltorzycki (1993: p. 35) claims, stakeholders are often not consulted about what they require from an activity, and 'as a result, companies end up measuring things their stakeholders don't care about – or failing to measure things critical to stakeholder satisfaction'. The point of stakeholder analysis, therefore, is to force organizations to be more responsive.

Mitroff (1982) explains that each stakeholder has a 'will of its own', and pursues its own goals as well as those of the system as a whole. The problem is that different stakeholders do not usually share the same definitions of an organization's 'problems', and therefore have different views on the solutions. People often perceive the same facts differently, interpreting them against their own background or interest, as they interpret the facts from very different backgrounds, each giving a different nature to the assumptions about the problem. He further states that, 'the state of an organisation at a certain point in time will be the result of the interaction of behaviour of all the organisation's stakeholders from the beginning of its history up to a particular point in time. This extended history may be referred to as the "culture" of the organization' (p. 38).

The Stakeholders of Purchasing

This approach can be modified for the purpose of the measurement of purchasing performance. Rather than concentrating on the external stakeholders of an organization, attention should be paid to the internal stake-holders of the purchasing process. These are likely to include not only the department which raised the purchase requisition in the first place – the user, or the internal customer – but also those other areas of the business which also have a 'stake' in the process. If a specific part is required, for example, by production or engineering, it is likely that marketing might have an interest in particular features or design; Quality control will want it to meet certain specifications in use; Finance will be concerned about the price, or total cost in use. Similarly, there will be certain purchasing or corporate procedures which must be followed, as well as regulations. If suppliers are considered to be the external resources of a company, and part of the extended organization (Lamming, 1993), they should be considered as legitimate internal stakeholders in the purchasing process. Using a simple input–output process model, as depicted in Figure 11.7, if all the activities of purchasing are broken down into the constituent parts, the use of the model will be able to identify the relevant stakeholders for each activity or area of responsibility. The boundaries of each of the areas in the diagram are characterized by a two-way flow of information.

Such an exercise might help in identifying the less obvious stake-holder, which might be overlooked in an unstructured analysis of internal customers. Such stakeholders have be termed 'snaildarters', following the delay in building a hydro-electric dam, which resulted in environmentalists protesting about an endangered species of fish. 'The lesson of the snaildarter is paramount. Just beneath the surface of the best laid and most rational plans swim forces of which people are entirely unaware and do not wish to consider. These seemingly tiny and insignificant forces, however, have a strange way of wrecking the most well-conceived pans and policies' (Mitroff, 1982: p. 45).

Cyert and March (1963) have identified *four* ways in which the stake-holders of a process derive their power and which provide a means to identify who the stakeholders might be in any given activity.

FIGURE 11.7 Purchasing Stakeholders

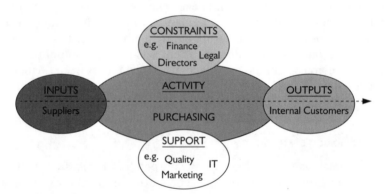

- Resource dependency.
- Involvement in implementation.
- Knowledge or skills critical to process success.
- Internal links in the process.

Accordingly, the internal stakeholders which are identified may then be ranked in terms of their 'importance' in the organization, and the nature of their 'stake' in purchasing activities, i.e. how important the level of purchasing performance in an agreed area is to the achievement of their strategic (and therefore corporate) objectives.

Regarding purchasing performance, Cavinato (1987) claims that 'one of the problems with the traditional accounting and operations-based performance measures is that, typically, they only travel upwards in a firm.' Through these chapters, purchasing's accomplishments do not reach many of the interfacing departments and other peer groups in the firm. He identifies *two* major problems with chaptering purchasing performance measures, based on organizational perceptions.

1. It can appear to be too easy, and paper-orientated. Few of the areas of effectiveness such as cost analysis, negotiation, or supply market management are made visible to their peers.

2. The measures are rarely regarded as relevant to other functional peers: they are often too tightly defined, with little relevance to the broader company picture.

The process of internal stakeholder identification will necessarily, in the course of the analysis, highlight what their respective interests, or stakes, in the purchasing process are, and therefore enable a more effective level of chaptering to the respective stakeholders, based on their information needs and eliminating irrelevant information. As Poltorzycki (1993: p. 41) says, 'once you have made relevant measurements, it is important to use them to improve performance and to communicate that performance to stakeholders ... companies that measure the right things and make those measurements both available and useful to the right people ... will contain their risks and discover valuable opportunities to gain competitive advantage.' Hedstrom and McLean (1993) describes the sequential process in which the appropriate chaptering approaches may come about (see Table 11.3).

In determining appropriate purchasing performance levels, therefore, stakeholder analysis provides a useful means by which to determine whether purchasing meets the needs of its internal stakeholder in an optimal way.

TABLE 11.3 Evolution in Communicating Performance

	Low	**Stage of Evolution**		**High**
Approach	Tell them what you have to	Tell them what you want to	Tell them what you think they want to know	Tell them what they have told you they want to know
Manifestation	Required disclosures	Good deeds descriptions	Programme implementation progress	Performance improvement

SOURCE: Hestrom and McLean (1993).

5. The Balanced Scorecard

5.1 The Concept Behind the Scorecard

The Balanced Scorecard, developed by Kaplan and Norton (1992; 1993), was originally conceived as a means of measuring corporate performance in a manner which would reflect not only financial indicators of performance, but also those other critical value drivers which enable an organization to compete successfully. The idea is that managers should not have to choose between financial and non-financial measures, as no single type of measure can provide a clear focus for attention. Therefore, a dynamic balance needs to be struck between the two types. The scorecard is based on *four* major areas: financial criteria, customer satisfaction, internal business processes and organizational learning (see Figure 11.8).

1. *Customer focus* is essential to an understanding of how customers view the business, because, without customers, no organization can create value. This area forces managers to translate their broad goals on customer service into measures that really matter to the customer. It is composed of such issues as time, quality, performance and service, and, essentially, tries to get managers to see the company from the customers' point of view.

2. *Internal business processes* refer to the way operations are carried out within the company, which enable the customer satisfaction to be achieved. The focus should be on the internal processes that have the greatest impact on customer satisfaction, and therefore which affect cycle time, productivity, quality and design, for example. A capable information system is vital to this.

3. *Organizational learning* is the ability to change and improve on a continuous basis. While customer and internal business processes

FIGURE 11.8 Balanced Scorecard Measures

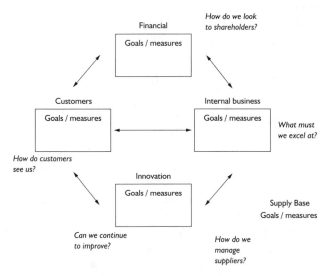

SOURCE: Kaplan and Norton (1992).

reflect the parameters which the company considers vital for success, continuous improvement is also necessary in an ever-changing business environment. It recognizes the intellectual assets which are inherent in any organization, and the importance of human resources.

4. The *financial perspective* reflects the extent to which the various initiatives contribute to the bottom line, and typically deals with the more traditional measures of corporate performance, focusing on profitability, cash flow, and shareholders – the results of actions already taken. The three other boxes relate to those indicators which contribute to financial performance, and which in turn depend on it.

The Balanced Scorecard focuses on strategy, drawing on the four different perspectives, and grounded in the company's particular view of the world and its perspective on key success factors. That view is then translated into a small set of coherent measurable objectives, which then cascade down into specific operational goals. The fact that there are only a few key measures is important, as this helps to avoid the proliferation of a number of less relevant indicators. It is a useful planning tool, which does not place undue emphasis on simple control measures, but rather pulls activities into

> *The Balanced Scorecard focuses on strategy.*

line with corporate strategy. The benefit of having a comprehensive focus of distinct, but related, activities is not only that it provides a focal point and common language for assessment for 'seemingly disparate elements of a company's competitive agenda' (Kaplan and Norton, 1992: p. 73), but that it makes visible any potential conflicts which may arise from pursuing certain courses of action. As such it guards against over- or under-optimization. Finally, and crucially, it provides a flexible approach to measurement, as objectives and priorities change over time to suit the business environment.

5.2 The Balanced Purchasing Scorecard

The scorecard approach provides a potentially useful way of approaching purchasing performance measurement. Purchasing needs to satisfy not only certain financial targets, such as cost reduction and price perform-ance, but also other important areas. On-time delivery, order cycle time, and waste elimination may all be measures of how well purchasing is satisfying the needs of its internal customers. Improved flexibility in terms of order scheduling systems or means of invoicing, or simply reduc-ing bureaucracy could fit into the internal business process focus, as they are all important in achieving internal customer satisfaction. Under orga-nizational learning, the levels of professional development, in terms of qualifications or the levels of training of staff may be important. Butler (1995) found that some companies were indeed using this type of approach in measuring purchasing performance, and has added a fifth box to the model for the use of purchasing (see Figure 11.7). Crucially, it relates to how well purchasing performs *vis-à-vis* its suppliers, and might examine such factors as supply market awareness and supplier development.

6. A Methodology for Approaching Purchasing Performance

6.1 Introduction

Based on the extensive literature search, the analysis of various purchas-ing models and performance measurement principles, and discussions with the collaborating companies of SCDP Group 2, a strategic method-ology for approaching performance measurement of purchasing has been developed. An overview of this is depicted in Figure 11.9.

The methodology addresses a number of key stages:

- The identification of the main internal stakeholders of purchasing.
- The identification and ranking of internal stakeholders' expectations of purchasing.
- The categorization of the general requirements for appropriate pur-chasing, according to the supply market.
- The plotting of a balanced range of objectives for purchasing, derived from a synthesis of internal expectations, and meeting the conditions of the supply market.

FIGURE 11.9 An approach to performance measurement of purchasing

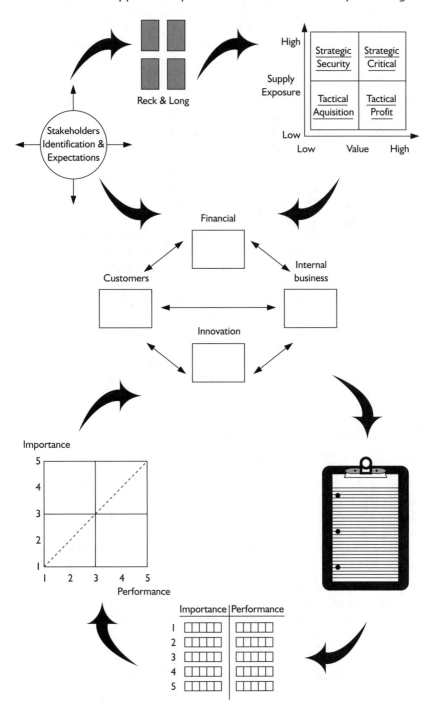

- The development of appropriate measures to support the objectives.
- Finding a means by which to gather information regarding the performance of purchasing against those measures.
- A simple representation of performance against the ranked expectations, which indicates areas of over- or under-optimization, and indicates any need to reallocate resources.

With reference to the various issues in the preceding discussion regarding performance measurement generally, and purchasing specifically, the methodology is designed to address particular criteria which should be considered in designing purchasing performance measures. These require that the measurement system should:

- place the measurement against agreed goals in the context of purchasing strategy and organizational culture;
- isolate a few critical activities worthy of evaluation;
- achieve a level of performance against a range of objectives, which do not concentrate solely on financial or efficiency-based measures;
- help the decision-making of purchasing personnel in their daily operations;
- ensure that both efficiency and effectiveness criteria are considered;
- allow tailored feedback to internal stakeholders;
- determine frequency, format and personnel;
- systematic (time series) data collection;
- recognize the relationships between means and ends;
- be flexible enough to adapt to the evolution of goals and objectives over time.

6.2 An Explanation of the Methodology

Identification of the main internal stakeholders of purchasing

Using the purchasing stakeholder model developed in Section 5, it should be possible to break down the activities of purchasing into specific areas, such as 'supplier development', 'cost control', or 'contribution to product innovation', for example.

In considering these activities, attention should be given to such questions as:

- What resources do we use – inputs?
- What services are produced – outputs?
- How are these services produced – processes?
- Who else do our actions affect – support?
- What constraints must we take into account – controls?

This should enable all the significant departments and areas of an organization which are in some way impacted by the activity to be identified.

FIGURE 11.10 Purchasing Stakeholders

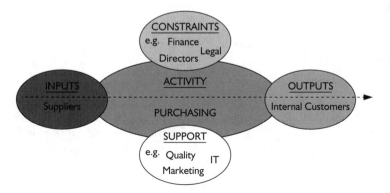

Identification and ranking of internal stakeholders' expectations of purchasing

The expectations collected at this stage should be based on the requirements for purchasing to provide the specified goods and services in such a way as to enable the internal stakeholder to meet its own strategic objectives.

Once the internal stakeholders have been identified, it will then be possible to approach them, asking for their broad expectations of purchasing. This could also be phrased in the negative, i.e. 'What is the most fundamental aspect of purchasing, the absence or failure of which would affect your ability to achieve your strategic objectives the most?' These expectations should refer to general requirements regarding their own objectives, but be specific enough to be attributed to more specific activities. For example, an expectation of 'brilliant purchasing' could not be broken down rationally. Anticipated responses at this stage might be 'reliable delivery', 'improved quality', 'to British Standard X', or 'improved responsiveness to requests for information', 'more involvement in product development', 'better provision of supplier information', or 'reduced purchasing lead times'.

Once these responses have been elicited, they can be 'ranked', according to their perceived level of importance, which might be determined in a number of ways, such as:

- according to where the 'power' lies in the organization;
- the impact on overall business objectives if the expectation is not met, i.e. the nature of the 'stake';
- using a variation of Pareto analysis;
- how easy the expectations are to meet.

Again, the method chosen will largely depend on the culture of the organization and the level of importance attached to purchasing in general. This stage might also give purchasing managers the information which they need to position themselves on the Reck and Long model, and develop appropriate strategies (see Section 3).

Categorizing the general requirements for appropriate purchasing, according to the supply market

Having ranked stakeholder expectations regarding provision of goods, services and expertise, the nature of the supply market needs be analyzed with respect to the products or services required. The Supply Positioning Matrix, as developed by Kraljic (1983), provides a useful means for this. It adopts a 'portfolio' approach to the market, based on a classification of products according to:

● the value added by product line, the percentage of purchased items in total costs and their impact on profitability;
● the complexity of the market, depending on scarcity of supply, the pace of technology, materials substitution, and monopoly or oligopoly conditions.

Issues to consider at this stage might include the suppliers' capacity utilization and flexibility, past variations in capacity utilization, the uniqueness of the product, volumes purchased and their expected demand, break-even stability, levels of technology employed, history of quality performance, and organizational culture. Such an analysis should enable the areas of significant opportunity, vulnerability and risk to be assessed, relative to an understanding of the power relationships between the firm and the relevant suppliers (for example if the company occupies a dominant or a secondary market role). As such, the organization should be able to build its own 'base scorecard' for each type of supply.

FIGURE 11.11 Supply Positioning Model

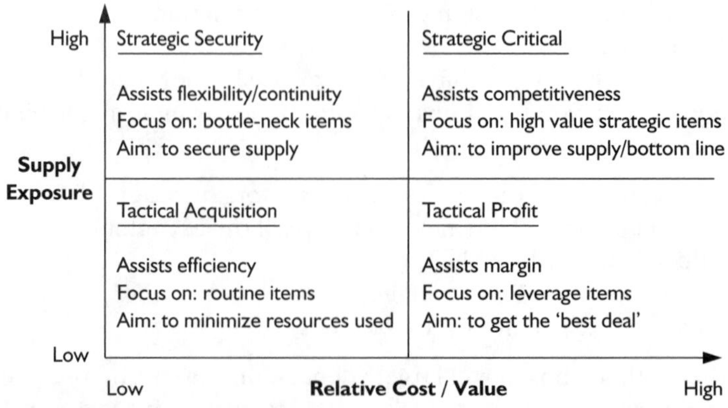

SOURCE: Kraljic (1983).

Plotting a balanced range of objectives for purchasing, derived from a synthesis of internal expectations, according to the conditions of the supply market

Such an analysis, combined with an understanding of internal stakeholder expectations, should enable a standard profile of activities to be identified in seeking to acquire types of product, and to 'spread' the expectations across certain areas of purchasing activity. Using the Balanced Scorecard Approach, expectations should be grouped according to the four criteria discussed in Section 5, specifically: Customer, Internal Business Processes, Innovation and Financial Performance. This process should enable managers to develop their specific objectives and enable customer expectations to be met in the most appropriate and effective way.

It is likely, for example, that the financial expectations for products which suit the Tactical Acquisition and Strategic Critical quadrants will differ widely: the former may require the most efficient acquisition of low cost materials, while expectations for products in the latter quadrant might require significant investment in a supplier's long-term capabilities, focusing on reductions in the Total Cost in Use. Similarly, the delivery or quality expectations for products will differ according to the strategic impact of the good upon the business process

Development of appropriate measures to support the objectives

As discussed in the main text, the operational measures chosen to support purchasing objectives will depend on the nature of the objectives, and their relation to purchasing and corporate strategy, and therefore the way in which they are to be used.

FIGURE 11.12   Balanced Scorecard Measures

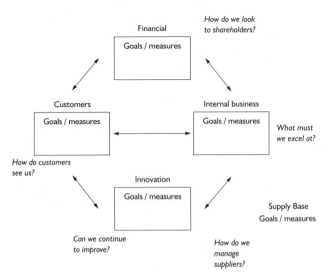

The model employs a comprehensive shopping-list of purchasing performance measures, developed by Lamming and Davis (1995) in research which identified a number of different types of measure employed in various blue chip organizations in the UK. This list has been updated with a number of other specific types of measure found in the literature, and from discussions with the participating companies, and can be found in Appendix B. The list has been divided into 'groups' of measure which might support different objectives. The intention here is simply to provide a stimulus to managers as they consider which measures will be useful for them to achieve the scorecard objectives, rather than to state absolutes. A significant consideration at this stage is to ensure that the measures adopted reflect an optimal balance between efficiency and effectiveness.

A means by which to gather information regarding the performance of purchasing against those measures

FIGURE 11.13 Importance and Performance 1

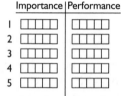

Once the measures have been decided, they can be assessed in terms of priority of achievement, according to the ranked expectations which gave rise to them initially. A simple questionnaire can then be sent out periodically to the internal stakeholders to determine the standard to which they perceive purchasing has been performed against their requirements, based on a simple ranking of 1 to 5. A format for doing this is provided in Appendix B. The performance indicators which it includes, derived from the list of grouped measures in Appendix C, are listed as examples, however, rather than the actual measures which should be used. The specific measures appropriate to an organization will be arrived at from the development of specific goals, developed from the approach described so far.

Performance can then be collected against the expectations of individual stakeholders, and at an aggregate level across all the stakeholders of purchasing in general.

A simple representation of performance against the ranked expectations, which indicates areas of over- or under-optimization and the need (or otherwise) to reallocate resources.

Once the levels of importance of the measures against which to perform have been ranked, and the performance achieved for each have been

FIGURE 11.14 Importance and Performance 2

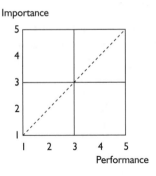

scored, it will be possible to 'plot' each measure on a simple graph, using the ranks and scores as 'coordinates'. Again, these can be plotted for individual stakeholders and for the aggregate. Assuming that resources are scarce, it follows that an organization cannot perform perfectly against all criteria all the time. Intuitively, it should perform best against the most important criteria, and less well against those of lesser importance. This is represented by the 45° line, running from points (1,1) to (5,5). Any deviance from the line represents either over-achievement or under-achievement against expectations, for a given indicator, and this has obvious implications for the way in which resources are allocated to particular activities and goals.

While this is an attractively simple tool to use, it must be recognized that the actual line running across the chart may, in practice, not be straight. The reason is that the measures which are deemed to be more important are likely to be of a more strategic nature, and therefore require proportionately more effort to be allocated to them in order to perform well. Similarly, relatively unimportant measures could require less effort and, therefore resource, in meeting the appropriate performance levels. To determine the realistic nature of this effort-resource line will require further research.

An alternative method of developing this information was initially attempted during the course of the research, which provided a valuable lesson. Respondents were given a list of potential activities for purchasing to perform well, and asked to rank their perceptions of how important each criterion was for purchasing to achieve. Next, they were asked to score purchasing performance against each criterion. In each case, the respondents were asked to allocate their marks 1 (low) to 10 (high) from a given total, i.e. to spread the total marks out across the criteria. This was to ensure that the respondents could not simply mark '10' for importance, and '1' for performance. For example, a total of only 50 marks would be available to allocate to 10 criteria. The intention was to encourage participants to make difficult choices, and force trade-offs in their allocation of

marks to different criteria, based on relative importance and performance. However, there were two significant problems with this approach.

1. The first problem arose in the collection of credible data. Initially,
   some questionnaires were distributed amongst key managers within
   two of the SCDP Group 2 companies. Because the concept behind the
   exercise was difficult to understand without a more detailed explanation, fewer responses than expected were received. In addition, of
   those received, less than 25 per cent were filled in correctly, as the
   respondents had misinterpreted the instructions and had simply
   ranked the criteria from 1 to 10, allocating fewer points than the total
   required, and not indicating relative preferences. In other cases, they
   had scored each criterion out of 10, allocating a total number of
   points far in excess of the total.

2. In the course of analyzing those responses which were completed correctly, and positioning them on the Importance-Performance chart, it
   was soon realized that an incorrect assumption had been made
   regarding the nature of the data collected and the way in which it was
   analyzed. The data collected was 'ratio' data, which was then being
   analyzed on a linear scale. In order to use this effectively would have
   required the use of logarithmic paper and further data manipulation,
   which undermined the reasons for having developed a 'simple' tool.

6.3 Implications of the Approach

If the methodology presented is undertaken systematically, significant
steps in developing purchasing performance measures which promote
activities to support key strategic objectives should have been achieved.
It provides for the systematic review of strategy and objectives in relation to the organization's internal and external environments, and their subsequent translation into meaningful measures covering both efficiency and effectiveness. These can then be chaptered back to the appropriate stakeholders and reviewed and updated over time. It also allows for the identification and promotion of purchasing's contribution across the organization.

If the methodology presented is undertaken systematically, significant steps in developing purchasing performance measures which promote activities to support key strategic objectives should have been achieved.

The methodology does not, however, explicitly enable performance to be 'benchmarked' against other companies, although it does provide the means by which to compare the expectations of purchasing against those of other companies which adopt this type of approach. The assumption made in the design of the methodology was that performance measurement in this field should be divided into two stages. The first, which this chapter addresses, is the review of activities undertaken by purchasing, and aligning these with the expectations and requirements of the stakeholders of purchasing within a strategic framework, while balancing internal expectations of purchasing with the conditions of the external supply market. In effect this addresses how well purchasing is doing in relation to its organizational goals. Once this has been implemented, the second stage, and potentially a subject of future research, could be the comparison of the resulting measures selected with those of external organizations. This would examine how well purchasing performance compares to other companies – i.e. how well it *could* be doing. Caution would be advised, however, to ensure that the analysis of the results of such an exercise take into consideration the strategic, cultural and structural differences between the organizations involved, and therefore the conclusions drawn.

7. Conclusion

7.1 Review of the Project and Further Research

The research at this stage has relied primarily on:

1. the available literature regarding performance measurement in general and purchasing performance in particular;
2. discussions with SCDP Group 2 managers regarding their own expectations and initiatives in this area.

Having derived the proposed methodology through continual reiteration and analysis of the principles, problems and potential of performance measurement in purchasing, an approach has been developed which should address most of these issues. However, it must be stated that this still requires rigorous testing in a real purchasing environment, to ensure its validity.

Further research on this approach might focus on any of the following areas:

1. The testing of each stage of the methodology, and identification of any practical problems regarding data collection and analysis.
2. A means by which to assess the curve of the line which depicts the optimum performance against levels of importance of the performance measures chosen, on the performance perceptions chart. This would consider the level of resource and effort required to achieve particular goals.
3. The potential for a limited 'benchmarking' between SCDP companies interested in testing this approach, identifying any broad similarities in measures chosen and the activities which they are designed to support.

Strategic Stages in the Development of a Purchasing Function

	PASSIVE
Definition	**Purchasing has no strategic direction and primarily reacts to the requests of other functions**
Characteristics	<ul><li>High proportion of purchasing time spent on quick fix and routine operations.</li><li>Purchasing function and individual performance are based on efficiency measures.</li><li>Little cross-functional communication takes place because of purchasing's low visibility.</li><li>Supplier selection in based on price and availability.</li></ul>

INDEPENDENT	
Definition	**Purchasing adopts the latest purchasing techniques and practices, but its strategic direction is independent of the firm's competitive strategy**
Characteristics	<ul><li>Performance is primarily based on cost reduction and efficiency measures.</li><li>Coordination links are established between purchasing and technical disciplines.</li><li>Top management recognizes the importance of professional development.</li><li>Top management recognizes the opportunities in purchasing for contributing to profitability.</li></ul>

SUPPORTIVE

Definition	**Purchasing supports the firm's competitive strategy by adopting purchasing techniques and practices which strengthen the firm's competitive position.**
Characteristics	● Purchasers are included in sales proposals teams. ● Suppliers are considered a resource which is carefully selected and motivated. ● People are considered a resource, with emphasis on experience, motivation and attitude. ● Markets, products and suppliers are continuously monitored and analyzed.

INTEGRATIVE

Definition	**Purchasing's strategy is fully integrated into the firm's competitive strategy and constitutes part of an integrated effort among functional peers to formulate and implement a strategic plan.**
Characteristics	● Cross-functional training of purchasing professionals is made available. ● Permanent lines of communication are established among other functional areas. ● Professional development focuses on strategic elements of the competitive strategy. ● Purchasing performance is measured in terms of contribution to the firm's success.

Characteristics of Each Stage of Development

	PASSIVE	INDEPENDENT	SUPPORTIVE	INTEGRATIVE
Nature of long-range planning	None	Commodity or procedural	Supportive of strategy	Integral part of strategy
Impetus for change	Management demands	Competitive parity	Competitive strategy	Integrative management
Career advancement	Limited	Possible	Probable	Unlimited
Evaluation based on	Complaints	Cost reduction and supplier performance	Competitive objectives	Strategic contribution
Organizational flexibility	Low	Limited	Variable	High
Computer system focus	Repetitive tasks	Techniques and efficiency	Specific decision requirements	Needs of decision-makers
Sources of new ideas	Trial and error	Current purchasing practices	Competitive strategy	Cross-functional info exchange
Basis of resource availability	Limited	Arbitrary/affordable	Objectives	Strategic requirements
Basis of supplier evaluation	Price and easy availabilty	Least total cost	Competitive objectives	Strategic contributions
Attitude towards suppliers	Adversarial	Variable	Company resource	Mutual independence
Professional development focus	Deemed unnecessary	Current new practices	Elements of strategy	Cross-functional understanding
Overall characterization	Clerical function	Functional efficiency	Strategic facillitator	Strategic behaviour

Purchasing Performance Measurement

Position: _____

Department: _____

> Score each **indicator's importance:**   I is low, 3 is average, 5 is critical.
> Score Purchasing **performance** against each indicator: I is poor, 3 is average, 5 is excellent.

Performance Indicators	Importance	Performance
1. Inventory Management / Cost of Working Capital	☐ ☐ ☐ ☐ ☐ 1 2 3 4 5	☐ ☐ ☐ ☐ ☐ 1 2 3 4 5
2. Lead Time Performance	☐ ☐ ☐ ☐ ☐ 1 2 3 4 5	☐ ☐ ☐ ☐ ☐ 1 2 3 4 5
3. Customer Delivery Service	☐ ☐ ☐ ☐ ☐ 1 2 3 4 5	☐ ☐ ☐ ☐ ☐ 1 2 3 4 5
4. Quality	☐ ☐ ☐ ☐ ☐ 1 2 3 4 5	☐ ☐ ☐ ☐ ☐ 1 2 3 4 5
5. Purchasing Skills	☐ ☐ ☐ ☐ ☐ 1 2 3 4 5	☐ ☐ ☐ ☐ ☐ 1 2 3 4 5
6. Purchasing Processes	☐ ☐ ☐ ☐ ☐ 1 2 3 4 5	☐ ☐ ☐ ☐ ☐ 1 2 3 4 5
7. Cost of Purchases	☐ ☐ ☐ ☐ ☐ 1 2 3 4 5	☐ ☐ ☐ ☐ ☐ 1 2 3 4 5
8. Impact on Profit	☐ ☐ ☐ ☐ ☐ 1 2 3 4 5	☐ ☐ ☐ ☐ ☐ 1 2 3 4 5
9. Purchasing Leverage	☐ ☐ ☐ ☐ ☐ 1 2 3 4 5	☐ ☐ ☐ ☐ ☐ 1 2 3 4 5
10. Continuous Improvement	☐ ☐ ☐ ☐ ☐ 1 2 3 4 5	☐ ☐ ☐ ☐ ☐ 1 2 3 4 5
11. Professionalism	☐ ☐ ☐ ☐ ☐ 1 2 3 4 5	☐ ☐ ☐ ☐ ☐ 1 2 3 4 5
12. Innovation	☐ ☐ ☐ ☐ ☐ 1 2 3 4 5	☐ ☐ ☐ ☐ ☐ 1 2 3 4 5

Performance Indicators and Potential Measures

1. **Inventory Management /
   Cost of Working Capital**
   Level of inventory
   Turnover ratio
   No. of stock-outs
   Inventory as a % of total
   purchases
   Inventory as a % of total sales
   Inactive inventory as a % of
   total inventory
   Amount of obsolescence
   (predicted usage)

2. **Lead Time Performance**
   Cycle time reduction
   No. of requisitions processed
   per period
   % of times products released
   to schedule

3. **Customer Delivery Service**
   Size of order backlog
   No. and frequency of
   complaints
   No. of deliveries on time
   No. and frequency of
   over/under deliveries
   % deliveries to rush order
   No. and value of invoice

adjustments
Customer satisfaction index

4. **Quality**
   % of rejections / rework
   Durability / reliability
   Ease of servicing
   % spend on scrap/salvage
   Quality of documentation

5. **Purchasing Skills**
   Team building
   Negotiation ability
   Commodity knowledge
   Level of purchasing analysis
   Supply market awareness
   Staff education levels /
   professional qualifications
   No. and type of training
   courses
   Training expenditure per
   head
   Productivity per head

6. **Purchasing Processes**
   Work load (suppliers/orders
   per buyer)
   Use of Vendor rating systems
   Supply base rationalization

Collaborative agreements
Technological capability (IT)
% total purchases processed
through EDI
% total purchase transactions
processed through EDI
% suppliers with whom EDI
is used.

7. Cost of Purchases
'Business ratio' (cost: spend)
Purchases / sales x 100
Total cost of ownership
Opportunity cost if invested
elsewhere

8. Impact on Profit
Actual vs. target price
Actual vs. market price
Price savings per period
% reduction in budgeted
spend
% return on sales / assets
Value of total cost reduction
through process
improvement
Credit terms
Payables
Payable days
Hedging / currency
management

9. Purchasing Leverage
Level of competition
achieved (by value and
volume)
No. of approved suppliers
Average order size (MOQ)
No. of new suppliers
contacted
Supply base review
No. of alternative supply
sources
Group strength consolidated

10. Continuous Improvement
Value analysis / value
engineering
No. supplier / joint
innovations generated
Time to bring new products
to market
Safety and Environment
quality ratings
Non-traditional purchasing
(% purchases handled by
purchasing department)
Share of preferred supplier
business
Scheduling improvements
(disruptions to suppliers /
vehicle waiting times /
demurrage)
No. of zero-defect status
suppliers
Suppliers per purchasing
employee
Suppliers per purchasing
professional
Order size constraints

11. Professionalism
Provision of order status
information
Internal customer contact
intervals
Ordering convenience
Documentation quality
No. of anchor people vs.
business managers
Response times to queries
Order confirmation time
Quotation response time

12. Innovation
Buyer targets for quality
improvement
Learning curve analysis
No. of cost saving ideas
Research funding

PART FOUR

Making the Change in Supply Management

Transparency in the Value Stream From Open-Book Negotiation to Cost Transparency[1]

The principle underpinning cost transparency in supply relationships is simple: for cost reduction at the interface to become reality and to be of benefit for both parties, there must be some degree of sharing of information about the two sets of internal operations (i.e. those within the supplier and the customer). This sharing must be conducted without jeopardizing the independent commercial stability and confidence of each party.

Little has been written about this subject. Occasional relevant passages, however, do provide an insight into how events have developed and how they might develop further:

> Manufacturers in the 1870's and 1880's used trade associations to devise 'increasingly complex techniques to maintain industry-wide price schedules and production quotas' (Chandler, 1997, p. 317). When these failed, the manufacturers resorted to the purchase of stock in each other's companies, which 'permitted them to look at the books of their associates and thus better enforce their cartel arrange-

---

[1] Prepared by Richard Lamming, Owen Jones and David Nicol. This chapter has not been published before, although a conference paper did cover the salient points (Lamming, R., Jones, O. and Nicol, D. (1996), 'Cost Transparency: A Source of Supply Chain Competitive Advantage?' Proceedings of the 5th International IPSERA Conference, U. of Eindhoven). Copies of the report giving a full account of this research, including detailed explanation of the methodology and results, are available from Richard Lamming at CRiSPS.

ment'. But they could not be certain that the company accounts to which they were given access were accurate. As with rail and telegraph, effective control required the next step – merger. (Williamson, 1985: p. 160)

Theory and Practice

Theory

In developing the concept of lean supply Lamming (1993) defined the notion of cost transparency (Figure 12.1), identifying it as essential to lean supply and providing a warning:

> Cost transparency means the sharing of costing information between customer and supplier, including data which would traditionally be kept secret by each party, for use in negotiations. The purpose of this is to make it possible for customer and supplier to work together to reduce costs (and improve other factors). ... Cost transparency is of no value ... unless it is two-way. (Lamming, 1993: p. 214)

Other literature on lean production and supply touches on subjects relevant to cost transparency (Womack *et al.*, 1990; Hines, 1994) and it finds a resonance in material on relationships between firms (Sako, 1992; Nishiguchi, 1994; Smitka, 1991; Cusumano, 1991; Macbeth and Ferguson, 1994; Carlisle and Parker, 1989).

In the most relevant texts, (Womack *et al.*, Hines, Sako, Lamming and Macbeth and Ferguson, Carlisle and Parker), the need for cost transparency is carried implicitly within the main thrust of the argument, the theme being the need to establish collaborative customer–supplier relationships founded on cooperation for mutual benefit and the optimization of the supply chain rather than individual organizations within the supply chain.

Traditional Practice

The concept of 'open book' negotiation is now commonplace in many industries, albeit with many variations upon the central theme. The idea is that the supplier should explain its process cost structures to the customer and that, in return, the customer will help the supplier to achieve cost savings. This notion is based upon the assumption that the customer is capable of helping the supplier – something which is clearly not always the case.

The concept of 'open book' negotiation is now commonplace in many industries.

In those sectors where the customer's operation is closely aligned to that of the supplier (such as the automotive industry) it may be assumed that a common understanding of, say, production

FIGURE 12.1   Cost Transparency in Lean Supply: a Combination of the Supplier's Value Chain and Part of the Customer's

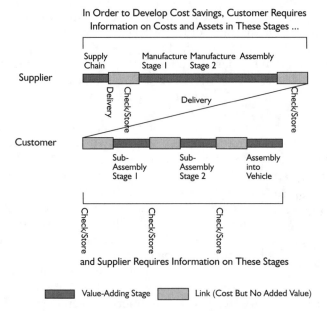

In Order to Develop Cost Savings, Customer Requires Information on Costs and Assets in These Stages ...

and Supplier Requires Information on These Stages

SOURCE: R. C. Lamming, *Beyond Partnership: Strategies for Innovation and Lean Supply*, © Prentice Hall 1993, p. 215.

engineering exists and may be more developed and better resourced in, say, a vehicle assembler than in a manufacturer of exhaust systems. Furthermore, in such an industry, if the customer firm is larger than the supplier, it may be assumed that the basic tenet of open-book negotiation applies – the customer should be able to help the supplier. In such cases, too, it will be simpler for the customer to in-source attractive business, and thus the supplier is naturally more wary of discussing details of production. This has led to the use of bogus accounts ('two sets of books') and, in some cases, a refusal to comply. These practices are, of course, examples of the 'guile' referred to in discussions on transaction cost economics (Williamson, 1975; 1985).

Given the need to change the shape of organizations towards lean enterprise, the threat of in-sourcing must be removed by the customer and a move towards genuine sharing of data accomplished. There is, however, a further requirement: given the logic of lean supply chains, the exchange of data must be two-way, in order for both organizations to concentrate – jointly – on the removal of duplications of capacity of effort in the value chain. Thus, in lean supply, the customer is prepared to divulge data on internal processes (value chain) to the supplier, at the same time as requiring open-book dealing. This is indicated in Figure 12.1.

In essence, cost transparency can be defined as a practice in supply in which the customer and supplier share detailed confidential information about their in-house activities, pertinent to the supply of goods and services which links them. It can be seen as an extension of open-book negotiation, the only difference being that the customer shares information on its activity with the supplier, in addition to the flow of information in the other direction. The objective of practising cost transparency is to reduce costs through the joint development of good ideas, thereby improving the mutual competitive position of both organizations.

It may not be necessary, desirable or practicable, to have symmetry in the transparency, i.e. one of the parties may need to know more about the other than vice versa. A principle of cost transparency is that any information requested of one side by the other should be clearly selected, justified and respected. A satisfactory balance (for the discussion in question) may be achieved with an unequal degree of revelation between the two parties.

The objective of practising cost transparency is to reduce costs through the joint development of good ideas.

This feature of lean supply represents a profit-sharing initiative – possibly a 50:50 arrangement on improvement activity. Just as the contract between customer and supplier (which may or may not be a written contract) will contain agreements on new product development, so there must be accord on productivity improvements, and therefore cost reductions, and perhaps annual price reductions.

Profit level, traditionally a bone of contention between customer and supplier, may need to be included in the discussion. In the short term, this may mean agreeing a desirable profit level (for the supplier) as a matter of principle. In the longer term, factors such as return on capital employed in the specific business may need to be discussed. Cost transparency may be combined with target costing (starting with the price the market will be prepared to pay and working backwards to the cost for which the item must be produced) and the techniques of value analysis/value engineering, once again requiring better collaboration between supplier and customer than has traditionally been the case in most instances.

Since customers may buy from suppliers in a variety of industrial and commercial sectors, it may be necessary to consider different cost regimes. For example, a supplier in the electronics industry may need to invest substantially in research and development to retain its position. In this case, a higher profit level may be necessary for the supplier than in other sectors (such as metal press work) which are less technologically consuming.

The subject of suppliers' profits may be expected to provide many difficulties in negotiations since, as costs are reduced, it is likely that the absolute profit margin will decline – the natural tendency is to protect this. If costs and therefore prices can be reduced, so absolute profits will follow. To reverse this apparently bad performance (in cold financial terms) for the supplier, it may be seen as desirable to increase the overall level of business. This is consistent with the practice of reducing the over-all number of suppliers with whom the customer deals – 'supplier base rationalisation' (Cousins, 1999) – a process which results in retained suppliers taking increased responsibility for satisfying the customer's needs. However, an increased volume of business on a reduced profit margin may be unacceptable to the supplier's shareholders and other ways of deriving benefits for the supplier may need to be found.

Developing Cost Transparency in Practice

The following primary objective was agreed for this project:

To ascertain whether or not, within the concept of 'lean' supply, the introduction of Cost Transparency would be of mutual benefit to the supplier and customer in minimizing overall costs.

The research was guided by the following enabling objectives:

- To define the term 'Cost Transparency' as related to the supply value stream.
- To ascertain the need for Cost Transparency in supply chain management.
- To determine the practicality of the introduction of Cost Transparency in the supply chain management.
- To review the structure within the supply chain and ascertain where the use of Cost Transparency might be considered.
- To determine the proportion of suppliers or customers with which Cost Transparency might be implemented.
- To identify the actual and perceived barriers which might inhibit the introduction of Cost Transparency.
- To examine the advantages and benefits which might accrue from the introduction of Cost Transparency.
- To identify the conditions necessary to set up a Cost Transparency interface between the supplier and customer.

The move from mass to 'lean' production has meant, more than ever, that the customer and supplier need to work in much closer harmony. Both have been more willing to share technical information within each other's domain but both, and perhaps more so the customer, have been less will-ing to declare costing details. The introduction of cost transparency could possibly enhance the strength of the supplier and customer relationship and its implementation could lead to an overall reduction in costs. How-ever, the sharing of such financial details, traditionally a guarded secret, could be seen as a major risk to companies in exposing sensitive information and strategies. Such a risk would require appropriate formal management.

Deliverables

It was intended that the project should culminate in the following deliverables:

- The development and implementation of a simple Cost Transparency Model.
- The issue of briefing papers on the conceptual research, a final report and end of project presentation.

Research Approach

It was realized from the outset that the novelty of this concept would be problematic in a questionnaire survey, in terms of response rate and, possibly, comprehension. The objective of the survey, however, was to canvass the views of as wide an industrial audience as possible and to elicit negative as well as positive responses.

To set the scene, the concept of cost transparency within the context of 'lean' supply was presented to the sponsor companies initially as a conceptual model and later within a workshop discussion to ascertain the need and relevance to them of such research. The workshop explored the need for cost transparency in supply chain management, the practicality of its introduction and the proportion of suppliers with which cost transparency might be practised. The group was also asked which approaches might be taken to explore the potential for cost transparency and which sectors, companies and products might form the most valuable focus. Finally, the group was asked to identify which barriers might inhibit the introduction of cost transparency and how these barriers might be overcome to enable cost transparency to be implemented.

Although the results or 'feelings' from the workshop do not form part of the analyzed findings within this chapter, the feedback from the workshop provided the stimulus for the research and was the basis on which the objectives were derived.

The two questionnaires (directed at Sales and Purchasing managers) were piloted with four companies and several academics, their responses and comments for improvements being subsequently included in the final version of each questionnaire. The changes involved some rework on the phraseology of questions and financial terminology and its relationship with different accounting periods.

The questionnaire was distributed to 600 companies (300 Purchasing Directors and 300 Sales and Marketing Directors). The companies, all private sector, were selected at random from the Gales Directory of UK Purchasing Managers.

Out of 600 companies selected at random from the Gales Directory, 40 (6.6 per cent) completed and returned the questionnaire. However, an additional 53 (8.8 per cent) companies replied giving many reasons why they could not or would not respond to the questions posed. These companies unwittingly or intentionally provided much useful information which has be included in the analysis. In all, the 93 responses represent a 15.5 per cent return.

Lastly, a series of interviews was held with managers within the SCDP sponsor companies, with particular reference to developing the model constructed after the questionnaire survey.

Findings

As one might expect, the project resulted in the collection of a large amount of qualitative and often complex information on the implementation of cost transparency within the value stream. The objective of this section is to explore the implications of the views that were expressed, and to provide a rational and coherent synthesis which will allow us to begin to draw conclusions from the primary research.

This discussion concentrates on *four* main subject areas which naturally coalesced as the research progressed. These subject areas are informed by and illuminate the issues which are contained within the objectives. The four areas are as follows:

- The Benefits and Dangers of Cost Transparency.
- The Cost Transparency Inhibitors.
- The Structural and Operational Classification of Inhibitors.
- The Enabling Mechanisms.

Practical Aspects of Cost Transparency

Benefits

One of the clear messages provided by the research project is that by far the greater number of those questioned felt that implementation of the cost transparency concept would significantly benefit their organization.

Although it is true that enthusiasm for cost transparency was greater within Purchasing functions than within Sales and Marketing departments (a point we shall return to in examining the influence of organizational culture), the relatively high support for cost transparency (even among sales and marketing managers) is remarkable, given the low profile of the concept and the natural reticence normally displayed toward innovation. The qualitative information reinforces the argument that cost transparency is seen as a potential source of competitive advantage. In particular, it is seen as the essential mechanism for making the strategy of supply chain optimization a practical reality. This belief is evinced directly in quotes such as:

> [Cost transparency would] assist in the elimination of non-value adding activities.

and would

> [help us to] … understand the cost drivers in the supply chain.

Many organizations are already collaborating with their supply chain associates to eradicate non-value-adding activities by seeking to understand the cost drivers of the supply chain. In these circumstances, cost transparency was credited with the ability to enhance effectiveness by providing:

> … More fact, less opinion.

and facilitating the improvement process as:

> [Cost transparency] … would reduce 'politics' by replacing it with objectivity.

One interviewee had the following to say on the subject:

> … One of the key benefits which I'm hoping is going to come out of this [cost transparency] is that, once you can generate true transparency of cost, you then have the opportunity to … view those costs through the eyes of the final consumer. … you can then make judgements; 'Is this cost adding value or isn't it?' A supplier may think 'Yes, this is adding value because we bundle our … we put a wrapper on with our brand name so you know it comes from us.' Now that's not adding value at all; as far as the consumer is concerned, it's an added cost. In terms of the transparency of the total pipeline cost, if we can get true transparency and look at it through the consumer's eyes, the real advantage … is that we can then start making collective decisions of whether the costs that we see are truly adding value to the final consumer or not, and … do something about it.

Cost transparency was seen as a mechanism for building relationships between supply chain trading associates.

Despite the fact that cost transparency was valued principally for the contribution it could make to the process of value stream optimization, there were clear indications that it is felt to have several other important contributions to make toward organizational effectiveness. In particular, cost transparency was seen as a mechanism for building relationships between supply chain trading associates and that it would:

> stimulate cross-functional processes and management initiatives.

Risks

It appears that the same individuals who felt that cost transparency might hold enormous positive potential for their organizations also felt that it posed significant potential dangers. This is the paradox that lies at the heart of the cost transparency issue and we will examine it in some detail later. The literature and the practical experience of the authors support this dual response to cost transparency. Many reduced forms of cost transparency exist, for example, in the UK construction industry, European Governmental procurement, and the worldwide defence industry. However, none of these references necessarily provides a good example of cost transparency leading to success in creating effective mutual relationships, or even competitive industrial practices. The lesson appears to be that cost transparency in itself is neither intrinsically positive nor negative. What determines its success is the manner in which organizations put it to use.

The research indicated that respondents (suppliers and customers) identified the principal dangers of cost transparency as:

- the exposure of sensitive information;
- the revealing of strategic plans.

The danger is that this information, shared in good faith, would be abused by the other party to the exchange, resulting in:

- lost competitive advantage;
- a loss of independence (particularly for the supplier).

Under these circumstances the fact that the sharing of commercially sensitive financial information with external organizations is felt to constitute a serious risk is not surprising. The fact that very few of the organizations conducted comprehensive cost transparency suggests that British industry is 'risk averse' in this area. The perceived dangers of cost transparency were viewed as outweighing the perceived advantages, with the result that those advantages are foregone. This view is supported by the fact that a large minority (47.8 per cent) of purchasers and a majority of sales and marketing managers (70.6 per cent) agreed with the contention that:

- the risk and uncertainty of relationships outweigh the perceived gain (from the introduction of cost transparency).

In short, the fear that cost transparency might damage the interests of the organization *inhibits* organizational adoption of the cost transparency concept even where the potential advantages of cost transparency are apparent. The nature of these *inhibitors* is important.

Cost Transparency Inhibitors

The inhibitors that emerged from the research appear to fall into three broad categories. There was a small minority who did not perceive any advantage in the application of cost transparency, and who indeed felt that cost transparency represented a contravention of sensible business practices (*absolute inhibition*). There was a second and much larger group who were supporters of cost transparency in principle, but who also recognized that, in practice, the implementation of the concept should be approached with caution (*operational inhibition*). Finally, there was a third, and again smaller group, who had embraced the cost transparency concept and felt able to introduce it with a number of their trading associates. These individuals were grappling with the practical structures which were required to make cost transparency a reality (*structural inhibition*). This distribution of responses is reminiscent of Rogers (1983) analysis of the adoption of an innovation – with its '*innovators*', '*early adopters*', '*early majority*', '*late majority*' and '*laggards*'.

From questionnaire returns and interview transcripts it is possible to differentiate the many reservations, suspicions and concerns which effectively inhibit the adoption of cost transparency. These are outlined below. The importance of these inhibitors within the cost transparency debate appear to be high: only by understanding and addressing the issues that they raise will progress be possible.

Culture

The research project identified organizational culture as a very strong factor inhibiting the acceptance of cost transparency. Indeed, one respondent felt that the successful adoption of cost transparency within UK industry would require:

> ... brain transplants for junior and middle managers throughout Britain.

It does appear that the received business culture within the United Kingdom is in many ways inimical to the concept and practice of cost transparency. Of purchasing managers 61 per cent, and 76 per cent of sales and marketing managers agreed that cost transparency was 'alien' to their company culture or philosophy.

Conventional wisdom seems to suggest that organizations should defend their independence vigorously, and sharing sensitive financial information was seen as tantamount to a 'surrender' to suppliers or customers who are viewed in an adversarial context. An illustration of the clash between cost transparency and organizational culture is given in the quote below:

> Our MD is completely hostile to the idea [cost transparency]. He would rather turn business away.

This feature of organizational culture appears, not surprisingly, to lead individuals to regard cost transparency with feelings of some trepidation. It was *expected* (i.e. not just feared) that sensitive commercial information would be abused by suppliers or customers. This abuse could take the form of leverage or misinformation within ongoing organization relationships and negotiations, or the betrayal of sensitive information to competitors, as in the respondent who saw cost transparency as just:

... another tool to negotiate gain.

Organizational culture informs the *actions and behaviour* of departments and individuals. If a culture of mistrust exists, then it is does so because past experience teaches managers that any other attitude could prove extremely detrimental to their individual and organizational interests. This is reflected in the following quotes which were given as part of the questionnaire survey:

> *Organizational culture informs the actions and behaviour of departments and individuals.*

[Cost transparency is not possible because of] ... mistrust justified over a time period ... BY US!

... Talk [within the industry] is now emerging of the need for stable relationships but bad examples on both sides abound.

While these cultural inhibitors did appear to be widespread, it was noticeable that they were not felt uniformly. In many organizations their influence was relatively weak and individuals and groups could contemplate new methods of doing business. In other cases the traditional, adversarial culture formed an apparently impenetrable barrier to innovation in the way customers and suppliers related to each other. An atmosphere of secrecy dominated, expressed in a refusal to record interviews (a very unusual occurrence) and in even to respond to a relatively innocuous questionnaire which at no point asked the respondents to supply confidential information:

It is company policy not to take part in research projects of this type because of the confidential nature of the details we would be passing on.

... I am unable to complete your questionnaire as much of the information required is company confidential.

... The questions are too searching in terms of confidential information. ... We as a company are very interested in building partnerships with customers and suppliers. We often exchange ... technical drawings, manpower and procedural information. We would not distribute pricing and cost data. ... The area of finance and accounting is sacrosanct.

It appears that managers who have been successful under the traditional culture and have been promoted as a result may have a vested interest in perpetuating the system they know and understand. Perhaps this is an explanation for the purchasing manager who felt cost transparency inappropriate as it curtailed his department's:

... Freedom to play the market.

and another who was resistant as cost transparency:

Removes [the need or scope] for competitive tendering.

Whatever the causes of this secretive, adversarial culture, the result is clear. The call for cost transparency is often regarded with suspicion. The unconvinced organization suspecting that the group calling for the sharing of sensitive information has ulterior motives. This is especially true where the group being asked to share cost information feels itself to have less power within the relationship than its associate. This view is represented strongly in quotes such as:

[the call to cost transparency] is viewed as a threat if not complied with.

and:

[there is] ... no true partnership with major vehicle manufacturers: partnership is a one way flow of information!

A respondent from the clothing industry had this to say:

[Cost transparency is] ... Driven by big brother!

But perhaps the most powerful quote of all came from a senior manager in an industry which will remain anonymous:

The whole partnership message is utterly devalued and corrupt out there. It's a joke and it's become a joke because all of the suppliers have experienced that what this is really about is the latest good technique for screwing down the supplier. One company in particular have done more to undermine this [partnership] than anyone. They say to the supplier, we want x% cost reduction. 'We don't know how to do it'. 'Well fine guys, if you still want the business in six months time you'll work out how to do it.

This mismatch in buyer/seller perceptions of cost transparency is illustrated clearly by the differential responses made to our questionnaire survey. Of respondents from the procurement function 73.9 per cent felt that the 'exposure of sensitive information' would be a barrier to the introduction of cost transparency with their suppliers. On the other hand, every single one (100 per cent) of the sales and marketing respondents felt that the need to expose sensitive information would form a barrier to cost transparency. However, 86.4 per cent of purchasing respondents felt that the introduction of cost transparency would improve competitiveness. This view was echoed by only 41.2 per cent of sales and marketing respondents.

This anomaly points to the fact that it is easier to ask another party to take a risk than to take that risk yourself. It may also mean that there is a persistent resistance to understanding cost transparency as a two-way sharing of information. Instead, the term 'Cost Transparency' is taken by managers within the supply chain to mean the transfer of sensitive cost information from the supplier to the customer. Of sales and marketing respondents 88 per cent felt that they would be reluctant to declare their profit margin, although interestingly only 59 per cent felt uncomfortable in declaring the rate of return desired by their organization. Indeed, one respondent described cost transparency as a 'lose-lose' situation: should the supplier be seen to be doing well, the customer would attempt to claw back some of the profit. Should the financial information present a poor picture, then the customer could move its custom to a more attractive supplier.

For whatever reason the nature of organizational cultures continues to be a prime factor inhibiting the implementation of cost transparency. Later in this discussion we shall return to the subject with strategies for overcoming the barrier represented by corporate culture.

Managerial Instability

The inhibiting action of instability was a recurring theme of the project. As explained above, it is clear that cost transparency is not without its risks. For the concept to be accepted within an 'established' business culture, individuals and organizations must believe that the 'bad old days' are over and future trading will take place in an atmosphere of collaboration for mutual gain. We came across several situations where managers who were being asked to share cost information were satisfied that their trading associates, at the level of the organization and the individual, were sincere and could be trusted not to abuse the information they would receive. However, a great problem still bars the path to cost transparency: how can one be sure that this benign environment will persist into the future?

The inhibiting action of instability was a recurring theme of the project.

When an organization is invited to institute cost transparency this concern is often reinforced by confusion. What is cost transparency? Is it a personal belief of a particular individual or group of individuals within the associate organization or is it official company policy? If it is only the former, what happens if a key individual leaves or loses political power? What happens if there is a change of senior management? Would the commitment to cost transparency continue or would the new management team revert to type and abuse the information which was shared in good faith? As an example, one procurement manager had this to say on what was required to enable cost transparency:

> [Develop] … Long-term contracts/agreements (suppliers are only people though, and people change).

For cost transparency to be successful, it appears that it should become an integral component of the organizational mission, so that even if key individuals do move to new positions, or suffer a sudden loss of enthusiasm, the organization's commitment – not to abuse information proffered in good faith – remains.

Practical Inhibitors

Even in those situations where supply chain associates are convinced of the need for cost transparency and are further convinced that sharing sensitive information will not lead to an abuse of trust, there is still the question of how to go about the mechanics of sharing cost information of a meaningful kind; who shares what information with whom, when and for what purpose? An interview quote illustrates both points, and the dangers faced when the sharing process suffers from a loss of momentum:

> People, as they get further into detail, start to take up defensive positions. 'My facts are better than yours'. 'No they're not'. ' My facts are perfectly OK'. You start to challenge their logic and thinking. You start to challenge something fundamental about them. What this does is generate conflict and we're finding a big problem in this area. We don't know how to get out of it by the way!

The research in this field distinguished between two related practical difficulties. The first involved actually obtaining the required information. This is not as simple as it might seem. Desegregating data to make it relevant to a single trading relationship is difficult unless the most simplistic of assumptions are acceptable as the basis of the exercise. The situation is aggravated when the profits from certain relationships go to subsidize the losses of others.

The other practical difficulty involves creating supply chain structures capable of using the information for process improvement when it is secured. The main limiting factor in this case is often not inter- but *intra*-organizational relationships. It was felt that for cost transparency to realize its full potential in terms of initiating action to optimize value stream activities, effective cross-functional management practices must be in place within organizations. To highlight this point, 74 per cent of the questionnaire responses from procurement functions and 65 per cent of those from sales and marketing departments felt that successful cost transparency required cross-functional management within the customer organization. Furthermore, 78 per cent of purchasing responses and 47 per cent of those from sales and marketing felt that cross-functional management was required within the supplier's organization. Without this advantage, political infighting between functions within the same organization could easily subvert the inter-organizational benefits generated by cost transparency.

The Structural and Operational Classification of Inhibitors

In attempting to define cost transparency inhibitors (as a first step to addressing their effects) the research team found it is extremely helpful to draw the distinction between *Structural* inhibitors and *Operational* inhibitors.

A structural inhibitor is one that arises as a consequence either of an integral aspect of a company's internal operation or its commercial relationships with external organizations. As one might imagine, such inhibitors are resistant to change and are very difficult to overcome. While it is possible to address the problem posed by structural inhibitors, the process of so doing may require an extended period of time to be successful.

An operational inhibitor, on the other hand, does not express the consequence of an integral aspect of a company's activity. Operational inhibitors are the result of tactical deficiencies in an organization's internal activities or its relationship with external organizations. As a result, operational inhibitors may be addressed over a much shorter time frame than is required for structural inhibitors.

It appears unlikely that organizations could implement successful cost transparency without addressing the effects of both types of inhibitor. To illustrate the distinction between structural and operational inhibitors, it is helpful to explore an issue which has great relevance to the cost transparency debate, that of 'trust and dependency'.

Trust and Dependency

There is at present a renewed debate on the nature of trust and the need for it within organizational relationships. The protagonists of trust argue that inter-organizational trust forms the basis of successful collaborative relationships. Sako (1992) has even gone so far as to identify *three* forms of organizational trust:

- Contractual Trust.
- Competence Trust.
- Goodwill Trust.

On the other side of the debate are those who feel that ascribing human emotions such as trust to commercial organizations is falsely anthropomorphic, such researchers preferring to talk of dependency as the driving force within collaborative relationships.

This research seems to show that respondents felt that both trust and dependency were very important prerequisites for successful cost transparency. Indeed, it would be very difficult to over-emphasize their perceived importance. Interviewees and questionnaire respondents repeatedly identified trust and dependency as being of crucial importance. However, it appears that trust and dependency exist on different levels. First, it seems imperative that dependency exists at the organizational level, i.e. the two organizations share a genuine community of interest in the marketplace that extends beyond the limits of the immediate transaction. This provides a genuine and independent practical justification for collaboration, one which allows both parties to contemplate the introduction of cost transparency.

At the same time, it appears just as important that individuals feel that they could trust their counterparts in the other organization. Without that personal bond of trust between individuals, it was felt extremely unlikely that cost transparency could be implemented, even between organizations which did share a community of interest. It was interesting to note the number of times interviewees began speaking of their relationships with another organization, 'Company x' or 'Company y', for example, but soon began referring to named individuals within those trading organizations, or 'the guys' at Company x or y. This need to 'personalize' organizational relationships has clear implications for the change to cost transparency.

Returning to the structural/operational classification of inhibitors, it may be that understanding might be furthered if interorganizational dependency (or the lack of it) was classified as a structural inhibitor, while a lack of trust between individuals working on behalf of their respective organizations should be classified as an operational inhibitor.

While it would take significant time and possibly some degree of structural change to develop a genuine community of interest, even if it was decided that such a development was desirable or practical, it would at least be possible to build a meaningful trust between individuals where a genuine organizational dependency already existed.

Therefore, the lack of interorganizational dependency can be thought of as a structural inhibitor, while the lack of interorganizational trust between individuals may be an operational inhibitor. This will have important implications for the introduction of cost transparency, as the number of customers or suppliers with whom an organization shares a genuine community of interest may be limited.

This illustration also serves to reinforce the finding of the research project that it is not sufficient to address either the structural or the operational inhibitors: for successful cost transparency both types of inhibitor must be overcome.

Enabling Mechanisms

The study concentrated not only on the potential advantages of cost transparency and the inhibitors to its adoption, but also the enabling mechanisms which would allow cost transparency to become a reality within the supply chain. Because of the low incidence of cost transparency within the referenced organizations, much of the information gathered on these enablers was of a speculative nature. Nevertheless, the results of the project in this area might provide valuable resource for other organizations that are contemplating the concept or are in the early stages of introducing cost transparency to their value stream. There appear to be two alternative routes to successful cost transparency implementation: the 'narrow steep path' and the 'wide easy path'.

On the one hand, a number of respondents felt that cost transparency could easily be instituted where one party to a relationship has the will, and sufficient power to enforce that will. A connected opinion appeared to be that the risk inherent in the sharing of sensitive financial information could be assured by the:

Signing of confidentiality agreements.

Variations on this contractual theme included:

Establish up-front contractual exclusivity.

and:

Tie in supplier contractually – confidentiality, exclusivity and non-compete clauses.

It appears, however, that this power-based, contractual route to cost transparency may be flawed. It seems to draw on the traditional adversarial culture and fails to recognize the true spirit of cost transparency (joint process improvement within a spirit of collaboration and mutual gain).

The alternative route to the implementation of cost transparency is more complex, requires a far greater level of effort, and demands a far longer time-scale for success. In its initial stages, rather than focus on cost transparency, it emphasizes the need to *create the conditions necessary for successful cost transparency*. This recognizes the reality, emphasized continually within the research programme, that to share sensitive cost information within a traditionally secretive, adversarial, opportunistic relationship, with no consideration given to the potential consequences, is an extremely dangerous course of action. A request for an external organization (whether supplier or customer) to do the same is likely to be met by refusal.

In the first instance, creating the conditions necessary for successful transparency means addressing the deficiencies within the organizational relationship caused by many years of operating under a traditional, secretive, adversarial culture. This fundamental change in business culture requires:

senior management commitment

and again:

Strong and inspired senior management and comprehension by financiers

and must represent an irrevocable change in company policy rather than a semi-private initiative on the part of an individual or single function. The study respondents displayed unanimity in identifying the only viable method for changing business culture as:

… Demonstration of integrity,

and

… Building trust over a period of time by actions not words.

It was recognized that this process of demonstration could take some time, thus implicitly acknowledging the earlier emphasis on managerial stability and the need to incorporate cost transparency into the organization's mission:

… The cultural issues are the strongest [most difficult] to change and both supplier and customer needs to put in effort over the long-term (24 months) …

… The act of placing trust in a supplier needs to be taken in small steps.

This would involve such actions as:

… very frank and open behaviour both internally and externally,

… Use internal resources to assist [the] supply base.

The creation of cross-functional supply chain teams would require training in change management and the exchange of employees:

… Send people to each other's organizations.

Once the cultural barriers have been addressed, advances in terms of achieving cost transparency proper can begin. Again there was remarkable unanimity among the study respondents as to how this challenge should be met. Many of them recommend the creation of pilot projects to be conducted in 'safe' areas of the business where, should initial failure occur, the negative effects would be limited. For example:

… Pilot on a small scale and then leverage to larger customers.

Respondents were also clear as to the principal criterion by which the success of the cost transparency pilot project should be judged; cost savings to the supply chain:

> ... Ensure that the [financial] gain [of cost transparency] is outstandingly attractive.

and

> ... Identify real benefits [money] from the practice of cost transparency.

> ... Proof that the increased admin. burden is outweighed by savings made by the exercise.

The responses to the survey would seem to emphasize the need to create the conditions necessary for successful cost transparency within the organization's commercial relationships. This will require both organizations to invest considerable time and effort in developing the type of relationship capable of sustaining cost transparency. When the relationship is prepared, and cost transparency has become part of the organization's mission, the respondents advocated a pilot cost transparency implementation. The success of which is seen as its ability to create cost savings to the supply chain.

As one interviewee put it:

> ... All can be solved if management wishes.

Summary

The objective of this section was to explore the implications of the research findings and provide a rational and coherent synthesis which will allow us to draw conclusions from the primary research. The section concentrated on three broad subject areas: the benefits and dangers of cost transparency; the inhibitors which tend to prevent the implementation of cost transparency; and the enabling mechanisms which organizations can adopt in order to make cost transparency a practical reality. The section also introduced the concept of the structural and operational classification of inhibitors. The main findings of the section are summarized below in the order in which they appear in the main body of the text.

1. The study respondents and interviewees feel that cost transparency holds great positive potential for their organizations.

2. This positive potential lies in the ability of cost transparency to identify non-value-adding activities, and hence to contribute to optimizing the supply chain.

3. The same respondents also identified cost transparency as being potentially dangerous for their organizations.

4. The negative potential lies in the possibility that trading associates will abuse the sensitive confidential information that they receive.

5. In the view of a large majority of the respondents the negative potential of cost transparency outweighed the positive. Respondents are 'risk-averse' and for the most part do not practise cost transparency.

6. There are a number of inhibitors which act as barriers, preventing the implementation of cost transparency. These include: cultural factors, managerial instability and practical considerations.

7. For the purposes of managing the change to cost transparency it is valuable to classify these inhibitors into those which are structural and those which are operational.

8. There are a number of enabling mechanisms (which are identified) which can allow organizations to overcome the barriers to cost transparency.

Conceptual Model

This section will introduce the cost transparency process model. The model was developed within the research project to facilitate the implementation of cost transparency within customer/supplier relationships. The model proposed within this chapter incorporates the knowledge accumulated over the course of the research project within a coherent framework designed to provide an aid to understanding the process and the basis for subsequent development of management tools.

The model is founded on the assumptions which were built into the research. It is assumed that cost transparency is not necessarily in itself a positive influence, but that it can be used for the mutual benefit in a supply chain, or abused in order to achieve advantage for one organization as the result of disadvantaging another. Cost transparency must therefore be viewed as a tool to be employed within a wider 'relationship management' initiative.

The research indicated that in implementing cost transparency, the crucial step is to 'create the conditions necessary' for successful positive (reciprocal) exchange of information. This will require the organizations to overcome the inhibitors identified earlier. Failure to put in place the conditions which effectively overcome structural and operational inhibitors should be taken as a sign that cost transparency, in the full sense of that term, may not be immediately appropriate. A failure to overcome structural inhibitors may signify that full and genuine cost transparency will not be appropriate for the foreseeable future. A failure to overcome operational inhibitors, given the required commitment, may preclude cost transparency only over the short to medium term.

Cost transparency must be viewed as a tool to be employed within a wider 'relationship management' initiative.

A final assumption which has been implicit throughout the research is that organizations are interested in positive cost transparency for mutual benefit. That is, they are *not* interested in obtaining sensitive financial information in order to enhance or abuse their relative power within their supplier/customer relationships.

Model Overview

Figure 12.2 shows diagrammatically an overview of the Cost Transparency Process Model.

FIGURE 12.2   The Cost Transparency Process Model Overview

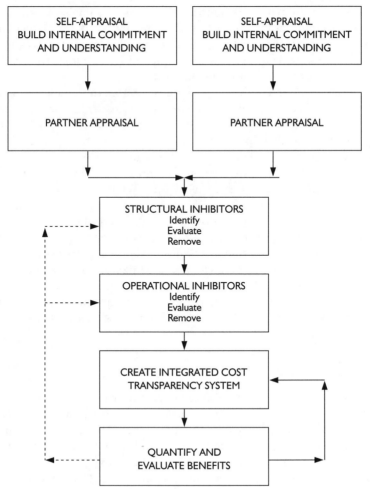

Process Steps

The principal feature of the model is that it contains two parallel strands which merge into a single process. This reflects the fact that cost transparency is a two-way process. It may be initiated by the supplier or the customer. This is also true of organizational relationships – they are made up of at least two parties. Therefore it must be recognized that there will be two perceptions of the same relationship. An effective relationship may require innovation from one's own organization as much as from customers and suppliers. The dual strands therefore represent organizational policies which are formed inside each partner company. The single strand represents a process shared between customers and suppliers, which is driven forward by a dialogue and a sharing of perceptions.

Step 1: Self-Appraisal

The first step toward implementing cost transparency is to build a commitment to, and understanding of, the concept within one's own organization. This process will call into focus the way the organization conducts its organizational relationships and may require that it should review its relationship management strategies.

It is also an opportunity to prepare responses to the questions which will inevitably be asked when the concept of cost transparency is introduced to suppliers or customers. For example: Why is cost transparency so vital? Why can't improvement be secured by some other method? What cost information is required? How exactly will it be shared? How will we integrate cost transparency into our existing business structure? What will the information be used for? What level of supply chain improvement is expected from cost transparency? Over what time-scale are improvements expected? How will we measure the improvements?

The initial responses to these questions raised within the organization will need to be modified as the implementation process receives the contribution of supplier or customer organizations. Nevertheless, it is extremely important that the initiating organization is clear at the outset of the project what it expects to gain from the introduction of cost transparency, how that gain will be achieved, and how success (or otherwise) will be measured.

Step 2: Partner Appraisal

Having built an internal commitment to cost transparency, the next step is to examine potential suppliers or customers with whom it is desired to introduce cost transparency. At this point the firm may wish to audit its entire supply base, identifying several suitable organizations which may make themselves immediately apparent. Alternatively, it may be decided to pilot the concept with a particular organization. The partner appraisal will have focused on the characteristics of particular relationships and their implications for the implementation of cost transparency. The conclusion of the partner appraisal should be the approach to the chosen organizations with the proposal that the cost transparency concept be considered. This may be either in the form of customer approaching supplier or vice versa. In either case it takes the form of a commercial proposition.

Step 3: Address Structural Inhibitors

Having begun to work together with another organization on the introduction of cost transparency, the first joint task is to assess the existence and nature of structural inhibitors. The model contains a three-stage approach:

1. Identify.
2. Evaluate.
3. Overcome.

Structural inhibitors are those which appear to be permanent features of the relationship. For example, does a true community of interest exist between the two organizations outside the limits of the immediate transaction? Without overcoming these structural inhibitors any cost transparency initiative may be vulnerable and likely to fail. It is also likely that overcoming existing structural barriers will require a significant amount of management time and commitment.

Step 4: Address Operational Inhibitors

Having examined and overcome any structural inhibitors, the implementation team will repeat the three-stage, identify–evaluate–overcome process for operational inhibitors. Operational inhibitors are more transient in nature than their structural counterparts: for example, a lack of interpersonal trust, the absence of appropriate channels of communication or the lack of departmental resources to conduct cost transparency. It may also be necessary to provide employees with additional skills to make cost transparency a practical reality. Again, overcoming the operational inhibitors is likely to require the commitment of management.

Step 5: Create an Integrated Cost Transparency System

Having removed the barriers to the cost transparency concept, the next task is to set up the cost transparency system itself. This involves far more than simply exchanging what was previously sacrosanct financial information. It involves providing practical solutions for build internal commitment. This includes: formalizing the benefits that it is expected cost transparency should achieve; identifying the information which is to be shared (and when it is to be shared); deciding on the individuals who will share it; and the action they will take, armed with the cost information and the wider organizational relationship within which the exchange will take place.

Step 6: Quantify and Evaluate Benefits

Having created a cost transparency system, integrated within the normal operation of the business, it is necessary to measure the relative ongoing success of cost transparency. This is vital to allow sceptics and enthusiasts alike to see the value of the concept in operation. The results of implementing cost transparency should be quantified, and expressed in the cash benefits they have brought to the supply chain. It is also important to evaluate the effectiveness of the integrated system and institute modifications where necessary, and periodically to re-evaluate the structural or operational barriers which have reappeared with time.

Summary

This section presented a six-stage process model for the implementation of cost transparency. The model was founded on the assumptions that cost transparency is not necessarily intrinsically a positive phenomenon. To ensure that its application results in mutual benefit (and not abuse by one or other of the parties) cost transparency must be applied as part of an overall relationship management strategy which emphasizes the need for collaboration between supply chain organizations.

The model concentrates on the need for organizations to build internal commitment to the concept of cost transparency and to follow this by creating the conditions necessary for the success of cost transparency within their own business culture and that of their organizational relationships.

The model also emphasizes the importance of integrating cost transparency into the established business ethos and activities of both organizations. Finally, it is imperative that the performance of cost transparency is quantified on a consistent basis in order to build enthusiasm for the process itself and also continually to recalibrate the systems and procedures which underpin the sharing of traditionally commercial cost information. This will entrench cost transparency as an essential driver of the supply chain's process improvement loop.

The Potential for Cost Transparency in Practice

To conclude the chapter, each of the enabling objectives will be addressed in turn and, in doing so, the responses will be used to provide an intellectually coherent answer to achieve the project's primary objective.

A Definition of Cost Transparency

Cost transparency was defined as a practice in supply in which the customer and supplier share detailed confidential information on their in-house activities, pertinent to the supply of goods and services which links them. It can be seen as an extension of 'open-book' negotiation, the only difference being that the customer shares information on its activity with the supplier in addition to a flow of information in the other direction. The objective of practising cost transparency is to reduce costs through joint development of process improvement, thereby improving the mutual competitive position of both organizations. This definition was used on both the Sales and Purchasing questionnaires to explain the concept of cost transparency.

The Need for Cost Transparency Within Supply Chain Management

The need for cost transparency is implicit in the principles of lean supply and supply chain management. The central theme of the supply chain philosophy suggests that it is the performance of the supply chain that should be optimized rather than the performance of individual organizations within the chain. The call to optimize the supply chain may be persuasive. However, the question remains: On what basis will the decision to optimize be made?

To make supply chain optimization a practical reality, organizations must share cost information pertaining to their business processes. This allows the process of supply chain optimization to be driven by objective 'fact' rather than an intuition which may be 'politically' motivated, or may prove wholly erroneous.

The need for cost transparency is implicit in the principles of lean supply and supply chain management.

The Advantages and Benefits of Cost Transparency

The study indicated that the prime advantage of cost transparency is its ability to form the basis of successful supply chain optimization. This belief is illustrated by the following quote:

> ... One of the key benefits which I'm hoping to come out of this [cost transparency] is that once you can generate true transparency of cost you then have the opportunity to ... view those costs through the eyes of the final consumer. ... You can then make judgements: Is this cost adding value or isn't it. ... If we can get true transparency and look at

it through the consumer's eyes the real advantage … is that we can … start making collective decisions of whether the costs that we see are truly adding value to the final consumer or not, and … do something about it.

The reward of successful supply chain optimization, facilitated by cost transparency included: enhanced competitiveness, increased profitability; cost minimization and more effective new product development. Furthermore, cost transparency could form an important mechanism in improving customer–supplier relationships and reduce the uncertainty which surrounds negotiations within established relationships. This could reduce the amount of time and cost expended on renegotiation and minimize the opportunity for conflict between the parties.

The Barriers Inhibiting the Introduction of Cost Transparency

The project highlighted that there were significant rewards to be gained from the introduction of cost transparency. Likewise, there were also significant dangers. These dangers were described within the project as cost transparency 'inhibitors'.

The abuse of sensitive information by trading associates was perceived to be a major inhibitor, as was the influence of organizational culture. Many of the contributors emphasized the disparity between established organizational culture (whether in their own organization or in the broader business environment) and the implicit requirements of cost transparency with regard to corporate culture. Traditional relationships were conducted in an arm's-length, adversarial and secretive manner. Several respondents admitted that cost transparency was 'alien to company culture' and that they might react with suspicion, particularly where the implementation of cost transparency was suggested by a customer who was perceived to posses a relatively large amount of power within the customer–supplier relationship. This feeling is illuminated obliquely by the quote:

> [Cost transparency is not possible because of] … mistrust justified over a time period … BY US!

The influence of managerial instability was mentioned at several interviews and within the questionnaire responses as an inhibitor. Trading associates might be reticent to cooperate with cost transparency initiatives, fearing that should key individuals be replaced, the commitment to cost transparency would be lost, possibly with the result that sensitive information could be abused. Some respondents suggested that individuals in receipt of sensitive information could seek employment with competitor organizations, thereby placing the former organization at a disadvantage.

Some practical barriers, such as lack of resources and number of skilled staff required, were also highlighted. Finally, the need to create, manage and operate an integrated cost transparency system was also viewed as a challenge, as evidenced by the following quote:

> People, as they get further into detail, start to take up defensive positions. 'My facts are better than yours!' ... 'No they're not!' ... 'My facts are perfectly OK!' You start to challenge their logic and thinking. You start to challenge something fundamental about them. What this does generate is conflict and we're finding a big problem in this area.

The Practicality of Cost Transparency

Of the questionnaire respondents, only 20 per cent of customers and 23 per cent of suppliers claim to use some form of cost transparency, and then only on a very limited basis. This would seem to provide a tacit acceptance of the *non*-practicality of cost transparency, at least given the current stage of development in inter-organizational supply relationships. On the other hand, only 10 per cent of customers and 30 per cent of suppliers rejected cost transparency out of hand. These are the minority of individuals and organizations who see cost transparency as an inevitable 'Lose-Lose' option: if the cost information is complementary, then they fear that the supplier will attempt to 'claw back' some of the profit. If the cost information is not complementary, the customer may examine the option of moving its business to what it perceives to be a more attractive supplier.

The disparity could signify that individuals and organizations are 'risk averse' with regard to cost transparency. The inhibiting effect of perceived dangers outweighs the potential reward of the benefits. The result is inaction which perpetuates the *status quo*. However, it does not prove that cost transparency is not practical.

The research appears to show, both from the significant minority of our questionnaire respondents and from the large majority of our interviewees who practise cost transparency that cost transparency is a practical option for organizations seeking to develop the competitive advantage they derive from commercial relationships with customers and suppliers.

The Conditions Necessary to Implement Cost Transparency

The research findings were unambiguous in their identification of the conditions necessary to implement cost transparency. This could involve reshaping corporate culture and its impact on the operation of the organization's commercial relationships. The process is likely to require the involvement of customer and supplier organizations to contribute to the other element of the relationship. The difficulty and time-scale of this process should not be underestimated, particularly when addressing the result of many years of operating within a corporate relationship founded on opportunistic, adversarial and secretive behaviour.

The concept and agreed practice of cost transparency needs to be written into the company's mission statement (i.e. not just its purchasing policy) to counter the fear of managerial instability across the business functions. Potential cost transparency partners may need to be assured, contractually or otherwise, that cost transparency is not dependent on individuals, but is part of the company's commitment (and culture).

> *The concept and agreed practice of cost transparency needs to be written into the company's mission statement.*

Having created the conditions necessary for cost transparency, the organization (in cooperation with other supply chain organizations) can begin to integrate cost transparency into its normal business processes. The cost transparency process model, discussed earlier in this chapter, emphasizes the need within both partner companies to overcome both *structural* and *operational* inhibitors jointly and to develop the cost transparency relationship. Its success should be judged by the amount of cost savings it produces within the supply chain, as confirmed by two respondents:

> … Ensure that the [financial] gain [of cost transparency] is outstandingly attractive!

> … Identify the real benefits (money) from the practice of cost transparency!

The Proportion of Suppliers and Customers With Whom Cost Transparency Might Be Implemented

The research could not identify an optimal proportion of trading associates with whom cost transparency might be implemented. However, the project did provide a guiding principle in this regard.

Initially it was felt that cost transparency should be limited to those customers and suppliers who were deemed to be 'significant'. This seemed to reflect the reality that where a customer was perceived as being relatively unimportant to a supplier (or vice versa) the implementation of cost transparency faced even greater difficulties than normal. The questionnaire respondents were asked to define significance. In general, the responses were disappointing, since no clear generic definition of significance emerged, except for the supplier whose sole customer was a major high street retailer.

It would appear that cost transparency should be limited to relationships where the two organizations *share a community of interest in the marketplace which extends beyond the immediate transaction*. In essence, the two organizations share a dependency which provides a strong rationale for both parties at least to *contemplate* collaboration in general and cost transparency in particular. Where two organizations do not share such a bond it would seem that cost transparency may not be viable and should not be contemplated.

The Supply Chain Locus at Which Cost Transparency Would Be Most Appropriate

The research project again found it impossible to be prescriptive in this area. Differences between supply chains meant that no generic rules could be drawn. However, the optimum tier for cost transparency would appear to be between the two supply nodes which account for the greatest proportion of 'value-added' within the supply chain.

However, if the objective is reversed, so that the aim is to identify supply chain *loci* where cost transparency is least appropriate, conclusions can also be drawn. The study indicated that the effectiveness of cost transparency was limited in circumstances where very large organizations trading commodity or commodity-like products were encountered – for example, steel producers, oil or agricultural produce. In these circumstances the purchasing relationship was driven by spot market prices and did not lend itself to the implementation of cost transparency.

Conclusion – the Primary Objective

The overall or primary objective of the research project was:

To ascertain whether, within the concept of lean supply, the introduction of Cost Transparency would be of mutual benefit to the supplier and customer in minimizing overall costs.

Cost transparency could have great potential for increasing supply chain competitive advantage. Its implementation could enable organizations to optimize their supply chain processes objectively and allow them to evaluate the potential for process improvement. The need to optimize the supply chain rather than individual organizations or functions within the supply chain is widely accepted. Cost transparency could allow managers (in the guise of supplier or customer) to measure objectively for the first time the effectiveness of the supply chain. As a consequence, subsequent supply chain optimization could be founded on rigorous comparative data rather than (at best) perception or (at worst) prejudice and self-interest.

The evidence and results of the cost transparency project are unambiguous. Cost transparency could hold the potential to minimize supply chain costs by identifying areas of non-value-adding activity. However, cost transparency does not exist in a vacuum. It exists within the context of an organization's relationship with its trading associates. For cost transparency to be successful, that relationship must be conducive to its application. For the most part, traditional organizational relationships, built around secrecy and opportunism, are inimical to the conduct of cost transparency. If the implementation of cost transparency is to be successful, commercial relationships within the supply chain may have to be re-shaped to *create the conditions necessary for cost transparency*. This will require the development of organizational relationships within which customers and suppliers feel comfortable, and with the assurance that the sensitive information they share will not be abused by either trading partner.

The challenge of creating such organizational relationships where they do not already exist and the implementation of cost transparency will undoubtedly require a great amount of commitment over an extended period of time. However, a joint commitment to cost transparency could be of mutual benefit to the supplier and customer in minimizing overall costs.

Further Research

As this book goes to press, a new research project is starting at CRiSPS, to take the concept of cost transparency further, working with a major global engineering group. This project, which takes the SCDP research as its starting point, will report in 2001.

CHAPTER 13

Supplier Development[1]

One of the main drawbacks in attempting to implement supplier development programmes is the perceived lack of benefit to the donor company. This usually results in a denial of the need for action and the entrenchment of value stream sub-optimization. As a result a decision-making tool is required that will help companies identify where this development work should take place and what the likely costs and benefits will be. This chapter gathers together the various theoretical research projects that were conducted within SCDP that address this important area. It goes on to summarize and demonstrate how one SCDP sponsor, RS Components, implemented these findings within an innovative supplier development programme.

Introduction

> *Nowhere in business is there greater potential for benefiting from ... interdependency than between customer firms and their suppliers. This is the largest remaining frontier for gaining competitive advantage – and nowhere has such a frontier been more neglected.* (Drucker, 1982)

Supplier development transforms problems into opportunities, weaknesses into strengths, costs into profits. Supplier development transforms the effectiveness of value streams (the network of final assembler and suppliers responsible for adding value to final products). Western industry is uncomfortable with the concept and practice of supplier development, to judge by the rarity of supplier development among indigenous organizations. This is largely the result of institutional barriers which act to inhibit

---

[1] Prepared by Peter Hines, Richard James and Owen Jones.

the initiation of supplier development. These institutional barriers include a lack of knowledge about how to develop suppliers, a lack of company buy-in into the process as well as a scarcity of exemplar cases for firms to emulate.

In addition, supplier development suffers from the absence of a financially credible investment appraisal technique. A technique is required, capable of supporting the adoption of supplier development as a mechanism for securing competitive advantage, since at present supplier development is often advocated on a vague or anecdotal basis. This places supplier development at a grave disadvantage compared with those competing calls for capital expenditure supported by sophisticated investment appraisal tools. In order to remedy this undesirable state of affairs, this chapter will review, *inter alia,* the testing and development of such an investment appraisal tool.

> *Supplier development transforms problems into opportunities, weaknesses into strengths.*

Background Literature

It is generally accepted that supplier development can trace its roots to the post-war rejection by the Japanese auto assemblers of the traditional, vertically-integrated industry structure favoured by US firms such as Ford and General Motors (Womack *et al.*, 1990). This is because the demands of the marketplace and competition intensified in Japan, requiring massive improvements in cost and quality from final assemblers and suppliers alike.

Various authors have given differing definitions of supplier development. For Watts and Hahn (1993), supplier development:

> refers to an organization's efforts to create and maintain a network of competent suppliers.

The arguments in favour of such supplier development are illustrated by Christopher (1992) who places an emphasis on the inherent ability of supplier development to impact positively on costs, quality, lead time, new product development and inventory along the value stream:

> there are many advantages to taking a pro-active approach to supplier development. ... For example, many companies are finding that an increasingly valuable source of innovation is the supplier. Either for product innovation or process innovation. ... Bearing in mind the fact that competitive advantage is increasingly a function of supply chain efficiency and effectiveness it will be apparent that the greater the collaboration, at all levels, between supplier and customer, the greater the likelihood that an advantage can be gained. ... The end result of such collaboration is more often than not measured in terms

of lower materials cost, higher quality, shorter lead-times of supply and lower inventories.

Newman and Rhee (1990) have identified the 'new' model for organizing the customer–supplier relationship in operation at the NUMMI Toyota/GM plant in California:

> A supplier becomes part of the team and, in turn, is responsible for structuring its operation to meet team requirements. Crossing traditional organization boundaries is acceptable because these boundaries really do not exist. Traditional functional responsibility has given way to responsibility for improvement and information flow.

Hines (1994a), has explored the mechanisms by which successful supplier development can be effected. In particular identifying the value of *Kyoryoku Kai* (supplier associations) as:

> a mutually benefiting group of a company's most important suppliers brought together on a regular basis for the purpose of co-ordination and co-operation as well as to assist all the members who benefit from the type of development associated with large assemblers. ... It is primarily through this mechanism that leading companies have integrated their value streams. Whilst doing this they share strategies within these value streams and start to adopt common approaches to problem solving and individual development.

In the view of Hines and Jessop reported in Hines (1994a), supplier development activities can be divided into those which seek to increase *inter-*organizational effectiveness and those which target *intra-*organizational opportunities for improvement. As Hines (1994a) clarifies:

> Supplier (or customer) development is a process where one partner in a relationship modifies or otherwise influences the behaviour of the other partner with a view to mutual benefit. This broad definition may be split into two parts: supplier co-ordination and individual supplier development. Supplier co-ordination refers to the activities made by a customer to mould their suppliers into a common way of working so that competitive advantage can be gained, particularly by removing inter-company waste. Individual supplier development refers to the activities made by a customer to help improve the strategies, tools and techniques employed by suppliers to improve their competitive advantage, particularly by removing intra-company waste.

However, despite the foregoing, Watts and Hahn (1993) have identified the paucity of academic literature relating to supplier development:

> In the final analysis, a firm's ability to produce a quality product at a reasonable cost, and in a timely manner, is heavily influenced by its supplier's capabilities. Consequently, without a competent supplier

network, a firm's ability to compete in the market can be hampered significantly. Yet, a careful review of existing textbooks and research articles appearing in the professional journals reveals that very little publication space has been devoted to the subject. In fact, most of the existing coverage of supplier development topics tends to be brief and lacks specifics.

In the years since the publication of the above statement, only slight progress has been made, notwithstanding the outputs of a few active researchers in the subject (such as Hahn *et al.*, 1990; Smitka, 1991; and Sako, 1992). Nevertheless, the situation in relation to the exposure given to supplier development within the academic and professional literature remains fundamentally, and disappointingly, unchanged.

Supplier Development in Context

In order to understand what supplier development is, where it might be used and what the specific problems are of undertaking such activity, it will be useful to place the topic within the broader context of buyer–supplier relationships. In order to do this the Network Sourcing model will be used as a datum (Hines, 1994a).

The Network Sourcing Model as shown in Table 13.1 is made up of ten

TABLE 13.1   The Network Sourcing Model

1. A tiered supply structure with a heavy reliance on small firms.
2. A small number of direct suppliers with individual part numbers sourced from one supplier but within a competitive dual sourcing environment.
3. High degrees of asset specificity among suppliers and risk-sharing between customer and supplier alike.
4. A maximum-buy strategy by each company within the semi-permanent supplier network, but a maximum-make strategy within these trusted networks.
5. A high degree of bilateral design employing the skills and knowledge of both customer and supplier alike.
6. A high degree of supplier innovation in both new products and processes.
7. Close, long-term relations between network members involving a high degree of trust, openness and profit sharing.
8. The use of rigorous supplier grading systems increasingly giving way to supplier self-certification.
9. A high level of supplier coordination by the customer company at each level of the tiered supply structure.
10. A significant effort made by customers at each of these levels to develop their individual suppliers.

SOURCE: P. Hines (1994a).

features that hide a closely interacting web of interrelationships leading to the excellent position exhibited today by many world-class companies, particularly from Japan's automotive, electronics and machine tool industries on which the model is based. The key elements within Network Sourcing that could be described as causal include supplier coordination and individual supplier development (Hines, 1996). These areas, in which Western firms have until recently shown little interest, are instrumental in bringing about the type of close long-term relationships prized by many western organizations.

The primary tools employed by the Japanese to implement supplier coordination and individual supplier development are cross-exchange of staff between buyer and supplier, one-to-one supplier development, but most importantly the *kyoryoku kai* or supplier association. The supplier association is used as the vehicle to help align suppliers with the policy set by the customer's senior management team. In addition it provides suppliers with the awareness of what they need to do to satisfy the customer as well, as an education on the individual techniques that they should use. This then subsequently helps to lead to the successful implementation and continued improvement of all members of the semi-formal, many-tiered, supplier networks.

However, the relationships should be viewed more widely than this and should include bilateral design and rapid supplier innovation in both technologies and manufacturing processes. In addition customers typically choose a small number of suppliers, although this does not necessarily, or even usually, result in single sourcing. Another important feature of the Japanese automotive and electronics industries is the tiering of supply with each firm in the various supplier tiers operating a maximum-buy strategy. This in turn helps lead to a highly tiered supply structure with each firm concentrating on what it is really good at.

Certainly in the early stages of developing such effective supplier networks, assemblers have played an important role in auditing or grading their suppliers and have indeed encouraged their suppliers to do the same to their suppliers. However, over time as trust is built, and competences improved, suppliers increasingly self-certify themselves. The relationships exhibited today involve a significant investment on the part of both customers and suppliers. In addition, suppliers are expected to make investments in customers through developing dedicated resources in factories, capital equipment, tools and even the training of staff. This mutual dependency tends to cement both partners into a long-term, mutually beneficial relationship – indeed, the type of relationship valued by many Western firms.

> *Another important feature of the Japanese automotive and electronics industries is the tiering of supply with each firm in the various supplier tiers operating a maximum-buy strategy.*

Comparing Supplier Development in the West With Japan

At this point it will be useful to gauge the gap between best practice in Japan and the situation in the UK, and more specifically with the SCDP companies. To establish the situation in Japan, a multi-industry survey was carried out involving a structured questionnaire and semi-structured verification interviews (Hines, 1995b). The findings within the supplier coordination and individual development area will be reviewed below.

Figures 13.1 and 13.2 describe the degree to which supplier co-ordination (feature 9 of Network Sourcing) and individual supplier development (feature 10) occur. It is not easy in practice to split these when asking a very small number of simple questions. However, as supplier associations are the major supplier coordination mechanism in Network Sourcing, their frequency has been used as a surrogate for supplier co-ordination. However, this would be to ignore their role in individual supplier development. As a result the degree of supplier development has been tested by simply adding up the different types of such activity either reported by the individual firms in the questionnaire or identified in the semi-structured interview.

Figure 13.1 shows somewhat surprisingly that the supplier association is used by all firms in the ten industries surveyed where data is available. With the exception of Nippon Steel it was possible to identify the number of meetings specifically concerned with supplier coordination per year (although for the more developed groups such as Toyota Motor there were in addition several hundred meetings per year that were specifically used for supplier development purposes).

Figure 13.2 shows the range of types of supplier support given by the surveyed firms. This generally ranged from 7 for the component industries, down to only 1 for the retailers, with the process manufacturers somewhere between. However, the range and depth of activities reported by Toyota Motor was not far short of astounding, with 15 different types identified. It is therefore possible to conclude that the range and complexity of supplier coordination and individual supplier development do vary considerably between industries in Japan, but also exhibit a generally high level of activity.

In contrast to this, Spiers (1997) conducted a comparative survey to the Japanese one in order to establish how the same industries in the UK performed. He found that the degree and sophistication of supplier co-ordination and individual supplier development being undertaken in the UK was far lower in all of the industries studied. Spiers concludes:

> that the above differences are not cultural, indeed the ... key areas (for the UK) to address, however, relate to suppliers taking more of a leading role in product design and the role of customers in terms of giving manufacturing and innovation assistance to suppliers. One

FIGURE 13.1   Japanese Survey Supplier Association Meetings per Year

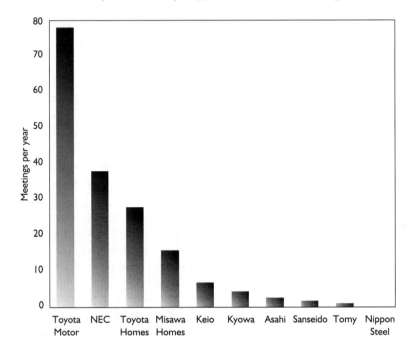

FIGURE 13.2   Japanese Survey Types of Supplier Support

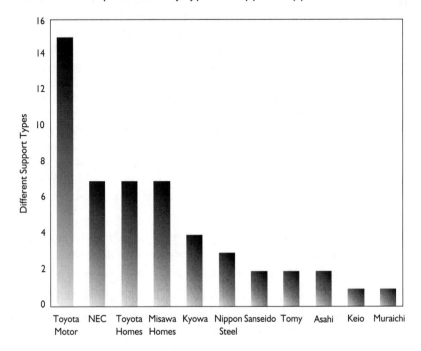

such method of driving both of these issues is through the Supplier Association, a competitive weapon yet to be employed (by Unipart) in the UK. (Spiers, 1997: p. 128)

In addition to these findings a questionnaire survey was conducted with the SCDP sponsoring companies which, *inter alia*, sought to establish their current general supplier development activities (Hines and James, 1994; James and Hines, 1994). Nine firms took part in the survey, with 7 recording some supplier coordination or individual supplier development activity. Within the supplier coordination area the achievement of on-time delivery and of high service level were found to be the most important areas, with improvement of incoming quality and cost control also being key. Three firms also wanted to reduce the supplier base in order to improve coordination.

In order to achieve this coordination, the firms generally held one-to-one meetings with the suppliers, although 4 did undertake supplier conferences in which they could either jointly target improvements or give suppliers targets. A majority of the firms surveyed reported significant but unquantified benefits from this type of activity.

Of the 9 firms questioned 6 reported that they had an individual supplier development programme and half of these had some permanent organizational structure to support this activity with projects generally chosen as a response to an individual supplier's recent poor performance. Thus, most of the activity was responsive and lacking a preventative focus. In terms of functional involvement in this area of work, all 6 firms reported that purchasing was involved, with quality taking part in 5 cases, materials management in 4 and production or engineering in 2 other cases. This showed a significant cross-functional involvement where individual supplier development was indeed taking place. The primary aim of this activity was to improve quality and general supplier service, with on-time delivery and reduced cost also key target areas. This targeting exercise was in general seen as a joint activity between buyer and supplier.

As a result of this exercise a number of central issues emerged from the research. The most important of these was the belief shown by the SCDP companies that further supplier coordination or individual supplier development would yield significant benefits to their organizations. However, a sponsor brainstorming exercise revealed that the two major reasons preventing this were:

1. a lack of accurate costing information that could be used to justify supplier coordination or individual supplier development;
2. a lack of clarity about the most effective activity to undertake.

Consequently, two parallel programmes were run inside SCDP which sought to help the companies in these areas. The results of these programmes will be reported in turn below.

Costing Supplier Coordination and Individual Supplier Development[2]

Unfortunately, supplier development[3] is not always a typical component of improvement programmes. Indeed, it is disappointing to note the frequency with which, for example, TQM is referred to as just 'a company-wide process'. This may be because the establishment of long-term relationships built on the principles of trust and mutual benefit may be anathema to purchasing, or simply the result of a lack of internal cross-functional collaboration to undertake such work.

Even in those organizations where particular individuals or particular functions both recognize the need for supplier development and feel confident of developing a cross-functional commitment, there are still other barriers to initiating supplier development. In the first instance, generally supplier development will require senior management to approve an initial expenditure to fund the programme. In this regard supplier development must compete with other prospective projects for the allocation of scarce investment capital. However, many, if not all, of the alternative projects put forward for consideration will benefit from the support of sophisticated investment appraisal techniques such as Discounted Cash-Flow (DCF) methods, or at least Break-Even Analysis. Such sophisticated investment appraisal techniques have the power to reassure senior management that their decisions can be justified as being rational in light of the information available. In the meantime, against the seemingly black-and-white benefits to be secured from a new piece of capital equipment, the benefits of supplier development can often only be represented to senior decision-makers in vague and/or anecdotal terms. Thus investment in supplier development is usually a leap of faith.

It would appear desirable to develop a tool which possesses the capacity to define the costs and benefits associated with supplier development. In concentrating on the twin aspects of cost and benefit (or investment and return), the tool will become an investment appraisal technique in itself. As a result, supplier development proposals will be placed on an equal footing with more conventional investment proposals.

The key to developing such a tool is the isolation of an appropriate costing methodology. The methodology must be capable of satisfying three basic criteria. First, it must capture the full range of costs which accrue to an organization as a result of supplier non-performance. Second, it must present the data in a manner which allows a ready distinction to be made between those costs which are best understood as

---

[2] A more detailed discussion of the Cost of Quality research undertaken can be found in Hines, James and Jones, 1995a.

[3] In this section we will use the term 'supplier development' to refer to a combination of supplier coordination and individual supplier development.

investments designed to reduce the overall expense of supplier non-performance, and those which are resultant and simply describe the magnitude of supplier non-performance. Finally, the methodology must be recognized by those in decision-making positions as possessing financial integrity.

Methodology Choice

Three possible methodologies were considered: accountancy, cost-benefit or Cost of Quality.

Accountancy

In general, traditional accounting systems are designed to report on a functional basis and we have already identified the cross-functional nature of the costs of supplier non-performance. In addition the accounting convention of 'conservatism' inhibits the accounts department from making all but the most direct connections between supplier non-performance and subsequent costs incurred by the organization. Therefore, while an accounting methodology does satisfy one of our criteria, namely that it is seen to possess financial integrity as a result of its origins in the accounts department, it fails to collect the necessary data, and also to present its data in a relevant manner.

Cost-benefit Analysis

Cost-benefit analysis is more usually associated with public sector investment decisions, such as road building schemes or the locations of new hospitals. The technique revolves around arbitrary mechanisms which seek to place tangible values on apparently intangible phenomena. Such a methodology appears apposite within the context of supplier development, as it may provide a method for quantifying the intangible benefits.

In its favour, this approach does represent an attempt to move away from purely anecdotal justifications for supplier development. On the other hand, the method is flawed in several important regards. Its reliance on arbitrary assumptions to calculate the benefit of supplier development renders it vulnerable to criticisms that it lacks financial integrity. In addition, most benefits of supplier development are tangible and so such an approach was rejected.

Cost of Quality

Fortunately, a costing methodology exists which is eminently suited to our needs. Unlike accountancy-based measures or cost-benefit analysis it satisfies each of the three criteria of a suitable costing methodology. It collates the necessary data, presents that data in a relevant manner and possesses financial integrity. Cost of Quality (COQ) (Dale and Plunkett, 1991), operates from the premise that organizations can actively measure their 'cost of quality' on an ongoing basis.

In many ways it is important to recognize the term 'cost of quality' as a misnomer. What we are really referring to is the cost of *poor* quality. This cost of poor quality can be calculated and compared with other organizational performance indicators. For example, the cost of poor quality can be given as a percentage of sales revenue. However, more important is the formula used by cost of quality theory to categorize the costs which accrue to the organization in the pursuit of quality.

Cost of Quality (COQ) operates from the premise that organizations can actively measure their 'cost of quality' on an ongoing basis.

The cost-of-quality methodology divides costs into four distinct categories. In so doing it establishes the basis of a supplier development appraisal tool. It must be accepted that an easy classification of costs into the four categories is not always a straightforward exercise. As an example, supplier assurance is given as a cost of appraisal by Crosby, but as a cost of Prevention by UK standard BS 6143. Moving beyond these minor reservations, the methodology is of great value in that it allows the differentiation of the various costs which accrue as a result of poor quality. It classifies the costs into:

- those which have the ability to influence the organization's cost of quality – that is, Prevention and Appraisal costs;
- those which accrue automatically as a result of poor quality and have no *causal* influence over the organization's overall cost of quality – that is, Internal and External Failure costs.

It further differentiates those costs which can influence the organization's overall cost of quality into proactive costs (Prevention), and reactive costs (Appraisal). Thus reactive Appraisal costs may be an effective short-term remedy for extremely expensive external failure, but (apart from goods inward inspection), will have little influence over internal failure. However, proactive Prevention costs will not only be able to reduce both types of failure costs but should also reduce the need for expenditure on appraisal. This relationship is demonstrated in Figure 13.3.

The cost-of-quality approach would appear to possess the necessary attributes to constitute a supplier development investment-appraisal tool. All that is required is to modify the focus of the methodology from the costs of poor quality in general to those costs which accrue specifically as a result of supplier non-performance. In establishing the methodology around the concept of supplier non-performance, we must first define what we understand as acceptable supplier *performance*.

FIGURE 13.3 The Costs Associated with Supplier Non-Performance

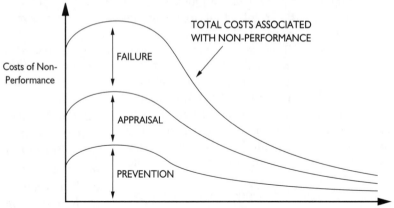

Supplier Performance

In attempting to define the level of supplier performance we deem as representing an acceptable and suitable target, we are faced with several alternatives. With reference to the model proposed here the overriding consideration must be that the standard should be viewed as being both reasonable and achievable by the greater part of the supplier network. Attempting to compare the organization's supplier base with that of a world-class organization was therefore thought to be unwise. Instead, we feel it preferable to set the standard at a more realistic (or less contentious) level. The target for supplier performance was defined as the level of the performance at the 10 per cent level (i.e. when a company has 100 suppliers, using the tenth best firm as a benchmark). Measuring the performance of the whole supplier base against this, we can define the potential benefit to be gained from addressing the issue of supplier non-performance against a realistic datum point.

Data Collection

Cost data is collected by identifying and quantifying those costs which accrue as a result of supplier non-performance. These are those costs which the organization would not have to bear if its entire supplier network operated as efficiently and effectively as the 10 per cent level firm. At this stage a decision must be made as to the amount of time and effort to be expended in collecting the information. The literature on the subject contains examples of organizations which take several months to ascertain their costs of quality (Dale and Plunkett, 1991; Grimm, 1981). We believe that this time-consuming approach is counter-productive and the data collection period should be measured in hours or days at most.

It must be remembered that the costing methodology is simply a means to an end. The ultimate goal is the reduction in the costs of supplier non-performance. This approach may produce marginally less accurate data, but the inaccuracy is just that, marginal. For most organizations a 10–15 per cent inaccuracy will not detract from the ultimate integrity of the model.

It is also necessary to collect data from organizations along the value stream. This is in recognition of the fact that different organizations within the value stream incur different costs from supplier non-performance. In addition, certain costs of supplier non-performance will only become apparent when one looks outside the organization.

Such an approach projects the costs incurred by an organization as a result of supplier non-performance, but does so in such a way as to distinguish between the costs of prevention, appraisal and failure. It is reasonable to expect that expenditure on preventative measures will ultimately reduce the costs of appraisal and failure. Therefore, in demonstrating the massive imbalances between prevention and failure costs which exist in the greater number of organizations, we are effectively making the case for supplier development. This is still one step short of true Discounted Cash-Flow methods of investment appraisal, as one cannot make the direct assumption that investment in Supplier Development will automatically reduce appraisal and failure costs. This can only be achieved by *successful* supplier development. Nevertheless, the strength of the approach lies in its ability to demonstrate the magnitude of the opportunity which exists for reducing the cost base of the value stream in general and the individual organization in particular.

It is important to embrace the dynamic nature of the model. Attempting to develop the capabilities of all suppliers to the level of the best will inevitably result in a retrospective focus. It therefore becomes an imperative to re-evaluate costs and targets periodically to retain the momentum of improvement. Thus supplier development becomes an open-ended process rather than a discreet programme which will conclude with the attainment of certain levels of achievement.

Testing the Approach

Although the identity of the organization used for testing will not be disclosed in order to maintain commercial confidentiality, we should emphasize that the organization has traded, and continues to trade, profitably and indeed to outperform its industry average. This is an important consideration which must be kept in mind when interpreting the costs incurred by the organization as a result of supplier non-performance.

The various costs resulting from supplier non-performance were identified on the basis of managerial experience held within the focus organization. This managerial experience was augmented by the use of such tools as *brainstorming* and *affinity diagrams*, facilitated by the academic research team. The necessity of establishing an exhaustive list of criteria made it desirable to supplement this experience-based approach with a checklist developed by the research team, which was used after the brainstorming of factors by the firm involved. Identifying the various ways in which costs accrued to the organization was relatively straightforward. Allocating those costs within the prevention, appraisal and failure framework was slightly more problematical. The data (presented in Table 13.2) reveals that it was sometimes necessary to split a particular cost between two categories. As an example, we identified both *preventative* and *failure-driven* expediting, but for simplicity recorded all the costs as preventative. In many ways, what is important is not the detailed nuances of what categories costs should be allocated to, but that all the (significant) tangible costs of supplier non-performance are recorded.

A dual approach was taken to the quantification of supplier non-performance. Managerial experience was employed to judge the fraction of a process cost, employees' time, or departmental effort which was caused by or given over to dealing with supplier non-performance. The costs of those activities were then calculated with the aid of financial cost data prepared by the accounts department. In this way the experience of management was consolidated by the financial integrity of the accounting function.

Several of the cost criteria established were intangibles such as the cost of lost business to the focal organization as a result of supplier non-performance. Although this could be estimated through discussions with customers, it was felt better to exclude such costs on the basis of conservatism, to ensure that the approach was not discredited by including costs which were difficult to substantiate. We therefore limited ourselves to overtly tangible costs of supplier non-performance, preferring to refer to the intangibles as footnotes in any presentation to senior management.

The process described above was completed in a single day at the focus organization and a series of half-days at a sample of the organization's value stream partners (customers and suppliers). Again, to inculcate financial credibility, subsequent work to validate the figures before their presentation to senior management would be prudent.

Results

Having drawn together the disparate strands of supplier non-performance costs, we are in a position to interpret and utilize our data (Table 13.2). The initial impression is the sheer magnitude of supplier non-performance. The overall costs to the organization exceed £32 million per annum. Putting this figure into perspective, supplier non-performance equates to 18 per cent of the focus organization's purchase spend (or almost 30 per cent where the costs incurred by the suppliers themselves

TABLE 13.2 Prevention, Appraisal and Failure Costs of Supplier Non-Performance at Focus Firm

	£.......000's	£.......000's	£.......000's
Cost of prevention			
Customer assistance	3		
Supplier development	500		
Supplier training	7		
Audit feedback	3		
Supplier suggestions	3		
Training (internal)	26		
Expedition	735		
Penalty clauses	<u>18</u>		
Total prevention costs		1,355	
Cost of appraisal			
Supplier audit (ongoing)	263		
Performance monitor	105		
Stock take (shortage)	<u>25</u>		
Total appraisal costs		393	
Cost of failure			
Lost business	?		
Lost prestige	?		
Stock excess (buffer)	15600		
Stock excess (other)	4950		
Stock discrepancies	3		
Double handling	120		
Re-sourcing	80		
Legal costs	54		
Price query	15		
Discrepancy claim	42		
Technical queries	22		
Rework	70		
Over-delivery	10		
Urgent transport	62		
Expediting / rush orders	923		
Customer queries	788		
Excess cost in market	<u>8000</u>		
Total cost of failure		<u>30,739</u>	
TOTAL COST OF SUPPLIER NON-PERFORMANCE			<u>32,487</u>

and the focus firm's customers are included). However, we previously argued that the true comparator of the costs of supplier non-performance is pre-tax profit. Under this comparison we find that the costs of supplier non performance are roughly the same as the present pre-tax profit of the focus firm (or nearly 170 per cent if costs to suppliers themselves and the focal firm's customers are included). At the limit, therefore, reducing the costs of supplier non-performance represent an opportunity to double the pre-tax profit of a relatively profitable firm.

Having realized the magnitude of these costs, we must turn our attention to the disproportion between the costs of prevention and failure. For every £1,000 spent on preventative measures, the organization incurs internally £23,000 in failure costs. Surely there can be no more eloquent,

The true comparator of the costs of supplier non-performance is pre-tax profit.

nor powerful argument in favour of supplier development than those made by these figures.

Several limitations to the approach discussed here, however, become immediately apparent. Those with the benefit of an accountancy training could be forgiven for questioning our data-capture methodology. Certainly the magnitude of supplier non-performance is an approximation. However if we accept that the actual figures for supplier non-performance may vary by plus or minus 10 per cent or even 15 per cent, the message of our model would not be altered substantially. Additionally, there is some difficulty in ascribing cost within the Prevention/Appraisal/Failure categorization. Finally, we must accept that the model is less financially rigorous than full DCF methods of investment appraisal. This is because we cannot draw a definite link between supplier development activity and a reduction in the costs of supplier non-performance.

As stated earlier such an approach is just a precursor for justifying supplier development activity. As such, an extended, dynamic, supplier-non-performance/development methodology is called for. This is presented in Figure 13.4. The ten-stage methodology uses the initial supplier non-performance costs (stages 1–4) as described above, together with a subsequent understanding on the specific causes of supplier non-performance (such as late delivery or unreliable quality through tools such as cause and effect diagrams) and the costs of different corrective programmes (stages 5–6).

This is the background within the model for a PDCA approach (stages 6–10) to address these costs and continually to reduce such costs especially in the failure area. This involves reviewing the amount of money spent on supplier development activities and making a case for a greater expenditure if this is warranted (stage 6). This is followed by a period of implementation of perhaps one year (stage 7), a checking of the benefits and re-running of the Cost of Supplier Non-Performance to gauge the potential benefits of future actions (stage 8). Lastly a re-analysis of the areas causing these costs and re-focusing of improvement activities (stages

FIGURE 13.4   Dynamic Supplier Non-Performance/Development
Methodology

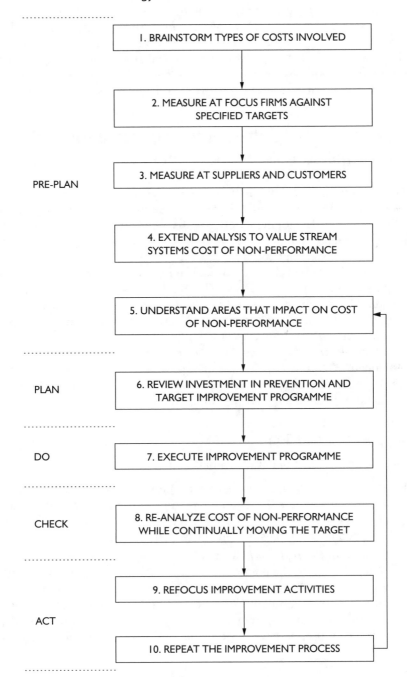

8-9) will allow for a loop-back (stage 10) to stage 5 for the implementation of further supplier development if this is proved to be beneficial.

Although this full new methodology has not been tested here, it should prove to be a useful framework for future testing and an aid for practical implementation. It provides the practitioner not only with a good framework for implementation but also a rigorous approach to improving the process of supplier development by periodically re-focusing attention to increase the effectiveness of given resources.

Effectively Focusing Supplier Coordination and Individual Supplier Development Activity[4]

The second major factor reported by SCDP sponsoring organizations as preventing them from undertaking more supplier coordination or individual supplier development activity was a lack of detailed knowledge as to how to focus such activity. There is, therefore, a clear need for some method or model that explains the scope of supplier development and gives an indication of the commitment required from a company wishing to pursue this type of strategy. The model must also help companies progress their strategy in a coherent manner and allow them to align their complete relationship with suppliers, rather than just individual segments of the buyer–supplier relationship.

In order to do this, a Supplier Development Positioning Matrix was developed (Figure 13.5). The Matrix provides a four-stage positioning approach for various characteristics within both supplier coordination (X axis) and individual supplier development (Y axis).

Supplier coordination

The four stages of supplier coordination are:

1. *No Coherent Strategy*: At this stage companies will be making little or no attempt to mould their suppliers into a common way of working. Buying criteria will be at lowest price with the supplier's role to provide goods or services that the customer cannot make.

2. *Piecemeal Coordination*: At this stage there will be some instances of a department in the company working with a relevant department at the supplier's. For instance, the designers may be using a modem link to transmit design data from their computer to the supplier's computer, or the supplier may be using the customer's containers when delivering product. Buying criteria at this stage will be lowest cost

---

[4] A more detailed discussion of the Supplier Development Positioning Matrix can be found in Hines, James and Jones (1995b).

FIGURE 13.5 The Supplier Development Positioning Matrix

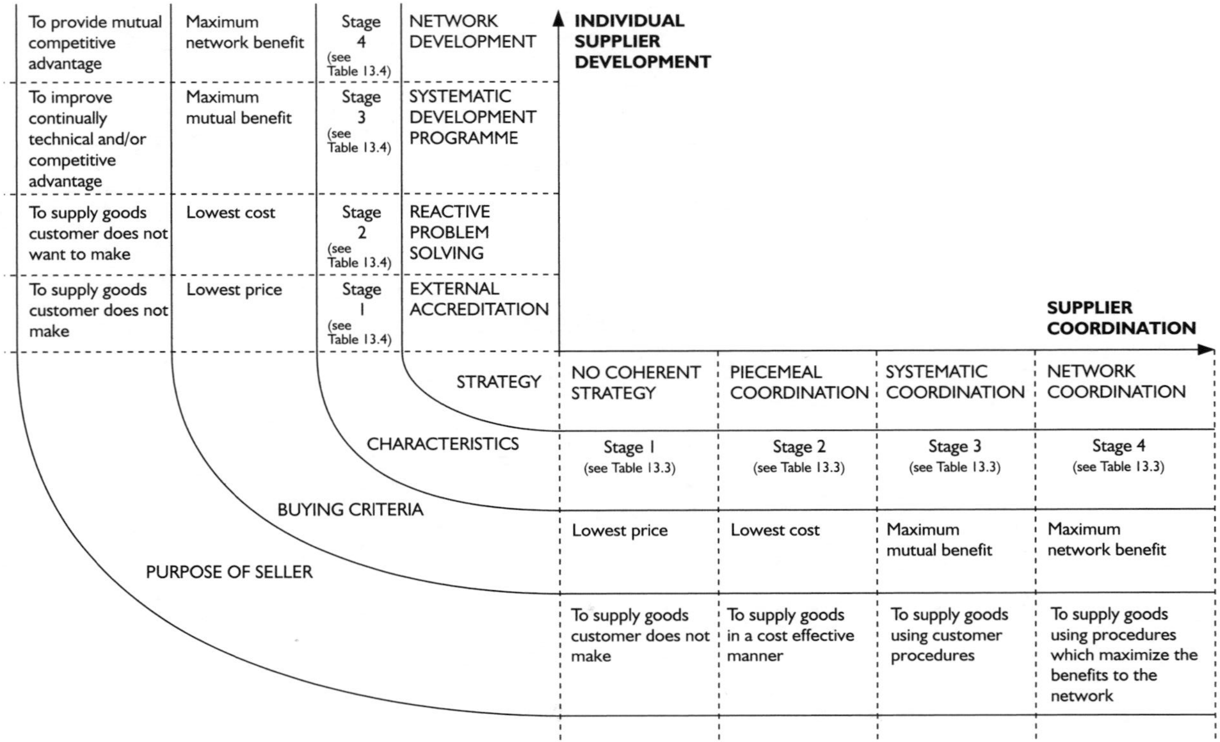

	NO COHERENT STRATEGY	PIECEMEAL COORDINATION	SYSTEMATIC COORDINATION	NETWORK COORDINATION
STRATEGY	Stage 1 (see Table 13.3)	Stage 2 (see Table 13.3)	Stage 3 (see Table 13.3)	Stage 4 (see Table 13.3)
BUYING CRITERIA	Lowest price	Lowest cost	Maximum mutual benefit	Maximum network benefit
PURPOSE OF SELLER	To supply goods customer does not make	To supply goods in a cost effective manner	To supply goods using customer procedures	To supply goods using procedures which maximize the benefits to the network

INDIVIDUAL SUPPLIER DEVELOPMENT

NETWORK DEVELOPMENT	Stage 4 (see Table 13.4)	SYSTEMATIC DEVELOPMENT PROGRAMME
	Stage 3 (see Table 13.4)	
	Stage 2 (see Table 13.4)	REACTIVE PROBLEM SOLVING
	Stage 1 (see Table 13.4)	EXTERNAL ACCREDITATION

CHARACTERISTICS	
To provide mutual competitive advantage	Maximum network benefit
To improve continually technical and/or competitive advantage	Maximum mutual benefit
To supply goods customer does not want to make	Lowest cost
To supply goods customer does not make	Lowest price

with the main role of suppliers to provide goods in a cost-effective manner.

3. *Systematic Coordination*: At this stage companies will be taking a proactive approach to working with their suppliers to eliminate waste. It will involve cross-functional working groups with long-term objectives. Buying criteria at this stage will be to maximize mutual benefit with goods supplied according to customer-defined criteria.

4. *Network Coordination*: At this stage companies will be taking a proactive role in developing common methods of working for mutual advantage throughout the supply chain. This will involve both direct and indirect suppliers, customers and even indirect customers. Buying criteria here will be to maximize the total supply network benefit with goods provided, using procedures that will ensure maximum benefit to the network.

Individual Supplier Development

The four stages of individual supplier are:

1. *External Accreditation*: At this stage a company will be doing very little to improve the competitiveness of its suppliers. At best it will be demanding that the suppliers have some form of third-party accreditation, such as ISO 9000. While this demand is made to give the customer some confidence in the supplier's ability, its by-product is to force the supplier to examine its own internal systems. At this stage suppliers are chosen on the basis of lowest price and are viewed as supplying products that the customer cannot made themselves.

2. *Reactive Problem-Solving*: At this stage companies will be willing to help their suppliers solve problems as they arise on an *ad hoc* basis. The response will range from quick fixes that overcome particular problems in the short term to more in-depth solutions that attempt to get to the real root cause of the problem, thus providing for a longer-term solution. At this stage the buyer's focus is on the lowest-cost supplier who will provide goods the customer does not wish to make.

3. *Systematic Development Programme*: At this stage companies will be taking a systematic approach to helping suppliers improve their own competitiveness with benefits to both parties. There will be a close working relationship involving many cross-functional participants, a sharing of information and technology as well as shared long-term objectives. As such, both parties will be seeking mutual benefit within a continual improvement framework.

4. *Network Development*: At this fourth stage companies will be taking a systematically proactive approach to improving the competitiveness of the complete supply chain. This will involve working with

both direct and indirect suppliers and customers. The goal here is maximum benefit to the complete supply network and the provision of mutual competitive advantage.

Relationship Characteristics

In order to allow a company to position itself, its various relationship characteristics should be used within the maturity grid provided for both supplier coordination (Table 13.3) and individual supplier development (Table 13.4). Thus a company adopting a Stage 1 Supplier Coordination response to supplier's delivery requirements would seek standard lead times, whereas a Stage 4 response would involve true JIT delivery. In the same way a Stage 1 Individual Supplier Development response to a supplier's quality would be to issue product specifications, whereas a Stage 4 response would be a TQM-style approach involving the supplier as well as the latter's own supplier base.

Use and Purpose of the Model

The model has *four* main uses:

1. To help companies to determine how advanced their present general stage of development is in both supplier coordination and individual supplier development.

2. To determine whether multiple strategies should be adopted by one company – for example, higher-stage methods with a few strategic suppliers, and lower stage approaches for less critical ones. If such multiple strategies are adopted, this may either be an interim strategy before the firm can adopt higher stage methods across a wider segment of suppliers or simply a sensible, long-term, segmented approach.

3. To determine whether they are adopting a misaligned strategy by adopting advanced methods for some aspects of activity and other methods likely to hold them back. An example of this would be a company having true JIT delivery from suppliers, but simply buying on lowest price criteria.

4. To prioritize further supplier coordination or individual supplier development activity in order to avoid misalignment and in general develop their supplier base.

For companies that are pursuing a strategy of supplier development in some form, the matrix will provide a checklist to help them optimize their efforts. For those companies that wish to advance their strategies the matrix will help them map out a sensible way forward. Although the model is a generalized industry one, a slightly refined approach based broadly on the matrix provided may be applied by firms in specific industrial areas. However, the general approach described above has proved robust where

TABLE 13.3 Maturity Grid for Supplier Coordination Response to Various Buyer–Supplier Characteristics

Strategy/ Characteristics	No Coherent Strategy	Piecemeal Coordination	Systematic Coordination	Network Coordination
Buying criteria	Lowest price	Lowest cost	Maximum mutual benefit	Maximum network benefit
Purpose of supplier	To supply goods customer does not make	To supply goods in a cost-effective manner	To supply goods using customer procedures	To supply goods using procedures to maximize the benefits to the network
Relationship type	Adversarial	Localized cooperation	Close	Strategic
Relationship length	Variable	Variable	Long	Lifetime
Customer involvement with suppliers	Small	Some, logistics	Frequent, mainly logistic	Frequent, many functions
Quality requirement	Product specification	Quality control	Quality assurance/TQM	TQM spread to own suppliers
Delivery requirement	Standard lead times	*Ad hoc* projects	Joint ventures timed deliveries	True JIT
Cost requirement	Lowest market price	Lowest cost	Stable reducing interaction costs	Target costing, share savings
Product design requirement	-------	-------	Some packaging and handling	Network packaging and handling
Technology sharing	None	Limited (mainly customer technology)	Customer sharing IT handling technology	Some reliance on predictive scores
Reliance on grading	None or external	Some reliance on reactive scores	Heavy reliance on reactive and predictive scores	Some reliance on predictive scores
Data interchange	Limited, operational only	Limited, mainly operational	Detailed and frequent	Detailed, some strategic, within network
Asset specificity	None/very low	Very low	Medium, e.g. designated trucks and handling equipment	Medium
Number of suppliers	High and unstable	High, relatively stable	Low and very stable	Very low and very stable
Frequency of interaction	Frequent, expediting-based	Frequent, *ad hoc*, mainly reactive problem-solving	Very frequent at operational level, planned regular meetings	Very frequent at operational level, spreading through network

TABLE 13.4 Maturity Grid for Individual Supplier Development Response to Various Buyer–Supplier Characteristics

Strategy/ Characteristics	External Accreditation	Reactive Problem Solving	Systematic Development Programme	Network Development
Buying criteria	Lowest price	Lowest cost	Maximum mutual benefit	Maximum network benefit
Purpose of supplier	To supply goods customer does not make	To supply goods customer does not want to make	To improve continually technical and/or competitive advantage	To provide mutual competitive advantage
Relationship type	Adversarial	Arm's-length	Close	Strategic
Relationship length	Short/variable	Variable	Long	Lifetime
Customer involvement with supplier	Small	Some, purchasing and quality	Frequent, many functions	Continuous and multi-functional
Quality requirement	Product specification	Quality control	Quality assurance/TQM	TQM spread to own supplier
Delivery requirement	Standard lead times	Standard lead time	Customer involved in shop floor lead time reduction	True JIT
Cost requirement	Lowest market price	Lowest cost	Stable/reducing product cost	Target costing, share savings
Product design requirement	Customer specification or catalogue product	Some joint input	Significant joint input	Integrated design capability within network
Technology sharing	None	Limited (mainly customer technology)	Frequent with two-way flow	Frequent within network
Reliance on grading	None or external	Some reliance on reactive scores	Heavy reliance on reactive and predictive scores	Some reliance on predictive scores
Data interchange	Limited, operational only	Limited, mainly operational	Detailed, often operational and some strategic	Detailed at both operational and strategic level
Asset specificity	None/very low	Low – medium	High	High through network
Number of suppliers	High and unstable	High, relatively stable	Low and very stable	Very low and very stable
Frequency of interaction	Infrequent	Infrequent, scheduled and reactive	Frequent proactive and reactive	Continuous

tested and has provided the basis for several SCDP firms in their supplier development activity. In particular it helped Nortel, Tesco, Clarks and Unipart to adopt various higher-stage solutions to their general supplier development strategies (Hoare, 1994; Watson, 1994; Taylor, 1994; Spiers, 1997). However, following later work within SCDP, various other methods and approaches have been developed from which later entrants to SCDP have also benefited. The remainder of the chapter will be confined to the supplier coordination and individual supplier development activity that was started at RS Components after a short period of initial Value Stream Mapping activity reported earlier in this text.

Putting it all Together: The RS Components Case[5]

Following the Value Stream Mapping programme at RS Components it was decided by the company to set up a Supplier Association as a framework for its programme of supplier development activity. For the purposes of this work the usual manufacturing definition of a Supplier Association (Hines, 1994a) was modified to fit the purpose required by RS Components. The definition used was that 'a Supplier Association is a group of companies, linked together on a regular basis to share knowledge and experience in an open and cooperative manner'. In order to implement the pilot scheme and in preparation for a later roll-out programme, a three-tier system of management was put in place (Dimancescu *et al.*, 1997). This cascading system (Figure 13.6) was employed with as many of the original group involved in the mapping as possible.

> *A Supplier Association is a group of companies, linked together on a regular basis to share knowledge and experience in an open and cooperative manner.*

At the highest level the steering board led by the head of the Strategic Purchasing unit was set up. This group consisted of the top managers from across the business. A key role of this group was to ensure that a critical target was set for the programme. This target was simply and unambiguously set at a doubling of stock turns within a three-year horizon. In addition, this group scheduled a series of bimonthly meetings to measure the progress of the work, to ensure that adequate resources were being employed and to make sure that nothing interrupted or disrupted the Supplier Integration process. The steering group made no attempt to tell the process development or product teams how to achieve the outline target that had been set, but provided the support to help them.

---

[5] This case first appeared as part of the paper: Peter Hines, Nick Rich and Ann Esain, 'Creating a Lean Supplier Network: A Distribution Industry Case', *European Journal of Purchasing and Supply Management* (1998). The authors would like to thank the editor and publishers of EJPSM for agreeing to its reproduction here in a modified form.

FIGURE 13.6   The Three-Tier System of Management

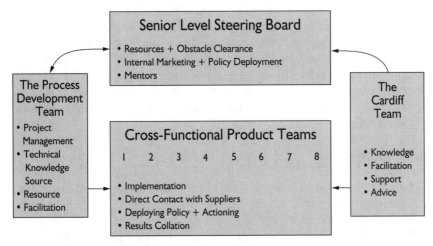

The process development team led by one of the staff within the Strategic Purchasing unit was formed from middle managers from various competency centres in the business. The team included representatives from inventory control, purchasing and a team leader for two of the individual product group teams. A key responsibility of this group was to develop a set of measures and performance gaps to motivate and guide the pilot product team and subsequent roll-out groups. The resulting measures together with initial data from the first pilot team are shown in Table 13.5. Around these goals the process development team designed the broad guidelines of an optimal Supplier Integration process and facilitated its subsequent dissemination to later product teams. It also ensured that ties between these product teams were created so that knowledge was shared between them of what did and did not work well.

TABLE 13.5   Balanced Benefit Benchmarking for RS Components Pilot Team

Metric	Target Performance	Current Performance	Gap
Average lead time	5 weeks	8.23 weeks	3.23
Average stock turns	6	3.6	2.4
Forecast accuracy	45%	38.2%	6.8%
Forecast variability ratio	1:2	1:3.1	–
Delivery on time	95%	74%	21%
Delivery correct quantity	95%	62%	33%
Rejections	1,000 ppm	5,314 ppm	4,314
Customer returns	10,000 ppm	60,815 ppm	50,815

The measures chosen were not designed to be a simple audit of supplier performance but were more designed to be a gauge of the degree of Supplier Integration, or what later became termed a 'Balanced Benefit Benchmark'. This was because some of the measures, such as 'forecast variability', were designed to be more a measure of RS Components' performance. Others, like 'delivery on time', were more aimed at suppliers' performance with a third group including average stock turns at RS Components – a reflection of how effectively the total Supplier Integration process was working.

The Pilot Supplier Association

The individual product teams were made accountable for attaining these targets with the process development team providing support when required. The first of the product teams dealing with industrial control equipment was created in early 1996, with members representing the internal value stream: a buyer, an inventory controller and a product (marketing) manager. They were supported by other individuals outside the process development team from other key support areas such as quality, goods inwards, accounting and packaging design. The team was led in this case by the buyer who had the greatest knowledge of the suppliers. The reason this product team was selected from the six teams that volunteered was the enthusiasm of the industrial control equipment team as well as the support given by their team leader.

The role of this team was to implement the Supplier Integration process with a group of their key suppliers. Of the 32 suppliers in this product area, a strategic group of 7 was chosen on the basis of expenditure as well as potential and its previous proactive stance towards RS Components. The seven represented around half of the external expenditure by the product group. The companies chosen were a mixture of European manufacturers and distributors of non-European products.

The seven companies were first brought together at a hotel near to RS Components in February 1996. Prior to this the team had undertaken a careful analysis of what they wanted to get out of the Supplier Association and how they might achieve it using the Value Stream Analysis Tool (VALSAT) (Hines, Rich and Hittmeyer, 1998), a modification of the Quality Function Deployment method (Mizuno and Akao, 1994). The method consisted of the RS Components product team brainstorming their wants from the programme and prioritizing them. With the help of the process development team they deliberated on different approaches to the achievement of these desired outcomes. They developed a correlation of the improvements required and possible methods to use, with a range of scores given depending on the closeness of correlation. They determined the total usefulness for each method by multiplying its weighting by the correlation score and summing the results by columns.

The result was a ranking of the top ten Supplier Integration methods to achieve the needs of the customer. This was presented to the Supplier Association members at the first meeting together with a briefing on the goals of the Supplier Association and how it could be used in the Supplier Integration programme. During this event, and in more detail afterwards, individual suppliers were asked to undertake a similar VALSAT exercise on what they wanted to achieve from the programme. This allowed for a balanced view between buyer and the suppliers before deciding what actually to do. The results of the exercise are shown in Table 13.6.

TABLE 13.6   Proposed Improvement Methods

Rank	Partsco's Suggested Improvement Methods	Suppliers' Suggested Improvement Methods
1	Self-certification	Co-managed inventory (CMI)
2	Due-date performance	Due-date performance
3	Vendor rating	Milk rounds (delivery)
4	Stabilize schedules	Ship to stock
5	Milk rounds (delivery)	Stabilize schedules
6	Co-managed inventory	Standard packs
7	EDI (Electronic Data Interchange)	Standard product information
8	Replenishment modules	Replenishment modules
9	Hotline to suppliers	EDI
10	Safety stock at suppliers	Self-certification

TABLE 13.7   Top-Rated Joint Improvement Methods and Inputs Required

	Improvement Methods	Inputs Required
1	Co-managed inventory (CMI)	Mostly supplier initiative
2	Due-date performance	Mostly supplier; better information from Partsco needed
3	Milk round	Mostly supplier; Partsco to coordinate
4	Self-certification	Shared work
5	Stabilize schedules	Partsco's initiative
6	EDI (Electronic Date Interchange)	Shared work

Although RS Components and the suppliers clearly had different requirements, there was a very close alignment of suggested improvement methods. Indeed, 7 were common to both top ten lists. However, only 6 of these were feasible in the short–medium-term horizon. Of these some would require joint input and others individual work by RS Components or the suppliers (Table 13.7).

The awareness-raising stage complete, it was then necessary to educate and share knowledge about how to effect these improvements and craft an action plan to meet the targets that had been set. This was done in a series of workshops held at rotating sites in early 1996. Participants drew up detailed plans permitting both RS Components and the key suppliers to implement the necessary improvements.

After only a few months and a continued monitoring of the Balanced Benefit Benchmarking results some rapid improvements began to emerge. The first area to feel change was the on-time delivery performance from suppliers which quickly rose from around 74 per cent to over 90 per cent. In addition, lead time also fell from over 8 week to around 7 and stock turns rose by 25 per cent for the products from the participating companies. It soon became obvious that the pilot was starting to produce the desired results. However, it also became apparent that the obstacles to further rapid development mainly lay more at RS Components rather than at the suppliers. Examples of these included RS Components' inability to order or accept deliveries more than once per month per product item due to IT constraints. In addition, a strengthening of the senior management support was required so that the steering board could be kept better informed and provide greater assistance and presence within the process. It was also increasingly obvious that, if the pilot scheme was to be rolled out to other product category areas, a more formal cost/benefit analysis would be required to ensure that initial decisions taken 'on faith' would actually produce the desired payback to RS Components.

The Roll-Out Programme

The roll-out programme involved starting a second product category Supplier Association in the summer of 1996 in the connector area. The group followed a very similar pattern to the first and indeed came up with an almost identical set of programmes based on the VALSAT analysis. As a result of this, the process development team decided to develop a fully-costed outline programme that could be followed by subsequent groups. Clearly it was important to learn from the first two pilot groups and produce a standardized approach to Supplier Integration, while still allowing new groups scope to fine-tune the approach according to the differing requirement of their individual product category areas.

1. Costing the Benefits

Based on detailed analysis of the first two groups a five-stage framework model was developed (Figure 13.7). The model consisted of discrete target steps towards a fully integrated final vision. It was felt that until at least stage 4 it would not be necessary to make significant changes to the suppliers' manufacturing processes, as there were easier-to-achieve and highly significant cost savings to be made broadly within the logistics area, as will be explained below.

FIGURE 13.7 A Framework Model for Roll-out of RS Component's Supplier Integration Process

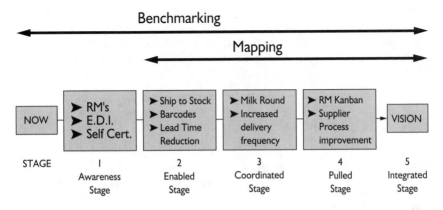

The '*Awareness*' stage involved setting up some basic systems at RS Components and the suppliers, such as the use of returnable modules or tote bins between the buyer and individual suppliers. This would remove the need for costly double-handling of products on delivery, together with the removal of the cost and environmental waste of the existing cardboard packaging. This first stage would also be accompanied by the introduction of EDI links and the development of self-certified product that would avoid the need for quality and quantity inspection at RS Components' goods inwards area. This first stage represented approximately where the first pilot Supplier Association group had reached by early 1997.

The second stage, called the '*Enabled*' stage, involved a further streamlining of the goods receipt and goods inwards process at RS Components, involving the bar coding of the returnable modules so that they would only require to be bar-code swiped on delivery before immediate put away. At the same time further lead time reductions are envisaged as the Supplier Association team move to focus on time compression. These first two stages will see progress continued to be monitored by the Balanced Benefit Benchmarking process.

The third stage of development, called the '*Coordinated*' stage, involved the development of a milk-round collection scheme with the key suppliers hand in hand with a dramatically increased frequency of deliveries. The frequency of deliveries for key suppliers at this stage will move from monthly (or less frequently) to weekly (or more frequently). This Coordinated stage is a prelude to the *'fully Pulled'* stage where supplier demand is linked to RS Components' customer demand by the use of a *kanban* pull system employing the returnable modules as physical *kanbans* in the system. At the same time suppliers will be encouraged to start addressing their manufacturing processes by the application of Value Stream Mapping which will help them pinpoint key areas for radical improvement internally.

The last, *'Integrated vision'*, stage appears at this point a long way off, but involves a further dramatic improvement in lead time, reduction in inventory within an almost stockless environment with demand on suppliers closely linked to customer demand. This vision is for RS Components still several years away. However, a justification for the actualization of this vision has been made by the benefit model shown in Table 13.8.

TABLE 13.8 A Benefits Projection

Stages	1 Aware Stage	2 Enabled Stage	3 Coordinated Stage	4 Pulled Stage	5 Integrated Stage
Service Level	96.5%	97%	97.5%	98%	100%
Lead Time	34 w/days	20 w/days	15 w/days	10.3 w/days	3 w/days
Inventory	77 w/days	46 w/days	34 w/days	20.6 w/days	5 w/days
Quality of Product	2,500 ppm	2,000 ppm	1,500 ppm	1,000 ppm	100 ppm
Delivery	50,000 ppm	20,000 ppm	10,000 ppm	10,000 ppm	1,000 ppm
Inventory Saving	1.41%	3.31%	4.05%	6.13%	7.56%
Service Level Saving	2.11%	4.21%	6.32%	8.42%	16.83%
Expediting Saving	0.01%	0.02%	0.02%	0.02%	0.05%
Customer Returns Savings	0.20%	0.24%	0.25%	0.27%	0.53%
Obsolete Stock Saving	0.10%	0.20%	0.30%	0.46%	0.56%
Total Cost Saving Index	3.83%	7.98%	10.94%	15.30%	25.53%
Equivalent Cost Saving (£M)	8.85	18.43	25.27	35.35	58.97

As can be seen in these illustrations, the Supplier Integration process will yield dramatic benefits to RS Components and their suppliers both in terms of improved customer service for RS Components' customers, better quality products and considerably reduced operating costs.

2. The New Supplier Associations

In order to achieve the vision it has been necessary to increase dramatically the number of product groups and suppliers taking part in the Supplier Association programme. As a result, during January and February 1997 a further six groups were started in separate product group areas. Thus, within a year of the start of the Supplier Association programme over 50 of the top suppliers have become involved out of a total supply base of around 1,500. However, this small number are responsible for around 25–30 per cent of RS Components' total purchases. Once these groups have had time to consolidate, a further wave of Supplier Associations will be started both in the UK and abroad so that around 50 per cent of RS Components' suppliers by value will be directly encompassed in their Supplier Integration process. This further roll-out is planned from 1998/1999.

Discussion and Conclusions

In little more than a year RS Components has developed from a situation where it had only a very limited Supplier Integration process to a strong system with a well-charted future development plan that is self-sustaining without significant outside facilitation support. This situation has been brought about by the application of a Lean Enterprise approach.

Of particular importance in the process has been the use of Value Stream Mapping to raise awareness of the needs for Supplier Integration together with the use of a multi-group Supplier Association. This approach has allowed RS Components to work with suppliers both more quickly and more effectively. It has also allowed development work to be carried out with competing suppliers, allowing in the early stages benchmarking data to be fed back using disguised names for the suppliers involved.

The work has been described by one senior RS Components executive as 'not rocket science but very effective … and who wants rocket science anyway?'. Another product group team leader, although strongly supportive all along, was concerned that they may risk upsetting or alienating the suppliers by asking too much of them. However, one important part of the work has been to remove this perceived fear of upsetting suppliers. The views of the suppliers towards the work have been very positive, and in many cases the initiatives and drive is coming from suppliers rather than RS Components. The programme has greatly improved communications between RS Components and their suppliers and has raised RS Components' presence within suppliers' thinking as well as the importance of Supplier Integration with RS Components' senior staff. As an unexpected side benefit, the performance of suppliers not in the Supplier Association programme also appears to be improving. This may be explained in two ways. First a spread effect is occurring as members of the product teams start informally to implement similar improvements, if at a slower rate with non-member firms. Second, as some firms may have initially been disappointed to have not been included in the activity, they may be putting in extra effort into their relationship with RS Components in order to try and become a member at a later date.

'Not rocket science but very effective ... and who wants rocket science anyway?'

Conclusion

This rather long chapter has sought to demonstrate various aspects of the supplier development research that have been carried out during SCDP. It has shown the importance of supplier development and, in particular, some gaps between the sophistication of supplier development in Japan and the West. It went on to give a picture of the existing supplier development at SCDP firms in 1994 together with some of the reasons why firms were finding it difficult to take this work further.

It transpired that two major problems were preventing further supplier development activity. The first of these was in terms of justifying supplier development when the benefits were often viewed within companies as either too vague or intangible. The second problem was that the firms lacked a framework within which to develop their supplier development activities. The middle section of this chapter developed a Cost of Quality approach to help solve the first problem and a Supplier Development Positioning Matrix to help with the latter.

The final section of the chapter has reported some more recent work carried out with RS Components that demonstrates how various aspects of research covered both in this and earlier chapters can be brought together in order, in this case, to run highly successful supplier development programmes.

CHAPTER 14

Vendor-Managed Inventory (VMI): A Systemic Approach[1]

Introduction

The current passion for supply chain innovation is founded upon time compression management (Stalk and Hout, 1990). The popularity of this movement is highlighted by the widespread application of time-based logistic and purchasing strategies. The automotive industry provided the birthplace of the concept of *Lean Production* (Womack, Jones and Roos, 1990). This has since diffused to other industrial sectors. We have also witnessed the rise of *Continuous Replenishment* (CRP), *Quick Response* (QR) in the textile industry and *Efficient Consumer Response* (ECR) in the retail sector (Christopher, 1992; Kurt Salmon, 1993). The common feature of each of these techniques is their treatment of inventory as a time-based support rather than a buffer against delay and disruption, as conventional practice would dictate. The new movement calls for the elimination, or at least minimization, of inter- and intra-company buffers and the use of inventory to manage the 'pull' of material from upstream to facilitate flow (Womack and Jones, 1996). It is this philosophy which has led to the concepts of the inventory-less warehouse and cross-docking becoming important.

> *The common feature of each of these techniques is their treatment of inventory as a time-based support.*

One such technique is Vendor-Managed Inventory (VMI). This represents a common denominator between various industrial contexts which aspire to time compression in the supply chain. VMI remains a largely illusive technique despite its potential impact on customer service and product availability. Part of its illusive nature stems

[1] Prepared by Richard James, Mark Francis and Nick Rich.

from a lack of definition and consensus on what it is and how it differs from other tactical inventory management techniques. In fact, an early literature review failed to establish a definition of VMI. This was the stimulus for the Vendor-Managed Inventory (VMI) project.

The purpose of the project was to synthesize pragmatic insight rather than to get involved in a semantic debate involving similarities and dissimilarities with other techniques. With this in mind the following project objectives were established:

1. To produce a working definition of VMI.
2. To produce a decision-support model for establishing the environment and enablers of an effective VMI system.

The decision-support model is designed to explain the scope and components of a VMI system, elaborating the above definition. It also provides an indication of the logical sequence of construction for such a system. An extension of the model is used to identify the circumstances favourable to VMI application and, by proxy, those circumstances which are unfavourable.

Methodology

The current body of literature regarding time-based competition and inventory management policies was reviewed broadly to define the area of VMI. Next, case studies were examined in order to understand the mechanics and principles of systems operated by various companies. After a period of review a second survey of companies operating derivatives of VMI in the automotive and food-retailing sectors was carried out and further cases developed from site visits. A model was derived from the findings, and characteristics and scenarios for potential VMI application were established.

During the process of the literature review it was discovered that empirical case material and studies provided adequate descriptions of time-based competitive strategies. However, relatively little empirical work had been undertaken on the tactical management of inventory, so little vigorous material existed on which to base empirical comparisons and to test existing hypotheses. The literature review therefore concentrated on case material, and focal theory was drawn from time-based competitive strategy literature.

Both quantitative and qualitative techniques were used during the site visits. Techniques included the use of structured interviews and semi-structured interviews, combined with secondary data relating to the operational performance of the company prior to and after the introduction of the vendor-managed system.

Some 20 diverse case studies were undertaken in total. Of these 5 were drawn from supplier organizations and 15 from customer organizations. During each case a cross-section of managers were first interviewed in a structured manner in order to understand the operation, advantages, limitations and contextual nature of VMI. The latter part of the interview was semi-structured and used to discuss the broader concept of VMI and the future of the technique within the context of the company's competitive strategy. The case studies included both large and small companies and involved a variety of industries. There was also a variety of enabling technologies used to communicate the necessary information, ranging from low technology (physically counting the inventory), to high technology (third-party computer specialist with dedicated programme and full time system support).

Data Analysis and Findings

The Dimensions of Inter-Organizational Inventory Management Relationships

Figure 14.1 describes the potential dimensions of any inter-organizational inventory management relationship. This model represents a simplification of an holistic relationship. Each dimension is interrelated.

A *sourcing agreement* may be single or multiple sourced and the *type of product* may fall into either category A, B or C. *Physical location* of the inventory may reside at the customer, supplier or third party premises. The *Ownership* of the inventory may reside with either the supplier, the customer or may be conducted on a consignment basis. If ownership

FIGURE 14.1 Dimensions of inter-organizational inventory management relationships

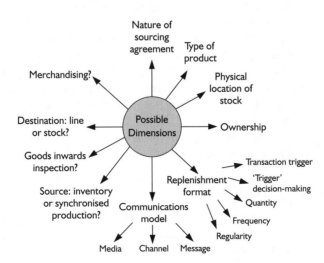

resides with the customer, the point of transference is an additional aspect. Ownership and physical location are primary dimensions. Inventory management responsibility and direct cost are conventionally associated with physical inventory location. Costs are then recovered in the transaction charge for supply. Theoretically, inventory management responsibility should reside with the party offering the lowest (real) cost of ownership.

The *replenishment format* can encompass techniques such as Economic Order Quantity (EOQ), Min-Max, *Kanban* or Fixed Order Quantity. The replenishment method can be further deconstructed. The replenishment *transaction trigger* can be generically a push (for example, from a customer-MRP-generated materials forecast) or a pull (for example, a *kanban* signal). The *trigger decision-making* could be automatic (for example, the MRP materials forecast or *kanban* signal) or manual (for example, a customer inventory controller or vendor merchandiser visually identifying a reorder point). *Replenishment quantity and frequency* are also inversely related. *Quantity* could be based on EOQ, fixed batch size, *kanban* replacement (use one, replace one) or a more reactive technique. *Frequency* could vary from minutes/hours for 'through the wall' operations to months/years for certain category 'A' items. For high frequency deliveries *regularity* becomes an additional factor.

The *communications model* can represent the broad continuum of formats encompassing manual (tally chart) to mechanized (Psion organizer) to automated (EDI system) configurations. The *communications model* components can be deconstructed to derive *media* (paper, electronic), *channel* (personal, phone, fax, EDI link, Internet) and *message type* (structured or unstructured) – where an example of a structured message type is an EDI transaction and an unstructured one an e-mail.

The supplier *source* can be finished goods inventory or synchronized production. The latter has obvious benefits from a supply chain cost inimization perspective. Another differentiator is the requirement or not for *Goods-In inspection*. This is an indication of the perceived quality and criticality of the inventory item from the perspective of the customer. The *destination* can likewise differ, ranging from direct to line (for JIT deliveries) to inventory (either directly or via some quarantine or intermediate). Finally there is the question of whether or not *merchandising* is to be performed.

Figure 14.1 represents a generic model. However such a model can be used as the basis for the development of a specific definition of VMI.

VMI: A Working Definition

Vendor-managed inventory can be generically characterized as a collaborative strategy between a customer and supplier to optimize the availability of products through a continuous replenishment approach to the management of inventory in the supply chain. The VMI technique is therefore a transference of management responsibility to the organization which can best manage the inventory in line with the commercial standards of service demanded by the customer. It does not absolve the customer from his responsibility, as it is he who is responsible for setting the framework within which the system operates and for continually monitoring and adjusting the characteristics of this framework. Ideally the two 'partners' in the system should be engaged in a process of continuous improvement, a form of cross-functional working cutting across the normal boundaries within which each firm normally operates.

> *The VMI technique is the transference of management responsibility to the organization which can best manage the inventory.*

The following working definition was therefore established for the purpose of the project. Key words are italicized for emphasis:

> VMI – a *collaborative* strategy between a customer and supplier to optimise the *availability* of products at *minimal cost* to the two companies. The supplier takes responsibility for the operational *management* of the inventory within a mutually agreed *framework* of performance targets which are constantly monitored and updated to create an environment of continuous improvement. (James, Rich and Francis, 1997)

The definition highlights the wide potential configuration of VMI relationships with the key determinant characteristic of supplier (vendor) responsibility for managing the inventory level and replenishment cycle. It is this characteristic which differentiates VMI from other techniques. From the dimensions discussed in the previous section, this differentiator can be interpreted as supplier-determined *replenishment format* – with the supplier acting as the replenishment trigger decision-maker, and determinant of replenishment quantity, frequency and regularity.

Inception – Capability Gaps and the Opportunity to Add Value

Research indicates that there are two modes of inception of a VMI type relationship which represent polar positions on a management style continuum. The first is *domination* and is based upon the leverage by the customer of his high power position with respect to the supplier. The driver is the customer and the style of negotiation is autocratic. At an extreme this may cynically be an attempt to reduce inventory management costs by pushing inventory upstream and off-loading the inventory management burden onto the supplier. This is not true VMI! It is this practice which has besmirched the reputation of VMI in the eyes of many suppliers.

A more moderate position on the *domination* continuum involves an attempt to negotiate a formal agreement. The terms are characteristically dictated and the resultant framework agreement is likely to be 'tight'.

The second mode of inception is *collaborative*. The basis for this relationship is trust. The driver is typically an innovative supplier who is looking to leverage his resource and expertise in a well-defined area to add value to the customer's business with an augmented product offering, and hence secure a long-term working relationship. The style of negotiation is typically democratic, based upon partnership and mutual benefit. It is this mode of inception which forms the basis the discussion outlined in the following sections.

The VMI Decision-Support Model – Overview

Figure 14.2 represents a decision-support tool for establishing the environment and enablers of an effective VMI system. The model is designed as a systems diagram (Checkland, 1981). There are six nested subsystem levels. The objective is for the proposal to qualify against the criteria established for each level and 'descend' to achieve the objectives and benefits sought at Level 1. The *six* levels are:

6. Capability and Product Category Characteristics;
5. Importance;
4. Ownership and Trust;
3. Framework Agreement;
2. Primary Enablers;
1. Objectives and Benefits.

The boundary of Level 6 represents the scope of the decision-support environment. Each descending level represents the boundary of a subsystem requiring increasingly refined qualification of the proposal in

FIGURE 14.2 The VMI decision-support tool model

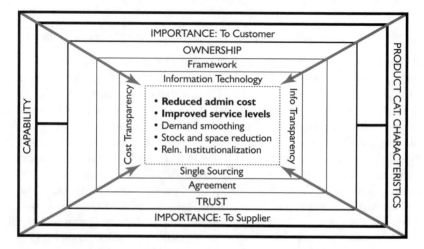

order to descend to the next level. For example, if the characteristics of the proposed product are congruent with those outlined in the *Capability and Product Category* sub-system (Level 6), then proceed 'inwards' to Level 5.

Levels 6–5 represent the *qualifying criteria*. Unless the proposal satisfies these criteria, it is highly improbable that it will deliver long-term benefits to both parties, and may result in respective disadvantages and prohibitive cost. Levels 4–2 represent the *winning criteria*. The more effective the components of these sub-systems the larger the potential business benefits which may accrue to both parties.

The arrowheads on the model converge on the inner sub-system at Level 1. This represents the desired benefits in the form of the primary reasons why organizations engage in a VMI relationship:

1. Reduced administrative costs (with maintained or improved inventory availability).

2. Improved service level.

Level 1 also indicates three secondary benefits which accrue as by-products of a well-engineered VMI system. The following sub-sections elaborate each of the descending sub-system levels of the decision support model.

LEVEL 6: Capability and Product Category Characteristics

The basic truism of any proposed business relationship holds that the proposal must offer perceived benefit to both parties. Once the perceived benefit is eroded, the relationship in its current form is likely to be ended or subject to renegotiation. The potential benefits of VMI to both parties are discussed below. At this point it is possible to state that these potential benefits originate from a *capability gap* with regard to a specific product/category. Phrased another way, it is the supplier's leveraging of a *core competency* (Hamel and Prahalad, 1995) to deliver a superior category of performance than is currently possible with the current configuration or vertically-integrated solution practised by the customer.

The basic truism of any proposed business relationship holds that the proposal must offer perceived benefit to both parties.

The opportunity for a VMI relationship occurs typically when the supplier realizes the possibility of offering the customer a value-added service based upon a 'gap' in respective capabilities for a specific product type or category. This is usually founded upon relative specialization (for example, an industrial fastener supplier) or an underdeveloped capability on the part of the customer resulting from a *product development* or *diversification* strategy (Ansoff, 1957). An example of the latter would include a supermarket multiple stocking best-seller books for the first time.

Figure 14.3 indicates that the capability gap can be present in the physical and/or information dimension, and can be founded upon capital and/or labour. For example, the fastener supplier leverages specialist material handling and storage equipment operated by staff who handle fasteners on a daily basis. The best-seller example is founded upon an information management capability. The (best seller) book market demonstrates unpredictable demand and often very short product life-cycles. The supplier's sales forecasting system has heightened sophistication compared with the multiple. This is based upon years of experience in the market with very large amounts of disaggregated sales data from multiple outlets. The supplier's sales forecasting system promises higher service levels and lower levels of waste – thus creating the VMI opportunity.

The capability gap provides the broader environment for the decision-support model, manifesting itself in a telltale 'footprint' of product category characteristics which lend themselves to a VMI relationship.

A high correlation was found between the presence of the product category characteristics listed in Table 14.1 and the potential for derived benefit from the resulting VMI relationship. These characteristics act as hygiene factors (Herzberg, 1966). Their presence does not guarantee the level of benefit, but their absence makes it highly unlikely that there is an opportunity for the supplier to add value. The proposal therefore fails to qualify. Table 14.1 accordingly acts as a screening checklist.

Unusual physical properties can be defined in terms of fragility, size, weight or dimensional criteria. Unusual characteristics necessitate unusual storage and handling and unusual skills. For example, a super-market multiple is predominantly geared to the management of square

FIGURE 14.3 Capability gaps within the physical and information dimensions

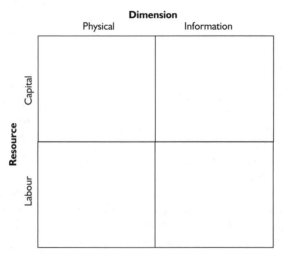

TABLE 14.1   The Seven-Point Product Category Qualifying Footprint

1.   Unusual physical properties.

2.   Low volume.

3.   Low (individual) cost/value.

4.   Low importance to the customer.

5.   Wide range and visual similarity.

6.   (Structural) unpredictability of demand.

7.   'Different' to the norm.

boxes of groceries. Books and carded products such as hosiery, batteries and films represent unusual physical dimensions and resulting problems. These unusual properties result in a disproportionately high handling and storage cost.

Low volume is another qualifying criteria. This encompasses retail products that are sold or replenished in 'singles', may demonstrate independent demand and are considered slow sellers (low inventory turns). In the manufacturing sector they are those products that can be serviced on a less than daily basis, such as Maintenance Repair and Operating (MRO) items.

When the third criteria (*low individual cost/value*) is taken in conjunction with *low volume* it yields a codification which is clearly tactical rather than strategic. The *Supply Positioning Model* (Kraljic, 1983) illustrated in Figure 14.4 provides a mechanism for managing the spectrum of product types. Within this model our product category would be categorized as *Tactical Acquisition.* The model suggests that the customer inventory manager would focus on efficiency (service level) and aim to minimize the resources used to manage the acquisition of such a product (minimum transaction cost). The inventory manager would therefore consider this category of *low importance.* Paradoxically, this is likely to

FIGURE 14.4   Supply Positioning Model

SOURCE: Adapted from Kraljic (1983).

result in low investment in capital equipment and labour for the storage and handling of this category, reinforcing qualifying criteria number 1 from Table 14.1.

Wide range and visual similarity cause their own problems from an inventory management perspective. For example, the range and similarity of carded hosiery result in a high incidence of picking and shelf-filling discrepancies by shop staff in a retail environment with some stock-keeping units (SKUs) straddling multiple shelf pegs, including those allocated to different SKUs. The effect is to generate a 'stock-out' with a negative impact on retail service level, even though the product may be available in store. Fasteners cause a similar problem in the manufacturing environment.

The final qualifying criterion is *(structural) unpredictability of demand*. The Systems Dynamics school, and particularly J.W. Forrester (1958) proved that the presence of independent inventorying locations in the supply chain lent itself to the amplification of perceived demand. This differs from the structural demand fluctuation witnessed by some products (such as best-selling books and fashion clothing) which are structurally unpredictable. The challenges of the latter are often best left to the experience and sophistication of the supplier to manage.

The product category characteristics represent only the outer level of qualification for a successful VMI relationship. However, contemporary VMI qualification has never seemed to progress beyond this level. For example, MRO items and fasteners have a long tradition of VMI application in the manufacturing sector. They are usually consumed in low volumes and exhibit almost negligible individual item cost, often being considered a commodity item. Demand is typically independent and the range is usually wide and similar in appearance – each size of bolt or screw looks visually similar. Fasteners in particular are notoriously difficult to control, suffering from split packs, spillage and high wastage as a result of return constraints for partially used packs. These characteristics place them low down the inventory manager's control list and help explain their VMI lineage.

Similarly, in the retail environment there is a long tradition of VMI applications for books, hosiery, films, baby products and herbs and spices. These share common characteristics. They are all slow sellers in relation to grocery products. In some cases they may be sold and replenished in singles. Storage and display is based upon low density 'card and peg' (or gravity rack for herbs and spices) with small frontage. Low sales volume and low value (per square foot of shelving) again correlate to low priority.

The product category characteristics of these two applications clearly *differ from the norm* and provide an opportunity for a niche specialist to add value and progress the relationship. However, this is by no means the only aspect of qualification, and these are by no means the only areas of VMI applicability.

LEVEL 5: Importance

If the product characteristics and supplier core competence lend themselves to progression, the next issue is one of relative *importance*. The above section indicates that from the perspective of the customer there is an *inverse* relationship between perceived importance (based upon volume and value) and the likelihood of a capability gap. However, in order to qualify for progression the proposal has to represent a high relative importance from the perspective of the supplier – implying that the volume of resulting business will represent a significant absolute percentage of the supplier's revenue stream and/or percentage of the demand for that category. It is these criteria which can then be flexed within the framework agreement to derive the supplier's benefits.

LEVEL 4: Ownership and Trust

Ownership of inventory affects the behaviour and expectations of both parties in a supply relationship. Ownership should ideally reside with the party who can offer the lowest (true) cost of ownership. However, deficiencies in intra-organizational costing systems (Kaplan, 1984 and 1988) and practical barriers to the achievement of true *cost transparency* (Lamming, Jones and Nicol, 1995) often prevent the true ownership cost from being ascertained.

The majority of cases saw ownership residing with the customer. In general, the customer controlled the total value of inventory, either by including a stock turn measure in the framework agreement or by monitoring the inventory levels. Pressure could be applied to the supplier to reduce inventory either by reference to the monitored figures or by an agreed programme of continuous improvement. Ownership by the customer consequently seemed to encourage him to maintain a role as an active participant in the overall management of the VMI inventory.

> **Ownership of inventory affects the behaviour and expectations of both parties in a supply relationship.**

Clearly the ownership issue will manifest itself in the *framework agreement* (Level 3), and these issues are unlikely to occur satisfactorily without a basis of trust and understanding between the two parties, not least because of the necessity for the customer to disclose more detailed and sensitive information to the supplier – for example, 'raw' Electronic Point of Sales (EPOS) data in the retail environment.

The *IMP Interactive Model for Buyer–Seller Relationships* (Hakansson, 1982) in Figure 14.5 describes the environment and interaction process between a customer and supplier. It explains the evolution of relationships as occurring via a series of exchanges of product, services, information, social activities and finance. These exchanges initially involve short-term 'exchange episodes' which evolve over the longer-term

FIGURE 14.5 The IMP Interactive Model for Buyer–Seller Relationships

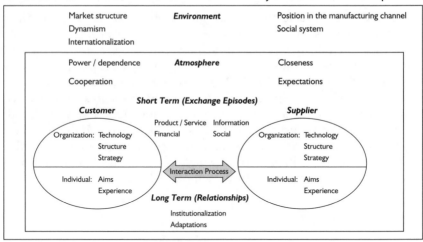

SOURCE: Adapted from Hakansson (1982).

into institutionalized or 'routinized episodes' (Ford, 1978) which then become a 'matter of expectation, with behaviour patterns which are taken for granted' (Lamming, 1993, p. 142). Such a model is useful for explaining the evolution of relationships and by proxy, the climate of trust required to nurture a VMI relationship.

Interestingly, the model can be adapted so that the exchange episodes are no longer perceived as interactions between participants (individuals and organizations); rather interactions between two respective sets of physical and information capabilities.

Sako (1992) classifies trust into three types (adapted from Hines, 1994):

- *Contractual Trust*: the mutual expectation that promises of a written or verbal nature will be kept.
- *Competence Trust*: the confidence that a trading partner is competent to carry out a specific task.
- *Goodwill Trust*: commitments from both parties that they will do more than is formally required.

Like the ownership issue, the prevailing 'type' of trust will be reflected in the framework agreement.

LEVEL 3: Framework Agreement

The framework agreement is the embodiment of the previous sub-systems, reflecting both ownership and apportionment of benefits, risk and cost. The agreement typically acts as a legal contract. Table 14.2 reflects framework content encountered in the case material. The scope and depth of the framework content define its level of prescription.

TABLE 14.2   Framework Agreement Content

1. Operational Constraints:
   - Max allocated storage space
   - Demand profiles
   - Delivery profiles:
     - Notification period
     - Min batch size
     - Delivery windows

2. Performance Measures:
   - Service level (incl. forecast demand and variation)
   - Customer ownership:
     - Inventory levels
     - Inventory turns

3. Responsibility:
   - Insurance
   - Obsolescence
   - Damage and deterioration

4. Termination Criteria

Clearly the type of trust has a major bearing on the nature of the agreement. The closer that the relationship is founded to a form of *contractual trust* (Sako, 1992), the more likely it is to be 'tight' or prescriptive in nature. A prescriptive agreement reduces supplier flexibility, and it is this flexibility which is a cornerstone for the creation of supplier benefit in a VMI relationship. There is therefore a relationship between the level of prescription of contract and equity of benefit and it is not surprising to find that contractual trust is the dominant type in a VMI relationship based on a *domination* mode of inception.

Conversely, the closer to a form of *goodwill trust*, the more obligational (Williamson, 1986) and thus the 'looser' the contract. From the previous argument it should be apparent that this offers flexibility opportunities to the supplier, and hence the potential to increase the equity of his benefit.

LEVEL 2: Primary Enablers

The primary enablers are those mechanisms which, when present, magnify the mutual benefit derived from the relationship.

Reference to the IMP model in Figure 14.5 illustrates that trading organizations conduct exchange episodes involving information. Such exchanges traditionally involve historic, summary data of a nature deemed non-sensitive by the customer. This conventional approach results in well-documented phenomena such as the demand amplification effects discussed by Forrester (1958) and Burbidge (1961).

Information transparency means unfettered access to relevant operational data (such as demand profiles, inventory levels and production forecasts) across the whole supply chain so that each party's production and supply operation is not sub-optimalized as a result of ineffective communication. Practically, this implies supplier access to more 'pure' (raw) demand data provided with greater frequency than would be made available in the conventional supply configuration. Potentially this could involve real-time data, *pulled* by the supplier rather than *pushed* by the customer. This has wide implications for computer security and corporate culture, regardless of the type and level of trust. Such configurations have demonstrated significant benefits in the case studies examined – resulting in reduced demand amplification and improved service level.

Cost transparency is analogous to information transparency, and has previously been mentioned. Its role as an enabler stems from the virtuous impact it has on trust, reinforcing the obligational aspect and hence facilitating flexibility (Lamming, Jones and Nicol, 1995)

Single sourcing is another important enabler. Clearly from the discussion raised so far, it is possible to deduce that an effective VMI relationship is possible without the supplier becoming the single source for that product or category. However, the single-source status generates economies of scale which reinforce the importance of the contract to the supplier and provide more flexibility for the provision of value-added services to the customer. For example, in the industrial fasteners case single sourcing was the springboard for the provision of a 'Total Fastener Management System' that evolved into the supplier representation on the customer's design team for engineering advice on the rationalization, applicability and appropriateness of fasteners in the customer's final product offering.

The application of *Information Technology* (IT) to a given scenario normally provides efficiency, rather than effectiveness, gains. In the VMI scenario this typically involves a computer-to-computer link to diagnose the customer's inventory level and consumption patterns from a distance. Traditionally this has involved establishing a (costly) Electronic Data Interchange (EDI) link. Increasingly, the Internet is being used as a low-cost vehicle for achieving this. The Internet method benefits from offering flexibility, based as it is either on structured or unstructured message types.

> *The efficiency gain offered by IT can then create a large enough capability gap to establish an exploitable opportunity.*

The research indicates that the necessity for the supplier to apply IT in order to establish a commercial opportunity arises in more 'mature' customer relationships. Here, the customer's capability may already be relatively 'high' with regard to the specific product category under consideration. The efficiency gain offered by IT can then create a large enough capability gap to establish an exploitable opportunity.

Potential Benefits of VMI

Introduction

A well-planned and well-implemented VMI system offers a number of advantages to customer and supplier alike. Taken in conjunction, these also derive holistic supply chain benefits, resulting in reduced supply chain costs and increased responsiveness. The major benefits all relate to the efficiency of operations between the two parties. Table 14.3 summarizes the benefits to each party:

Supplier Benefits

The move to allow suppliers to manage inventories which were previously the responsibility of the customer creates a system which eliminates one link or decision point in the supply chain and provides greater transparency of information to the supplier. Forrester (1958) argued that each ordering point or independent stocking position can amplify demand fluctuations, thus causing inefficiencies in the supply chain. The larger the number of decision points and the greater the level of myopia at each decision point, the larger the demand amplification witnessed. Thus decision-point elimination and information transparency tend to *smooth demand*, enabling the supplier to anticipate future demand and manage such inventory more efficiently.

   With suppliers in the manufacturing sector the transparency of information frequently provides an opportunity to combine inventory levels

TABLE 14.3   Supplier and Customer Benefits of a Well-engineered VMI System

Supplier Benefits	Customer Benefits
Demand smoothing	Reduced administrative costs
Increased operational flexibility	Improved service levels
Higher customer switching costs	Reduced inventory
Information impactedness	Reduced risk
	Improved cashflow
	Off balance sheet and dedicated assets
	Draw on specialist expertise in design

with operational postponement policies so that the product supplied can be managed against shorter lead times. The use of VMI therefore allows the supplier to be more *flexible*. The conventional order received by a supplier details quantity and due date. Where the supplier is aware of the 'real' (non-aggregated and filtered) demand, he can often adjust the timing and actual quantity of the order to suit his own situation, reconfiguring load sizes and delivery timings within the framework agreed. It allows him to make better use of the inventory available both to him and to the customer, reducing buffer stock and space and freeing up working capital (Coyle, Bardi and Langley, 1992).

Improved demand accuracy and increased flexibility represent operational benefits, but VMI also offers the supplier potential *strategic* benefits. The consummation of the VMI relationship by necessity involves a tighter bonding of the customer and supplier. The supplier's system is more closely integrated with the customer's at numerous levels, including the integration of procedures, training and capital investment. Where primary enablers such as single sourcing and IT applications such as EDI are involved, the level of integration and investment can be high. There are high *switching cost* associated with a customer move to an alternative supplier. This represents a heightening of the barriers to entry for a prospective competitor (Porter, 1980).

An additional potential benefit arises in the form of *information impactedness* (Williamson, 1975). Williamson argues that a supplier firm which is actively transacting with a customer will be party to a wide range of potentially useful information via the exchange episodes which make up its operational and social contact with the customer firm. When it becomes time to renegotiate the contract, it is consequently in a stronger negotiating position, whether that is in order to re-tender the business or to strengthen its position with the customer.

Customer Benefits

All cases indicated a significant *reduction in administrative cost* as a result of the elimination of a large number of formal transactions. Taking the industrial fastener case as an example, a single monthly itemized invoice was provided by the supplier for the aggregated category consumption over the period. This eliminated the conventional purchase-ordering cycle and associated purchasing activity. Where information technology enablers were in place, further administrative savings were made.

Only in one of the initial case studies was inventory reduction named as a significant reason for adopting VMI, and even here it was not identified as the primary reason. However, in most cases the introduction of VMI was accompanied by a period of very limited inventory re-ordering which drained the system of inventory but was accompanied by an improvement in *service levels* and availability. At the end of this period the service levels experienced by the customers were significantly higher than before VMI, and with usually a far *lower inventory* and significant reduction in storage space. With reduced inventory came reduced risk of obsolescence, damage and deterioration as well as improved cashflow.

As the main objective of the customer was to reduce administration costs while improving service levels, reduction in inventory and storage space was an unexpected bonus. It should be noted that the magnitude of cost and space savings were relatively small due to the nature of the product categories encompassed within the relationship (predominantly category 'C' items).

A less tangible financial benefit of the relationship involved *off-balance-sheet and dedicated assets*. Off-balance-sheet assets are those assets which the organization has the right to use or rent, which are not owned and therefore not listed on the balance sheet. These assets may or may not be dedicated by the supplier for the sole application to the customer's account. Ownership implies cost (of purchase, operation and maintenance). An example would include dedicated inventory owned by the supplier and held on consignment to ensure service level achievement within the demand profiles established within the framework agreement. The specialist nature of the VMI supplier's proposal often necessitates the application of specialist storage and materials management equipment as well as specialist staff. The acquisition of such equipment and staff by the customer would require capital investment and would impact on the organization's gearing ratio.

> *Reduction in inventory and storage space was an unexpected bonus.*

The final area of customer derived benefit originates from his ability to draw upon the supplier's *specialist expertise* in the design process, involving supplier staff on a cross-functional development team (Kurogane, 1993).

Potential Disadvantages of VMI

While a well-thought-out and constructed VMI system can derive significant supply chain benefits, an ill-conceived system can damage supply chain competitiveness and this should be recognized. Table 14.4 summarizes these disadvantages. They stem predominantly from the *domination* mode of inception.

In a relationship conceived from a customer power position where the inventory management burden is intentionally off-loaded to the supplier (domination mode), the supplier is likely to incur both increased administration and inventory costs with a negative impact on liquidity and cashflow. In an extreme case, where the customer represents a significantly large percentage of the supplier's business, this may entail the additional burden of 'acquiring' the necessary physical/information capability in

TABLE 14.4 Supplier and Customer Disadvantages of a Badly-engineered VMI System

Supplier Disadvantages	Customer Disadvantages
Increased inventory.	Increased dependence on supplier (risk).
Increased inventory management burden.	Disclosure of potentially sensitive commercial information.
Reduced cashflow and bloated assets.	
Increased administration.	
Cost of 'capability acquisition and development'.	

order to placate the customer and meet their demands – for example, the installation and equipping of additional warehouse space or the implementation and operation of an EDI link.

While the supplier can suffer the calculated decision to off-load the stock management burden in the above scenario, it can also work in the opposite direction with the customer becoming the repository of superfluous or obsolete inventory. Additional disadvantages are associated with risk. For example, the customer embraces a heightened level of risk due to increased dependency if the relationship entails single sourcing with the VMI partner. Risk is also apparent in the requirement to disclose an increased volume of raw demand data, often 'pulled' by the supplier. Such information can be commercially sensitive, especially if the supplier also supplies a key competitor. The customer must satisfy themselves that effective 'Chinese walls' are in place during such an arrangement.

Such information can be commercially sensitive, especially if the supplier also supplies a key competitor.

Potential customer disadvantages therefore originate from those associated with the primary enablers and inappropriate levels of obligational trust (Williamson, 1986) in the relationship. The need to qualify the proposal via a decision-support mechanism such as the model proposed earlier therefore becomes acute.

Termination of a VMI Relationship

The VMI arrangement is likely to endure while both parties obtain a perceived benefit. It is a truism that the relationship will be ended by a party when that party perceives that it no longer receives the level of (cost) benefit necessary to fuel the arrangement. Mutual benefit is based upon an identified capability gap for a given product category. This gap fluctuates over time. Figure 14.6 illustrates the capability gap in the outer subsystem or 'environment' of the decision-support model in Figure 14.2.

FIGURE 14.6   The capability gap in the outer sub-system

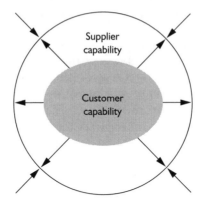

Product Category Characteristics (Environment)

The supplier constantly attempts to improve his offering by maintaining or extending the capability gap and by differentiating his offering through the provision of added value services to the customer. Further supplier improvement opportunities are based largely upon the benefits derived from the relationship, namely information transparency and increased operational flexibility. However, the supplier is already a specialist in this product category area. There are therefore only a finite number of improvements which can be made. After effectiveness improvements to the underlying process are exhausted, the only route open for gap extension and efficiency gains is via the application of increased automation and information technology.

While the customer's internal capability with regard to the product category can actually decrease as a result of the VMI relationship, there is far greater probability of accrued organic capability growth over time. This capability growth can be planned, or result as a by-product of a general capability improvement.

Planned capability growth is stimulated by an increased importance in the product category in the eyes of the customer, so eroding the attraction of the relationship. Using the example of carded products in the retail sector, the stimulus could be the increased sales volume of the product range. Turning to the MRO example from the manufacturing sector, the stimulus could be a focus on MRO items as a result of *kaizen* activity (all the 'easy' improvements having previously been made). A more likely reason for customer gap erosion is unplanned growth as a by-product of generic improvement activity. For example, an amendment could be made to the inventory control software which enables the storage and management of 'singles'.

The erosion situation may never arise and the relationship may be institutionalized subject to periodic review. However, if the situation does arise, there must come a point of decision. Coase in *The Nature of the Firm* (1937) proposes a 'Theory of the Firm' based upon transaction cost. During his discussion he forwards two competing strategies for minimizing the transaction costs incurred by the firm: the *hierarchical* solution (make) and *market* solution (buy). It is possible to adapt Coase's theory so that the termination decision point occurs when the perceived cost of organizing one extra transaction (for this product category) using the hierarchical approach (customer capability) equates to the cost of organising the VMI relationship (market approach).

Conclusion

The research indicates that, as a result of the low relative importance of the product categories which have traditionally been the subject of VMI relationships, the role of VMI in the management of modern supply chains has largely been overlooked. While a number of companies have actual experience of working with such systems, they have failed to understand the underlying concepts and hence failed to grasp the potential of applying these concepts in their inventory management of category 'A' and 'B' products which also fulfil the criteria outlined in the decision-support model. VMI therefore offers great latent potential.

VMI is well established in certain sectors of 'C' class category items. Here, the advocates tend to be suppliers rather than customers. The main benefits to the customer of a successfully implemented system are improved service levels with reduced administration. Inventory reduction is not a primary objective, due to the 'C' class status of the product categories in question. However, inventory reduction is usually a by-product of a well-engineered VMI system.

The benefits to the supplier are based upon flatter and more accurate demand data. These benefits can be significant. They do however require a supplier who is capable of capitalizing on these aspects.

Interestingly, the act of organizing and operating a VMI system can improve the relationship between the two parties. More than one case noted an improvement in the quality of relationship on termination, even though the VMI system was deemed to have failed as measured by the key performance indicators used to drive the system.

Two modes of inception were identified. The *collaborative* mode was seen as offering the greatest potential for a successfully implementing a VMI system. However, even if inception is based upon *domination*, there is still potential for derived value stream benefit if the dominated supplier is highly 'capable'. In such a situation the level of benefit will, by definition, be sub-optimal owing to the implied constraints (for example, access to raw demand data), with the customer deriving a disproportionate benefit from the relationship.

Where the capability gap is relatively wide, the use of IT offers the opportunity to obtain efficiency gains, but is usually non-essential for the creation of mutual benefit. When dealing with a 'mature' customer, or when natural gap erosion has occurred, the IT takes on added importance. In such a scenario, the application of IT often represents the only opportunity for the supplier to add value.

VMI also offers benefits to the purchasing and materials management infrastructure. The 'unusual' product categories typically subject to VMI agreements take a disproportionate effort (and cost) to control. Outsourcing this provision to a specialist will reduce fire-fighting and expediting time, enabling purchasing and materials management professionals to focus on the 'vital few' (Juran, 1979) value-adding activity such as sourcing new materials and suppliers, negotiation and supplier development.

In summary, Vendor Managed Inventory offers supply chain benefits when used in context. This research has provided a decision-support mechanism for establishing this context. An opportunity exists for substitute inventory with information in traditionally problematic product categories.

Environmentally Sound Supply Chain Management: Environmental Strategies in Supply and Sourcing[1]

Pressures are mounting on businesses, from consumers, regulators and the stock market, to take more responsibility for their environmental performance. These pressures appear to fit a cyclical trend, which is closely correlated with economic prosperity (Downs, 1973). Accordingly, as the effects of pollution become more visible and affect more people over time, it is likely that the peak of concern at the last cycle will form the base level of concern for the next cycle.

In North America, 75 per cent of consumers say that their purchasing decisions are affected by a company's environmental reputation, while 80 per cent would pay more for environmentally 'friendlier' goods (Drumwright, 1994). In the UK, the results of a recent Department of the Environment survey on public attitudes show that concern about the environment survived the years of recession and grew in line with the economic recovery; it is now third on a list of the most important issues that the public believes government should be addressing, second only to unemployment and health, and above crime, education and the economy in general. The survey also showed a dramatic shift in public opinion to favour the 'polluter pays' principle, even if this means paying higher prices for goods and services (62 per cent). Of respondents, 87 per cent wanted more information

> *The environment is now third on a list of the most important issues that the public believes government should be addressing.*

[1] Prepared by Richard Lamming and Jon Hampson.

from companies on the environmental impact of their products, and 88 per cent wanted better labelling to enable them to make more informed buying decisions (ENDS 232 1994). Other studies have produced results that show that, while consumers may state these preferences in surveys, in practice their buying activities do not reflect this. However, it appears likely that, faced with a choice between two otherwise identical products, they would buy the more environmentally sound of the two.

Furthermore, while consumers may not explicitly state that they want 'environmentally sound' goods, they *expect* them; that is, although they do not ask for them, they expect that their goods have been produced in the least damaging way possible. If they find out, or suspect, that this is not the case, then they are 'disappointed'. Disappointment is a far cry from the aims of 'customer satisfaction', and even further from that of 'customer delight or excitement', which are the criteria required to make consumers come back and buy again, and also to tell their friends. In terms of market image, therefore, environmental issues are quite evidently a business issue. We will argue that this is the case in other respects, also.

Environmental problems are intrinsically linked to supply chains: their manifestation may be at one point in the chain – typically, but not exclusively, the end consumer – but their cause may be two or three links earlier in the chain. Thus, the supply manager's perspective must include provision for potential problems – and opportunities – up and down the chain, and policies and strategies must be formulated accordingly.

In order to formulate sourcing and supply strategies to equip companies with competitive positions, it is necessary to understand the concepts that underlie environmentally sound behaviour and to synthesize them into comprehensive, practicable frameworks.

This section focuses on these issues, examining some techniques and approaches that may be employed in addressing them.

Purchasing and Supply

Purchasing and supply activities are concerned with the regulation of the flow of materials and information between customers and suppliers, and with balancing the requirements of organizations' output strategies with the necessary input requirements. Employing the view that purchasing, even in its strategic mode, is essentially a service function which relates supply market factors and business environment issues to the needs, wishes and perceptions of its customers, it can be understood that the quality of the output of one stage in a process is dependent upon the quality of the input of not only that stage but also the previous one. It is clear that one potentially effective way of managing a company's environmental policy is by linking it closely with the activities of the Purchasing function, since Purchasing managers will often determine the nature of the materials and services which are bought into an operation. It would appear, then, that diffusing environmental management techniques backwards or forwards through the supply chain might be a very effective way of developing the general environmental performance of an industry.

Issues and Concepts

What does 'Environmentally Sound' mean?

The environmental pressures that affect business are derived from a number of disparate sources, both internal and external to the firm. The external ones include industry requirements (including customers and suppliers), financial institutions, regulatory authorities, and public bodies, including local, national, regional and even global parties. These pressures constitute the external environmental context in which the business operates, and which overall strategy should be designed to address. However, internal pressures are of increasing importance, whether from marketing people who want to 'green' the organization's image, health and safety inspectors, board members who are concerned with the issues, or employees who are either beginning to feel the effects of pollution personally or who do not wish to be associated with recognized polluters; employee motivation is a key factor in business productivity.

In viewing opportunities and threats in this context, therefore, it is clear that organizations have to be accountable to several groups of people, in order to be truly effective. Each of these groups will have its own agenda and definition of what is meant by 'environmentally sound', or 'green'. As the scientific evidence does not yet exist to determine the real environmental impact of business activities, companies which accept that environmental management, and therefore environmentally sound purchasing, is a desirable objective, need to appreciate what each of these 'stakeholders' understands by these terms. Developing environmentally sound supply chain strategies to address the related market needs, therefore, requires a clear understanding of each of the stakeholder's perspectives and priorities, coupled with a way of fitting them into some framework which may be used to guide the firm's activities. This unique framework becomes the firm's environmental supply strategy and should be able to predict the outcome of any chosen path, with regard to environmental consequences and their likely impacts upon the business itself.

Companies may be expected to have the capacity to withstand these pressures to a degree but there are limits to this resilience (Cramer, 1996). As the various definitions and understandings will differ between groups, and over time, we should understand 'green' as 'a continuous process with respect to improving environmental performance. It would be erroneous to suggest that green is a fixed state that users of the environment can eventually reach ... Companies do not become green; they become greener.' (Miller and Szekely, 1995)

Environmental soundness, therefore, refers to the degree to which the activity undertaken (or the strategy that surrounds and introduces that activity) complies with the composite framework of requirements a firm identifies on the part of its stakeholders.

The Environment and Quality

Pollution can be broadly defined as matter that is out of place. The first law of thermodynamics says that matter can neither be created nor destroyed – it is simply converted from one medium into another, so that the actual weight of the world remains the same. For example, burning wood does not destroy it, it simply turns it into billions of smaller particles, i.e. smoke. Similarly, using gas scrubbers to reduce sulphur dioxide emissions from a smoke stack does not eliminate the problem, it just converts pollution in one medium into an environmental problem in another, i.e. from gas to liquid. When the liquid is precipitated, it becomes a problem of solid waste. This is described in Figure 15.1. This thinking is, of course, identical with the basis of supply chain thinking – every item must have a source and destination.

Pollution can be broadly defined as matter that is out of place.

The second law of thermodynamics says that matter is becoming increasingly diluted and dispersed. The problem here can be described using the example of a bag of cash: it is probably far more useful in this state, perhaps as a down payment on a house, or as an investment in a new piece of machinery. It is far less useful in individual £5 notes, for example. In environmental terms, parallels can be drawn with the value of natural resources in concentrations, particularly in the extraction industries.

In economic terms, it is clear that pollution often represents a form of economic waste. Peter Jones, of Biffa, refers to the 10:1 ratio in the British economy of raw material inputs which are used to produce the nation's consumable outputs. (Jones, 1996) Put simply, pollution is indicative of some business inefficiency, showing that resources have been used incompletely, inefficiently or ineffectively. It also requires additional cost, for example, in terms of dealing with hazardous materials, double handling of returned or recycled products, and disposal or clean-up activities, all of which add cost, but little value. 'Like defects, pollution often reveals flaws in the product design or production processes' (Porter van der Linde, 1995). That traditional costing systems have ignored these 'external costs', they might not impact on the business, and thus might not need to be attributed to the product (e.g. the cost to the environment of dumping the packaging in landfill sites). As regulation changes this (e.g. landfill taxes and the rights of consumers to

FIGURE 15.1   Matter cannot be destroyed, only converted

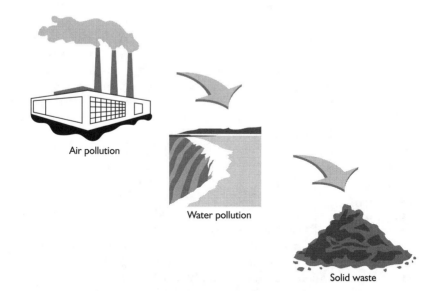

Air pollution

Water pollution

Solid waste

return packaging to the manufacturers), the external costs cease to be negligible and must be added to the direct costs of the product. In effect, the supply chain implications of the product must be managed at the primary costing level (a factor that will have repercussions right along the supply chain if not properly managed).

The implication of this is that environmental issues should be dealt with in the same manner as, say, the design, logistics or quality improvement processes, that is, by integrating the issues into overall management, and assigning management responsibilities and goals, on a continuous improvement basis, which will minimize the possibility of mistakes occurring.[2] This does not mean that no environmental impact will occur, but rather that no management mistakes will be made, which might lead to an environmental 'incident'. This approach has been dubbed 'Total Quality Environmental Management' (TQEM), (Shrivastava, 1995). The parallels with quality principles are clear: it is more expensive to return a faulty product for repair after it has left the factory; it is less expensive to inspect the quality at the end of the production line; but it is most cost-effective of all to design any faults out of the system initially. Quality is essentially about limiting the cost of failure: 'when a product fails, you must replace it or fix it. In either case, you must track it, and apologise for it. The losses are much greater than the costs of manufacturing it; none will recover your

---

[2] This is the purpose of the environmental quality management systems, BS 7750, the Environmental Management and Audit Scheme (EMAS), and ISO 14000, all of which are based on the principle of continuous improvement.

reputation, leading to the loss of market share'. Similarly, with environmental quality it will be more costly to pay for clean up and fines after a spillage or a leak, for example (assuming regulatory frameworks operate effectively). It will be less expensive to use pollution abatement technology to minimize any pollution that is produced. The most effective solution, however, is to eliminate the risk of problems occurring by designing those problems out of the system in the first place. In terms of market image, any business process that is inherently wasteful, risky or controversial could be argued to be poor quality, by definition.

> *The most effective solution is to eliminate the risk of problems occurring by designing those problems out of the system in the first place.*

Taking a process view of a system (Figure 15.2) it can be seen that, as a company uses inputs from suppliers to produce outputs for its customers and end users, it will pollute the three environmental media of land, water and air. This apparently obvious analysis is in fact the practical basis for an assessment of the environmental impact caused by a company or its supply chain, and is reflected in the legislation with which firms must comply. The management system needs to address each of these stages, by translating customer requirements back up to suppliers, and by combining with the various functions and other parties within the extended organization (i.e. including suppliers and customers where appropriate), to manage and control the outputs.

This view of environmental management fits well with the concept of 'lean'. If a lean enterprise seeks to produce goods and services using significantly lower levels of input (materials, time, labour, space) and avoiding all forms of waste, it is likely to adopt the principles of

FIGURE 15.2 A Process View of the Business Organization

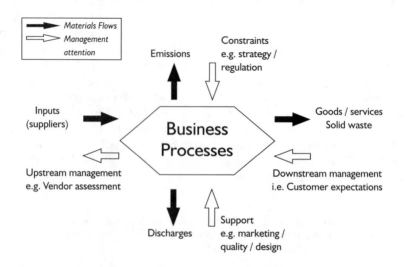

environmentally sound supply easily. This is recognised by Warhurst: 'the elimination of all costs incurred that do not add competitive value to a product. Secondary principles include the reduction of waste, utilisation of space, the elimination of inventories, and the integration of quality control within the production process' (Warhurst, 1994). The same is true of lean supply (Lamming, 1993). If organizations are to produce greater product value from fewer resources, and with less waste (the 'more from less' approach) (Hindle, 1993), then environmental management is an integral part of this – the use of fewer natural resources should be a key aim of environmental strategies.

Plastic moulder, Holden Hydroman, for example, removed a wasteful activity in their process – the practice of throwing away test samples taken from the mix, rather than replacing the sample in the mix after testing – and consequently saved £8,000 in a year. Protagonists claim that, just by looking at processes it is possible to identify a saving in terms of the cost of waste – a similar conclusion to that reached by observers of lean production. For example, it has been estimated that 40 per cent of trucks on UK roads are travelling empty – a clear example of a business inefficiency with a corresponding environmental impact. In response to this realization, companies such as Nissan, Ford and Rank Xerox have initiated Nominated Carrier Schemes, and cross-docking initiatives, in order to reduce the problem, with significant financial and economic benefits. Expressing environmental issues in the language of quality and lean principles brings them into the mainstream of business activity, on the basis of efficiency and cost savings.

Rather than concentrating on pollution control and clean-up, therefore, companies should perhaps examine the potential for pollution avoidance, which is ultimately related to improved resource productivity, and understanding the opportunity costs of pollution. In this sense, recycling, although commonly understood as a 'green' activity, is an 'end-of-pipe' solution, in that it deals with pollution and waste only after it has been produced. When one considers that all 'waste' was once bought into the company as an asset (or part of one), it becomes logical to think about minimizing the amount of waste produced. Environmental improvement therefore, may be achieved within a hierarchy of *five* main levels of approach (see Figure 15.3), each of which provides opportunities to improve process efficiency and product value:

1. Reduction of the total amount of resource (materials, energy, etc.) used in the production and use of a unit of service or goods;

2. Extension of the life of that unit;

3. Reduction of the unwanted side-effects of the unit throughout its life, including pollution and waste;

4. The reuse, recycling or incineration with energy recovery at the end of a product's normal useful life, instead of disposal to landfill.

FIGURE 15.3   The Waste Hierarchy

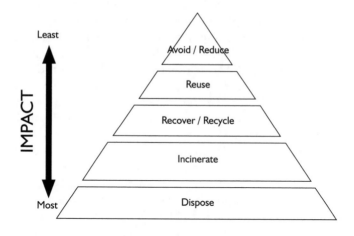

It is important to retain a market focus in dealing with environmental management. Traditionally, 'green' products have sold on the basis of what they do *not* contain, as opposed to what they do. Frequently, this resulted in a loss of functionality (and therefore value to the consumer) in the product, i.e. 'less from less'. The 'more from less' approach can only be realized if the improved product sells in place of its less environmentally sound competitors. If it does not, the improvements will have been made in vain (Hindle, 1993).

The Role of the Supply Chain

Supply Chain Management encompasses supplier management, purchasing, materials management, production scheduling, facilities planning, logistics, and customer service. The principal aim of supply chain management is to minimize the costs and non-value-adding activities associated with each stage of the chain, while increasing the value-added, with a primary focus on the end user. In environmental terms, there appears to be a clear link between supply chain management and product stewardship (Figure 15.4). This concept illustrates that the extent of a company's influence lies well beyond the traditional boundaries of a firm: it includes the environmental impacts of goods upstream and downstream in the supply chain, from raw materials extraction to end-of-life disposal. To understand the full impact of products throughout their whole lifecycles, therefore, proactive companies need to examine not only their own processes, but also those along the full chain of materials sourcing, production, distribution and use (Smart, 1992).

It is therefore useful to view environmental management strategies in two broad categories: those dealing with the organization's own structure and activities (its core competencies), and those relating to the supply

FIGURE 15.4   The Product Stewardship Concept

chain. In principle, suppliers need to be drawn into the process of environmental improvement, if an organization is to make substantial improvements in the environmental performance of its products and processes: suppliers' own sourcing decisions and activities determine the nature of the inputs into a system, and are also integral to the competitive survival of the organization in the business environment. Purchasers are interested in reducing the Total Costs of Ownership (TCO) of goods and services. The TCO comprises all the costs associated with the acquisition, use, maintenance and disposal of a good or service, from pre-transaction to post-transaction stages. The principle behind this is that poor quality, or products which are incompatible with their processes, for example, will require extra time and attention to sort out. In many cases it makes financial sense to pay a slightly higher prices, than to pay less, and in doing so receive unreliable products which will cost the firm more in the medium term.

> *Poor quality, or products which are incompatible with their processes, will require extra time and attention to sort out.*

In this respect, the 'Polluter Pays Principle' – a fundamental driver behind much environmental legislation – is a misnomer. If the polluter is not caught, then 'society' pays, in the form of external costs. If the polluter is caught, however, and fined, then these additional costs may be passed down the chain to customers, who are in effect paying for that supplier's poor environmental management, i.e. buying at prices that reflect the cost of production and waste (Burt and Los, 1995). This will also be the case, even if the supplier is complying with legislation, but is still producing unnecessary waste.

The challenge, then, is to urge suppliers to improve their environmental performance at each stage of the supply chain, through implementing the appropriate features of the waste hierarchy at each stage. Some of the key areas (Burt and Los, 1995) to address in this process include:

- customer specification;
- quality requirements;
- interface waste due to distance, and differing customer–supplier processes;
- company internal processing of materials: scrap, stock, and transport requirements;
- progression to the next processing / manufacturing firm in the value chain;
- post-consumption waste, not consumed by the end user.

With each of these, the aim should be to instil a philosophy of continuous improvement, without simply pushing particular environmental problems either back up or down to the next stage in the supply chain – thus avoiding a transference of the immediate risk of penalties, rather than an improvement in the overall environmental performance of a product. What would be the point, for example, of eliminating transport packaging, which as a result causes more damage or breakages to goods in transit? As noted above, 'green' is not a fixed state – organizations can only become 'green*er*', and so companies should focus on the quality of supply as a whole (which will include environmental issues) rather than just the constituents of the product. Standards, legislation, expectations and competition will only become tighter and more stringent over time, so continuous improvement is key to succeeding in this area of business. Many large firms already have quality improvement programmes in place with their major suppliers, of which environmental management forms a part, and guidelines for the role of TQM relationships in the supply chain are beginning to emerge (Bessant *et al.*, 1993).

> *The aim should be to instil a philosophy of continuous improvement.*

Collaboration in Supply Chains

The benefits of collaboration between different companies in supply chains are broadly accepted. The applicability of collaboration to optimize overall environmental performance of a product or service is equally valid. It is worthwhile noting, however, that companies which are placed at different stages in the supply chain are likely to face different environmental pressures, depending upon the priorities of their various stakeholders. For example, retailers and their immediate suppliers are likely to feel the effects of consumer demands far more strongly than, say, an automotive components manufacturer, which may be more concerned with legislation on emissions levels, and production efficiency.

Suppliers should be able to help customers to understand environmental effects and their causes, in relation to their own competitive concerns, while customers may help suppliers understand the related issues such as potential competitive advantage and the criteria used for evaluation and rating. This joint working should create the best results, giving a more cost effective environmental solution overall, and better market opportunities for suppliers to embed their business in customers' value chains. In addition, environmental standards in purchasing should motivate suppliers to look at activities of their own suppliers, and so on. Cases abound of companies who have taken this approach with their trading partners and, in some cases, competitors. For example, in 1994, Rover piloted a scheme with six suppliers, to help them improve their environmental performance through implementing an environmental management system. Suppliers involved in the scheme achieved annual cost savings of between £10,000 and £100,000. Rover did not demand a share of this, recognizing that these savings help to make the suppliers more cost-effective, a benefit which then comes through to the company as cost improvements (Lamming *et al.*, 1996). BT is reconsidering its policy on lubricants and other fluids for its extensive vehicle fleet. In the future, it may effectively rent the oil from suppliers, returning it to them for cleaning and reprocessing after a specified period of use.

Improving the dialogue amongst the actors in the value chain is clearly essential in allowing them to choose the materials and techniques with the least impact, and for effective product stewardship to be a real possibility. For example, 'there is no benefit from claiming that a product is recyclable if the manufacturer chooses inappropriate materials for which no market exists, or uses manufacturing techniques that do not lend themselves to a "clean" break-up of the end-of-life product, and hence, relatively clean, reusable material . . . the manufacturer should be aware of the limitations of the material that he chooses, and the effect that his choice has on the rest of the recycling chain' (Roy and Wheelan, 1992). Internal collaboration is equally essential. There is little point in embarking upon an environmentally sound purchasing initiative if internal users are unaware of the intended benefits, and purchasing people lose visibility of purchased products and services once they have entered the system. Similarly, dialogue with internal customers may highlight opportunities for further cost improvements: BT found that the batteries which they use for their payphones were actually classed as hazardous waste, and that consequently, because of Duty of Care obligations, they were costing the company twice as much to dispose of as they were to buy initially. Once this was realized, a recycling scheme was set up to minimize costs.

The main 'virtues' of collaboration, in this respect include:

- fostering innovation through the cross-fertilization of skills and complementary knowledge of markets and technology;
- sharing costs and risks;
- improving information exchanges, in the absence of legislation-driven information exchange.

Supply chains often appear to suffer from a plethora of poorly organized information and many barriers to communication. This is particularly the case with environmental issues, which are multi-sectoral in nature and relate to different elements of organizations. As the nature of environmental problems is uncertain in the future, and the focus of future legislation unclear, intra-value chain cooperation would appear to be a fundamental element of any environmental strategy. As a result of such a policy, suppliers should be more confident of protecting their markets, and more able to employ the expertise of their customers and their own suppliers to develop innovative products with improved environmental qualities.

Purchasing Risks

Environmental issues therefore pose a number of risks to supply chain managers.

Non-compliance with Legislation / Protocol

Any non-compliance is likely to lead to company fines, the threat of imprisonment for directors, and potentially the loss of public and market place 'goodwill'. If suppliers are having problems with compliance, then it is likely that they are passing these costs down the chain to customers.

Bought-in Liability

Customers must be confident that the goods which they buy into their own processes will not cause them to pollute once they are in use. This is related to the Duty of Care principle, which states that any company that produces, holds or is concerned with controlled waste (commercial or industrial) is responsible for its safe passage downstream through the supply chain. Contract cleaners, for example, may expose a company to duty of care legislation if they are responsible for disposing of some wastes.

Security of Supply

This is perhaps the major issue which the environment poses for purchasing managers. Legislation will increasingly restrict the availability of certain key items. Types of available packaging may be one example. Another is that of the UK dry cleaning industry in the 1980s, which, unaware of the impending ban on CFC manufacturing, proceeded with investment decisions in equipment which was dependent upon using those CFCs. As production capacity has declined subsequently because of the ban, so the price of CFCs has risen by over 800 per cent per litre. These companies also face the possible early obsolescence of that relatively new capital equipment (Business in the Environment, 1995). Similarly, the requirements of the Clean Air Acts have led some states in the USA to demand the reformulation of gasoline to include more methanol. As a result, the anticipated increase in consumption has caused a tighter supply, and short- or medium-term price increases. Those companies with more secure sourcing arrangements might be expected to cope better during this period – before new production boosts capacity – than those with less foresight (Colby, 1995).

Resource Productivity

As mentioned previously, the management of resources – and deriving the maximum possible value from the minimum input – is becoming increasingly important. Indeed, with the growth in global sourcing and the intensity of competition, it is no longer enough simply to own or have access to resources – the key is how they are managed and how to get the most out of them (Porter van der Linde, 1995). The opportunity cost of not maximizing this while competitors do so may affect the cost performance of products in their end markets.

Loss of Competitive Positioning

Major industrial and corporate customers are increasingly asking questions of their suppliers regarding their environmental performance and, in some cases, how they assess their own suppliers' environmental performance. Those suppliers which can respond to these questions proactively, and demonstrate improved resource efficiency and cost-effectiveness will be able to realize some benefits *vis-à-vis* their competitive positioning.

Developing an environmental purchasing policy is, therefore, not about buying 'green' goods, with sub-standard performance, to be socially responsible: it is about working to minimize a growing strategic business concern, simultaneously reducing costs and improving added value.

Implementation Issues

Measuring Environmental Effectiveness

If it is accepted that environmentally sound purchasing is a desirable objective (based on some of the ideas we have outlined in the preceding section) then it becomes necessary to develop techniques for measuring the purchasing function on its performance in meeting these objectives.

As the nature of purchasing changes, so what constitutes good performance in purchasing must also be redefined. This issue must be considered in the light of the wider debate on performance measurement in purchasing: the move from traditional methods that tend to focus on operational aspects (throughput of paperwork, etc.) to more conceptual approaches that try to capture strategic performance – success in developing strong relationships, for example, or perhaps the ability to add value.

Performance measurement of any activity should be designed to bring about improvement in that activity. It involves the development of goals and their related measures, combined with the appropriate mechanisms of feedback, which reflect the operating assumptions of the organization in terms of culture, strategy and operational processes. When measures are not related to specific organizational goals, there is a tendency for them either to be misused, or not used at all. Too often, business units end up with measures which reflect results, but which do not indicate how those results occurred, or what management should do differently. This is an important point: it is often not so much *what* the actual measures are that make a difference, but *how* they are being used. Any performance measurement system needs to be derived from corporate strategy, synthesizing an analysis of the external environment, with internal capabilities which reflect the purpose, technology available, and the nature of the activity; and which focus on long-term competitiveness rather than short-term considerations. The aim should be to develop a system whereby the goals of one stage in the organization become the means of the next stage. Overall strategy provides the context in which these goals are set, so that personnel on the ground have a view of the activities to which they are contributing, rather than just buying 'from the hip'.

> *Too often, business units end up with measures which reflect results, but which do not indicate how those results occurred, or what management should do differently.*

Measurements in organizations have an important motivational influence, which shapes employees' perceptions of what is important for them to concentrate on (although measures should never become ends in themselves). Poorly designed measurement systems will encourage the wrong goals and reward the wrong achievements; lip service may be paid to the stated priority, but actions will always be directed first towards achieving the target on which personnel are measured.

In supply management and purchasing, measurement has traditionally concentrated on measures of efficiency data, e.g. how much it costs to achieve a goal, while typically ignoring those measures of effectiveness, the information describing the extent to which a goal can be met using a certain course of action. It is the effectiveness of purchasing – the areas where purchasing can really add value (supplier development or value analysis, for example) which is often overlooked. While it is difficult to quantify such areas, these are often the types of activity which need to be monitored and stimulated, in order for purchasing to deliver the appropriate goods and services to internal users. It is important to strike a balance between understanding the cause, and measuring the symptoms of the problem.

The benefits of a well-planned performance measurement system which supports strategic objectives at every organizational level should therefore include: improved decision-making; better visibility of activities, their consequences and any areas of waste or duplication; and improved workforce motivation. The aim should not only be to help senior managers to pull information upwards, so that they can duly impose policies downwards, but to help employees – those 'nearest to the action' – to monitor and improve their own performance.

An environmental purchasing policy must be supported by open, credible, stated measurements which reflect the goals of that policy: otherwise, it will become sidelined. There appear to be many companies that claim to have implemented an environmental purchasing policy, but which have actually achieved little in terms of improvements, because measurements have not been put in place against which buyers may be assessed. For example, it is pointless to state that the company will only buy from suppliers that can demonstrate that they have taken significant steps towards addressing their own environmental performance, if the prevailing measurement system simply assesses purchasing on the amount of savings made compared to the previous period. In addressing these issues, the longer-term competitive implications (such as total cost of ownership, quality improvements and continuity of supply), with which environmental improvements might be associated, need to be considered. As such, the development of an effective performance measurement system which reflects the environmental priorities (derived from top-level strategy) requires a shift in management attitude.

Companies can measure environmental performance on many levels. The most basic of these would be on the number of incidents or prosecutions faced by the company over time, as most companies which publish environmental reports disclose. However, such measures can be deceptive: 'they are equivalent to tracking your personal automobile driving record by counting the number of tickets you have received. What this measures is not how well you drive, but how many times you've been caught' (Hedstrom and McLean, 1993). More sophisticated systems include progress against corporate goals, improvements against environmental audit results, waste tracking, etc., and develop a balance between process, and results-based measures.

Supplier Assessment

Life Cycle Inventory (White, 1995) is potentially one tool which could enable buyers or purchasing managers to build an 'impact profile' for suppliers, forming a baseline for assessing their future performance. Another method, used by the British DIY retailer, B&Q, is based on the management practices of suppliers. The practices reviewed are translated into buyers' appraisals, and may ultimately affect their bonuses. Once a general profile has been constructed of the key actors in the supply base, however, appropriate actions need to be in place for dealing with the information received: there is little point in investing time in setting up such an activity, if plans for what to do with the information do not exist.

A useful exercise would be to analyze all the sources of supply, integrating environmental concerns with regular commercial analysis. One approach to this might be to develop existing supply management tools to incorporate environmental considerations. For example, the well-known Supply Positioning Matrix (Kraljic, 1983) adopts a portfolio approach to the market, traditionally based on a classification of products according to:

- the value added by product line, the percentage of purchased items in total costs, and their impact on profitability;
- the complexity of the market, depending on scarcity of supply, the pace of technology, materials substitution, and monopoly or oligopoly conditions.

This might be extended to add a 'third dimension' for environmental costs in each sector (see Figure 15.5).

Issues to consider in using this matrix, with which most purchasing managers have been familiar for many years, would typically include the supplier's capacity utilization and flexibility, past variations in capacity utilization, the uniqueness of the product, volumes purchased and their expected demand, levels of technology, quality history and organizational culture. The consideration of environmental issues (derived from an analysis of internal and external stakeholder concerns and requirements) may well cause some suppliers to be positioned in different areas of the

FIGURE 15.5   Development of Kraljic's Model to Incorporate Environmental Concern

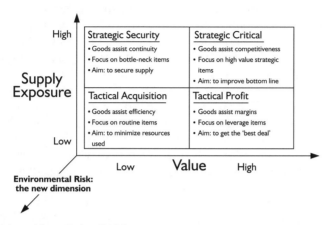

SOURCE: Adapted from Kraljic (1983).

grid, according to the strategic impact of the environmental issue. For example, in the case of the dry cleaning industry mentioned above, CFC suppliers may have moved from the Tactical Acquisition box to the Strategic Critical box, and would therefore require buyers to deal with such suppliers in an entirely different manner from that with which they were accustomed.

Strategy and Senior Management Commitment

As with most management initiatives, the need for a senior management figure – a 'champion' – to promote the cause, both within the organization, and to customers and suppliers, is vital to the long-term success of pursuing environmental soundness in supply chains. It appears that this is not always the case: a recent survey showed that although most UK environmental managers claim to have board-level approval for their work, 74 per cent cite the lack of senior management commitment as the key obstacle in their work (ENDS 241, 1995). This issue also relates to the importance attached to those factors which are measured; the prominence of such a senior manager will help to communicate the message that the initiative is important to the company, and worthy of senior management time. Environmentally sound sourcing decisions may initially give rise to increased costs, posing difficulties for departments assessed financially at a local level. This would be difficult for purchasing to support as an initiative, without the endorsement of

The prominence of such a senior manager will help to communicate the message that the initiative is important to the company.

senior management. Rover, for example, as an 'act of faith' have made a commitment to buy only recycled paper, to show that they are serious about this issue, although it is currently more expensive and requires the standardization of photocopiers, etc. throughout the organization. The company reasons that the paper will soon become much cheaper anyway, and in the meantime is sending a clear message to its own organization and its suppliers.

There is naturally a danger associated with this, of being seen as a 'corporate seagull' – somebody who simply imposes yet another requirement onto an already busy purchasing team and its much-harried suppliers. This is why strategic alignment with the overall environmental goals of the organization, and their relation to what purchasing can do in this respect, is vital. Effective implementation requires that the environmental objectives be integrated with day-to-day activities, as part of overall business performance, rather than as a separate add-on.

As with any project which introduces something new into working practices, requiring a change in attitudes, it is important to produce successful results in the short term. In this way, general confidence and credibility for the project and the concept may be created. The way to do this is to identify potentially successful pilot projects – small-scale, with high visibility, and well-supported, to 'harvest the low-hanging fruit'. Waste management practices provide many opportunities to remove costs, simply through corrective action. As discussed above, poor quality products that do not work are a waste of resources, and vice versa. For example, improvement processes applied by packaging engineers at Xerox, to reduce the impact of supplier and product packaging, have enabled the company to avoid 10,000 tonnes of waste, and save $15 million per year (Smart, 1992). One useful initial measure, as part of a waste audit, might be to compare the quantity of waste produced by the organization, with the purchase value of those wasted products (Biffa, 1994). This would not only highlight the cost savings potential of such initiatives internally, but also bring together disparate parts of the organization, focusing not only on the symptoms (i.e. excess waste) but on the causes.

Once the appropriate management and measurement system has been constructed, and short-term improvements have been realized, it is important to use those results to communicate the performance to all stakeholders, including suppliers, based on their respective needs for information (as opposed to what purchasing *thinks* those stakeholders want to know). A sequential process of the appropriate reporting stages in environmental performance is described in Figure 15.6 (Hedstrom and McLean, 1993).

Supplier Development

Since purchasing is responsible for managing external resources, it has the double issue of dealing with suppliers. From one point of view this is an advantage, since the supplier may be a source of information (e.g. technical data on a product) which may be used to strengthen Purchasing's case with internal customers. From the opposite side, however, the supplier may be reluctant to change its ways to become environmentally sound, thus giving purchasing managers the double task of convincing parties upstream and internally. Convincing suppliers of their obligations may be difficult, but a number of companies, notably B&Q, Rover and BT, have undertaken this challenge, marketing the benefits to suppliers, particularly in terms of the continuation of business with the customer company, and demonstrating the potential cost savings to be realized.

The ways in which organizations generally approach their supply bases for supplier development vary. Two opposite strategies used can be distinguished as 'cascade' and 'intervention' (see Figure 15.7).

The cascade metaphor is not new in management terms: the suggestion is that some decision is taken at a 'high' level and the implications flow down to lower levels which, in turn, pass them on to their subordinates, and so on, like a cascading fountain. It is a term frequently used in practice, in the field of policy-making. Its use in the area of supply, however, requires acceptance of the customer occupying a higher position than the supplier (the 'vantage point').[3]

The cascade strategy in supply chain management thus entails passing the customer's ideas to the supplier, assuming that they will pass 'downwards' to the supplier's suppliers, and so on. The customer sits atop

FIGURE 15.6 Evolution in Communicating Performance

	Low	Stage of Evolution		High
Approach	Tell them what you have to	Tell them what you want to	Tell them what you think they want to know	Tell them what they have told you they want to know
Manifestation	Required disclosures	Good deeds descriptions	Programme implementation progress	Performance improvement

[3] It is a curious anomaly that proponents of supply chains frequently use two directly conflicting terminologies simultaneously. The suppliers are upstream of the customer (who should thus look 'up' to them) and yet ideas and requirements may be passed, or cascaded, down to suppliers. It may be that preoccupation with the Japanese 'tiered' model is responsible for this. The jargon of strategy compounds the issue, speaking of backward integration when referring to a takeover of a supplier's operation – a *horizontal* metaphor.

FIGURE 15.7 Cascade and Intervention Strategies in Supplier Development

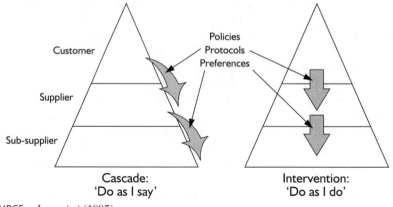

SOURCE: Lamming (1997).

a pyramid of companies, each of whom is 'washed' with the same policy which originates on high.

Forgetting for a moment the invidious implications of this rather crude hierarchical model, let us consider the likely effects of this approach.

Firstly, the cascade model assumes that it is sufficient for the customer to dictate and to delegate responsibility for implementation of the policy. This would be the case in a statement such as: 'All our suppliers are required to become certified to BS7750. After 1 January 1995 we shall only buy from suppliers who have achieved this.' A similar case would be represented by the substitution of a company-specific environmental assessment scheme in place of BS 7750.

An apparently more justifiable cascade approach might be 'The supplier's competitive position is his own concern: we will deal only with those suppliers who can meet our requirements and survive in a competitive market.' The practical manifestation of this policy, of course, is traditional competitive tendering.

The effect of either of these strategies is to emphasize the divide between customer and supplier. This is a competitive position between parties who need each other to survive. The supplier will react accordingly to the message such as strategy imparts: traditional interaction is based upon the assumption that the other party (customer or supplier) will employ guile. Taken to the extreme, this situation can paralyze entire industries (Lamming, 1994).

The cascade strategy has clear potential as a 'weeding out' tool, a necessary item for many purchasers in the process of *rationalizing* their supply bases (Cousins, 1999). Despite its shortcomings in a more mature situation, however, it is still widely used in supply chain management.

The alternative to cascade is intervention. This strategy is based upon the belief that the customer is able to intervene in the supplier's business operations and bring about change for the better – so-called 'supplier development'. As noted above, this term has paternalistic overtones – implying that it is only the supplier that needs to develop (or be developed) and that the customer can see how to do this (from the vantage point).

In practice, two sorts of intervention strategy are apparent. In the first, the customer takes the paternalistic role ('We send a team of experts to the supplier to sort out his business and recommend action'). In the second, the approach is more cooperative – the customer's experts work side by side with the supplier's personnel, in order to develop improvements through joint effort.

The UK automotive industry provides an example of this. Two of the key vehicle manufacturers (VM-A and VM-B) currently operate intervention schemes that appear similar until examined closely. Both have the concept of a quick response improvement – identifying an opportunity for improvement in a day or two of discussions and implementing it in a further three days. A large part of the efficacy of this technique is due to the sense of urgency which it creates. As happens with some crash diets, however, unless the work done is consolidated, it is likely that the benefits will be short-lived. The policy of VM-A is to intervene for three days, in which time the supplier and customer identify an opportunity, implement the improvement and measure the benefit. Following this, VM-A withdraws and expects the supplier to carry on the good work – a switch from intervention to cascade. VM-B has the same initial technique, but follows the intervention with a further team visit some days later. The members of this second team remain with the supplier until everyone is satisfied that the improvement has been integrated into working practices. Thus, intervention may be seen to be more than the opposite of cascade: it is a multi-stage strategy, with different types of intervention being employed, as appropriate.

The cases of Marks and Spencer and Tesco provide other examples of intervention strategies. In the mid-1980s, this was noted in the context of Marks and Spencer by Tse:

> In order to carry out his task, the [M&S] technologist is seldom found in the office. Apart from visiting the stores, he spends a tremendous amount of his time at the suppliers' plants. He works closely with the manufacturer's technical personnel and is readily available for consultation and advice. To Marks and Spencer, a manufacturer supplying merchandise to the company is regarded almost as part of the operation. (Tse, 1985)

At the time, Marks and Spencer had a team of 350 technologists. Other retailers learnt the lesson also: for example, in developing a new Brazilian wine for its low price market between 1991 and 1994, Tesco spent very significant amounts of time and effort in perfecting, not only the taste of the product, but also changing the way the vineyard was managed. The efforts transformed the wine from unpalatable (to Europeans) to a major UK success.

In both cases, the customer may be said to have adopted a benevolent approach, the results of which left the supplier arguably better suited not only to that customer's requirements but also to the wider demands of the market in general.

Sound environmental practice in supply chain management might therefore be expected to include some mix of strategies – cascade and intervention – designed in contingent fashion to be adapted to the needs of the relationship. The customer must ensure that the supplier is not insulated from the consumer market forces (as might happen, for example, in the case of vertical integration – which might be characterized as a 'total intervention' strategy), but must also recognize the common interests which may be served by a shared response to competitive pressures.

> **The customer must ensure that the supplier is not insulated from the consumer market forces.**

An overall environmental framework has been developed internally within Proctor & Gamble, to meet the goal of environmental and economic sustainability. This framework is built around *four* main elements, each of which is associated with a number of different management tools for achieving sound environmental performance (White, 1995):

1. Human and environmental safety.
2. Regulatory compliance.
3. Efficient resource use and waste management.
4. Addressing societal concerns.

The first two elements in this framework are really prerequisites for doing business – effectively those factors that give businesses their licence to operate. The second two, however, are understood to be vital to the long-term competitiveness and sustainability of the business. It should be evident that if this is the case, all companies would ideally have all of their suppliers not only complying, but operating for long-term sustainability and competitiveness. This is a major challenge for most organizations, however, and it would seem appropriate to cascade the first two elements to suppliers so that they must at the very least be complying with legislation in order to win the company's business. The second two elements, however, might be better brought about through intervention, working with other companies in the supply chain, understanding each other's business needs and concerns, to bring about overall waste and cost reduction, improved efficiency, and mutual business advantages.

'Where do you draw the line?'

There remains the problem of extent of influence, responsibility and interest – of how far upstream an organization's purchasing activities should be expected to probe. There is no clear answer to this. Some companies provide evidence of following supply chains all the way back to raw material processing. For others with longer and more complex supply chains, this may not be immediately possible, and they may focus just on first-tier, and possibly second-tier, suppliers.

Ideally, all companies in the supply chain should be practising good environmental management as a matter of course, as it makes inherently good business sense. Practically, though, with the pressures on modern business as they are, and with the relatively low levels of environmental 'literacy' in many companies, Purchasing's responsibility should extend as far as possible, within the requirements of its corporate objectives, to the level where a positive influence can still be made apparent. The key constraint must be cost, however: for the whole strategy to work effectively, the firm must benefit economically, and this will depend, both on the time horizons the firm is willing to consider in terms of payback, and also on the nature of that payback (e.g. price reductions, quality improvements, costs of waste disposal, improved market positioning, improved supplier relations, elimination of regulatory non-compliance, etc.) The commercial organization exists to provide profits, products and services, and work: limiting its environmental impact is a sound business requirement, but not the ultimate reason for doing business – all business activities will always necessarily impact in some way on the environment, be they 'positive' or 'negative'. The extent to which to pursue an environmental purchasing policy must therefore ultimately depend on what is 'fit for purpose' for the particular company, based on the requirements of internal users and the expectations of the final customer.

Leaving Somewhere to Go Somewhere Else

Developing environmentally-sound purchasing is an example of innovation. Innovation is concerned with bringing about improved organizational change, through creativity, novelty, risk, and challenges. One of the words rarely associated with innovation, however, but which is vital to its success is *destruction* – removing old systems in order to build the new. Examples might include dismantling a computer system, or changing functional boundaries within the organization, or the shape of the organization itself. Something has to go, in order for something new to find its place. Advocates of Business Process Reengineering, for example, advise managers not to automate existing activities or systems, but to replace them with newer, more efficient ways: 'innovate, don't replicate'. Innovation is rarely a pleasant process: those with an established interest in the *status quo* may be expected to protect their investments, and others will remain unconvinced. The innovator, therefore, has to battle on both fronts. Management thinking is largely influenced by the rational model, whereas management of innovation and organizational change has more in common with contingent practices. Hurst has linked the concept of the ecocycle with the need to manage the irrational processes that occur in organizations during major change or upset. He suggests that rational management is of little use where significant innovation is necessary (Hurst, 1995).

The Search or Selection Environment (see Figure 15.8) is a widely recognized concept in studies on innovation. It may be viewed as a network of contacts and connections available to an organization, from which it learns about new technologies, etc. Environmental soundness in purchasing is a prime example of innovation and the need to learn proactively. The purchasing function is a potential gatherer of intelligence through the supply base and may, by careful design of the search environment, develop the organization's knowledge of risks, legislation, good practices, and opportunities for competitive advantage of which suppliers are aware.

Purchasing managers and buyers may not become technical experts in the scientific subtleties of suppliers' goods, services and processes, but through judicious use of a search environment they may acquire a base knowledge of the issues – legislative, environmental and commercial – and how these relate to corporate strategy, and their own specific roles within that. They will increasingly be expected to know how and where to look within and outside the organization, and which resources to draw upon to monitor these issues.

This activity naturally leads to involvement in cross-functional teams within the company, since environmental management issues are not simply a problem for the purchasing function, or any other single function. They span the functions in an organization, as each function will affect and be affected by environmental issues in different ways. Pur-

FIGURE 15.8 The Search or Selection Environment

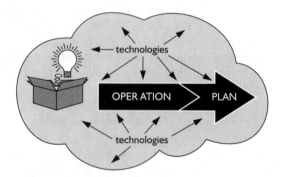

chasing must be able to provide the necessary advice regarding the relevant environmental issues for purchased goods and services to all internal users. In much the same way as purchasing is increasingly considered as a process rather than a function, so environmental management should be envisaged, drawing on all the stages within an organization. Developing this perspective will require significant investment in training and education for individuals in purchasing.

A decision to source materials, products or services on the basis of sound environmental factors must be taken in accordance with purchasing policies concerned with costs and social aspects. There follows the challenge of disseminating this complex policy throughout the organization. The approach to this will naturally depend upon the way in which purchasing is organized (e.g. centralized/decentralized), the relationship between purchasing and other functional areas and process/project teams, the general awareness of the organization, and so on. The economic consideration is linked to the market image that the organization wishes to portray.

Relationship Assessment

As indicated above, sound environmental practice in supply chain management has about it many features which find resonance in other developing purchasing practices – especially those to do with partnership sourcing and lean supply. One aspect of the latter is Relationship Assessment Process (RAP™) (Lamming et al., 1996). In RAP™,[4] both parties to a supply relationship work together in assessing the relationship and the potential for improvement for mutual benefit. The principle of sharing responsibility for performance of the inter-firm connection (as part of the value chain or flow) has clear implications for the approaches to sound environmental supply chain management. While at an early stage, it is clear that the development of RAP™ could provide a valuable context for environmental assessment techniques.

Conclusion

Sound environmental management in supply chains may now be classed as an essential business requirement. Although the full effects of the various pressures may take some time to filter through to purchasing in some industries, in others it is already a mainstream issue. Companies that consider environmental issues (and, perhaps, related public image issues) to be 'strategic' will not wait for the repercussions of inactivity to have an effect – they will seek proactively for the potential impacts on their busi-

---

[4] The rights to RAP are now owned by A.T.Kearney Inc., Chicago, IL.

Sound environmental management in supply chains may now be classed as an essential business requirement.

ness and attempt to minimize the risk before it is fully manifested. There is no quick fix, and there are still many uncertainties in the area. It is likely, however, that as with cars, which are sold on the merits of such technologies as side-impact bars, airbags, ABS brakes, and other safety features, so sound environmental management will become a defining feature for the goods and services of modern companies. The competitive pressure that this market development may be expected to place upon firms will surely find its way rapidly to supply chain management.

PART FIVE

Making the Change
in Other Linked
Processes

CHAPTER 16

Managing Promotions Within the Value Stream[1]

Introduction

Promotions of one sort or another are an ever-increasing event in the high streets and shopping precincts of the UK. There is promotional activity to accompany the launch of every new product or the re-launch of an existing one. There are promotions to increase the exposure of the product range or of the company itself. There are promotions which rely solely on advertising, others which rely on price reductions and many other variations which fall between these two extremes. There are indeed probably just as many reasons for running a promotion as there are different types of promotion. Products are promoted to increase sales, to maintain sales, to stop the competition from increasing sales. 'The prevailing assertion in marketing and retailing textbooks is that price promotions help attract shoppers who purchase regular price merchandise' (Ghosh, 1990). Thus price promotions will have an effect not only on the item being promoted but also on the overall sales volume in the store.

Whatever the reason for running a promotion, a great deal of time and money can be spent on the market research, the marketing effort and on calculating the best way of presenting the product in the store and in the media. Promotions tend to be the responsibility of the sales or marketing department, who decide when to do it, how to do it, how much it will cost and what gains it will make. The debate in the advertising and marketing press is ongoing about the benefits and costs of promotions while new and more complicated means of promoting products are being introduced.

However, what is rarely taken into account in this debate is the true

---

[1] Prepared by Richard James, Daniel Jones, Peter Hines and Nick Rich.

cost to the supply chain of managing promotions. The production department will probably be asked if they can manage the potential increase in demand, and risk analysis may be undertaken to evaluate the cost of potential stock surpluses. However, little work has been done on evaluating the possible increase in waste in the system, especially on similar products not on promotion, or on the risk and potential cost of overstocking these products. Moreover, while the actual cost of point-of-purchase advertising can be established, the actual cost of physically locating this material is difficult to calculate. It would need a sophisticated Activity Based Costing (ABC) analysis to estimate accurately the management time (and grey hair) that should be allocated to the cost of a promotion. Even in their report on collaboration in supply chain management, the Coca-Cola Retailing Research Group (1994) concentrate on the marketing benefits, with only a small reference to the supply chain where they recommend the elimination of special packaging.

In summary, little research has been carried out on the effects of promotions on the supply chain, and companies are making decisions about the launching of promotions without a clear idea what will be the overall cost to their supply chain and, eventually, to them.

Thus, the purpose of the research detailed in this chapter has been to investigate the wastes incurred in one particular supply chain in food retailing and to see what improvements could be made. While the details are specific to that particular supply chain, inferences can be drawn that relate to similar ones.

The Promotions Environment

Food Retailing was the example chosen as this was the sector in the UK that seemed to be making most use of promotions and one in which the UK had well-developed supply chains. The majority of the promotions were rather simple in nature, mainly involving price discounting without media advertising, which in turn would make analysis of cause and effect somewhat easier. Also the willingness of both customers and suppliers to take part in the research meant that we would have reasonable access to the key players in the promotional process.

In the competitive retail environment of the UK the promotions battle is fought out every day of the week as the major retailers offer more and more promotions. One of the leading UK retailers was chosen for this research activity. The retailer 'Foodco' has around 2000 different promotions at any one time. Recent research by Nielsen estimates that items under promotion make up 20.3 per cent of the average British shopping basket, an increase of 1.6 per cent over the previous year. The range of promotions being used is also on the increase, from the simple money-off offer through to the complex cross-product offers where, if you buy one product, you get another product free or at a major discount. This is not only difficult to forecast but is extremely difficult to manage in-store if the products are from totally different product ranges or managed by different buyers and inventory controllers.

An added complexity is the degree of advertising that accompanies a particular promotion within a retailer. The supplier may be supporting the promotion with national advertising. The retailer might include the details of the promotional offer in his own national or local advertising. Foodco, for example, run corporate image advertising which may have an effect on a current promotion, but tends to have a more long-term influence. However, they also run advertisements highlighting some of their current promotions. With some promotions, 'this form of retailer support can increase the demand for the product by a factor of two or three' (Stock Control Manager, Foodco).

> *Items under promotion make up 20.3 per cent of the average British shopping basket.*

There are also the different players in the process each with a different motive for running a promotion. The retailer is looking to offer the customer the 'best buy' and in the words of one Foodco executive, *'promotions bring excitement to their store'*. The suppliers, on the other hand, may have completely different reasons, such as maintaining, increasing or gaining shelf space in the retailer's stores. So there are the various suppliers offering various promotions to the retailer, and the retailer demanding promotions from the supplier. Nonetheless, despite the potential problems to the supply chain, both parties are willing participants in the promotional process.

Retail Supply Chain

The research involved Foodco, one of the UK's leading food retailers and four multi-national suppliers. At the time of the research,[2] Foodco had an annual turnover in excess of $10 billion, a range of 30000 products and operated with a stock turn of over 30, basically 10 days' stock in the system. They estimated that they could reduce this by another one or two days without reducing customer service, but it would mean their stores operating with half-empty shelves, which they do not want for obvious marketing reasons. Although they do have overseas links, their main operations are in the UK where they are currently running over 500 stores. These stores are supplied by over a dozen Regional Distribution Depots, half of which are classed as 'composite', stocking both ambient, chilled and frozen. They

---

[2] This research work was carried out in 1995 and so all figures concerning Foodco and their supply chain date from this period. Since this time Foodco has undertaken considerable activity within the promotions area in order to optimize the consumer offering, eradicate or reduce waste and optimize inventory levels.

have about 2000 suppliers, most of whom are connected by EDI. The EDI-linked suppliers account for 95 per cent of deliveries by value.

Each of the suppliers in this research project has a turnover close to the $1 billion per annum level and all trade multinationally. Each one is a subsidiary of a larger company and all of them deal almost exclusively in branded products where they are market leaders in many of the product categories.

Research

Despite the efficiency of their supply chain management, promotions still caused Foodco problems and it was the awareness of this that prompted their active involvement in the research project. The first stage of the research was to map out the actual promotions process, including activities at both supplier and retailer and both physical and communications links between the two. This involved both the official process and the informal communications and decision-making that went on throughout the promotional period. To this end interviews were carried out with the

FIGURE 16.1 The Supply Chain Decision-Makers

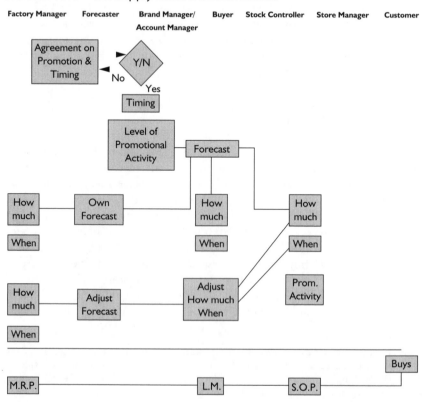

key decision-makers at the retailer and the supplier, both at strategic and operational level. It also involved a number of interviews with key personnel at some of the suppliers' suppliers. From these interviews it was possible to map out (Figure 16.1) the actual flow of information during the whole promotional process, the key decision points in the process and how, when and with what information these decisions are made (Kurt Salmon Associates, 1993; Coca-Cola Retailing Research Group, 1994).

The second stage in the research was to analyze the movement of stock through the supply chain for eight different products before, during and after a three-week promotion period in late 1995. The products chosen were viewed as those where there was likely to be a significant uplift in sales and where there were no or only a few other promotions in the same product group. This involved actual stores sales, store demand on depots, stock at depots and delivery from suppliers to depots. The inclusion of stock at the supplier was considered but, as the majority of items included in the study were branded goods rather than own-label, it would not have been possible to calculate the proportion of stock being held for the one retailer. Unfortunately, the stock levels for the stores, even at an aggregate level, were not available.

The two main areas of interest in promotions were the amount of management time they believed that they spent on controlling promotions and the prospect of either having too much stock or of running out of stock.

The two main areas of interest in promotions to both Foodco and the four suppliers were the amount of management time they believed that they spent on controlling promotions and the prospect of either having too much stock or of running out of stock. The supply chain management functions at both retailer and suppliers – the groups who were supporting the research – all believed that the way they ran promotions was inefficient. However, each believed that the problem lay with other functions or with their customer (for the suppliers) or with the suppliers (for the retailer). Each thought that forecasting was the key but that their partner in the promotional process was getting it wrong. Within the retailer, the supply chain function believed that, even if they got the forecast correct, the demand from the stores (over which they had no control) would still cause both stock-outs and overstocking during the promotion. Thus both supplier and retailer were keen to analyze the promotional process but each had preconceived ideas about where the research would lead.

Research Findings

The research findings will be divided into *six* subject areas, each briefly discussed in turn before examining the results altogether in the following section.

1. Complementary Products

It was found that a promotion on a particular product seemed to have little significant effect on complementary products (e.g. turkey and stuffing), unless they were physically linked or co-located in a store. Indeed, in store interviews none of the interviewees could recall a past example where a complementary promotion had had a significant effect on the non-promoted item except when it was linked to a seasonal event such as Christmas. In this case, arguably, the effect was more closely linked to Christmas than the promotional activity.

2. Effect on Substitute Products

The promotion of a particular product seems to have little significant visible effect on the sales of other products in the same product group. This was particularly true for short-shelf-life products as shown in Figure 16.2. At any one time there was at least 1 and sometimes 2 products on promotion in the same group. In the 5 product groups containing short-shelf-life products, all the main lines examined showed very steady sales during the nine weeks covered by the analysis unless they were on promotion at some time during that period. The sales were significantly higher during their promotional period and slightly higher in the week following their promotion.

FIGURE 16.2 The Substitution Effect

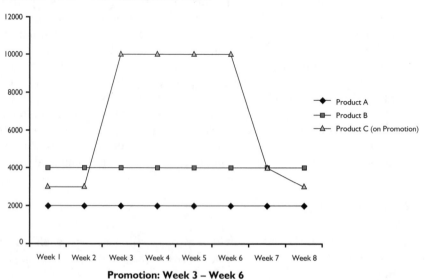

Promotion: Week 3 – Week 6

FIGURE 16.3   Sales and Waste After Promotion

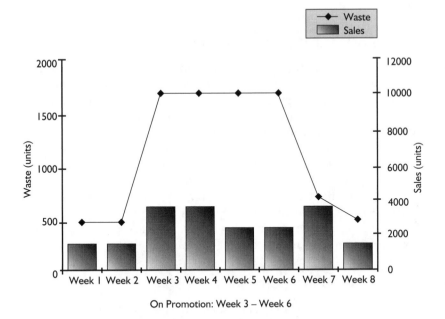

On Promotion: Week 3 – Week 6

3. Future Sales of a Promoted Product

A promotion seems to have little or no effect on the future sales of the item. However, typically, the sales figures for the week following the promotion are slightly higher than normal but then revert back to normal in the week after that (Figure 16.3). This phenomenon is linked to discounting or remaindering by store managers, who are keen to reduce unsold promotions particularly if the product has a short shelf life. The survey found no evidence of a 'sales nadir' effect where customers had stocked up during the promotion and were, in effect, de-stocking their cupboards in the following weeks. This effect, however, was felt to be more likely to occur with non-perishable goods.

4. Waste After Promotion

Waste levels for promoted products were significantly higher in the week after the promotion, typically by a factor of between 3 and 5 (Figure 16.3). For the 5 short-shelf-life products, deliveries to the store in the week after the promotion were 25–40 per cent higher than usual, possibly caused by de-stocking at the National Distribution Centres. Thus in the week following the promotion there were higher deliveries, higher sales and far higher waste. This waste was especially high where the promotion uplift had been very high (600–1000 per cent) as a small forecasting error towards the end of the promotion often created a very large excess stock quantity.

5. Levels of Waste During a Promotion

The level of waste at the start of the promotion is generally very low, both in absolute and percentage terms, and continues at this level for the first four to five days (Figure 16.4). Indeed, waste here is lower in absolute terms than normal. Wastage then peaks at the first weekend and continues to peak for four to five days. After this, wastage during the promotion tends to fall to around normal levels. Taking the promotion period as a total, actual waste levels increase over the norm but are lower as a percentage of sales. This pattern may be due to the early uncertainty of ordering, with tight early stocks leading to a big uplift in orders above realistic sales levels, leading in turn to overstocking and wastage. Another factor may be the more economic use of large pack quantities in smaller stores that would normally have higher wastage levels.

6. Sales Peak During Promotions

In every case there is a considerable sales peak due to the promotion. However, in many cases the sales peak was remarkably stable (Figures 16.2 and 16.3), although in other cases there was a peaking in the first week. This slight decline in later weeks may be a result of reduced ordering during this time to reduce the risk of excess stock and subsequent wastage.

Discussion

Sales Analysis

The results from the analysis of the data showed the typical demand amplification or Forrester Effect (Forrester, 1958) but with an interesting variation. Before the start of the promotion, deliveries from the supplier to the depots increased sharply followed by increased orders from the stores. These increases were based on forecasts made approximately six weeks earlier when the promotion had been decided. If the stores' sales were as predicted, the demand on the supplier declined sharply towards the end of the promotional period. If, however, the sales were lower than predicted, demand on the supplier dropped within the first week and took up to five weeks to return to normal. Stock in all parts of the supply chain increased, sometimes to 10 times normal levels.

The supply was very dependent on the accuracy of the forecast, yet little cross-functional work was done between the various decision-makers to maximize the use of the information available in the system.

FIGURE 16.4 Typical Waste Pattern During a Promotion

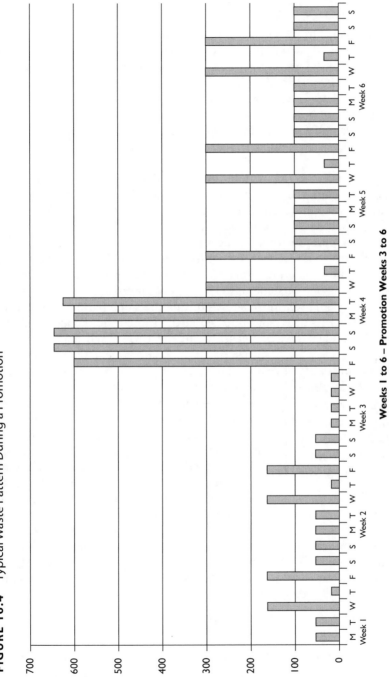

For example, the first day's sales was a reasonable indicator for the whole 4-week period. Adjusting for the normal weekly pattern where, for instance, Monday's sales are roughly 10 per cent of the week's sales, a weekly forecast based on the first day's sales would have been within +/- 20 per cent, in 95 per cent of cases, for the 4-week promotional period. This should be compared to an accuracy level +/- 20 per cent for only 24 per cent of the promoted items made by the stock controllers and worse than +/- 100 per cent for 20 per cent of the forecasts. Forecasts based on the first day's sales were possible because the weekly variation of sales during a promotion was of a similar level to that when prices are stable. For over half (55 per cent) the promotions, the first week's sales were within +/- 3 per cent of the average for the four weeks and 80 per cent were within +/- 5 per cent.

Thus, the sample results suggested that, while the accuracy of forecast was poor, the sales during the promotion followed the same weekly pattern as a non-promotion period. Following on from that, the first day's sales could be (but were not) used to forecast the remainder of the promotional period with some accuracy. There was also strong evidence of the Forrester Effect that in turn led to a certain degree of overstocking.

All the promotions were for a fixed number of week periods starting and ending on the same day. There were approximately 1800 other promotions being run in the stores during the same period, the vast majority of which started and finished at the same time. Foodco has over 10 million square feet of sales area in the UK, spread amongst over 500 stores. Half of these are large, modern, single-storey superstores, stocking all the main products, and benefitting from their own car parking. A typical large store would have in excess of 25000 square feet of sales area and stock approximately 22000 stock keeping units (SKU's). A number of other smaller store formats are also used by Foodco, with a more limited SKU range. There is a wide range of store sizes, which meant that not all the stores stocked the same ranges. However, during a promotion, the individual store manager was allowed to bring into his range any item that was on promotion. This in turn meant that the forecasters did not know how many stores would be stocking the promoted item – not a major problem for a popular line that would be stocked by nearly all the stores throughout the year, but a major one for the less popular item that was normally stocked by, say, only half the stores.

While the accuracy of forecast was poor, the sales during the promotion followed the same weekly pattern as a non-promotion period.

Process Analysis

The main finding from the mapping process was that, despite Foodco's advances in the use of EDI for information (or more accurately data) transmission, and their wholehearted support for the concept of working in partnership with suppliers, the quality of the information flow at the time of the research in 1995 showed considerable room for improvement. The informal systems in place did allow for a fast flow of relevant data, but advantage was rarely taken of this facility. The major breakdown in communications was normally between the retailer and his suppliers but there were also major barriers between the stock controllers and the stores. Part of the problem within the retailer was the functional outlook taken by most of the key players, although there were increasing attempts to tackle many of the problems cross-functionally (Kurogane, 1993). An example of the poor quality of information flow was that the forecasters at the suppliers complained that they did not receive promotion forecast updates from Foodco despite the fact that Foodco sent weekly updates to the suppliers. Unfortunately, these forecasts normally went to the account manager who did not pass them on to the people responsible for forecasting. This was true of all four suppliers.

A promotion was normally agreed eight weeks in advance between the account manager of the supplier and the buyer from the relevant product group from Foodco. However, the level of in-house promotion activity took up to another two weeks to agree. Apart from the very few promotions that were featured in Foodco advertising, the most important in-house activity was the use of 'gondola ends'. These were the shelves or cabinets at the end of each aisle that were used to feature the 'best' promotion. This normally gave the item two separate locations in the store, the end-of-aisle one being considered a prime position. The use of a 'gondola end' could more than double the sales expected of a normal promotion.

Also, despite generally fixing promotions six weeks in advance, little attempt was made to gather the views from the stores as to how well the promotion would go. This was particularly important for those items that were not normally sold in all stores, as store managers were in the habit of ordering these out-of-range items when the promotion offered a significant discount. Many of these lower volume items could enjoy an uplift of 1000 per cent during a promotion and so any inaccuracies in forecast could have serious effects on the supply chain.

The main problems for both the retailer and the suppliers of the various promotions were the amount of management time taken up by promotions and the increased possibility both of running out of stock and of overstocking, which was particularly relevant with short-shelf-life products.

However, despite the fact that the retailer tried to measure nearly every activity and characteristic of his operation, he had no way to quantify the effects of these problems using existing data.

Characteristics of a Promotion

Combining the qualitative and quantitative data, a model was built (The Doomsday Scenario) highlighting the major characteristics of a promotion that could have an adverse effect on the supply chain.

1. Special Pack

Where a packaging design created specially for the promotion was used, this caused problems for the supplier, especially if his own process time was long. As a result of the lead time in obtaining the packaging, he normally had to commit himself to a specific quantity before the promotion started. This led to waste of unused packaging, stock-outs where the promotion exceeded forecasts and surplus stock at the supplier if the forecast was over-optimistic (Coca-Cola Retailing Research Group, 1994).

2. Very Good Offer

Where the price reduction is great, this will, as expected, produce a bigger uplift. Unless the same or a very similar offer has been made before, it makes the forecasting more difficult. Also, the major increase in produc-

TABLE 16.1 The Doomsday Scenario

	Characteristic	Effect on Promotion
1	Special Pack	Problem for supplier in forecasting demand for packaging
2	Very Good Offer	Uplift likely to be high, less predictable
3	Slow Seller	Uplift likely to be high, less predictable, possible problem with supplier's capacity
4	Impulse Product	Difficult to forecast
5	Short Shelf Life	Excessive waste if forecast inaccurate
6	Chosen for Gondola End	Increases uplift but also the difficulty of forecasting
7	Product is Physically Small	If put on gondola ends, needs a high initial stock
8	Not Generally Listed	Difficult to forecast
9	Appeals to Store Managers	Out-of-range demand, extra in-store activity
10	Featured on TV Advertising	Can create significant extra demand causing forecast difficulties
11	Long Lead Time from Supplier	Cannot react quickly to demand in excess of forecast without stockholding

tion required can cause problems for the supplier: 'In a normal workplace, the more the flow of things varies, the greater the incidence of creating waste' (*Just-In Time at Toyota*, Ohno and Mito, 1986).

3. Slow Seller

If the product is normally a slow seller and it has an attractive offer, this will cause forecasting problems. A slow seller will not normally be listed in all the stores. An attractive offer will encourage other stores to take it for the duration of the promotion although the initial forecasts can only guess at how many. A further problem caused by stores taking products not listed for them is that they have no history to use in placing their initial orders. On many occasions they have grossly over ordered, causing even more fluctuations in the supply chain.

4. Impulse Product

Again there is great difficulty in forecasting these products. The uplift can be potentially high but a lot will depend on the manner in which they are displayed in the stores, something that is down to the initiative of the store personnel. By its very nature, the location of an impulse product will have a great effect on its sales.

5. Short-Shelf-Life Product

Any forecasting errors on the optimistic side will result in increased wastage. High uplift and use of gondola end will increase this problem.

6. Chosen For Gondola End

This automatically increases the potential uplift by having two locations in the store, one of which is considered a prime position. It also increases the initial order through the supply chain in order to fill the extra shelf space allocated to the product. A further potential forecasting problem is introduced as the initial forecasts are made with the knowledge of the gondola end decision. However, stores are only advised on the products to go on the gondola ends, and do not have to abide by the plans. From the survey, 90+ per cent do place the product on gondola end if advised, but it does not always get the planned amount of shelf space.

7. Physically Small Product

If the product is chosen for a Gondola End, it may require possibly two or three weeks stock just to fill the location. This in turn causes a major disruption in the supply chain.

8. Not Generally Listed

If the offer is attractive, many stores may take it although not listed for it. This causes major forecasting problems.

9. Appeals To Store Managers

Store managers have a great deal of discretion over what products they will stock and promote. If the offer appeals to the store managers they may take it even though it is not listed for their store. They can give it a prominent position in the store and they may even over-order so that they can carry on the promotion after the end of the official promotion period. All of this can upset the accuracy of the initial forecasts.

10. Featured On TV Advertising

If the retailer is featuring the promotion in his national campaigns, this can cause a major uplift in the promotional sales. Unfortunately, the stores and the forecasters are not always informed. Thus the original forecast may not include the possible effect of the advertising and/or the stores may not take it into consideration when making the initial orders, leading to stock-outs.

11. Long Lead Time From The Supplier

Where a supplier cannot react quickly to unforeseen changes in demand, he is forced to build up stock in anticipation. Provided there is not a shelf-life problem, he will normal try to ensure that he does not run out by overproducing against forecast. Thus we have amplified the fluctuations in the supply chain initially caused by the promotion. The supplier will normally finish the promotional period with surplus stock that may take weeks to run down or may require re-packing. This not only upsets the normal loading on his production facility, but is passed up the supply chain to his own suppliers.

Thus the characteristics of the promotion can have a significant influence on the efficiency of the promotional process. The larger the uplift, the greater can be the disruption to the supply chain with stocks being built up in advance and overall production levels being affected. Inaccuracies in the forecast can lead to either overstocking or stock-outs. Again, suppliers might tend to overstock to ensure that they did not run out of stock, thus amplifying the disruptions to the supply chain. Where the lead time to react to changes is slow, as in the case of special packaging, the supplier will often have to rely solely on the original forecast and will be unable to adjust with the benefit of feedback from the first few days of the promotion.

Conclusions

Promotions cause disruptions in the supply chain. The characteristics of the promotion can amplify these disruptions. The major problem areas, at least to supply chain management, are the level of the uplift and the uncertainty of the forecasts. While a high uplift can be planned for, it is the uncertainty that causes the problem. Unfortunately, the higher the uplift, the greater are the disruptions caused by the forecasting errors.

Promotions cause disruptions in the supply chain.

Good communications between the key players in the process is vital. Involvement and feedback of the latest information and planned actions can do much to mitigate the effects of the inability to forecast accurately. At present promotions are planned by the sales and marketing functions and treated as a necessary evil by the supply chain management. Recognizing the waste involved to the supply chain from promotions, involving key functions in the initial planning stages and in the design of the process itself should help reduce this waste. The current process at Foodco and, according to the four suppliers, also at the other major retailers is one in which each function carries out 'their bit' and then passes it on to the next function.

Further Research

Many possible solutions to the problem of reducing the waste caused by the promotional process can be developed from the current research findings (Figure 16.5). Each of these possible solutions would require further empirical testing and research. These could be divided into *three* separate sections:

1. *Improve the forecasting* – at present this is carried out both by stock controllers at the retailer and forecasters at the suppliers, normally on the basis of past demand and an educated guess as to the effect of the promotional offer. No attempt is made to involve two of the key decision-makers in the process, the stores and the customer. In the case of the stores, they could be asked to forecast their ordering on depots three or four weeks in advance of the promotion. This would allow 500 experienced managers to have an input into those promotions considered to be potentially volatile. It would also feed back the information on those stores planning to take non-listed items. In the case of the customers, trial promotions could be run for two or three days in a selected group of stores, four weeks before the promotional period. Care would be needed with seasonal lines, but, with the right choice of representative stores, these trial promotions might succeed in giving a more accurate forecast for a wide range of different promotions.

FIGURE 16.5 Relationship Between Observations, Conclusions and Recommendations

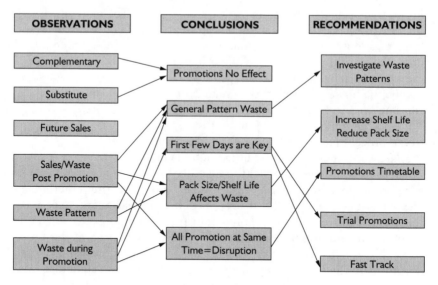

2. *Improve the supply chain's ability to react to changes* – obviously, the more accurate the forecasting, the smaller the changes in demand against forecast. However, we should attempt to reduce the reliance of the supply chain on forecasting. The system is most vulnerable in the first few days of a promotion and this is the area we should concentrate on. A feasibility study could examine a 'fast track' process for the first week of a promotion. This would involve reduced lead times from the supplier and feedback of sales data based on the first half-day's trading figures.

3. *Improve the promotions process* – the current process involves decisions and information passing between functional units, each with their own set of objectives. A pilot study could be set up to explore the practicality of a cross-functional promotions management team involving key decision-makers from both the retailer and the supplier. The first team would probably involve two or three suppliers with similar product offerings. The purpose of the team would be to look at the most efficient ways of running the process and implementing the necessary changes without the necessity of considering functional objectives.

While this research has basically involved a specific case study, we believe that the findings and the further research suggested both have applicability to other similar supply chains.

CHAPTER 17

Managing New Product Introduction and New Product Development[1]

Traditionally, new product development has been viewed as a discrete activity carried out within the design department being controlled either by designers' technological skills (technology push) or market needs (market pull). However, the view taken within the SCDP programme was that new product development is, for most companies, a key intra- or inter-company process that must be measured, improved and managed in much the same way as other key processes, such as the order fulfilment process that the majority of this book is concerned with.

Much of the classic marketing focused new product development literature with its standard innovation stage models, such as those provided by Kotler (1986), have been bypassed in the work demonstrated here. However, on the basis of past practical experience in developing new products, a number of key principles have been found to run through successful projects (Hines, 1994; Dimancescu and Dwenger, 1996; Dimancescu *et al.*, 1997). These principles are:

- a three-tier, process-based strategy/process/actioning structure (like the one described at RS Components in Chapter 13);
- cross-company teaming;
- performance metrics;
- rewards and recognition;
- suppliers as partners;
- three-track technology management (corporate (10 year), group (3–5 year) and business unit (3 year));
- relationship mapping;
- capturing the voice of the customer;

[1] Prepared by Peter Hines, Ann Esain, Mark Francis and Owen Jones.

- rigorous gates and design reviews;
- shared knowledge systems.

A review of some of the world's leading product developers, such as Hewlett Packard and Sony carried out by Dimancescu and Dwenger (1996) found that those firms that had a deliberate policy of spending considerable time before the traditional product development cycle occurred on pre-planning or developing the pre-concept were particularly successful in bringing high-rate success products to market rapidly. Two other major factors were also identified among these best-in-class companies. These were that there was an early involvement of downstream players (such as purchasing) and that considerable R&D activity was undertaken off-line. These points are illustrated in Figure 17.1.

> **For many of the SCDP companies there was not a single clear design or introduction process.**

However, early within the research process, when looking at what was initially termed 'new product introduction' (Esain and Hines, 1997), it soon became obvious that for many of the SCDP companies there was not a single clear design or introduction process. Indeed, in many of the firms taking part three distinct processes could be identified within this general area, which can be defined generically.

1. *New Product Introduction (NPI)*: where either a very slight variant of an existing product was being brought to market (for instance, an own label food product introduced to a second supermarket company where only the label was being changed) or where an already developed product was being brought to market (as in the case of 'black box'-designed and manufacturer-branded products being offered to a supermarket).

FIGURE 17.1 Key Aspects of Production Development

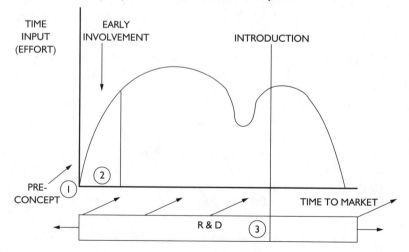

2. *New Product Development (NPD)*: where a truly new product was being conceived, designed and developed for the market.
3. *Research and Development (R&D)*: where new technologies were being developed, not for a particular new product, but on the basis that they can later be incorporated into a future new product and its consequent new product development process.

The interrelationship of these different processes are best illustrated within the traditional product life-cycle in what became known as the 'Batman' diagram (Figure 17.2). The diagram illustrates the way in which before product launch the product is developed (New Product Development, NPD), then introduced to the market (New Product Introduction, NPI), sold in large quantities (Order Fulfilment, OF) and then the remainder of stock or redundant inventory is sold or disposed of before sales cease (Old Product Retirement, OPR). Running in parallel with the three selling processes (NPI, OF and OPR) is a possible extra process, namely Promotion, with a tendency to increase sales when the product under consideration is promoted (or when complementary products are promoted), or to decrease sales when competing products are promoted. The promotions process was the subject of the last chapter. In addition to this, the Research and Development process continues on regardless of the particular life-cycles of individual products.

FIGURE 17.2 Key Business Processes Within Product Life-Cycle (the Batman Diagram)

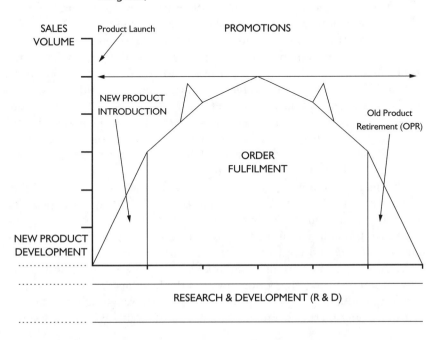

As this area of product introduction and development received a relatively small research time budget compared to other areas, this chapter will present a series of theoretical and practical applications that will be the subject of further development and refinement by the Cardiff team in subsequent research programmes. However, this chapter will first describe work concerned with the New Product Development (NPI) process and will then present a conceptual model of how the original mapping approach may be used within New Product Development (NPD) more generally.

New Product Introduction

The first work carried in this area was a result of a concern raised by one of the SCDP sponsors, RS Components, who at the time had an unacceptable level of redundant stock, primarily as a result of the New Product Introduction process not working as well as it might. This problem was reducing the effectiveness of an otherwise highly successful company. In addition, although the problem was not causing great difficulty, it was felt that, since the number of products being introduced was rising rapidly, any problem that did exist would multiply further if it was not cured. In this case, although the symptoms of the problem was manifested within the Old Product Retirement (OPR) process, the problems lay more, in the way it introduced products, as will be discussed below.

The product life-cycle of the failing products is shown in Figure 17.3. As can be seen, this life-cycle starts with a marketing function involving the decision whether the product should be selected for catalogue sale. Then follows the purchasing function of price negotiation, estimation of sales and order placement. The latter stages of the cycle involve the control of inventory during the early sales period and ongoing re-purchase period. However, often the problem of market failure could not be seen until near the end of this cycle when the product, by definition, was overstocked. In terms of the processes described above in Figure 17.2, this cycle could be seen as New Product Introduction up to the start of sales, Order Fulfilment during the period when the product was not remaindered and Old Product Retirement thereafter.

If this life-cycle is analyzed crudely to show where the cost of this overstocking is incurring, some estimation can be made of the point at which it would be most sensible to try to reduce the number and consequence of the failures. In order to do this a Cost of Quality approach is employed (Dale and Plunkett, 1991; Grimm, 1981). As shown in Figure 17.4, the first four stages, up to and including sales estimation, are in the 'prevention zone', i.e. the period in which the firm has the opportunity to prevent products that will ultimately fail from reaching the market. During this period the cost incurred in the product life-cycle is very small

FIGURE 17.3   Product Life-Cycle of Failed Products

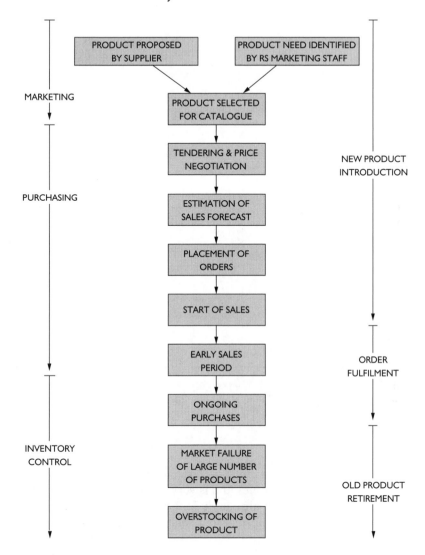

for the catalogue company as it has only really incurred staff time for marketing and purchasing people. However, once it places orders, the consequential costs rise rapidly as the company is committed to a certain amount of stock. Thus, here there is a *step-change* in committed cost. During this time-period and up to and including the early sales period, the firm can be considered to be in a period of Appraisal as this is the time when the company is appraising whether the product will ultimately succeed or not. While committed costs are high here, they are not as high as in the 'failure zone'.

FIGURE 17.4   The Cost of Market Failure

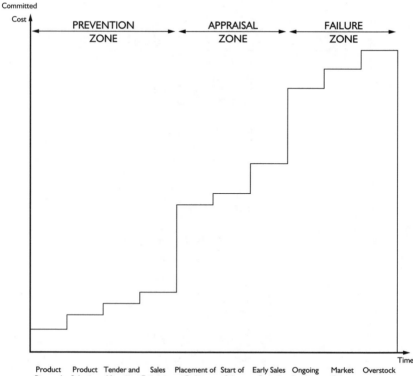

The 'failure zone' of ongoing purchase, market failure and overstocking is the last of the three zones and is very costly to enter. Reaching this zone for products that will ultimately fail should clearly be avoided if at all possible. However, the most serious waste is where a product that will ultimately fail is reordered, and it is at this point that the second major *cost step-change* occurs.

In order to look a little more closely at the causes of these failures, a cause-and-effect diagram or fishbone analysis was used (Bicheno, 1994) as shown in Figure 17.5. As can be seen from Figure 17.5, the 'effect' here is excess of redundant new product stocks. The 'causes' of this failure can be estimated to lie in one of four areas, namely, the prevention, appraisal or failure zones or as a result of a lack of integration between the different functions involved in the process. In each case, a brainstorm activity yielded the potential reasons within each of the cause areas. Examples of these possible causes include: a 'lack of market understanding' in the prevention zone; 'no early sales feedback' in the appraisal zone; 'supplier will

FIGURE 17.5 The Causes of Market Failure

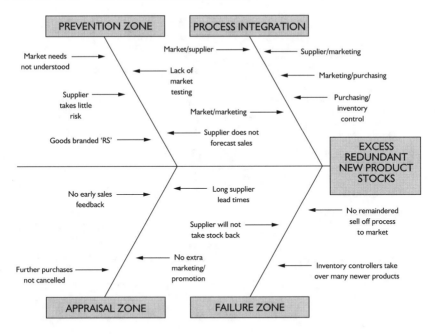

not take back redundant stock' in the failure zone; and a 'lack of integration between marketing and purchasing' in the process integration area. At this point the potential causes of failure were discussed with the company so that an estimation could be made of which of these causes was the most serious.

Subsequent to this, a counterpart solutions analysis was conducted by reversing the cause and effect analysis shown in Figure 17.5. Thus, in Figure 17.6 the 'effect' of excess redundant new product stock is linked to a number of potential 'solutions' to the problem. To illustrate this, in the prevention zone one method that could be used to reduce failure and particularly to understand the market better is the use of 'Quality Function Deployment' (Hines, 1994) where the needs of the customer are translated into effective product offerings. As mentioned above, if problems can be caught at this early stage then the consequential costs are very low.

An example of a method that would make improvements in the appraisal zone is the 'introduction of an early feedback loop' to analyze sales patterns within the early sales period. Although some costs would have been incurred here, this early feedback would prevent more product being ordered and so incurring more cost. Although, strictly speaking, not itself an appraisal method, the 'reduction of supplier lead time' fits into this zone, as a shorter supplier lead time would allow more time for appraisal before subsequent orders are placed and so would help minimize the ordering of extra stocks of products that will ultimately fail.

FIGURE 17.6 The Solutions to Market Failure

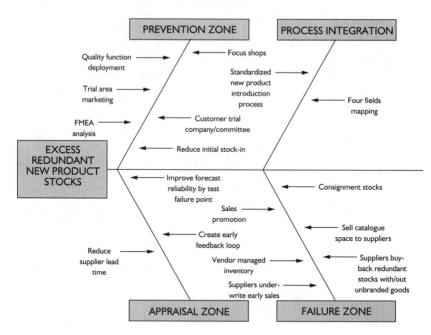

Once a product has reached the failure zone, most or all of the costs have been incurred and the worst of the damage done. Any actions in this area are reactive to a problem that has already happened. This means that working in this zone is often highly demoralizing for the people involved as they 'clear up someone else's problem'. However, if a product does enter this zone, a number of choices of method are available including the 'supplier underwriting early sales' or 'promoting the redundant stock' to sell out the excess.

The last of the four solution areas was the 'process integration' area. Within this there were two suggested activities: the first was 'the use of mapping methods' in order to visualize the product life-cycle; and the second the 'introduction of a standard new product introduction process'. For each of the solutions further analysis was used to estimate the difficulty, timescale, likely success rate as well as who would have to take part. As this data is company-specific and sensitive it will not be presented here. However, after a period of reflection, the company decided to map out the product introduction process in order to develop a standardized process using a cross-functional team over a short period of time in what was seen as a relatively easy activity. This activity was facilitated by a member of the Cardiff team and built on the firm's early experience of Value Stream Mapping activity described in an earlier chapter. This approach, the company decided, would give them the facts with which to make any further improvement decisions.

Mapping the New Product Introduction Process

A cross-functional team at RS Components was brought together in late 1997 under the project coordination of Nikki Rainey who had been involved in the early Value Stream Mapping of the Supplier Integration process. The objectives were:

1. to analyze and review the current New Product Introduction processes identifying key areas of value/non-value-adding activities, delay areas in process and opportunities for improvement;

2. to design a common New Product Introduction Process which could logistically cope with the increased volume of products being introduced and ensure that all products identified for the catalogue are available for Day 1 sale;

3. to ensure that the processes designed to achieve the above objectives also reduce the overall NPI cycle time, optimize resource and incorporate purchasing best practice.

In order to do this, a variant of Process Activity Mapping (Hines and Rich, 1997) was employed, termed here 'Information Flow Mapping', which was similar in nature to the method discussed in Chapter 4 on Mapping Information Flows. However, each activity was split into four types: waiting, communication, operation and decision, with actual time recorded against each of these. The times for each of these activities at the time of mapping are recorded on an index basis in Table 17.1. As might be expected for an information-flow mapping exercise, around 99 per cent of the time is recorded as waiting, with only a small amount within operation, communication or decision-making. The full details of this activity were recorded on a large flow diagram.

Once this had been done, the investigating team sought to identify improvement possibilities, of which three were chosen. Again the details of these improvements are company-specific and sensitive. However, to summarize, it was identified that there were two types of new product introduction. The first of these started with a new product offering from a supplier and the second from a point where the product had already been

TABLE 17.1 Current New Product Introduction

ACTIVITY	NUMBER OF STEPS	TIME (100 = INDEX) %
OPERATION	24	0.59
COMMUNICATION	9	0.03
WAITING	21	99.11
DECISION	2	0.28
TOTAL	56	100

quoted for. The benefits in terms of time reduction that could be produced from these activities are recorded in Tables 17.2 and 17.3. In the case of a totally new product, a new standardized process could cut introduction time by a third, and for a previously quoted product the time reduction could be over half. This order of change will have a significant effect on the ability of RS Components to respond to customers, reduce unnecessary inventory and remove wasted time, effort and cost. As a result it will allow the company, in effect to introduce increased volumes of new products into the business while maintaining visibility of the product status at all times.

New Product Development

The practical programme with RS Component described above proved the benefits of applying a version of Value Stream Mapping to the New Product Introduction process. However, the research team also felt that it would be appropriate when applied to the broader New Product Development process. However, the work within this area was undertaken only over the end stages of SCDP, and so the following section only presents a

TABLE 17.2 Proposed Process For New Products

ACTIVITY	NUMBER OF STEPS	TIME (100 = CURRENT TOTAL TIME) %
OPERATION	15	0.37
COMMUNICATION	12	0.03
WAITING	12	67.21
DECISION	4	0.28
TOTAL	43	67.89

TABLE 17.3 Proposed Process For Products Previously Quoted For

ACTIVITY	NUMBER OF STEPS	TIME (100 = CURRENT TOTAL TIME) %
OPERATION	13	0.31
COMMUNICATION	8	0.01
WAITING	8	45.99
DECISION	3	0.22
TOTAL	32	46.53

theoretical reworking of the Value Stream Mapping approach.[1] Further practical testing of the method is being undertaken within the Lean Processing Programme (LEAP), a programme based at Cardiff addressing the 'leaning' of the upstream automotive industry (Hines *et al.*, 1998).

For four of these maps the original Value Stream Mapping method translates directly: Process Activity Mapping, Quality Filter, Demand Amplification and Decision Point Analysis. For further details of these tools the reader should refer to Chapter 2. In addition, two further maps – Value Analysis Time Profile and the Relationship Map – are drawn from further development of the original Value Stream Mapping tools that was undertaken within the LEAP programme (Hines *et al.*, 1998). This leaves a further five maps that have been designed specifically for the New Product Development Process, namely: New Product Development Responsiveness, Product In Process Funnel, Human Structure Mapping, Skills Constraint Funnel and the Committed Design Cost Curve. Each of the latter seven maps will be briefly discussed in turn.

The first of these is the Value Analysis Time Profile (VATP). The method is partly derived from the Cost-Time Profiles used by Westinghouse (Bicheno, 1994; Fooks, 1993), but develops this company-specific approach further to include an analysis of the relative waste and value

TABLE 17.4 Maps For New Product Development

No.	Map	Original Value Stream Map	Extended Value Stream Map	Additional NPD Map
1.	Process Activity Mapping	✔		
2.	New Product Development Responsiveness			✔
3.	Product In Process Funnel			✔
4.	Quality Filter	✔		
5.	Demand Amplification	✔		
6.	Decision Point Analysis	✔		
7.	Human Structure Mapping			✔
8.	Value Analysis Time Profile		✔	
9.	Skills Constraint Funnel			✔
10.	Committed Design Cost Curve			✔
11.	Relationship Map		✔	

[2] The theoretical perspective here was developed together with Donna Samuel of the Cardiff Lean Enterprise Research Centre and James Sullivan of British Steel Strip Products.

content of the total cost of product development over time. This new tool as illustrated in Figure 17.7 (in this case in an order fulfilment setting) is a time-based value analysis tool which allows for the plotting of both the total cost and value as a product moves along the process under consideration (Hines *et al.*, 1998).

In Figure 17.7, a hypothetical pressings industry case, the raw material and components are bought in at value 'a' (here assuming that there is no waste upstream of the firm concerned: an area that would be checked if the supplier integration process was also being mapped). During the various value-adding steps its value is raised (for instance during the value-adding parts of the blanking, pressing and assembly activity) from 'a' to total value 'b' over the period it is in the company. However, during this same period its cost has risen further from point 'a' to 'c'. The cost

FIGURE 17.7 Value Analysis Time Profile

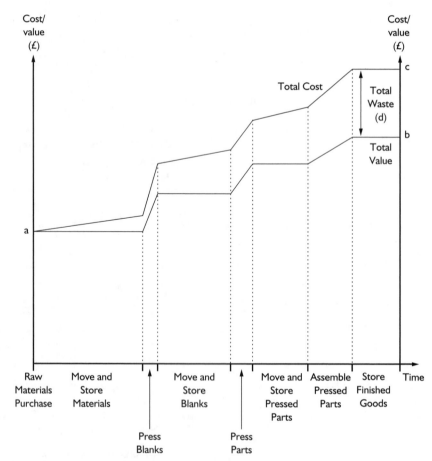

SOURCE: Hines *et al.* (1998).

(which may bear little relation to the selling price) that has been added reflects both value added and the waste. In this example waste is added during the various non-value-adding steps of movement, storage and the setting-up of the various processing machines. The total waste in this case is the distance 'd'. The tool therefore allows the researcher to get a very good idea of where waste is being added over time and helps pinpoint (if, for instance, linked to Pareto analysis) where major improvement efforts might effectively be focused. In addition it is also helpful in showing where time may be reduced for the various activities charted on the horizontal axis, providing a simple-to-understand time-compression tool.

The second of the new extended Value Stream Mapping tools is the Relationship Mapping. This map simply charts the major interactions and relationships between the different departments or sub-areas within the process being mapped. It is a widely used method, but in this case the approach adopted by Alber and Walker is being followed (Alber and Walker, 1997). Figure 17.8 gives a simple example of the use of this approach for the order fulfilment process. In this case, details are shown of the internal part of the process with the relevant links to suppliers and customers. In many cases the method is extended to include the relevant members or departments within other companies within the Value Stream. The method is quick to undertake and provides a useful insight into the existing relationships, forming a firm basis for understanding which of these are working well, whether there are too many or too few

FIGURE 17.8 Relationship Map

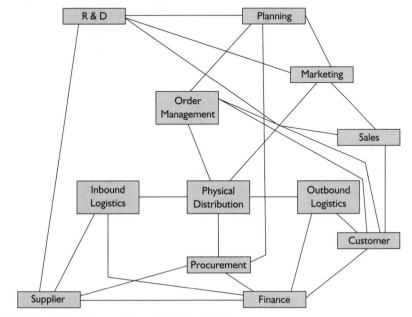

SOURCE: Adapted from Alber and Walker (1997).

FIGURE 17.9 New Product Development Responsiveness

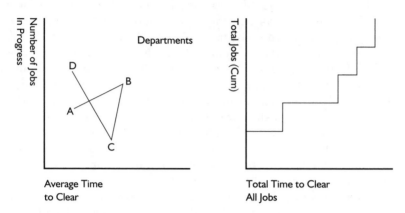

relationships and perhaps who is likely to champion change or obstruct it.

The first of the additional New Product Development maps is the New Product Development Responsiveness map illustrated in Figure 17.9. This map has two parts to it. In the first part (left-hand side) the number of new product development jobs in progress are plotted against the average time taken to clear a job through a particular department. Thus, the number of jobs and time through department A are small and short respectively. In contrast, the opposite is true for department B, showing that this department is a bottleneck. Department C, in contrast again, although taking a long time to clear jobs, does not have a great number of jobs in progress at any one time, with department D having a short clearance time but many jobs in progress. Clearly, when this information is

FIGURE 17.10 Product in Process Funnel

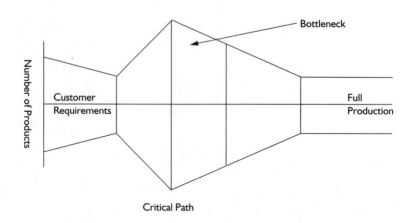

mapped, individual bottlenecks and excessive work-in-progress quantities can easily be identified and the bottlenecks removed or at least planned around.

The left-hand side of Figure 17.9 shows the total number of cumulative jobs plotted against the total time to clear all jobs through different departments. It therefore acts in a similar way to the Supply Chain Responsiveness map (see Chapter 2) by helping to identify where large portions of inventory (total jobs) and lead time (total time to clear jobs) can be removed. The Product In Process Funnel (Figure 17.10) is used in a very similar way to the Product Variety Funnel (see Chapter 2), inasmuch as it maps the number of products being developed over time and where they stand in the different new product development steps. It is also useful in identifying where bottlenecks are occurring along the critical path.

Human Structure Mapping is broadly derived from Physical Structure Mapping (see Chapter 2). In the left-hand side of Figure 17.11, the number of people is mapped for different departments or design stages (either in one, or a series of companies). In addition the map records how many of these are direct workers (those directly working or operating on the new product development) and how many are indirect or support workers (such as secretarial support). The right-hand figure translates the cost of these direct and indirect human resources into cash terms. The tool in its totality is, therefore, useful in measuring productivity of labour, and also helps in discussions of the appropriate percentage split between direct and indirect workers through the new product development process.

The Committed Cost Curve approach has already been used in the above section on the new product introduction process at RS Components with an estimated curve shown in Figure 17.4. The method as shown in Figure 17.12 has two dimensions. The first is a map of the cost of the design process over the whole new product development cycle. This is the lower dome-shaped curve. The second is the committed cost curve which,

FIGURE 17.11   Human Structure Mapping

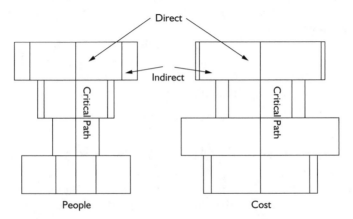

FIGURE 17.12 Committed Cost Curve

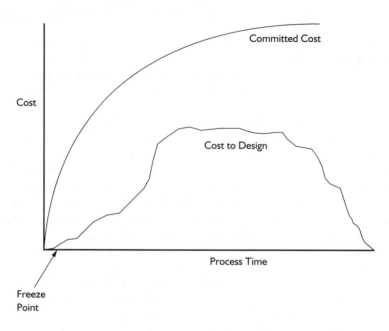

as can be seen in Figure 17.12, rises far more quickly than the cost to design curve. Although this feature is well known in the design literature, it almost always comes as a surprise when mapped for a particular company. One of the lessons that this approach helps to teach is that early involvement of downstream activities (such as purchasing) is vital, as inadequate up-front planning can rarely be corrected later.

The last of the new maps is the Skills Constraint Funnel illustrated in Figure 17.13. This approach maps the number of skilled people along the critical process sequence so that skill gaps or requirements for multi-skilling can be identified. This is of particular use when used in combination with the Product In Process Funnel, as it may help to explain process bottlenecks.

The value of this total 11-piece toolkit is not in using one tool on its own but, like the original Value Stream Mapping approach discussed in Chapter 2, it is the combination of tools that helps triangulate and validate where waste exists and highlights where improvement efforts should be concentrated.

Conclusions and Further Work Agenda

This chapter has sought to demonstrate how the Value Stream Mapping approach may be extended to the new product development area. In

FIGURE 17.13   Skills Constraint Funnel

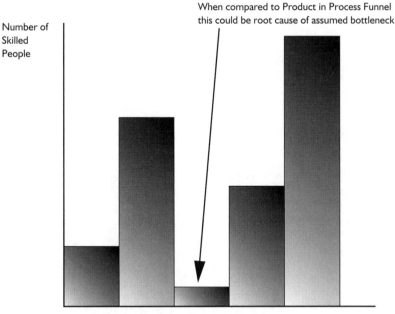

doing this, a distinction has been drawn between several different, but related, processes within the broad design area. In particular, attention has been focused on the New Product Introduction and New Product Development processes.

Various approaches to reviewing the New Product Introduction process were illustrated in a practical way using the example of the work within SCDP with RS Components. The methods employed included the use of Cost of Quality, Cause, Effect and Solution Analysis and Information Flow Mapping. The use of these methods helped the company to devise a radical breakthrough programme within the NPI area.

The use of these methods helped the company to devise a radical breakthrough programme within the NPI area.

The second half of the chapter demonstrated in a theoretical way the tools that may be used to apply the general Value Stream Mapping approach within the New Product Development process. The 11-strong toolkit is either directly drawn from the existing Value Stream Mapping toolkit, the extended approach that has been developed elsewhere, or are modifications to the existing toolkit or new additions specific to New Product Development. While it is believed that this new toolkit can be of great value in reviewing the NPD process, the tools still require further testing and practical validation.

CHAPTER 18

Managing Distribution Within the Value Stream[1]

Introduction

Distribution systems transmit demand information from an end customer to supplier, and in response deliver products from the supplier, usually via intermediaries, to the end customer. This chapter uses *case study material* correlated to a *conceptual framework* to define the key concepts of *Lean Distribution* in the *Value Stream*.

Case Study Material

The main source of primary research data are distribution organizations in the Supply Chain Development Programme. In considering how typical a view of distribution these cases provided, their maturity was considered in the context of culture for change. Hammer and Champy (1993) describe three modes of change motivation:

> First are companies that find themselves in deep trouble. They have no choice …
> Second … are not yet in trouble but … see trouble coming
> Third … are in peak condition … they seek to raise the competitive bar and make life even tougher for everyone else

Distribution systems transmit demand information from an end customer to supplier, and in response deliver products from the supplier, usually via intermediaries, to the end customer.

On this continuum of distribution change achievement, the Supply Chain Development Programme (SCDP) cases lie in the

[1] Prepared by David Simons.

second and third modes. To achieve a balanced analysis, covering all three types of organization, further examples are drawn from an After-Sales study conducted as part of the International Car Distribution Programme (ICDP) (Kiff *et al.*, 1998). This study benchmarked the main automotive manufacturers parts supply systems in four European markets, and simulated the effectiveness of their distribution systems.

The cases described in three sections of this chapter are:

- *Automotive After Sales* based on Unipart from SCDP and a number of car manufacturers from ICDP;
- *Fast Moving Consumer Goods* based on Tesco from SCDP;
- *Chilled Ready Meals* a Value Stream Mapping (Hines and Rich, 1997) study from supplier to retail shelf.

Information and Physical Flow in the Value Stream

Throughout this chapter, information and physical flows are linked to the phenomena of demand amplification. The link between the respective flows and the two fundamental demand amplification effects ('Burbidge' and 'Forrester') are described below:

- Information discussion focuses on the characteristics of end customer demand, and how transmission of these characteristics are distorted by the process of single company demand noise or 'Burbidge Effect', described by Naim (1997) as 'The Burbidge Effect ... relates to operational decisions ...with regard to schedules, batching policies, order priorities'.
- Physical flow discussion looks at overall distribution structures, and their constituent parts, principally storage and transport. Demand amplification is discussed in the wider inter-company context of the 'Forrester Effect', described by Naim (1997) as 'The Forrester Effect ... relates to the structural dynamics of the supply chain and is caused by planning policies ... stock holding requirements ...'.

Conceptual Framework for Value Stream Improvement

The conceptual framework, used to analyze the case study material emanates from a system dynamics paradigm. Naim and Towill (1994) identified supply chain strategies and measured their systemic effects on factory demand based on extensive research in the electronics, automotive and construction industries. The conceptual framework is a derivation of this work, which yields a sequence of *four* stages for supply chain improvement:

- *Control*: Ensure every replenishment decision in the supply chain is consistent in timing and logic. Improve the algorithm eliminating unnecessary safety stock. Apply standard operations to physical distribution.

- *Time*: Order more frequently, and remove delivery delays from the system.
- *Centralization*: Introduce visibility of stock throughout the supply chain. Rationalize ordering to one decision point, ideally at the production stage.
- *Structure*: Eliminate unnecessary echelons in the supply chain.

Automotive After-Sales

Automotive suppliers are selected during the new vehicle product development process on the basis of their capability to satisfy production criteria. As a result, the manufacturer's after-sales distribution system is often saddled with suppliers that have little flexibility for some producing volumes in the after-market. Supplier lead times are long requiring large stocks at central warehouses. As vehicle models are taken out of production, supplier batches tend to increase as after-sales then becomes the sole customer. For slower moving parts, batches frequently exceed the projected demand for the remaining vehicles on the road, requiring after-sales to make 'all time-buys' of several years stock.

Performance

RS Components (Dimancescu *et al.*, 1997) focus their service success on *order fill*. So if RS have a *line fill* of 99 per cent, this translates to 97 per cent (i.e. 99 per cent x 99 per cent x 99 per cent) for *order fill* if there are three products required. In automotive after-sales (Kiff *et al.*, 1998), all echelons of the supply chain have a 90 per cent plus key performance indicators based on *line fill*. However, customer vehicles on average need four parts per repair, resulting in *order fill* sometimes dipping below 70 per cent (this is not often measured though!).

Structure

To service this requirement, typically an automotive after-sales system has three echelons (Figure 18.3), a European Central Warehouse, a series of Regional Warehouses and a network of dealers.

Daily Ordering and Dealer Control

Most regional after-sales warehouses are some way through the process of moving from weekly to daily ordering. The associated physical response

FIGURE 18.1 European Automotive After-Sales Network

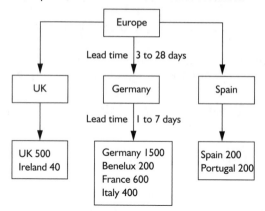

time to pick and deliver the order ranges from 1 to 3 days depending on the franchise. The research shows that those franchises that have moved to 1-day response time have much greater benefits in terms of stock levels, service levels and demand amplification.

By value, a third of stock is at central warehouses and half is at dealers' sites. The dealers have depth of stock with just 5 per cent of part numbers. At the central warehouse there are a set of experts monitoring and optimizing stock levels to maximize availability at least cost. At the dealer echelon, by contrast, there is a diversity of control. The best dealers manage stock in a similar way to the central warehouse, but there is then a continuum of deteriorating dealer stock management practices including:

- partial use of order opportunities;
- amendment of computer-generated orders on 'market hunches';
- economic order quantity (EOQ) mindset balancing transaction and holding costs.

Manufacturers in the UK have invested heavily in delivery lead *Time* cycle improvements. However, *30 per cent* of the benefits are lost due to the lack of dealer *control* described.

To overcome this issue of dealer control, one UK franchise has centralized stock control. A bespoke stock profile is created for each dealer based on the dealer's demand history, which is held centrally. Each day, stock is fed into dealers to top-up stock to the required profile. The warehouse has an accurate stock count in the whole market, allowing it to make responsive orders on its suppliers that reflects true demand.

Warehouse Operations

As part of the research, the seven manufacturing wastes of the Toyota production system (Shingo, 1989) were defined for a distribution envir-

TABLE 18.1 Seven Manufacturing Wastes of the Toyota Production System

Manufacturing definitions	Distribution definitions
Overproduction	Faster than necessary pace
Waiting	Waiting
Unnecessary motion	Unnecessary motion
Transport	Conveyance
Inappropriate processing	Processing
Defects	Correction of mistakes
Inventory	Excess stock

onment (Jones, 1995) and tested in an automotive warehouse (Simons *et al.*, 1997).

Overproduction is regarded as the most serious waste in manufacturing. *Faster than necessary pace* was found to correlate with this in distribution as analysis of the following wastes demonstrates:

- *Waiting*: Significant investment in information technology ensured rapid accurate transfer of order information. However, the waste of waiting was evident before and after many of these high velocity activities: Pick lists were transmitted and printed instantaneously, but then waited to go to the pick face until the printer table was full!

- *Faster than Necessary Pace* or 'Picking too Soon' was a result of releasing the orders from the system before a despatch vehicle was ready to be loaded. This increased the size of the physical buffer area needed for goods 'waiting' to be loaded. This, in turn, increased 'conveyance' distance from the pick face to the loading dock. Thus, picking operation control needs to be at a pace to suit waiting despatch vehicles, ultimately eliminating the double handling of a 'Goods Out' buffer. Warehouse employee bonuses (found in other non-automotive case studies) directed at pick rate were found to magnify this waste.

> *The information waiting waste was sometimes outweighed by reduction of the more significant waste of Faster than Necessary Pace.*

Thus the information *waiting* waste was sometimes outweighed by reduction of the more significant waste of *Faster than Necessary Pace*.

Fast-Moving Consumer Goods

In the early 1980s major grocery retailers such as Tesco and Sainsbury received supplies into small local warehouses or direct to store. In the mid-1980s these companies restructured their distribution chains, replacing local warehouses with much larger RDCs (Regional Distribution Centres) with approximately 10 throughout the UK per retailer. Since then suppliers have predominantly delivered to these hubs and the retailer consolidates loads into stores.

This change in distribution chain structure has been a key enabler to delivering phenomenal growth in volume for these major grocery chains. For Tesco throughput has increased from 76 million cases in 1983 to 813 million cases in 1996 (Booth, 1997), a compound annual increase of 20 per cent.

As part of this improvement process, stockholding and supplier lead times have dropped dramatically. This has allowed the retailers to replace depth of stock with breadth of stock.

There has clearly been a huge reduction in stock in the lower tiers of the distribution chain. However, there is evidence of some of this reduction being transferred up the distribution chain to supplier warehouses. As a result, major grocery manufacturers have invested in NDCs (National Distribution Centres) to channel products from different manufacturing locations. Britvic's decision to operate such an NDC was driven by its major grocery retailer customers service requirements (Green, 1997):

... daily deliveries to each of their RDCs ...
... all their products on a single vehicle ...
... delivery effectively within 24 hours ...

Applying the analogy of river flow (Womack *et al.*, 1990), the system stock can be represented as in Figure 18.2.

Most automotive systems deliver all products through the same distribution system. By contrast in FMCG (Fast Moving Consumer Goods), Tesco have two process routes:

- *Pick by store*, where product is put away and retrieved at RDC level.
- *Pick by line*, where product enters the RDC and is picked for store on the same day without being put away.

TABLE 18.2   Tesco

	Stock Depth (Weeks)	Stock Breadth (Lines)	Supplier Lead Time (Days)
1983	4.5	5,000	15
1990		15,000	8.5
1996	2.5	40,000	2

SOURCE: Tesco (Booth, 1997).

FIGURE 18.2   System Stock

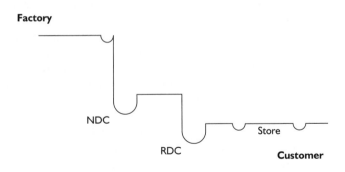

Information

Store data is collected electronically several times per day. Overnight, the store orders are created *centrally* using order rules tailored to each store. The stores are given a few hours to enter any amendments they require, usually due to system stocks not equating to actual stocks (reasons may include damage, shrinkage, etc.). Hence, FMCG unlike automotive, has consistent *control* of the ordering process.

The Tesco Information Exchange System (Galloway, 1998) is currently being introduced to improve information flows with suppliers. One of the functions of this system is to give real time sales and stock data by product line. Thus, a supplier can instantly see real time information to forecast demand and plan production. Tesco with their service supplier GE Systems, see the benefit of making this an industry standard allowing everybody to see vertically-orientated information but with strict control of horizontal information. Thus a branded producer will be able to see all subscribing retailers' data, but retailers will be barred from seeing each others' data.

Transport

Transport is a highly visible and expensive part of distribution. Vehicle capital and running costs make large vehicles most attractive. Most organizations have vehicle fleets consisting of tractor/trailers with a gross weight of 38 tonnes. In FMCG, this expensive asset is optimized using vehicle routings computer software to maximize vehicle fill and minimize distance travelled. However, because vehicles often return empty, the industry achieves only a 50 per cent fill rate overall.

Such focus on transportation for one perishable goods supplier meant that one day of shelf life was lost to optimize vehicle movements and fill. 'Factory A' finished production at midnight, shipped to 'Factory B', where product was consolidated at the expense of much double handling. The product did not start 'value-adding activity' (Monden, 1993) transport towards the customer until fourteen hours after being produced. Ironically, despite the outward optimization, the vehicles returned empty, except for return pallet bases.

The focus on transport optimization manifested itself in another practice. When the number of cages exceeded the vehicle floor area, non-fragile product was decanted from the excess cages and thrown on top of the load. On arrival at the destination retail store this resulted in double handling of the product and slower vehicle turnaround.

Optimization of transport invariably increase costs in other parts of their business and in other parts of the supply chain. Full loads introduce a batch constraint which results in more handling and storage requirement. This translates internally into bigger storage areas. Furthermore, if supply chain responsiveness is significantly reduced, an extra echelon might be incurred with resultant capital and operational costs.

Third-party logistics networks provide shared user networks to overcome this imbalance between transport cost and batch size. Murray and Ferguson (1997) summarize shared user networks as:

> use of a shared user network … can overcome the problem of moving small consignments where a dedicated vehicle would not be justified and thus enable smaller material flows …

Storage and handling

Wherever possible, input to warehouses is in pallets. Vehicles are unloaded either by fork lift truck or automated unloaders. Pallets are then put away by conveyors and automated cranes, or by fork lift trucks. Outbound goods from warehouses are picked for each point of sale, usually by the case. The products are assembled in roll cages. Typically, orders received at warehouses are sorted into carefully designed picking routes. Operators are assigned picking tasks with clearly defined targets, often linked to bonuses. Thus the picking operation at this level is tightly controlled.

Vehicles arrive at the retail outlet loaded with cages of mixed product and are unloaded to a secure goods in area, and subsequently decanted from case to single units at the point of sale. To do this many more people are employed to handle product in retail stores rather than in the warehouse. However, in contrast to the warehouses, the retail network in FMCG has low levels of *operations control*, as standard operations and times are not monitored for putaway and picking tasks. A frequent response to the subject of standard operations from retail managers referred to a culture that was highly focused on customer service. A highly disciplined operations environment would reduce the flexibility for operatives to deal with customers.

FMCG organizations are beginning to recognize these operational issues at the retail store through analysis of the high proportion of supply chain costs in this area.

FMCG organizations are beginning to recognize these operational issues at the retail store through analysis of the high proportion of supply chain costs in this area. Anecdotal evidence suggests that Sainsbury incur more than half of their total logistics costs in this retail environment. In response to this the industry is cooperating on the design and implementation of containers with better handling characteristics. These deliver benefits at the retail store but generally incur extra cost for manufacture and transport firm. As a result there is a need to negotiate transfer of cost between parties to realize a holistic benefit.

Chilled Ready Meals

Chilled ready meals were the subject of Value Stream Mapping (Hines and Rich, 1997) for a single product and for the whole range produced by a particular supplier. The Value Streams were mapped from the supplier through the RDC and retail store to the end customer.

Chilled Ready Meals Mapping

The main steps of the process were:

- Day 1: Store orders product.
- Day 2: Product made.
- Day 3: Product shipped to RDC.
- Day 4: Product shipped to store.

The biggest issue detected was that of demand amplification resulting in two apparently opposite wastes:

- Too little product giving incomplete availability to the customer.
- Too much product creating waste due to the sell by date being exceeded.

Analysis of chilled food demand showed that 50 per cent of product lines in stores sold less than 6 per day. This relatively low daily movement was found to hold true for FMCG goods in general and for the automotive after-sales. Figure 18.3 shows that about 80 per cent of product lines sell less than 6 units per day, but that this accounts for only 20 per cent of volume:-

The assumption was made that for this 80 per cent of product lines that move slowly the Poisson distribution can be used to model base demand. Poisson, the nineteenth-century French mathematician, derived a discrete distribution to model random events. For an average occurrence, the Poisson distribution gives the probability of a series of actual occurrences. So, for an average daily demand of 2 units, Poisson says the actual demand will be 0 on 13 per cent of days, 1 on 27 per cent of days, 2 on 27 per cent of days, etc (Figure 18.4).

FIGURE 18.3 Point-of-Sale Demand

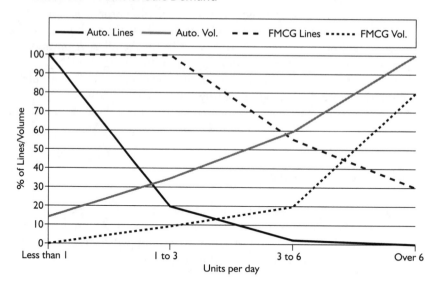

Forecasting demand for the next day (0 days lead time) could simply be based on topping stock up to a level of 5 to achieve 99 per cent availability to the customer. However, for a 1-day lead time the top up level is 8, for a 2-day lead time the top up level is 9, etc.

For a chilled meal that sold exactly 2 per day in a store, a case of 6 meals would last 3 days, which is the shelf life of the product. However if demand is random like the Poisson distribution, then there are lots of scenarios that can occur, including:

- a 40 per cent chance of selling 1 or less per day. This means that in any 3-day period there is a 6.4 per cent (40 per cent x 40 per cent x 40 per cent) chance of wasting half a case or more;
- a 17 per cent chance of selling 3 or more per day. So at the end of 2 days, there is about 3 per cent (17 per cent x 17 per cent) chance of having no stock at the start of Day 3.

So, when stores are constrained to ordering boxes of 6, on some days they would be lucky and the right number of customers would come in for the product. However, more often than not, either too many or too few would arrive, resulting in non-availability or wasted product.

Real life is even more complicated than this Poisson distribution: end customer demand can be distorted by a whole range of influences, including weekly sales patterns, weather and promotional activities. This makes reduction in batch size even more important.

FIGURE 18.4 Poisson Distribution For Mean of 2 Per Day

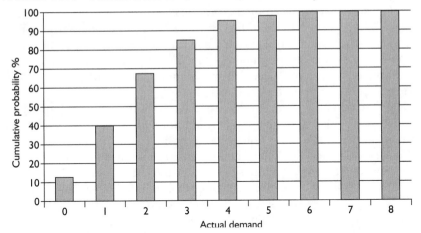

Lean Chilled Ready Meals

As a starting point, an unconstrained Lean System was proposed, assuming information and physical flows could be completely redesigned. The principle changes proposed were:

- the cardboard case constraint is removed allowing single-piece flow.
- product is made to order on Day 2, shipped overnight, and is available at Point of Sale on Day 3.

In the factory, at the start of each production run, demand and stock data is 'pulled' from every individual point of sale. A forecast requirement is made for each store for Day 2 and Day 3 (the forecasting period has been cut by at least 33 per cent). Each requirement is then printed to a pick card for the particular store and product. The card shows the destination store, product line and quantity in a highly visible format (no codes, no small print!), and has a barcode for system recording. This card follows the product through the value stream, it is the picking list, delivery note and invoice trigger.

For the fast-moving products going to large stores, packers fill 'Green Trays' (like those used for fruit and vegetables in supermarkets) straight from the production line according to the data on the card. When the product is in the 'Green Tray', the packer scans the barcode to record despatch on the system, and attaches the card to the 'Green Tray'. The system records when and by whom the product was packed, and the card

FIGURE 18.5 Pick Card

OXFORD
300g Tikka Massala
4

goes with the 'Green Tray' to its destination.

For slower-moving products, the ideal order quantities may be less than a 'Green Tray'. To avoid the 'Burbidge' effect, suppliers who deliver several such product lines should have multiple product lines in 'Green Trays'. So slow-moving products coming off different production lines are consolidated into one 'Green Tray'. Standardization of product single packaging is important to allow such a mix.

At the end of Day 2, for each store there will be a quantity of 'Green Trays', some filled with just one product line, others with multiple product lines with single piece flow where required.

A key enabler for Lean Manufacture is mobility of machines and products in a factory. Machines on wheels allow the layout to be changed quickly without the requirement of complex handling systems. Within FMCG, an industry standard 'dolly' has been developed with a footprint two 'Green Trays'. Potentially it is possible to wheel from the Supplier to the Point of Sale without any intermediary handling or delays. For a large retail stores, a dedicated 'Dolly' to Point of Sale will be possible. For smaller retail stores 'Dollies' will need to be consolidated to some extent at the RDC.

A key enabler for Lean Manufacture is mobility of machines and products in a factory.

The transport system used should be as direct as possible. Third-party logistics are likely to be able to consolidate locally and deliver direct to one RDC. The 'Dollies' of 'Green Trays' then travel through the RDC and into store, being routed by the original pick card, a type of postal system. The only inspection that should take place anywhere in the system is that there is a pick card attached to the 'Green Tray'. When the 'Green Tray' arrives at the Point of Sale, its contents should be checked by the shelf filler. If it agrees, then the pick card should be scanned, triggering the retailer's payment system.

A card discrepancy at the 'Point of Sale' should trigger a thorough investigation of the process. Based on the principle of 'Five Whys' (Shingo, 1989), the fault in the process should be detected and corrected with a failsafe device. The route cause in the process must be corrected, not another inspection introduced.

Chilled Meals Implementation

Implementation of the Lean System has raised a number of interesting change management issues. The route agreed was that of evolution rather than revolution through a pilot evaluation of 'Green Trays' – a change from 6 meals in a cardboard box to 6 meals in a 'Green Tray'. Achieving this first step was seen as a key enabler.

Negotiation of cost/benefit ground rules and Activity Based Costing methods were a major part of the project, requiring senior management input. Once agreed, the cost/benefits included:

TABLE 18.3 Costs and Benefits

Cost	Benefit
Tray hire vs. Cardboard	Supplier ease of packing
Reduced supplier vehicle fill	Warehouse handling
	Product visibility
	Reduced damage
	Reduce shelf fill times
	Recycling

Using only 'Green Trays' there was a benefit, but this required movement of some cost along the supply chain from the retailer towards the supplier. The next step planned is to pilot the smaller batch-size cases of 3 to 4 (production is taking time to buy in to mixed trays). Providing the benefits meet expectations, the next step will be to move towards single piece flow.

Lean Distribution

From the case study material there have been clear examples of the concepts of the framework, *control, centralization, time* and *structure*. To conclude the major practical points and framework are summarized.

Availability Measurement

In terms of performance measurement of demand, most organizations measure the availability at various points in the distribution chain. For an individual product line, the only point that really counts is the point of sale, the other measurements being causal. There are few instances in which a customer enters a point of sale with a requirement for one product; invariably the customer wants a basket of products. So measurement of *line fill* (availability of one product line) provides a proxy for customer service, whereas measurement of *order fill* (the basket of products) relates directly to customer need and is therefore a more useful measure.

Information Flow

Since Forrester identified the demand amplification phenomenon in 1961, there have been great advances in order transmission procedures. In most organizations orders are transmitted virtually instantaneously via Electronic Data Interchange (EDI) links. However, value stream mapping of this information flow showed that there were delays either side of the sender and recipient information buffers.

These delays are occupied by companies dedicating expertise and computing resource to forecast algorithms to predict the resultant demands. At a macro level this can provide valuable information on production requirements. At the point of sale, however, such forecasting is only beneficial to the faster moving lines, selling more than 10 per day where lead times are very short. Forecasting should focus on *variability* not *uncertainty,* as defined by (Bhattacharya *et al.*, 1996):

> variability measures changes in demand over a given sequence of time buckets uncertainty measures the changes in demand for a given time bucket.

So the technology is available to transmit information quickly, but it is being delayed by intermediary decision points and is being distorted by intermediary forecasts. Supply chain visibility through real time availability of information between companies is the solution. Tesco and pioneering automotive after-sales companies are introducing systems to achieve this objective. This will *centralize* information to suppliers, allowing *control* of manufacture in real time, free of the 'Forrester effect'.

Manufacturing Batch Size (Burbidge Effect)

Across industries, single units of product are predominantly packed into cardboard boxes. The number of 'singles' contained in a 'cardboard outer' is dominated by cost at the point of packing, taking factors such as:

- cardboard outer price;
- ergonomics of packing;
- pallet fill.

Companies that tend toward the latter options succeed in achieving a good intra-company decision. However, given the low demands discussed for 80 per cent of product lines, this can restrict point-of-sale stocking policy. So, for these products where there is a high chance of waste due to deterioration or obsolescence, single piece flow is an imperative.

Physical Flow

Distribution storage to the point of sale lead times ranged between:

- *Traditional* – order weekly receive delivery one week later;
- *Advanced* – order daily receive delivery the next day;
- *Leading* – order start of shift, receive delivery start of next shift (8 hours).

Simulation of simple 'Poisson' demands of 1 to 6 per day (i.e. 80 per cent product lines) showed that the *Traditional* policy could not practicably deliver 100 per cent availability, without extremely high levels of stock cover. By contrast the *Advanced* policy could deliver 100 per cent service with significantly lower stocks. Our sponsor research supported these findings with reductions of up to 70 per cent in stock levels.

To approach *Leading*, the supplier needs to implement lean production with fast set-up times to allow every product to be made each day. Faster moving products are more predictable than slow movers. The slow movers should be the last products made to minimize the forecasting period, and hence increase forecast accuracy. Hence, the criteria for sequencing production is fast mover to slow mover, and not traditional set-up constraints, e.g. light to dark chocolate to reduce cleaning time.

For suppliers that can fill a vehicle each hour, direct transport is a good solution. However, where suppliers have a small number of loads or need to consolidate loads between factory sites, a third-party shared user network is best. Few organizations have this critical mass to organize their own transport and achieve high levels of transport efficiency through backhaul. During the research, several automotive after-sales suppliers transferred to third-party logistics. The rationale behind this was to enable a more responsive system (daily vs. weekly delivery), and thus remove stock from the system.

Faster moving products are more predictable than slow movers.

In all sectors, the Retail echelon's Operations Control needs to become slick enough to empty a vehicle to shelf in minutes, not hours. The Toyota Production System has shown that machine set-ups can be reduced from many hours to less than 10 minutes by 'Single Minutes Exchange of Dies' (SMED). A Formula 1 motor racing tyre change and refuel in 10 seconds is an application of SMED thinking. At the retailer echelon these techniques offer the opportunity to make product available for customers quicker. Equally important, the Goods In area can be reduced, so freeing up more retail space, giving the opportunity to increase customer choice through more stock lines.

Flexible Process Routes and Single Stocking Points

Potentially, with sufficiently responsive systems, only one stocking point is needed as a buffer within the distribution system. There is enormous opportunity to eliminate stocking echelon for those who can:

- develop relationships and achieve demand visibility and centralized control;
- increase responsiveness of manufacturing and continuity of supply;
- employ flexible transport systems to eliminate delays in the flow of goods.

By identifying generic 'value streams' (Womack and Jones, 1996) based on customer requirements and product characteristics, a set of generic distribution routes can be identified. A starting point for defining such routes is the analysis of movement rates, and defining the stocking points for four generic process routes:

FIGURE 18.6 The allocation of stocking points

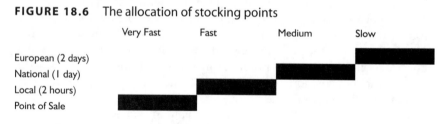

The next step is to balance customer expectation with the responsiveness of the system. In the automotive sector a medium moving line (e.g. a body panel) is satisfactory next day. However, in FMCG a medium moving line (e.g. a spice) needs to be available at the point of sale. The compromise solution may be a less optimal stocking point or, more likely, a second stocking point.

After, improving *control, centralization* and *time* a more responsive distribution system can be created. Within this system, different generic customer expectations can be satisfied via different process routes. The number of storage locations in each process route will be a balance of system responsiveness and customer expectation.

Conceptual Framework

So, within the conceptual framework, *time* is being compressed between distribution echelons. However, there is clear evidence that the preceding step in the framework, *control* is not being implemented rigorously, and as a result a major part of the *time* benefit is being lost. In the major organizations visited, warehouse stock control and operations management were implemented precisely. However, at point of sale practices were more varied and less controlled.

Centralization of ordering is evident in some organizations and is a key enabler to removing *control* problems to ensure uniform point-of-sale ordering and flow. This gives more level warehouse picking schedules, ultimately eliminating demand amplification at the factory.

When distribution *structures* were mapped, up to five stocking points were detected in the system – finished goods, supplier warehouse, retailer warehouse, point-of-sale storage area and point of sale display. These structures are a result of incomplete implementation of *control, centralization* and *time* due to intra-company optimization mindsets and technological barriers to supply chain visibility. This is changing due to a trend towards inter-company optimization and improvements in Internet-based technologies. As a result *structures* evolve and simplify naturally as requirements are driven by the need to move product toward a point of sale by the fastest possible route.

CHAPTER 19

Conclusion[1]

This book has attempted to discuss a wide variety of issues relating to the area of supply chain management. The work has evolved from our four-year industrial sponsored research programme. It has encompassed the combined efforts of two universities, a large team of researchers and a host of company representatives, all of whom have played a significant role in allowing us to complete a successful research project.

The concepts explored in this book have led us to conclude that no one area of supply chain improvement will allow an organization to optimize its supply chain. Rather, it is the combination of the ideas, concepts and models presented in this text that will allow firms to achieve increased competitive advantage from its supply activity. We have termed the synthesis of this approach, 'Value Stream Management' (VSM). This incorporates the focus and alignment of the various value-adding processes that exist both intra- and inter-organizationally, allowing firms to become more effective and efficient in their handling of the supply chain.

We see VSM focusing at the strategic, managerial and operational levels within the firm (see Table 19.1). At the strategic level we have introduced concepts to allow firms to concentrate on understanding performance measurement alignment, thinking about where value is added and focusing on strategic procurement.[2] At the managerial level we have suggested ways for thinking managers to analyze their value flows, examine inventory implications, construct performance measurement and benchmarking systems and to map the level of strategic capability of their purchasing organization. Finally, at the operational level we have suggested methods and approaches to investigate and measure change within organizations.

We see VSM as an approach for data capture, analysis, planning and implementation of effective change within the core cross-functional or cross-company processes required to achieve a truly lean enterprise.

[1] Prepared by Peter Hines and Paul Cousins.
[2] Strategic in this sense is defined as being proactive as opposed to reactive. It involves the firm having a planning process and linking those plans and objectives to the overall corporate plan.

Table 19.1   Value Stream Mapping (VSM)

Level	Focus	Tools & Techniques
Strategic	• Assessment of supply process • Alignment of performance measures • Fit of purchasing structure • Assess value components	• Strategic positioning tools • Performance measurement tool kit • Purchasing structure mapping • Value stream mapping
Managerial	• Development of skills profiles • List of measures and approaches – benchmarking • Measure and assess current purchasing ability • Assessment of value components	• Skills mapping profile sheets • Practical measures and benchmarks for assessment • Comparison to best practice firms – data available • Value stream mapping of detail
Operational	• Implementation of skills programme – align to measures • Measures and benchmarks built into assessment systems • Feedback mechanisms • Apply to value components	• Skills profile tree – examine courses, etc. • Link to measures • Use of balanced scorecard approach and benchmarking mechanism • Application of staged model • Value stream mapping tool

We started the journey through this book by outlining *ten* key elements of a lean value stream. These are reproduced in Table 19.2 and are indeed the objective of applying the Value Stream Management way of thinking. VSM is therefore an approach that facilitates data capture, analysis planning and implementation of effective change with inter- and intra-organizational process to facilitate improved supply chain performance. We see VSM as an approach for data capture, analysis, planning and implementation of effective change within the core cross-functional or cross-company processes required to achieve a truly lean enterprise (Hines *et al.*, 1998).

TABLE 19.2   The Ten Key Elements of the Lean Value Stream

1. Specifying what does and does not create *value* from the customer's perspective and not from the perspective of individual firms, functions and departments.

2. Identifying all the steps necessary to design, order and produce across the whole *value stream* to highlight non-value-adding waste.

3. Make those actions that create value *flow* without interruption, detours, backflows, waiting or scrap.

4. Only make what is *pulled* by the customer just-in-time.

5. The creation of a dynamic *transparency* of strategies, costs and information in the value stream.

6. Address competitive advantage at the value stream *network* level, moving past simple buyer–supplier partnership rhetoric.

7. The use of a new toolkit called *value stream mapping* for analysis, daignosis and implementation of change.

8. The need to focus on key *processes*, not just separate business departments.

9. The need to address *whole industries* over the long-term rather than on short-term improvement of individual firms.

10. And finally strive for *perfection* by continually removing successive layers of waste as they are uncovered.

Going Lean: A Framework

In order to go lean it is necessary to understand customers and what they value. To get your company focused on these needs, you must define your internal value stream and later the external one as well. In order to meet customer aspirations, you need then to eliminate all the waste that exists in your organization.

When you have done this, the next step is to determine a way of setting the direction, targets and finding a way to see if your change is working or not. You then need an internal (and later external) framework to deliver value for your customers, as well as a toolkit to use to make the change.

If you can do this effectively you won't need to benchmark competitors to set some arbitrary and often incomparable target; perfection or the complete elimination of waste should be your goal. Sounds good, but back to the real world a minute; if it was so easy why don't others think this way?

Sometimes we ask ourselves this question, and when we have gathered a few facts about a company, we ask them. The answer they give is usually something like 'yes, that makes a lot of sense but we never saw it that way'. The reason was that firms were often unable to get into this

FIGURE 19.1 Going Lean

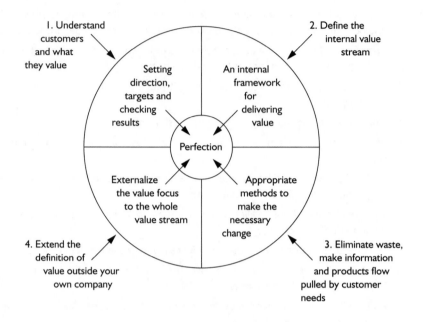

virtuous circle of improvement. This text is designed to help organizations to do this.

The Starting Point

The starting point is to design an internal and external system that can create sustainable competitive advantage. In our travels across five continents we have found that there a *four* key differentiators of the leanest companies:

- Policy Deployment.
- Process Based Management.
- Lean Tools and Techniques.
- Supply Chain Integration.

It is highly unusual to find a company that is 'excellent' in all of the value-generating areas. During our four-year study we have found only one firm that has come reasonably close. It appears that the reason for this is often that firms tend to be unitary with goal-setting. That is, they will focus on reducing suppliers and building long-term relationships, but ignore measurement systems and the requisite skills and competences required to make the strategy work. They will implement an inventory reduction exercise, but not focus on the value-adding (or indeed non-value-adding)

FIGURE 19.2   Lean Differentiators

processes that are creating high inventory. Finally, these approaches are often conducted at the exclusion of understanding the customers' needs and requirements.

In order to address this unitary perspective, we have presented the concept of Value Stream Management. This process is designed to allow firms to make advances, based on strategic need, in a coherent and multiple-goal approach. This method, now validated and perfected by application to the SCDP sponsoring companies, is, we feel, the secret of success in unlocking your firm's innate ability to be world class.

The starting point is to design an internal and external system that can create sustainable competitive advantage.

The Future

During our joint programme at Cardiff University and the University of Bath the research team found that we had an insightful and synergistic research approach, as the supply chain aspects were covered by the former and purchasing by the latter. With future work that is under way at the time of writing, and indeed with future planned activity, this essential different but complementary research focus is being maintained.

At Cardiff a series of research projects are underway, for instance, in the steel-based upstream automotive, the food and grocery industry and a programme covering the whole automotive industry from dealer through to raw material suppliers. New research is also being started in a number of other sectors, such as construction, medical and service industries. A series of further outputs within the area of Value Stream Management are planned including a detailed 'how to' workbook aimed at industry (Hines *et al.*, 2000) and a casebook of outputs from the automotive industry research work that has followed SCDP (Brunt *et al.*, 2000).

The work at Bath has followed the strategic and operational work pioneered within SCDP. It is following the development of inter-company relationship assessment and the development of environmentally-friendly purchasing. Further research is being undertaken into the area of performance measurement and trends within supplier/buyer relationships (Cousins, 1999a; 1999b).

References

Chapter 2

Akiyama, K. (1989), *Function Analysis: Systematic Improvement of Quality and Performance*, Cambridge, MA, Productivity Press.

Beesley, A. (1994), 'A Need for Time Based Process Mapping and its Application in Procurement', Proceedings of the 3rd Annual IPSERA Conference, University of Glamorgan, pp. 41–56.

Bicheno, J. (1994), *The Quality 50*, Buckingham, PICSIE Books.

Burbidge, J. (1984), 'Automated Production Control with a Simulation Capability', Proc. IFIP Conf. WG 5–7, Copenhagen.

Forrester, J. (1958), 'Industrial Dynamics: A Major Breakthrough For Decision Makers', *Harvard Business Review*, July–August, pp. 37–66.

Forza, C., Vinelli, A. and Filippini, R. (1993), 'Telecommunication Services For Quick Response in the Textile-Apparel Industry', *Proceedings of the 1st International Symposium on Logistics*, The University of Nottingham, pp. 119–126.

Hammer, M. (1990), 'Re-engineering Work: Don't Automate, Obliterate', *Harvard Business Review*, July–August, pp. 104–112.

Hines, P. (1994), *Creating World Class Suppliers: Unlocking Mutual Competitive Advantage*, London, Pitman Publishing.

Hines, P., Rich, N. and Hittmeyer, M. (1998), 'Competing Against Ignorance: Advantage Through Knowledge', *International Journal of Physical Distribution and Logistics Management*, Volume 28, Number 1.

Hoekstra, S. and Romme, S. (eds) (1992), *Towards Integral Logistics Structure – Developing Customer Oriented Goods Flows*, New York, McGraw-Hill.

Ishiwata, J. (1991), *Productivity Through Process Analysis*, Cambridge, MA, Productivity Press.

James, R. (1995), 'Promotions Update', *Supply Chain Development Programme I Workshop 8*, Lutterworth, Britvic Soft Drinks, 6–7 July.

Japan Management Association (1985), *Kanban: Just-in-Time at Toyota*, Cambridge, MA, Productivity Press.

Jessop, D. and Jones, O. (1995), 'Value Stream Process Modelling: A Methodology For Creating Competitive Advantage', Proceedings of the 4th Annual IPSERA Conference, University of Birmingham.

Imai, M. (1986), *Kaizen: The Key to Japan's Competitive Success*, New York,

McGraw-Hill.

Jones, D. (1995), 'Applying Toyota Principles To Distribution', Supply Chain Development Programme I, Workshop #8 Workbook, Lutterworth, Britvic Soft Drinks, 6–7 July.

Macbeth, D. and Ferguson, N. (1994), *Partnership Sourcing: An Integrated Supply Chain Approach*, London, Pitman Publishing.

Miles, L. (1961), *Techniques of Value Analysis and Engineering*, New York, McGraw-Hill.

Monden, Y. (1993), *Toyota Production System: An Integrated Approach to Just-In-Time*, 2nd Edn, Norcross, GA, Industrial Engineering and Management Press.

New, C. (1974), 'The Production Funnel: A New Tool for Operations Analysis', *Management Decision*, Vol. 12, 3, pp. 167–178.

New, C. (1993), 'The Use of Throughput Efficiency as a Key Performance Measure for the New Manufacturing Era', *The International Journal of Logistics Management*, Vol. 4, 2, pp. 95–104.

Practical Management Research Group (1993), *Seven Tools For Industrial Engineering*, PHP Institute, Tokyo.

Rich, N. (1995), 'Supply Stream "Responsiveness" Project', *Supply Chain Development Programme I Workshop 6*, Tesco Stores, Ponsbourne Hotel, Hertford, 25–26 January.

Senge, P. (1990), *The Fifth Discipline: The Art & Practice of the Learning Organization*, New York, Doubleday Currency.

Shingo, S. (1989), *A Study of the Toyota Production System from an Industrial Engineering Viewpoint*, Cambridge, MA, Productivity Press.

Wikner, J., Towill, D. and Naim, M. (1991), 'Smoothing Supply Chain Dynamics', *International Journal of Production Economics*, 22, pp. 231–248.

Womack, J. and Jones, D. (1994), 'From Lean Production to the Lean Enterprise', *Harvard Business Review*, March–April, pp. 93–103.

Chapter 3

Andersen Consulting (1992), *The Lean Enterprise Benchmarking Project*, London, Andersen Consulting.

Bicheno, J. (1994), *The Quality 50: A Guide to Gurus, Tools, Wastes, Techniques and Systems*, Buckingham, PICSIE Books.

Cox, A. (1995), 'Pro-Activity, Value Engineering and Strategic Procurement Management', *Proceedings for the First Worldwide Research Symposium on Purchasing and Supply Chain Management*, R. Kemp and R. Lamming (eds), IFPMM/CIPS/PMAC/NAPM, Tempe, Arizona.

Dimancescu, D., Hines, P. and Rich, N. (1997), *The Lean Enterprise: Designing and Managing Strategic Processes for Customer-Winning Performance*, New York, AMACOM.

Hines, P.(1994a), *Creating World Class Suppliers: Unlocking Mutual Competitive Advantage*, London, Pitman Publishing.

Hines, P., Rich, N. and Esain, A. (1998), 'Creating a Lean Supplier Network: A Distribution Industry Case', *European Journal of Purchasing and Supply Management*.

Monden, Y. (1993), *Toyota Production System: An Integrated Approach to Just-In-Time*, 2nd Edn, Norcross, GA, Industrial Engineering and Management Press.

Womack, J., Jones, D. and Roos, D. (1990), *The Machine that Changed the World*, New York, Rawson Associates.

Chapter 4

Andersen Consulting (1992), *The Lean Enterprise Benchmarking Project*, London, Andersen Consulting.

Andersen Consulting (1994), *Worldwide Manufacturing Competitiveness Study*, London, Andersen Consulting.

Dimancescu, D. (1992), *The Seamless Enterprise: Making Cross Functional Management Work*, New York, Harper Business.

Edwards, C., Ward, J. and Bytheway, A. (1995), *The Essence of Information Systems*, 2nd edn, London, Prentice Hall.

Goldratt, E. and Cox, J. (1993), *The Goal*, 2nd edn, Aldershot, Gower.

Hammer, M. and Champy, J. (1995), *Reengineering the Corporation: A Manifesto for Business Revolution*, London, Nicholas Brealey.

Hines, P. (1994), *Creating World Class Suppliers: Unlocking Mutual Competitive Advantage*, London, Pitman Publishing.

Hines, P. and Rich, N. (1997), 'The Seven Value Stream Mapping Tools', *International Journal of Operations & Production Management*, Vol. 17, 1, pp. 46–64.

Hines, P., Rich, N. and Esain, A. (1997), 'Creating a Lean Supplier Network: A Distribution Industry Case', *Conference Proceedings: Logistics Research Network*, University of Huddersfield, Huddersfield, 16–17 September.

Inger, R. (1997), 'Performance Measurement Issues in the Supply Chain', *Logistics Research Network Workshop*, Cranfield University, Cranfield, 15 April.

James, R., Rich, N. and Francis, M. (1996), 'Vendor Managed Inventory: A Processual Approach', *Proceedings of the 5th International IPSERA Conference*, Eindhoven University of Technology (TUE), Eindhoven, Netherlands.

Jones, O. (1997), 'Information in the Supply Chain: Media and Message', in: A. Cox and P. Hines (eds), *Advanced Supply Chain Management: The Best Practice Debate*, pp. 207–230, Boston, UK, Earlsgate Press.

Levit, S. (1994), *Quality is Just the Beginning: Managing for Total Responsiveness*, New York, McGraw-Hill.

Martin, J. (1995), *The Great Transition: Using the Seven Disciplines of Enterprise Engineering to Align People, Technology, and Strategy*, New York, AMACOM.

Mintzberg, H. (1979), *The Structuring of Organizations*, London, Prentice Hall.

Monden, Y. (1983), *The Toyota Production System*, Atlanta, GA, Institute of Industrial Engineers.

Monden, Y. (1993), *Toyota Production System: An Integrated Approach to Just-In-Time*, 2nd Edn, Norcross, GA, Industrial Engineering and Management.

Ohno, T. (1988), *The Toyota Production System: Beyond Large-Scale Production*, Portland, OR, Productivity Press.

Shingo, S. (1989), *A Study of the Toyota Production System from an Industrial Engineering Viewpoint*, Portland, OR, Productivity Press.

Womack, J., Jones, D. and Roos, D. (1990), *The Machine That Changed the World*, New York, Rawson Associates.

Womack, J. and Jones, D. (1994), 'From Lean Production to the Lean Enterprise', *Harvard Business Review*, March–April, pp. 93–103.

Womack, J. and Jones, D. (1996), *Lean Thinking: Banish Waste & Create Wealth in Your Corporation*, New York, Simon & Schuster.

Chapter 5

Beesley, A. (1994), 'A Need for Time Based Process Mapping and its Application in Procurement', *Proceedings of the 3rd Annual IPSERA Conference*, University of Glamorgan, pp. 41–56.

Bouverie-Brine, C. and Rich, N. (1997), 'Cross Functionality, Organisational Decision Making & The Role Of Purchasing: IT Procurement In London Underground Limited' in: A. Cox and P. Hines (eds), *Advanced Supply Management: The Best Practice Debate*, pp. 255–301, Boston, UK, Earlsgate Press.

Clausing, D. (1994), *Total Quality Development: A Step-By-Step Guide to World-Class Concurrent Engineering*, New York, ASME Press.

Delbridge, R. and Kirkpatrick, I. (1994), *Theory and Practice of Participant Observation*, in: V. Wass and P. Wells (eds), *Principles and Practice in Business Management Research*, Aldershot, Dartmouth Publishing, pp. 35–62.

Drucker, P. (1992), *Post-Capitalist Society*, Oxford, Butterworth Heinemann.

Forza, C., Vinelli, A. and Filippini, R. (1993), 'Telecommunication Services For Quick Response in the Textile-Apparel Industry', *Proceedings of the 1st International Symposium on Logistics*, The University of Nottingham, pp. 119–126.

Glaser, B. and Strauss, A. (1967), *The Discovery of Grounded Theory*, Chicago, Aldine.

Harrison, A. (1992), *Just-In-Time Manufacturing In Perspective*, London, Prentice Hall.

Hill, T. (1985), Production/Operations Management: Text and Cases, New York, Prentice Hall.

Hines, P. (1994), *Creating World Class Suppliers: Unlocking Mutual Competitive Advantage*, London, Pitman Publishing/Financial Times.

Hines, P., Rich, N. and Hittmeyer, M. (1998), 'Competing Against Ignorance: Advantage Through Knowledge', *International Journal of Physical Distribution and Logistics Management*, Vol. 28, 1.

Jessop, D. and Jones, O. (1995), 'Value Stream Process Modelling: A Methodology For Creating Competitive Advantage', *Proceedings of the 4th Annual IPSERA Conference*, University of Birmingham.

Kobata, T. (1995), *Managing By Fact: The Results-Oriented Approach to Quality*, Tokyo, Asian Productivity Organization.

Kotler, P. (1988), *Marketing Management: Analysis, Planning, Implementation and Control*, 6th Edn, Englewood Cliffs, NJ, Prentice-Hall.

Mizuno, S. and Akao, Y. (eds) (1994), *QFD The Customer-Driven Approach to Quality Planning and Deployment*, Tokyo, Asian Productivity Organisation.

Monden, Y. (1983), *Toyota Production System: An Integrated Approach to Just-In-Time*, 1st Edn, Norcross, GA, Industrial Engineering and Management Press.

New, C. (1993), 'The Use of Throughput Efficiency as a Key Performance Measure for the New Manufacturing Era', *The International Journal of Logistics Management*, Vol. 4, 2, pp. 95–104.

Nonaka, I. and Takeuchi, H. (1995), *The Knowledge-Creating Company*, New York, Oxford University Press.

Ohno, T. (1988), *Toyota Production System: Beyond Large-Scale Production*, Cambridge, MA, Productivity Press.

Ozeki, K. and Asaka, T. (1990), *Handbook of Quality Tools*, Cambridge, MA, Productivity Press.

Parikh, R. (1992), 'Contextual Inquiry', *Proceedings of International Association for Electronic Product Development (IAEPD) Workshop #7 Product Definition*, Minneapolis, MN, June.

Quinn, J. (1992), *Intelligent Enterprise: A Knowledge and Service Based Paradigm for Industry*, New York, Free Press.

Reich, R. (1991), *The Work of Nations*, New York, Alfred A. Knopf.

Rich, N. (1995a), 'Quality Function Deployment: A Decision Support Matrix For Location Determination', *Proceedings of the 2nd International Symposium on Logistics*, University of Nottingham, pp. 295–300.

Rich, N. (1995b), 'Partner, Associate Or Enemy?: The Use of Quality Function Deployment For Supplier Evaluation', *Proceedings of the 4th Annual International Purchasing & Supply Education and Research Association*, University of Birmingham.

Saaty, T. (1980), *The Analytical Hierarchy Process*, New York, McGraw Hill.

Stalk, G. (1988), 'Time-The Next Source of Competitive Advantage', *Harvard Business Review*, July–August, pp. 41–51.

Stalk, G. and Hout, T. (1990), *Competing Against Time: How Time Based Competition is Reshaping Global Markets*, New York, Free Press.

Suzaki, K. (1987), *The New Manufacturing Challenge*, New York, Free Press.

Toffler, A. (1990), *Powershift: Knowledge, Wealth and Violence at the Edge of the*

21st Century, New York, Bantam Books.

Womack, J. and Jones, D. (1994), 'From Lean Production to the Lean Enterprise', *Harvard Business Review*, March–April, pp. 93–103.

Chapter 6

Achrol, R. (1991), 'Evolution Of The Marketing Organisation: New Forms For Turbulent Environments', *Journal Of Marketing*, October, pp. 77–93.

Ackroyd, S., Burrell, G., Hughes, M. and Whittaker, A. (1988), 'The Japanisation Of British Industry?', *Industrial Relations Journal*, Vol. 19, 1, pp. 11–23.

Andersen Consulting (1992), *The Lean Enterprise Benchmarking Project*, London, Andersen Consulting.

Andersen Consulting (1994), *Worldwide Manufacturing Competitiveness Study*, London, Andersen Consulting.

Belcher, J. (1987), *Productivity Plus*, Houston, Gulf Publishing Co.

Bicheno, J. (1991), *Implementing JIT*, London, IFS Publications.

Blois, K. (1971), 'Vertical Quasi-Integration' *Journal Of Industrial Economics*, Vol. 20, pp. 253–272.

Cox, A. (1995), 'Pro-Activity, Value Engineering and Strategic Procurement Management: An Entrepreneurial Contractual Model For The Firm', *1st WorldWide Research Symposium On Purchasing & Supply Chain Management*, NAPM.

Dimancescu, D., Hines, P. and Rich, N. (1997), *The Lean Enterprise: Designing and Managing Strategic Processes for Customer-Winning Performance*, New York, AMACOM.

Ford Motor Company (1995), *The Ford Production System*, Ford Motor Company, Dearborn, Detroit.

Hammer, M. and Champy, J. (1993), *Re-Engineering The Corporation*, London, Brearley.

Hanan, M. (1992), *Growth Partnering*, New York, AMACOM.

Hill, T. (1995), *Manufacturing Strategy: Texts & Cases*, London, Macmillan.

Hines, P. (1994), *Creating World Class Suppliers: Unlocking Mutual Competitive Advantage*, London, Pitman Publishing.

Imai, K. (1986), *Kaizen*, New York, McGraw-Hill.

Ishikawa, K. (1976), *What Is Total Quality Control ? The Japanese Way*, London, Prentice Hall.

Japan Union of Scientists and Engineers (1988), *Standards Book*, Tokyo, JUSE.

Johnson, G. and Scholes, K. (1988), *Exploring Corporate Strategy (2nd Edn)*, London, Prentice Hall.

Jones, D. (1990), 'Beyond The Toyota Production System: The Era Of Lean Production', *5th International Operations Management Association Conference On Manufacturing Strategy*, Warwick University, pp. 1–13, 26–27 June.

Kanter, R. (1989), *When Giants Learn To Dance*, New York, Simon & Schuster.

Keuning, D. and Opheij, W. (1994), *Delayering Organisations*, London, Pitman Publishing.

Lamming, R. (1993), *Beyond Partnership: Strategies for Innovation and Lean Supply*, London, Prentice Hall.

Lawrence, P. and Lorsch, J. (1967), *Organisation And Environment*, Boston, Harvard University Press.

Likert, R. (1967), *The Human Organisation*, New York, McGraw-Hill.

Merli, G. (1991), *Co-Makership*, Cambridge, MA, Productivity Press.

Newman, R. and Rhee, K. (1990), 'A Case Study Of NUMMI & Its Suppliers', *Journal of Purchasing & Materials Management*, Vol. 26, 4, pp. 15–20, Fall.

Ohno, T. (1988), *The Toyota Production System: Beyond Large-Scale Production*, Portland, OR, Productivity Press.

Peters, T. and Waterman, R. (1982), *In Search Of Excellence*, New York, Harper Row.

Porter, M. (1980), *Competitive Strategy*, New York, The Free Press.

Quinn, J. (1992), *Intelligent Enterprise*, New York, The Free Press.

Rich, N. (1998), *TPM: The Lean Approach*, Wirral, Tudor Business Publishing.

Rich, N. and Armitage, S. (1998), 'Policy Deployment: Aligning The Organisation For Competitive Advantage', *Lean Enterprise Research Centre Working Paper*, Cardiff, LERC.

Rich, N. and Hines, P. (1998), 'Purchasing Structures, Roles, Processes and Strategies: Is It A Case Of The Tail Wagging The Dog', *European Journal Of Purchasing and Supply Management*, Vol. 4, 1, pp. 51–63, March.

Senge, P. (1990), *The Fifth Discipline*, New York, Century Business Publishing.

Shiba, S., Graham, A. and Walden, D. (1993), *A New American TQM*, Portland, OR, Productivity Press.

Simon, H. (1947), *Administrative Behaviour*, New York, Macmillan.

Stalk, G. and Hout, T. (1990), *Competing Against Time*, New York, The Free Press.

Stevens, G. (1989), 'Integrating The Supply Chain', *International Journal Of Physical Distribution & Materials Management*, Vol. 19, 8.

Suzaki, K. (1987), *The Manufacturing Challenge*, New York, Free Press.

Taylor, F. W. (1911), *The Principles Of Scientific Management*, New York, McGraw-Hill.

Womack, J. and Jones, D. (1996), *Lean Thinking: Banish Waste and Create Wealth in Your Corporation*, New York, Simon & Schuster.

Womack, J., Jones, D. and Roos, D. (1990), *The Machine That Changed the World*, New York, Rawson Associates.

Chapter 7

Andersen Consulting (1992), *The Lean Enterprise Report*, London, Andersen Consulting.

Andersen Consulting (1994), *World Wide Manufacturing Competitiveness Study: The Second Lean Enterprise Report*, London, Andersen Consulting.

Cox, A. (1995), 'Pro-Activity, Value Engineering and Strategic Procurement Management: An Entrepreneurial Contractual Model For The Firm', *1st World-Wide Research Symposium On Purchasing & Supply Chain Management*, NAPM.

De Meyer, A. (1994), *Creating Product Value*, London, Pitman Publishing.

Dimancescu, D., Hines, P. and Rich, N. (1997), *The Lean Enterprise: Designing and Managing Strategic Processes for Customer-Winning Performance*, New York, AMACOM.

Dobler, D., Burt, D. and Lee, L. (1990), *Purchasing & Materials Management*, 2nd Edn, New York, McGraw Hill.

Hammer, M. and Champy, J. (1993), *Re-Engineering The Corporation*, London, Brearley.

Harrison, A. (1992), *Just In Time In Perspective*, London, Prentice Hall.

Hayes, R. and Pisano, G. (1994), 'Beyond World Class: The New Manufacturing Strategy', *Harvard Business Review*, January/February.

Hayes, R. and Wheelwright, S. (1984), *Restoring Our Competitive Edge: Competing Through Manufacturing*, New York, John Wiley.

Hill, T. (1995), *Manufacturing Strategy: Texts & Cases*, London, Macmillan.

Imai, K. (1986), *Kaizen*, New York, McGraw Hill.

Japan Union of Scientists and Engineers (1988), *Standards Book*, Tokyo, JUSE.

Kanter, R. (1989), *When Giants Learn To Dance*, New York, Simon & Schuster.

Keuning, D. and Opheij, W. (1994), *Delayering Oorganisations*, London, Pitman Publishing.

Kotler, P. (1988), *Marketing Management: Analysis, Planning, Implementation and Control*, 6th Edn, Englewood Cliffs, Prentice-Hall.

Kurt Salmon (1993), *Efficient Consumer Response*, Washington, Kurt Salmon Associates.

Lawrence, P. and Lorsch, J. (1967), *Organisation And Environment*, Boston, Harvard University Press.

Merli, G. (1990), *Co-Makership*, Cambridge, MA, Productivity Press.

Peters, T. and Waterman, R. (1982), *In Search Of Excellence*, New York, Harper & Row.

Porter, M. (1980), *Competitive Strategy*, New York, Free Press.

Quinn, J. (1992), *Intelligent Enterprise*, New York, Free Press.

Rich, N. (1998), *TPM: The Lean Approach*, Wirral, Tudor Business Publishing.

Rich, N. (1995) 'Partner, Associate Or Enemy?: The Use of Quality Function Deployment For Supplier Evaluation', *Proceedings of the 4th Annual Inter-*

national Purchasing & Supply Education and Research Association, University of Birmingham.

Rich, N. and Francis, M. (1998), 'Overall Supply Chain Effectiveness', *Logistics Research Network Annual Conference*, September.

Skinner, W. (1985), *Manufacturing: The Formidable Competitive Weapon*, New York, John Wiley.

Slack, N. (1991), *The Manufacturing Advantage*, London.

Stalk, G. and Hout, T. (1990), *Competing Against Time: How Time Based Competition is Reshaping Global Markets*, New York, The Free Press.

Storey, J. (1994), *New Wave Manufacturing*, London, Paul Chapman.

Womack, J. and Jones, D. (1996), *Lean Thinking: Banish Waste and Create Wealth in Your Corporation*, New York, Simon & Schuster.

Womack, J., Jones, D. and Roos, D. (1990), *The Machine That Changed The World*, New York, Rawson Associates.

Chapter 8

Andersen Consulting (1992), *The Lean Enterprise Report*, London, Andersen Consulting.

Andersen Consulting (1994), *World Wide Manufacturing Competitiveness Study: The Second Lean Enterprise Report*, London, Andersen Consulting.

Argyris, C. (1964), *Integrating The Individual & The Organisation*, New York, Wiley.

Burns, T. and Stalker, G. (1966), *The Management Of Innovation*, Tavistock, Tavistock Publications.

Crozier, M. (1964), *The Bureaucratic Phenomenon*, Tavistock, Tavistock Publications.

Fayol, H. (1949), *General & Industrial Management*, London, Pitman.

Grimsdale, P. (1990), 'Genius Behind The Japanese Miracle', *Independent On Sunday*, London, 11 November.

Imai, K. (1986), *Kaizen*, New York, McGraw Hill.

Lawrence, P. and Lorsch, J. (1969), *Organisation And Environment*, New York, Irwin.

Maslow, A. (1943), 'A Theory Of Human Motivation', *Psychological Review*, Vol. 50, July, pp. 370–396.

Ohno, T. (1988a), *Toyota Production System: Beyond Large-Scale Production*, Portland, OR, Productivity Press.

Ohno, T. (1988b), *Workplace Management*, Portland, OR, Productivity Press.

Rich, N. (1998), *TPM: The Lean Approach*, Wirral, Tudor Business Publishing.

Roethlisberger, F. and Dickson, W. (1939) *Management & The Worker*, Harvard, Harvard University Press.

Silverman, D. (1970), *The Theory Of Organisations*, London, Heinemann.

Taylor, F. (1947), *Scientific Management*, New York, Harper & Row.

Toyota Motor Corporation (1992), *The Toyota Production System*, Toyota Motor Corporation, Toyota City.

Trist, E. (1963), *Organisational Choice*, Tavistock, Tavistock Publications.

Womack, J. and Jones, D. (1996), *Lean Thinking*, New York, Simon & Schuster.

Womack, J., Jones, D. and Roos, D. (1990), *The Machine That Changed The World*, New York, Rawson Associates.

Woodward, J. (1980), *Industrial Organisation: Theory & Practice*, 2nd Edn, Oxford, Oxford University Press.

Chapter 9

Burt, D. and Soukup, W. (1985), 'Purchasing's Role in New Product Development', *Harvard Business Review*, September–October pp. 90–96.

Caddick, J. and Dale, B. (1987), 'The Determination of Purchasing Objectives and Strategies: Some Key Influences', *International Journal of Physical Distribution and Materials Management*, Vol. 17, 3, pp. 5–16.

Carlson, P. (1990), 'The Long and the Short of Strategic Planning', *Journal of Business Strategy*, May–June, pp. 15–19.

Cavinato, J. (1987), 'Purchasing Performance: What makes the magic?', *Journal of Purchasing & Materials Management*, Fall.

Cousins, P. (1998), 'The Snake and The Old Woman: A Study of Inter-Firm Relationships', *World-Wide Purchasing Symposium*, London, UK, Chartered Institure of Purchasing and Supply.

Cousins, P. (1999), *Strategic Supply: Report on trends and developments in Supply Management*, Bath, University of Bath, pp. 1–63.

Ellram, L. and Carr, A. (1994), 'Strategic Purchasing: A History and Review of the Literature', *International Journal of Purchasing and Materials Management*, Spring.

Farmer, D. (1972), 'The Impact of Supply Markets on Corporate Planning', *Long Range Planning*, Vol. 5, 1, pp. 10–15.

Farmer, D. (1981), 'Seeking Strategic Involvement', *Journal of Purchasing and Materials Management*, Vol. 17, 3, pp. 20–24.

Hines, P. (1994), *Creating World Class Suppliers: Unlocking Mutual Competitive Advantage*, London, Pitman Publishing.

Kraljic, P. (1983), 'Purchasing Must Become Supply Management', *Harvard Business Review*, September–October.

Lamming, R. (1993), *Beyond Partnership: Strategies for Innovation and Lean Supply*, Hemel Hempstead, Prentice Hall.

Laneros, R. and Monckza, R. (1989), 'Co-operative Buyer-Supplier Relationships and a firms competitive strategy', *Journal of Purchasing and Materials Management*, Vol. 25, 3, pp. 9–18.

Macbeth, D. and Ferguson, N. (1994) *Partnership Sourcing: An Integrated*

Supply Chain Approach, London, Pitman Publishing.

Monczka, F. (1992), 'Integrating Purchasing and Corporate Strategy', *NAPM Conference*, NAPM, USA.

Nishiguchi, T. (1994), *Strategic Industrial Sourcing: The Japanese Advantage*, Oxford, Oxford University Press.

Quinn, J., and Mintzberg, H. (1988), *The Strategy Process: Concepts, Contexts and Cases*, New Jersey, Prentice Hall.

Reck, R. and Long, B. (1988), 'Purchasing: A Competitive Weapon', *Journal of Purchasing and Materials Management*, Fall.

Schonberger, R. (1986), *World Class Manufacturing*, New York, The Free Press.

Speckman, R. (1989), 'A Strategic Approach to Procurement Planning', *Journal of Purchasing and Materials Management*, Spring.

St John, C. and Young, S. (1991) 'The Strategic Consistency between Purchasing and Production', *International Journal of Purchasing and Materials Management*, Spring, pp. 15–20.

Steudel, H. and Desruelle, P. (1992), *Manufacturing in the Nineties: How to Become a Mean, Lean, World-Class Competitor*, New York, Van Nostrand Reinhold.

Syson, R. (1992), *Improving Purchase Performance*, London, Pitman Publishing.

van Weele, A. (1984), 'Purchasing Performance Measurement and Evaluation', *Journal of Purchasing and Materials Management*, Fall.

Womack, J. and Jones, D. (1996), 'From Lean Production to the Lean Enterprise', *Harvard Business Review*, March–April.

Womack, J., Jones, D. and Roos, D. (1990), *The Machine That Changed The World*, New York, Rawson Associates.

Chapter 10

Chandler, D. (1962), *Strategy and Structure*, Massachusetts, MIT.

Cox, A. (1995), 'Pro-Activity, Value Engineering and Strategic Procurement Management: An Entrepreneurial Contractual Model For The Firm', *1st World-Wide Research Symposium On Purchasing & Supply Chain Management*, Tempe, Arizona.

Dimancescu, D. (1992), *The Seamless Enterprise: Making Cross-Functional Management Work*, New York, HarperBusiness.

Dimancescu, D., Hines, P. and Rich, N. (1997), *The Lean Enterprise: Designing and Managing Strategic Processes for Customer-Winning Performance*, New York, AMACOM.

Farmer, D. (1995), 'Purchasing Myopia – A Touch of Mr Magoo', *Proceedings of the 1st Worldwide Research Symposium on Purchasing and Supply Chain Management*, pp. 63–71.

Hammer, M. and Champy, J. (1993), *Re-Engineering The Corporation*, London, Brearley.

Hines, P. (1994), *Creating World Class Suppliers: Unlocking Mutual Competitive Advantage*, London, Pitman Publishing.

Humby, S. (1995), 'Purchasing Evolution', *Proceedings of the 1st Worldwide Research Symposium on Purchasing and Supply Chain Management*, pp. 7–14.

Joag, S. and Scheuing, E. (1995), 'Purchasing's Relationships with its Internal Customers', *1st World-Wide Research Symposium On Purchasing & Supply Chain Management*, Tempe, Arizona.

Jones, O. (1997), 'Multi-Site Purchasing Report', *SCDP Workshop Meeting #6*, Welsh Health Supplies, Cardiff.

Kanter, R. (1989), *When Giants Learn To Dance*, New York, Simon & Schuster.

Keuning, D. and Opheij, W. (1994), *Delayering Organisations*, London, Pitman Publishing.

Merli, G. (1991), *Co-Makership*, Cambridge, MA, Productivity Press.

Reck, R. and Long, B. (1988), 'Purchasing: A Competitive Weapon', *International Journal Of Purchasing & Materials Management*, Fall.

Stuart, I. (1996), 'Purchasing's Role in Corporate Strategy: Do Strategic Supplier Alliances Make A Difference?', *Proceedings of the 5th IPSERA Conference*, pp. 1–12, Eindhoven University of Technology.

Womack, J. and Jones, D. (1996), *Lean Thinking*, New York, Simon & Schuster.

Chapter 11

Bleinkinsop, S. and Burns, N. (1992), 'Performance Measurement Revisited', *International Journal of Operations & Production Management*, Vol. 12 (10).

Butler, R. (1995), 'What You Measure is What You Get – an investigation into measurement of the value added by the purchasing function', *Proceedings from 4th Annual IPSERA Conference*.

Cannon, J. (1995), 'Auditing the Purchasing and Contracts Function', *Purchasing & Supply Management*, June.

Cavinato, J. (1987), 'Purchasing Performance: What Makes the Magic?', *Journal of Purchasing & Materials Management*, Fall.

Chao, C., Sheuing, E. and Ruch, W. (1993), 'Purchasing Performance Evaluation: An Investigation of Different Perspectives', *International Journal of Purchasing and Materials Management*, Summer.

Christopher, M. (1992), *Logistics and Supply Chain Management*, London, Pitman Publishing.

Cox, A. (1995), 'Relational Competence and Strategic Procurement Management: Towards an Entrepreneurial and Contractual Theory of the Firm', *1st Worldwide Research Symposium on PSCM*, Arizona, March.

Cyert, R. and March, J. (1963), *A Behavioural Theory of the Firm*, Englewood Cliffs, Prentice-Hall.

Dumond, E. (1991), 'Performance Measurement and Decision Making in Purchasing Environment', *Journal of Purchasing and Materials Management*, Spring.

Dumond, E. (1994), 'Moving Towards Value-Base Purchasing', *International Journal of Purchasing & Materials Management*, Spring.

Dumond, E. (1994), 'Making Best Use of Performance Measures and Information', *International Journal of Operations and Production Management*, Volume 14 (9).

Ellram, L. and Carr, A. (1994), 'Strategic Purchasing: A History and Review of the Literature', *International Journal of Purchasing & Materials Management*, Spring.

Freeman, V. and Cavinato, J. (1990), 'Fitting Purchasing to the Strategic Firm: Frameworks, Processes and Values', *Journal of Purchasing & Materials Management*, Winter.

Geanuracos, J. and Meiklejohn, I. (1994), *Performance Measurement: the New Agenda – using non-financial measures to improve profitability*, London, Business Intelligence.

Ghobadian, A. and Ashworth, J. (1994), 'Performance Measurement in Local Government – concept and practice', *International Journal of Operations & Production Management*, Vol. 14 (5).

Ghorpade, J. and Chen, M. (1995), 'Creating Quality Driven Performance Appraisal Systems', *Academy of Management Executive*, Vol. 9, 1.

Hedstrom, G. and McLean, R. (1993), 'Six Imperatives for Excellence in Environmental Management', *PRISM*, Third Quarter.

Johnson, G. and Scholes, K. (1980), *Exploring Corporate Strategy (2nd edn)*, London, Prentice-Hall.

Kanter, R. (1989), *When Giants Learn to Dance*, London, Simon & Schuster.

Kaplan, R. and Norton, D. (1992), 'The Balanced Scorecard – Measures that Drive Performance', *Harvard Business Review*, January– February.

Kaplan, R. and Norton, D. (1993), 'Putting the Balanced Scorecard to Work', *Harvard Business Review*, September–October.

Kraljic, P. (1983), 'Purchasing Must Become Supply Management', *Harvard Business Review*, September–October.

Lamming, R. (1993), *Beyond Partnership: Strategies for Innovation and Lean Supply*, Hemel Hempstead, Prentice-Hall.

Lamming, R. and Davies, L. (1995), 'Performance Measurement in Purchasing', *Centre for Research in Strategic Purchasing and Supply*, Working Paper.

Lynch, R. and Cross, K. (1991), *Performance Measurement Systems*, in: B. Brinker, *Handbook of Cost Management*, New York, Warren, Gorham & Lamont.

Meyer, C. (1994), 'How the Right Measures Help Teams Excel', *Harvard Business Review*, May–June.

Mitroff, I. (1982), *Stakeholders of the Organisational Mind – towards a new view of organisational policy making*, Boston, Jossey-Bass Publishers.

Poltorzycki, S. (1993), 'Measurement for Environmental Effectiveness', *PRISM*, Third Quarter.

Reck, R. and Long, B. (1988), 'Purchasing: a Competitive Weapon', *Journal of Purchasing & Materials Management*, Fall.

Ringwald, K. (1995), 'Does Public Sector Purchasing Measure Up?', *Proceedings from 4th Annual IPSERA Conference*.

Saunders, M. (1994), *Strategic Purchasing and Supply Chain Management*, London, Pitman Publishing.

Simons, R. (1995), 'Control in an Age of Empowerment', *Harvard Business Review*, March–April.

Stanley, L. (1993), 'Linking Purchasing Department Structure and Performance – toward a contingency model', *Journal of Strategic Marketing*, 1.

Syson, R. (1995), *Improving Purchase Performance*, London, Pitman Publishing.

van Weele, A. (1994), 'Purchasing Performance Measurement and Evaluation', *Journal of Purchasing and Materials Management*, Fall.

van Weele, A. (1994), *Purchasing Management: Analysis, Planning & Practice*, London, Chapman & Hall.

Zenz, G. (1994), *Purchasing and the Management of Materials (7th edn)*, Chichester, John Wiley & Sons Ltd.

Chapter 12

Carlisle, J. and Parker, R. (1989), *Beyond Negotiation: Redeeming Customer–Supplier Relationships*, Chichester, Wiley.

Chandler A. (1997), *The Visible Hand: The Managerial Revolution in American Business*, Cambridge, MA, Harvard Business Press.

Cousins, P. (1999), 'Supply Base Rationalisation: Myth or Reality', *European Journal of Purchasing and Supply Management,* forthcoming, Vol. 5.

Cusumano, M. (1991), *Japan's Software Factories: A Challenge to US Management*, New York, Oxford University Press.

Hines, P. (1994), *Creating World-Class Suppliers: Unlocking Mutual Competitive Advantage*, London, Pitman/Financial Times.

Lamming, R. (1993), *Beyond Partnership: Strategies for Innovation and Lean Supply*, New York, Prentice-Hall.

Macbeth, D. and Ferguson, N. (1994), *Partnership Sourcing*, London, Pitman Publishing.

Nishiguchi, T. (1994), *Strategic Industrial Sourcing: The Japanese Advantage,* New York, Oxford University Press.

Rogers, E. (1983), *Diffusion of Innovation,* (3rd Edn) New York, Free Press.

Sako, M. (1992), *Prices, Quality and Trust: Inter-Firm Relations in Britain & Japan*, Cambridge, Cambridge University Press.

Smitka, M. (1991), *Competitive Ties: Subcontracting in the Japanese Automo-*

tive Industry, New York, Columbia University Press.

Williamson, O. (1975), *Markets and Hierarchies*, New York, The Free Press.

Williamson, O. (1985), *The Economic Institutions of Capitalism,* New York, The Free Press.

Womack, J., Jones, D. and Roos, D. (1990), *The Machine that Changed the World,* New York, Rawson Associates.

Chapter 13

Andersen Consulting (1992), *The Lean Enterprise Benchmarking Project*, London, Andersen Consulting.

Christopher, M. (1992), *Logistics and Supply Chain Management: Strategies for Reducing Costs and Improving Services*, London, Pitman Publishing.

Dale, B. and Plunkett, J. (1991), *Quality Costing*, London, Chapman & Hall.

Dimancescu, D., Hines, P. and Rich, N. (1997), *The Lean Enterprise: Designing and Managing Strategic Processes for Customer-Winning Performance*, New York, AMACOM.

Drucker, P. (1982), *The Changing World of the Executive*, New York, Heinemann.

Grimm, A. (ed.) (1981/1997), *Quality Costs: Ideas & Applications: A Collection of Papers Vol. 1 & 2*, New York, Quality Press.

Hahn, C., Watts, C. and Kim, K. (1990), 'The Supplier Development Program: A Conceptual Model', *Journal of Purchasing and Materials Management*, Vol. 26, 2, pp. 2–7, Spring.

Hines, P. (1994a), *Creating World Class Suppliers: Unlocking Mutual Competitive Advantage*, London, Pitman Publishing.

Hines, P. (1995b), 'Can Network Sourcing Work Outside the Automotive Industry? A Comparative Study of Buyer-Supplier Relationships in Japan', *Proceedings of the 4th International Annual IPSERA Conference*, University of Birmingham, 10–12 April.

Hines, P. (1996), 'Network Sourcing: A Discussion of Causality Within the Buyer–Supplier Relationship', *European Journal of Purchasing and Supply Management*, Vol. 2, 1, pp. 7–20.

Hines, P. and James, R. (1994), 'Supplier Development', *Supply Chain Development Programme I*, Workshop 2, University of Bath, 20 January.

Hines, P., James, R. and Jones, O. (1995a), 'A Cost-Benefit Model for Decision Making in Supplier Development Activities', *Proceedings of the 4th International Annual IPSERA Conference*, University of Birmingham, 10–12 April.

Hines, P., James, R. and Jones, O. (1995b), 'The Supplier Development Grid: A Tool for Awareness Raising, Acceptance and Successful Implementation', *Proceedings of the 2nd International Symposium on Logistics*, The University of Nottingham, 11–12 July, pp. 87–94.

Hines, P., Rich, N. and Esain, A. (1998), 'Creating a Lean Supplier Network: A Distribution Industry Case', *European Journal of Purchasing and Supply Management*.

Hines, P., Rich, N. and Hittmeyer, M. (1998), 'Competing Against Ignorance: Advantage Through Knowledge', *International Journal of Physical Distribution and Logistics Management*, Vol. 28, 1.

Hoare, A. (1994), 'Northern Telecom – Supplier Association', *Supply Chain Development Programme I*, Workshop 5, Van den Bergh Foods Limited, Burgess Hill, 14–15 September.

James, R. and Hines, P. (1994), 'Report on Supplier Development', *Supply Chain Development Programme I*, Workshop 3, Cardiff Business School, 21 April.

Mizuno, S. and Akao, Y. (1994), *QFD The Customer-Driven Approach to Quality Planning and Deployment*, Tokyo, Asian Productivity Organisation.

Newman, R. and Rhee, K. (1990), 'A Case Study of NUMMI and Its Suppliers', *Journal of Purchasing and Materials Management*, Vol. 26, 4, pp. 15–20, Fall.

Sako, M. (1992), *Prices, Quality and Trust: Inter-Firm Relations in Britain & Japan*, Cambridge, Cambridge University Press.

Smitka, M. (1991), *Competitive Ties: Subcontracting in the Japanese Automotive Industry*, New York, Columbia University Press.

Spiers, J. (1997), 'The Theory and Practice of Buyer-Supplier Relationships: A Sectoral and Unipart Perspective', in: A. Cox and P. Hines (eds), *Advanced Supply Chain Management: The Best Practice Debate*, pp. 107-136, Boston, Lincs, Earlsgate Press.

Taylor, E. (1994), 'Clarks International Company Overview', *Supply Chain Development Programme I*, Workshop 3, Cardiff Business School, 21 April.

Watson, P. (1994), 'Logistics Development Groups', *Supply Chain Development Programme I*, Workshop 2, University of Bath, 20 January.

Watts, C. and Hahn, C. (1993), 'Supplier Development Programmes: An Empirical Analysis', *International Journal of Purchasing and Materials Management*, Vol. 29, 2, pp. 11–17, Spring.

Womack, J., Jones, D. and Roos, D. (1990), *The Machine that Changed the World*, New York, Rawson Associates.

Chapter 14

Ansoff, I. (1957), 'Strategies for Diversification', *Harvard Business Review*, September–October, p. 114.

Burbidge, J. (1961), 'The New Approach to Production', *The Production Engineer*, Vol. 40, 12, pp. 769–784.

Checkland, P. (1981), *Systems Thinking, Systems Practice*, Chichester, Wiley.

Christopher, M. (1992), *Logistics and Supply Chain Management*, London, Pitman Publishing.

Coase, R. (1937), 'The Nature of the Firm', *Economica (NS)*, Vol. 4, pp. 386–405.

Coyle, J., Bardi, E. and Langley, C. (1992), *The Management of Business Logistics*. 5th edn, New York, West.

Ford, I. (1978), 'Stability Factors in Industrial Marketing Channels', *Industrial*

Marketing Management, Vol. 7, pp. 410–422.

Forrester, J. (1958), 'Industrial Dynamics: A Major Breakthrough for Decision Makers', *Harvard Business Review*, July–August, pp. 37–66.

Hakansson, H. (1982), *International Marketing & Purchasing of Industrial Goods: An Interaction Approach*, Chichester, Wiley.

Hamel, G. and Prahalad, C. (1995), *Competing for the Future*, Harvard Business School Press.

Herzberg, F. (1966), *Work and the Nature of Man*, London, Staples Press.

Hines, P. (1994), *Creating World Class Suppliers: Unlocking Mutual Competitive Advantage*, London, Pitman Publishing.

James, R., Rich, N. and Francis, M. (1997), 'Vendor Managed Inventory: A Processual Approach', *Proceedings of the 6th International IPSERA Conference*, University of Naples 'Frederico II', Iscia (Naples), Italy, 24–26 March.

Juran, J. (1979), *The Quality Control Handbook*, 3rd edn, New York, McGraw-Hill.

Kaplan, R. (1984), 'Yesterday's Accounting Undermines Production', *Harvard Business Review*, July–August, pp. 95–101.

Kaplan, R. (1988), 'One Cost System Isn't Enough', *Harvard Business Review*, January–February, pp. 61–66.

Kraljic, P. (1983), 'Purchasing Must Become Supply Management', *Harvard Business Review*, September–October.

Kurt Salmon (1993), *Efficient Consumer Response*, Washington, Kurt Salmon Associates.

Kurogane, K. (1993), *Cross-Functional Management: Principles & Practical Applications*, Tokyo, Asian Productivity Management.

Lamming, R. (1993), *Beyond Partnership: Strategies for Innovation and Lean Supply*, Hemel Hempstead, UK, Prentice-Hall.

Lamming, R., Jones, O. and Nicol, D. (1995), *Cost Transparency – Final Report*, Supply Chain Development Programme.

Porter, M. (1980), *Competitive Strategy*, New York, The Free Press.

Sako, M. (1992), *Prices, Quality & Trust: Inter-Firm Relations in Britain & Japan*, Cambridge, Cambridge University Press.

Stalk, G. and Hout, T. (1990), *Competing Against Time*, New York, The Free Press.

Williamson, O. (1975), *Markets & Hierarchies*, New York, The Free Press.

Williamson, O. (1986), *Economic Organization: Firms, Markets and Policy Control*, Brighton, Wheatsheaf.

Womack, J., Jones, D. and Roos, D. (1990), *The Machine that Changed the World*, New York, Rawson Associates.

Womack, J. and Jones, D. (1996), *Lean Thinking: Banish Waste and Create Wealth in Your Corporation*, New York, Simon & Schuster.

Chapter 15

Bessant, J., Lamming, R., Levy, P. and Sang, R. (1993), 'Managing successful total quality relationships in the supply chain', *European Journal of Purchasing and Supply Management*, Vol. 1, 1, pp. 7–17.

Biffa Waste Services Ltd. (1994), *Waste: A Game of Snakes and Ladders?*, UK.

Burt, D. and Los, R. (1995) 'A Value Chain Approach to Pollution Avoidance', *Proceedings of the Strategic Supply Management Forum*, University of San Diego, September.

Business in the Environment (1995), *Supply Chain: the Environmental Challenge*, London.

Colby, E. (1995), 'The Real Green Issue: Debunking the Myths of Environmental Management', *The McKinsey Quarterly*, 2.

Cousins, P. (1999), 'Supply base rationalisation – Myth or Reality', *European Journal of Purchasing and Supply Management*, forthcoming.

Cramer, J. (1996), 'Experiences with Implementing integrated chain management in Dutch industry', *Business Strategy & the Environment*, Vol. 5, pp. 38-47.

Downs, A. (1973), 'Up and Down with Ecology: The Issue-Attention Cycle', in: J. Barns (ed.), *Environmental Decay*.

Drumwright, M. (1994), 'Socially Responsible Organisational Buying: Environmental Concern as a non-Economic Buying Criterion', *Journal of Marketing*, Vol. 58.

ENDS 232 (1994), 'Public concern for the environment rides the recession'.

ENDS 241 (1995), 'Environmental Managers call for greater support from the boardroom'.

Hedstrom, G. and McLean, R. (1993), 'Six Imperatives for Excellence in Environmental Management', *PRISM*, London, Arthur D. Little.

Hindle, E. (1993), 'Achieving Real Environmental Improvements Value Impact Assessment', *Long Range Planning,* Vol. 26, 3.

Hurst, D. (1995), *Crisis and Renewal: meeting the challenge of organisational change*, Boston, MA, Harvard Business School Press.

Jones, P. (1996), 'Producer Responsibility and Resource Recovery from Waste: the Grave'.

Kraljic, P. (1983) 'Purchasing must Become Supply Management', *Harvard Business Review*, September/October.

Lamming, R. (1993), *Beyond Partnership: Strategies for Innovation and Lean Supply*, Hemel Hempstead, UK, Prentice-Hall.

Lamming, R. (1994), *A review of the relationships between vehicle manufacturers and suppliers*, London, UK, DTI Vehicles Division/SMMT.

Lamming, R. (1997), 'Squaring Lean Supply with Supply Chain Management', *International Journal of Operations and Production Management*, Vol. 16, 2.

Lamming, R., Cousins, P. and Notman, D. (1996), 'Beyond Vendor Assessment:

Relationship Assessment Programme', *European Journal of Purchasing and Supply Management*, Vol. 2, 4.

Lamming, R., Warhurst, A. and Hampson, J. (1996), *Purchasing and the Environment: Problem or Opportunity?*, Stamford, UK, CIPS.

Miller, J. and Szekely, F. (1995), 'What is Green?', *European Management Journal*, Vol. 13, 3, September.

Porter, M. and van der Linde, C. (1995), 'Green and Competitive: Ending the Stalemate', *Harvard Business Review*, September–October.

Roy, R. and Wheelan, R. (1992), 'Successful Recycling Through Value Chain Collaboration', *Long Range Planning,* Vol. 25, 4.

Shrivastava, P. (1995), 'Environmental Technologies and Competitive Advantages', *Strategic Management Journal,* Vol. 16, pp. 183–200.

Smart, B. (1992), *Beyond Compliance*, World Resources Institute, USA.

Tse, K. (1985), *Marks and Spencer: Anatomy of Britain's most efficiently managed company*, Oxford, Pergamon Press.

Warhurst, A. (1994), 'The Limitations of Environmental Regulation in Mining'.

White, P. (1995), 'Environmental Management in an International Consumer Goods Company', *Resources, Conservation and Recycling*, Vol. 14, pp. 171–184.

Chapter 16

Coca-Cola Retailing Research Group (1994), *Supplier-Retailer Collaboration In Supply Chain Management*.

Forrester, J. (1958), 'Industrial Dynamics-A Major Breakthrough for Decision Makers', *Harvard Business Review*.

Ghosh, A. (1990), *Retail Management*, Chicago, Dryden Press.

Kurogane, K. (1993), *Cross Functional Management*, Tokyo, Asian Productivity Organisation.

Kurt Salmon Associates (1993), *Efficient Consumer Response,* The Research Department Food Marketing Institute.

Ohno, T. and Mito, S. (1986), *Just-In-Time: For Today and Tomorrow*, Cambridge, MA, Productivity Press.

Chapter 17

Alber, K. and Walker, W. (1997), *Supply Chain Management: Practitioner Notes*, Falls Church, VA: APICS Educational & Research Foundation, October.

Bicheno, J. (1994), *The Quality 50: A Guide to Gurus, Tools, Wastes, Techniques and Systems*, Buckingham, PICSIE Books.

Dale, B. and Plunkett, J. (1991), *Quality Costing*, London, Chapman & Hall.

Dimancescu, D. and Dwenger, K. (1996), *World-Class New Product Development: Benchmarking Best Practices of Agile Manufacturers*, New York, AMACOM.

Dimancescu, D., Hines, P. and Rich, N. (1997), *The Lean Enterprise: Designing and Managing Strategic Processes for Customer-Winning Performance*, New York, AMACOM.

Esain, A. and Hines, P. (1997) 'Responsiveness in Product Introduction', *SCDP Workshop*, University of Bath, 15–16 January.

Fooks, J. (1993), *Profiles for Performance*, Boston, Addison Wesley.

Grimm, A. (ed.) (1981/1987), *Quality Costs: Ideas & Applications: A Collection of Papers Vol 1 & 2*, New York, Quality Press.

Hines, P. (1994), *Creating World Class Suppliers: Unlocking Mutual Competitive Advantage*, London, Pitman Publishing.

Hines, P. and Rich, N. (1997), 'The Seven Value Stream Mapping Tools', *International Journal of Operations and Production Management*, Vol. 17, 1, pp. 46–64.

Hines, P., Rich, N., Bicheno, J., Brunt, D., Taylor, D., Butterworth, C. and Sullivan, J. (1998), 'Value Stream Management', *International Journal of Logistics Management*, Vol. 9, 2.

Kotler, P. (1986), *Principles of Marketing*, New Jersey, Prentice Hall International.

Chapter 18

Bhattacharya, A., Jina, J. and Walton, A. (1996), 'Product market, turbulence and time compression: three dimensions of an integrated approach to manufacturing systems design', *International Journal of Operations and Production Management*, Vol. 16, 9, pp. 34–47.

Booth, G. (1997), 'Leaning Retailing: The Tesco Story', *The First European Lean Enterprise Summit*, National Motorcycle Museum, Birmingham, UK, 17–18 June, pp. 237–264.

Dimancescu, D., Hines, P. and Rich, N. (1997), *The Lean Enterprise*, pp. 159–164, New York, AMACOM.

Galloway, J. (1998), 'Changing Structures Within the Company: Remodelling Relationships and Results of ECR initiatives', *3rd Official ECR Conference*, Hamburg, 1–2 April.

Green, M. (1997), 'Britvic Soft Drinks: Development of a major distribution centre', in: D. Taylor (ed.), *Global Cases in Logistics and Supply Chain Management*, London, International Thomson Business Press, pp. 205–216.

Hammer, M. and Champy, J. (1993), *Reengineering the Corporation*, London, HarperCollins.

Hines, P. and Rich, N. (1997), 'The seven value stream mapping tools', *IJOPM*, Vol. 17, 1, pp. 44–62.

Jones, D. (1995), 'Applying Toyota principles in distribution', *Supply Chain Development Programme I*, Workshop #8, Britvic Soft Drinks Ltd, Lutterworth, 6–7 July.

Kiff, J., Chieux, T. and Simons, D. (1998), *Parts Supply Systems in the Franchise*

After-Market in France, Germany, Italy, UK, International Car Distribution Programme Research Report 7/98, May.

Monden, Y. (1993), *Toyota Production System: an Integrated Approach to Just-in-Time*, 2nd Edn, Norcross, GA, Industrial Engineering and Management Press.

Murray, W. and Ferguson, J. (1997), *The role of shared user networks in supply chain re-engineering, Logistics Research Network Conference*, Huddersfield University.

Naim, M. (1997), 'The book that changed the world', *Manufacturing Engineer*, pp. 13–16, February.

Naim, M. and Towill, D. (1994), 'Establishing a Framework for Effective Materials Logistics Management', *International Journal of Logistics Management*, Vol. 5, 1, pp. 81–88.

Shingo, S. (1989), *A Study of the Toyota Production System from an Industrial Engineering Viewpoint*, Cambridge, MA, Productivity Press.

Simons, D., Francis, M. and Jones, O. (1997), 'Value Stream Mapping in a distribution environment', *Supply Chain Development Programme I*, Combined Workshop, Welsh Health Supplies, 17–18 September.

Womack, J., Jones, D. and Roos, D. (1990), *The Machine that Changed the World*, New York, Rawson Associates.

Womack, J. and Jones, D. (1996), *Lean Thinking*, New York, Simon & Schuster.

Chapter 19

Brunt, D., Butterworth, C. and Taylor, D. (2000 (forthcoming)), *Value Stream Management: A Casebook*.

Cousins, P. (1999a), 'Trends in high value, buyer, supplier relationships', University of Bath, School of Management report.

Cousins, P. (1999b), 'The Snake and the Old Women: Managing Inter-Firm Relationships', *Long Range Planning*.

Hines, P., Bicheno, J. and Rich, N. (2000 (forthcoming)), *Value Stream Management: A Workbook*.

Hines, P., Rich, N., Bicheno, J., Brunt, D., Taylor, D., Butterworth, C. and Sullivan, J. (1998), 'Value Stream Management', *International Journal of Logistics Management*, Vol. 9, 2, pp. 25–42.

Further reading

Adams, F. and Niebuhr, R. (1985), 'Improving Individual Productivity in Purchasing', *Journal of Purchasing and Materials Management*, Winter.

Akbar, N. and Lamming, R. (1996), 'Federal Organisation Of Purchasing: A Reverse Thrust Organisation', *Proceedings 5th International IPSERA Conference,* Eindhoven, pp. 422–437.

Ammer, D. (1989), 'Top Management's View of the Purchasing Function', *Journal of Purchasing & Materials Management*, Spring.

Amus, D. and Griffin, J. (1993), 'Harnessing the Power of Your Suppliers', *The McKinsey Quarterly*, 3.

Bales, W. and Fearon, H. (1993), *CEOs'/Presidents' Perceptions and Expectations of the Purchasing Function*, Centre for Advanced Purchasing Studies, Arizona.

Bicheno, J. (1994), *The Quality 50: A Guide to Gurus, Tools, Wastes, Techniques and Systems*, Buckingham, PICSIE Books.

Brown, M. and Laverick, S. (1994), 'Measuring Corporate Performance', *Long Range Planning*, Vol. 27 (4).

Cairncross, F. (1995), *Green Inc.: A Guide to Business and the Environment*, London, Earthscan.

Central Unit on Purchasing (1989), *Measuring Performance in Purchasing: Guidelines No. 14*, London, HMSO.

Collins, T. and Harris, G. (1992), 'Implementing New Performance Measures', *Insights*, September.

Cousins, P. (1992), 'Purchasing A Professional Approach', *Purchasing and Supply Management*, September, pp. 20–23.

Cox, A. (1995), 'Pro-Activity, Value Engineering and Strategic Procurement Management', *Proceedings for the First Worldwide Research Symposium on Purchasing and Supply Chain Management*, R. Kemp and R. Lamming (eds), IFPMM/CIPS/PMAC/NAPM, Tempe, Arizona.

Cox, A. (1996), 'Relational Competence and Strategic Procurement Management. Towards an Entrepreneurial and Contractual Theory of the Firm', *European Journal of Purchasing & Supply Management*, Vol. 2, 1, March, pp. 57–70.

Cunningham, M. (1982), 'Purchasing Strategies in Europe: An Interaction Perspective of Industrial Buyer Behaviour', *International Journal of Physical Distribution & Materials Management*, Vol. 12 (4).

Cusumano, M. (1985), *The Japanese Automobile Industry: Technology and Management at Nissan and Toyota,* Cambridge, MA., Harvard University Press.

Dimancescu, D. (1992), *The Seamless Enterprise: Making Cross Functional Management Work,* New York, Harper Business.

Dimancescu, D., Hines, P. and Rich, N. (1997), *The Lean Enterprise: Designing and Managing Strategic Processes for Customer-Winning Performance*, New York, AMACOM.

Dion, P. and Banting, P. (1987), 'Effective Buyers – are they cunning or co-operative?', *Journal of Purchasing and Materials Management*, Winter.

Dobler, D. *et al.* (1990), *Purchasing & Materials Management: text & cases (5th edn)*, New York, McGraw-Hill.

Ellram, L. and Carr, A. (1994), 'Strategic Purchasing: A History & Review Of The Literature', *International Journal of Purchasing & Materials Management*, Spring, pp. 10–18.

Farmer, D. (ed.) (1985), *Purchasing Management Handbook*, Basingstoke, Gower Publishing.

Farmer, D. and van Amstel, R. (1991), *Effective Pipeline Management: How to Manage Integrated Logistics*, Basingstoke, Gower Publishing.

Felch, R. and Felch, R. (1988), 'Controlling Purchase Price Performance', *Journal of Purchasing & Materials Management*, Fall.

Freeman, R. (1984), *Strategic Management: A Stakeholder Approach*, London, Pitman.

Gore, A. (1993), *Creating a Government that Works Better and Costs Less – the Chapter of the National Performance Review*, New York, Plume.

Handy, C. (1992), 'Balancing Corporate Power: A New Federalist Paper', *Harvard Business Review*, November–December, pp. 59–72.

Hahn, C., Watts, C. and Kim, K. (1990), 'The Supplier Development Program: A Conceptual Model', *Journal of Purchasing and Materials Management*, Vol. 26, 2, Spring, pp. 2–7.

Hines, P. (1994b), 'Internationalization and Localization of the Kyoryoku Kai: The Spread of Best Practice Supplier Development', *International Journal of Logistics Management*, Vol. 5, 1, pp. 67–72.

Hines, P. (1994c), 'Supplier Associations', *Supply Chain Development Programme I*, Workshop 2, University of Bath, 20 January.

Hines, P. (1995a), 'New Developments in Japan', *Supply Chain Development Programme I*, Workshop 6, Tesco Management Training Centre, Ponsbourne Park, 25–26 January.

Hines, P. (1996), 'Creating Your Own World Class Supply-Chain', *Logistics Focus*, Vol. 4, April.

Hines, P. and Rich, N. (1997a), 'The Seven Value Stream Mapping Tools', *International Journal of Production and Operations Management*, Vol. 17, 1, pp. 46–64.

Hines, P. and Rich, N. (1997b), 'Purchasing Structures, Roles, Processes and

Strategy: Is it a Case of the Tail Wagging the Dog?', *Proceedings of the 6th International Annual IPSERA Conference,* T 5/3 1–17, University of Naples 'Frederico II', Ischia (Naples), Italy, 24–26 March.

Hines, P. (1998), 'Toyota Supplier System in Japan and UK', *Long Range Planning.*

Hines, P. and Rich, N. (1998), 'Outsourcing Competitive Advantage', *International Journal of Physical Distribution and Logistics Management.*

Hines, P., Rich, N. and Hittmeyer, M. (1998), 'Competing Against Ignorance: Advantage Through Knowledge', *International Journal of Physical Distribution and Logistics Management,* Vol. 28, 1.

Hittmeyer, M. (1994), *Focusing Development Efforts in the Supply Chain – A Kenyan Case Study,* University of Wales, September.

Ishikawa, K. (1976), *What Is Total Quality Control? The Japanese Way,* New York, Prentice-Hall.

James, R. (1994), 'Supplier Development Positioning Matrix', *Supply Chain Development Programme I,* Workshop 5, Van den Bergh Foods Limited, Burgess Hill, 14–15 September.

Johnson, G. and Scholes, K. (1988), *Exploring Corporate Strategy,* 2nd Edn, Englewood Cliffs, Prentice-Hall.

Jones, D., Hines, P. and Rich, N. (1997), 'Lean Logistics', *International Journal of Physical Distribution and Logistics Management, Lean Logistics Special Edition,* Vol. 27, 4, pp. 153–173.

Jones, O. (1994), 'Quantifying Supplier Non Performance: An Investment Appraisal Model for Evaluating Supplier Development', *Supply Chain Development Programme I,* Workshop 5, Van den Bergh Foods Limited, Burgess Hill, 14–15 September.

Kaplan, R. and Norton, D. (1992), 'The Balanced Scorecard–Measures That Drive Performance', *Harvard Business Review,* January–February, pp. 71–79.

Lamming, R., Cousins, P and Notman, D. (1996), 'Beyond Vendor Assessment. Relationship Assessment Programmes', *European Journal of Purchasing & Supply Management,* Vol. 2, 4, pp. 173–182.

Lamming, R., Jones, O. and Nicol, D. (1996), 'Cost Transparency: A Source of Supply Chain Competitive Advantage?' *Proceedings of the 5th International IPSERA Conference,* University of Eindhoven.

Lamming, R. and Cox, A. (eds), *Strategic Procurement in the 1990s: Concepts and Cases,* Boston, UK, Earlsgate Press.

Lamming, R. and Hampson, J. (1996), 'The Environment as a Supply Chain Management Issue', *British Journal of Management,* Vol. 7, March Special Issue.

Le Saint-Grant, F. (1992), 'Performance Evaluation: all the answers?', *Management Accounting,* April.

Lovell, R. (1994), *Managing Change in the New Public Sector,* Longman.

Macbeth, D. and Ferguson, N. (1994), *Partnership Sourcing – An Integrated Supply Chain Approach,* London, Pitman Publishing.

Marschan, R. (1994), 'New Structural Forms In Multinationals: Decentralisation At

The Expense Of Personal Communication Networks', *10th IMP Annual Conference Proceedings*, pp. 21–37, September–October.

Mintzberg, H. (1979), *The Structuring Of Organisations*, New York, Prentice-Hall.

Mizuno, S. and Akao, Y. (1994), *QFD The Customer-Driven Approach to Quality Planning and Deployment*, Tokyo, Asian Productivity Organisation.

Monczka, R. and Morgan, J. (1993), 'Today's Measures Just Don't Make It', *Purchasing*, 21 April.

Monden, Y. (1993), *Toyota Production System: An Integrated Approach to Just-In-Time*, 2nd Edn, Norcross, GA, Industrial Engineering and Management Press.

National Audit Office (1996), *Supplies Procurement: Introduction To The Audit*, Audit Commission.

Neely, A., Gregory, M. and Platts, K. (1995), 'Performance Measurement System Design: A literature review and research agenda', *International Journal of Operations & Production Management*, Vol. 15 (4).

Ouchi, W. and Macguire, M. (1980), *Organisational Control: Two Functions in Litterer J A Organisations Structure & Behavior*, 3rd Edn, New York, Wiley.

Pearson, J. (1991), 'Essential Elements of Strategic Planning', *NAPM Insights*, 6 May.

Pheasey, D. (1991), 'Measuring for Success', *BPICS Control*, June–July.

Power, S. (1993), 'Thoughts on Performance Appraisal', *Purchasing & Supply Management*, October.

Quayle, M. (1990), 'Measuring Purchasing Performance', *Purchasing & Supply Management*, March.

Rich, N. (1996), 'Evidence Of A Watershed In The Purchasing Profession – A Case Of Deja Vu?' *Proceedings 5th International Annual IPSERA Conference*, Eindhoven, pp. 593–607.

Rich, N. and Hines, P. (1997), 'Supply-Chain Management and Time-Based Competition: The Role of the Supplier Association', *International Journal of Physical Distribution and Logistics Management, Lean Logistics Special Edition*, Vol. 27, 4, pp. 210–225.

Rich, N. and Hines, P. (1998), 'Purchasing Structures, Roles, Processes and Strategy: Is it a Case of the Tail Wagging the Dog?', *European Journal of Purchasing and Supply Management*.

Rummler, G. and Brache, A. (1990), *Improving Performance: How to Manage the White Space on the Organisation Chart*, San Francisco, Jossey-Bass.

Sako, M. (1992), *Prices, Quality And Trust: Inter Firm Relations In Britain & Japan*, Cambridge, Cambridge University Press.

Scott, C. and Westbrook, R. (1991), 'New Strategic Tools for Supply Chain Management', *International Journal of Physical Distribution & Logistics Management*, Vol. 21, 1, pp. 23–33.

Slack, N. (1994), 'The Importance–Improvement Matrix as a Determinant of

Improvement Priority', *International Journal of Operations & Production Management*, Vol. 14 (5).

Spekman, R. (1989), 'A Strategic Approach to Procurement Planning', *Journal of Purchasing & Materials Management*, Spring.

Stalk, G. and Hout, T. (1990), *Competing Against Time*, New York, The Free Press.

Steele, P. and Court, B. (1988), 'The Procurement Marketing Concept – Buyers Become Sellers', *Purchasing & Supply Management*, June.

Strauss, B. (1995), 'Internal Services: Classification and Total Quality', *International Journal of Service Industry Management*, Vol. 6, 2.

Symonds, J. (ed.) (1994), *Total Quality Measurement in the Oil Industry*, London, Blackie Academic & Professional.

van Weele, A. (1995), 'Myths and Truths in Purchasing and Supply – Some Provocative Ideas and Thoughts', *Proceedings of the 4th IPSERA Conference*, 'Manufacturing and Production Procurement Volume', University of Birmingham.

Warhurst, A. and Hampson, J. (1996), *Purchasing and the Environment: Problem or Opportunity?* Stamford, UK, CIPS.

Welford, R. and Gouldson, A. (1994), *Environmental Management and Business Strategy*, London, Pitman.

Womack J., Jones, D. and Roos, D. (1990), *The Machine That Changed The World*, New York, Rawson Associates.

Womack, J. and Jones, D. (1994), 'From Lean Production to the Lean Enterprise', *Harvard Business Review*, March–April, pp. 93–103.

Womack J. and Jones D. (1996), *Lean Thinking: Banish Waste and Create Wealth in your Corporation*, New York, Simon and Schuster.

Zairi, M. (1992), 'Measuring Success in AMT Implementation Using Customer–Supplier Interaction Criteria', *International Journal of Operations & Production Management*, Vol. 12 (10).

Index